Benjamin Klatt

Consolidation of Customized Product Copies into Software Product Lines

The Karlsruhe Series on Software Design and Quality
Volume 16

Chair Software Design and Quality
Faculty of Computer Science
Karlsruhe Institute of Technology

and

Software Engineering Division
Research Center for Information Technology (FZI), Karlsruhe

Editor: Prof. Dr. Ralf Reussner

Consolidation of Customized Product Copies into Software Product Lines

by
Benjamin Klatt

KIT Scientific Publishing

Dissertation, Karlsruher Institut für Technologie (KIT)
Fakultät für Informatik
Tag der mündlichen Prüfung: 23. Oktober 2014
Referenten: Prof. Dr. Ralf Reussner, Prof. Dr. Uwe Aßmann

Impressum

KIT Scientific Publishing

Karlsruher Institut für Technologie (KIT)
KIT Scientific Publishing
Straße am Forum 2
D-76131 Karlsruhe

KIT Scientific Publishing is a registered trademark of Karlsruhe Institute of Technology. Reprint using the book cover is not allowed.

www.ksp.kit.edu

Print on Demand 2016

ISSN 1867-0067
ISBN 978-3-7315-0368-2
DOI: 10.5445/KSP/1000046821

Consolidation of Customized Product Copies into Software Product Lines

zur Erlangung des akademischen Grades eines

Doktors der Ingenieurwissenschaften

der Fakultät für Informatik
des Karlsruher Instituts für Technologie

genehmigte

Dissertation

von

Benjamin Klatt

aus Solingen

Tag der mündlichen Prüfung: 23. Oktober 2014
Erster Gutachter: Prof. Dr. Ralf H. Reussner
Zweiter Gutachter: Prof. Dr. Uwe Aßmann

Abstract

In software development, project constraints, such as limitations of time and budget, lead to customer-specific variants by copying and adapting the original product. During such copy-based customizations, modifications are performed in an ad hoc manner and scattered all over the code. Such an approach provides flexibility and efficiency in the short-term to include new customer-specific features. But in the long-term, a Software Product Line (SPL) approach with managed variability has proven to be valuable for achieving goals such as cost reduction, improved time-to-market, and improved quality attributes [33, 67].

To take advantage of the speed of copy-based customizations and managed variability of an SPL, companies and developers have to cope with the challenge of consolidating the customized product copies into a valuable SPL. Therefore, developers have to understand the differences between copies, find those that belong together, design desired SPL variability and integrate the implementations of the copies.

Today, generic difference analysis tools are typically used in context of a consolidation. They confront developers with a lot of fine-grained and unrelated differences. There is no support for further interpreting the differences and designing the variability of the future SPL. Doing this manually is tedious as all differences must be reviewed one after another and, thus, consolidations are often performed ad hoc and with a limited scope only.

This thesis presents a novel approach named SPLEVO for supporting the consolidation of customized product copies into an SPL. In short, the contributions of my thesis are:

- A **Variability Analysis** to support the variability design
- A fully automated **Difference Analysis** specific for consolidations of product copies

- A **Refactoring Specification Concept** for consistent implementations of variability
- A **Consolidation Process** for structured guidance of developers
- An **Evaluation** of the benefits and industrial applicability of the approach

The SPLEVO approach detects the differences between product copies, relates them to each other, and identifies those contributing to a common product feature. In addition, a semi-automatic process guides developers in iteratively creating a variability design by recommending refinements. This process considers guidelines for implementing variability, such as expressing variability only at the level of exchangeable classes. Based on an approved variability design, the refactoring of the customer-specific product copies into the future SPL is initialized. The SPLEVO approach clearly identifies the software elements to modify and allows for manual and automated refactorings. The approach has been validated on publicly available and documented variants of the modeling tool ArgoUML as well as copies of an industrial software product provided by a partner in the KoPL research project.

The contributions of my thesis have been published as part of several peer-reviewed publications [100, 101, 99, 104, 105, 102, 97, 97] and can be summarized as follows:

Variability Analysis for Detecting Related Program Modifications Customizations are typically performed as modifications scattered all over the implementation. To relate these modifications to each other, a variability analysis has been developed that exploits existing approaches for program analysis and evaluates relationships between the modifications. This allows for supporting developers in iteratively developing the variability design and reducing their manual efforts. In addition, a variation point model has been developed to allow for deriving variation points from differences and iteratively aggregating them. Furthermore, it allows for individually specifying the variability characteristics of each variation point.

Difference Analysis for Customized Product Copies A difference analysis for detecting copy-specific modifications in context of a consolidation has been developed. It considers specific requirements of a consolidation, such as typical practices of copy-based customization. Furthermore, it allows for a fully automatic and reliable analysis as well as for deriving a variation point model that represents an initial variability design. Hence, this step is completely transparent for developers.

Specification Concept and Recommendation System for Consolidation Refactorings Clearly specifying program refactorings has been proven to be valuable for a better comprehension and automation of refactorings. However, existing specification concepts do not support the consolidation of several program copies while introducing variability mechanisms at the same time. A novel specification concept for program refactorings has been developed that allows for selecting and implementing variability in a traceable and consistent manner. Based on this specification concept, a recommendation system has been developed for automatically selecting appropriate variability mechanisms to implement for individual variation points.

Definition of a Structured Consolidation Process A semi-automatic process to guide developers in designing the variability of the future SPL has been specified. Furthermore, an SPL Profile has been developed that allows for capturing SPL guidelines to further automate the process. First, a difference analysis is performed to receive an initial fine-grained variation point model. Next, variability analyses are iteratively performed to recommend variation point aggregations to the developers. To consider soft criteria such as organizational constraints and product strategies, developers finally decide about the recommendations and can specify preferred variability characteristics. The resulting variability design is enhanced with decisions about how to implement the variability. Finally, the variability design is processed by the consolidation refactoring and the clear identification of affected code locations allows for manual and automated refactorings.

Evaluation of the Benefits and Industrial Applicability of the Approach Different program analyses have been adopted to be executed as part of the

SPLEVO Variability Analysis and to evaluate their benefit within case studies. Therefore, variants of the publicly accessible modeling tool ArgoUML have been analyzed. The code of the variant-specific features is documented and provides a benchmark for the analyses. In addition, an industrial case study with the CAS Software AG and customer-specific copies of their commercial product has been performed to evaluate the approach under industrial conditions. Interviews and an online survey have been performed to evaluate the appropriateness of the approach for the state of the practice. The evaluation confirmed the approach to be applicable under realistic conditions. The SPLEVO Difference Analysis and SPLEVO Variability Analysis have been proven to be valuable for reducing the manual effort of a consolidation. At the same time, a need for adapting and optimizing existing program analyses to be used for copy consolidations as well as differing benefits for the individual analyses have been identified.

The automated analyses support software developers in comprehending customizations and designing variability. Considering company guidelines allows for ensuring consistent designs and implementations of variability. Furthermore, the tool-supported process allows developers without specific knowledge in program analysis for performing consolidations while benefit from the analyses. Accordingly, a consolidation for exploiting long-term advantages of software product lines becomes more attractive for companies in terms of required efforts and commercial risks.

Zusammenfassung

In der Software-Entwicklung führen Rahmenbedingungen wie Zeit- und Kostendruck oft dazu, dass bestehende Software-Produkte kopiert und an individuelle Kundenanforderungen angepasst werden. Hierbei werden änderungen typischerweise ad hoc und verstreut im Quellcode vorgenommen. Kurzfristig bietet ein solches Vorgehen Flexibilität und Entwicklungsgeschwindigkeit, langfristig ist aus Wartungs- und Produktsicht jedoch meist eine flexible Produktlinie mit geordneter Variabilität sinnvoller.

Um die Vorteile beider Strategien nutzen zu können, stehen Unternehmen und Entwickler vor der Herausforderung, kundenspezifisch angepasste Produktkopien nachträglich in eine zentrale Produktlinie zu konsolidieren. Neben dem aufwändigen Verstehen der Unterschiede zwischen den Produktkopien erfordert auch der Entwurf der zukünftigen Variabilität tiefgehende Kenntnisse der einzelnen Kopien.

Wenn heutzutage Konsolidierungen von Produktkopien durchgeführt werden, kommen in der Regel generische Werkzeuge für einen Quellcodevergleich zum Einsatz. Diese konfrontieren Entwickler mit einer großen, nicht aufbereiteten Menge feingranularer Code-Unterschiede. Eine darauf aufbauende Unterstützung bei dem Entwurf der zukünftigen Variabilität fehlt gänzlich. Als Folge des entstehenden Aufwands werden Konsolidierungen oftmals gar nicht oder nur ad hoc und in einem eingeschränkten Umfang durchgeführt.

In meiner Arbeit schlage ich einen neuen Ansatz namens SPLEVO zur Unterstützung der Konsolidierung kundenspezifisch angepasster Software-Produktkopien zu einer Produktlinie vor. Die Beiträge meiner Arbeit lassen sich wie folgt zusammenfassen:

- Eine **Variabilitätsanalyse** zur Unterstützung des Variabilitätsentwurfs
- Eine vollautomatisierte **Differenzanalyse** für die Konsolidierung angepasster Produktkopien

- Ein **Spezifikationskonzept** für Programm-Restrukturierungen zur Einführung von Variabilität
- Ein **Konsolidierungsprozess** zur strukturierten Gestaltung und Einführung von Variabilität
- Eine **Evaluation** des Nutzens und der industriellen Anwendbarkeit der Beiträge

Der SPLEVO Ansatz erkennt die Unterschiede zwischen Produktkopien, bringt diese zueinander in Verbindung und identifiziert diejenigen Unterschiede, die zu einer gemeinsamen Produkteigenschaft beitragen. In einem semi-automatischen Prozess werden Entwickler mittels Vorschlägen für sinnvolle Variabilitätspunkte zu einem Variabilitätsentwurf geführt. Dabei werden auch mögliche Vorgaben zur Umsetzung der Variabilität, beispielsweise nur durch den Austausch ganzer Klassen, berücksichtigt. Mit einem von den Entwicklern akzeptierten Variabilitätsentwurf wird in einem letzten Schritt die überführung der kundenspezifischen Produktkopien in die zukünftige Produktlinie initiiert. Hierzu werden die zu modifizierenden Teile der Software eindeutig identifiziert, sodass sowohl manuelle als auch technisch unterstützte Umstrukturierungen möglich sind. Zur Validierung des Ansatzes dienen öffentlich verfügbare und dokumentierte Varianten des Modellierungswerkzeuges ArgoUML sowie Produktkopien eines Industriepartners aus dem Forschungsprojekt KoPL.

Die Beiträge meiner Arbeit wurden bereits im Rahmen verschiedener Publikationen [100, 101, 99, 104, 105, 102, 97, 97] veröffentlicht und lassen sich wie folgt zusammenfassen:

Variabilitätsanalyse zur Erkennung zusammenhängender Programmänderungen Kundenspezifische Anpassungen manifestieren sich in der Regel als änderungen an vielen verstreuten Programmstellen. Um diese miteinander in Beziehung zu setzen, wurde eine Variabilitätsanalyse entwickelt, die existierende Verfahren zur Programmanalyse erschließt und Beziehungen zwischen Programmänderungen auswertet. Dies erlaubt es, Entwickler bei der iterativen Erstellung des Variabilitätsentwurfs zu unterstützen und ihre manuellen Aufwände zu reduzieren. Zudem wurde ein Variationspunktmodell entwickelt, das es erlaubt, Variationspunkte aus Differenzen abzuleiten sowie zusammengehörende Variationspunkte iterativ zu aggregieren und ihre gewünschten Variabilitätseigenschaften zu spezifizieren.

Spezifische Differenzanalyse für angepasste Produktkopien Es wurde eine Differenzanalyse zur Erkennung kopie-spezifischer Anpassungen entwickelt, die spezielle Anforderungen der Konsolidierung, wie typische änderungsmuster bei der Kopie-Erstellung oder Namenskonventionen, berücksichtigt. Die Differenzanalyse erlaubt eine vollautomatisierte Erkennung der Unterschiede zwischen den Kopien sowie die automatische Ableitung eines initialen Modells für den Entwurf der Variabilität der zukünftigen Produktlinie. Die Differenzanalyse kann somit für Entwickler vollständig transparent durchgeführt werden.

Spezifikationskonzept für Programm-Restrukturierungen zur Einführung von Variabilität Die Spezifikation von Programm-Restrukturierungen innerhalb eines Programms hat sich in der Software-Entwicklung durch die bessere Nachvollziehbarkeit und die Möglichkeit zur Automatisierung bewährt. Bestehende Spezifikationskonzepte unterstützen jedoch nicht die Zusammenführung mehrerer Programmkopien und die gleichzeitige Einführung von Variabilität. Daher wurde ein Konzept zur Spezifikation von Restrukturierungen von Programmen entwickelt, das eben dies ermöglicht und es im Rahmen einer Konsolidierung erlaubt, Variabilität einheitlich und damit nachvollziehbarer und wartbarer zu implementieren. Zudem wurde auf Basis des Spezifikationskonzeptes ein Vorschlagssystem entwickelt, das Entwicklern die manuelle Auswahl von Variabilitätsmechanismen für die einzuführenden Variationspunkte abnimmt.

Konsolidierungsprozess zur strukturierten Gestaltung und Einführung von Variabilität Es wurde ein semi-automatischer Prozess entwickelt, der Entwickler bei der Erstellung eines Variabilitätsentwurfs leitet. Zudem wurde ein Profil erarbeitet, in dem Produktlinien-Vorgaben zur stärkeren Automatisierung des Prozesses erfasst werden können. Zu Beginn wird eine Differenzanalyse durchgeführt und ein initiales Variationspunktmodell daraus abgeleitet. Iterativ werden nun Variabilitätsanalysen auf dem Modell durchgeführt und den Entwicklern Vorschläge zur Aggregation von Variationspunkten unterbreitet. Um weiche Faktoren, wie organisatorische Rahmenbedingungen und Produktstrategien, zu berücksichtigen, liegt die letztendliche Entscheidung für eine Aggregation bei den Entwicklern. Der so entstehende Entwurf wird mit Entscheidungen zur technischen Realisierung der Variabilitätspunkte versehen und als Eingabe an die Restrukturierung der Implementierung übergeben. Hierbei werden die betroffenen Programmstellen identifiziert und die jeweils zu implementierende Variabilität definiert, sodass sowohl manuelle als auch automatisierte Restrukturierungen möglich werden.

Evaluation des Nutzens und der Anwendbarkeit der Beiträge in der Praxis Im Rahmen meiner Arbeit habe ich verschiedene Programmanalysen und deren Optimierungsmöglichkeiten in Fallstudien untersucht. Hierbei wurden zum einen Varianten eines frei zugänglichen Modellierungswerkzeuges untersucht, deren variantenspezifischer Code dokumentiert und damit als Maßstab verfügbar ist. Zum anderen wurde zur Untersuchung der Anwendbarkeit des Ansatzes in einem industriellen Szenario eine industrielle Fallstudie mit der CAS Software AG und kundenspezifischen Kopien eines ihrer Produkte durchgeführt. Darüber hinaus wurden Befragungen und eine internetbasierte Umfrage zur Angemessenheit des vorgeschlagenen Ansatzes in Bezug auf den heutigen Stand der Praxis durchgeführt. Die Evaluation hat die Angemessenheit des Ansatzes für reale Bedingungen bestätigt. Zudem wurden der Nutzen der Variabilitätsanalyse insgesamt zur Reduzierung des manuellen Aufwands sowie der Mehrwert des strukturierten Prozesses für eine konsistentere Umsetzung der Variabilität bestätigt. Gleichzeitig hat sich die Notwendigkeit der Anpassung und Optimierung bestehender Programmanalysen für deren Anwendung im Rahmen einer Konsolidierung herausgestellt. Damit verbunden wurde auch ein unterschiedlich großer Nutzen der untersuchten Programmanalysen deutlich.

Zusammengefasst konnte festgestellt werden, dass die automatisierten Analysen Software-Entwickler, im Rahmen einer Konsolidierung unterstützen können kundenspezifische Software-Anpassungen besser zu verstehen und die einzuführende Variabilität zu entwerfen. Die Berücksichtigung von Unternehmensvorgaben, wie die erlaubten Variabilitätsmechanismen, ermöglicht es eine einheitliche Gestaltung und Umsetzung der Variabilität sicherzustellen.

Darüber hinaus unterstützt der werkzeuggeführte Prozess auch Entwickler ohne spezielle Vorkenntnisse im Bereich der Programmanalyse, kundenspezifische Produktkopien in eine variable Produktlinie zu überführen. Eine Konsolidierung zur Nutzung langfristiger Wartungs- und Produktvorteile wird somit für Unternehmen hinsichtlich der Aufwände und Risiken attraktiver.

Preliminary Remarks

Use of genders When a specific gender is used in this thesis, this is done for the sake of legibility and does not exclude any genders.

Use of "we" For the sake of the flow of words, the term "we" is used instead of "I" in this thesis. However, the work presented represents my own contributions, and any work done in cooperation has been marked explicitly.

KoPL project This thesis was partly conducted in the KoPL [107] research project and partly funded by the German Federal Ministry of Education and Research (BMBF), grant No. 01IS13023 C. The KoPL research project takes up results from this thesis. Accordingly, parts of the results have been published and cited in the according project deliverable. The consolidation process and stakeholders defined in this thesis have been reused in the KoPL deliverable "D2.1 Requirements Specification for the KoPL Tool Chain". The architecture of the prototype and the concept of technology-specific adaptations defined in this thesis have been reused in the KoPL deliverable "D3.1 Architecture Specification for the KoPL Tool Chain". The industrial case study and the interview workshop have been performed in cooperation with the consortium of the KoPL project.

Contents

List of Figures

List of Tables

Listings

Part I.

Customized Product Copies

1. Introduction

Copying existing software products as a starting point for new projects is a frequently used approach in software development, as recently surveyed by Dubinsky et al. [45] and described by Riva and Del Rosso [157]. Copying a product and adapting it to customer-specific needs allows for flexible and efficient software customization in the short-term. However, in the long-term, such copies cause barriers of growth because of redundant maintenance efforts, not taking advantage of synergy effects, or cross selling features. In contrast, a Software Product Line (SPL) [33] approach with a single code base and explicitly managed variability allows overcoming such barriers and benefit from effort reduction, quality improvements, and time-to-market reduction as summarized by Schmid [169].

Starting with an SPL approach requires additional upfront investment and lowers the time-to-market, which is often not acceptable from a business perspective. However, starting with customized copies and consolidating them into an SPL later is challenging. Consolidating customized copies requires to identify and combine their varying features by introducing variability mechanisms [113, 162]. For example, identifying relevant differences between those customized copies requires to review a lot of code and to understand which modifications belong to each other [165, 4].

State of the art software difference analyses are not designed for SPL consolidation. They neither consider characteristics specific for copy-based customizations (e.g., copy creation practices such as change patterns and naming conventions) nor support interpreting differences (e.g., identifying relationships between thousands of low-level code differences). Furthermore, deriving a reasonable variability design which structures the features of an SPL requires specific expertise, and is not a software developer's everyday task.

This thesis proposes a novel approach for consolidating customized product copies. It contributes software analyses and a development process for reducing manual efforts of such consolidations and achieving consistent variability with less coordination overheads.

1.1. Motivation

When it comes to consolidating customized product copies, one cannot assume a complete and reliable documentation of all modifications performed in the copies. As confirmed by an industrial case study performed in the context of this thesis, one cannot even assume a list of custom features that have been implemented for a certain product copy. Furthermore, the developers, who originally introduced the copies might not be available anymore, as it was the case in the industrial case study as well.

Relevance in practice If done the naive way, a product copy consolidation results in a lot of manual effort and high complexity. For example, consolidations considering only parts of a copy and performed in an unstructured manner come with the risk of too many unrelated and insufficiently documented variability. Svahnberg et al. [183] describe such variability as a threat to the manageability of an SPL in practice. The high effort and complexity reduce the advantages of introducing an SPL.

A survey performed as part of this case study confirmed that companies are aware of the disadvantages of customized product copies but do not actively target their consolidation (Section 8.5.3).

Limitations of related research directions Existing SPL engineering approaches either follow a top down approach (i.e., designing the SPL first), or do not support the consolidation of existing copies to an SPL in an implementation-aware manner. Existing approaches for analyzing differences and merging them into a single code base do not allow for designing and introducing variability. On the other side, approaches in the field of clone detection allow for identifying commonalities within one or more code bases.

However, having the commonalities at hand, the approaches do not support developers in transforming the rest of the implementations into reasonable variability.

Scientific challenges described in literature Due to the limitations of existing directions of research, it is still an open scientific question which type of information and guidance allows for supporting developers in consolidating copies into SPLs. In recent years, this scientific question raised additional awareness as several groups started to investigate this topic, such as Rubin et al. [165, 160, 162], Meister [129], Eyal-Salman et al. [57], or Alves et al. [4], and the research community started according events such as the International Workshop on Reverse Variability Engineering (REVE [123]). Rubin and Chechik [161] recently published a survey on feature location techniques and motivated their potential for a transition to SPLs. They concluded their survey with the demand for adapting and evaluating the benefit of feature location techniques for such transitions, which matches to the contributions of this thesis.

1.1.1. Example Scenario

Copy-based customization of existing software solutions is not limited to a specific domain or type of system. One can assume, the higher the need for customization, the lower the experience with variability, and the stronger the project constraints are, the more often customized product copies exist. To give an example, an online shop used in an e-commerce scenario as shown on the left side of Figure 1.1.

Starting position A software vendor has for example developed an integration of a shop with a product database and an Enterprise Resource Planing (ERP) system for the customer operating the shop. The product database provides information about the products sold in the shop and the ERP system provides real time stock and price information. The solution is successfully deployed and used.

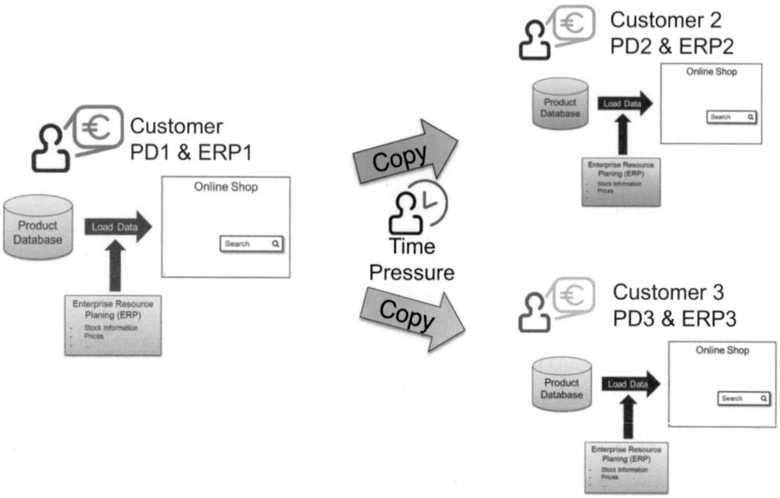

Figure 1.1.: E-Commerce example of customized product copies

Customization need and project pressure Now, customer 2 and customer 3 request similar solutions but operate different product databases, different ERP systems, and adaptations in their data processing. These adaptions are not foreseen configuration options and require source code changes. Furthermore, it is summertime already and the customers need to have these integrations before the Christmas business starts. As this time will be the peak of their business, the integrations will be useless if they are not available in advance. To cope with this time pressure, copying the existing software solution allows for two teams working in parallel on adapting the integration to the customer-specific needs.

Consolidation need When the Christmas time is successfully passed and the new year has started, the management of the software vendor decides to offer such integrations for varying ERP systems and databases as a product. In particular, they want to offer the solution with the ability to support any combination of product databases and ERP systems supported so far. Thus, the software vendor needs to consolidate the customized copies into an SPL flexible enough to support this strategy. However, at the same time, the effort required for this consolidation must be as low as possible to finance the strategy and to offer the future SPL in a reasonable time frame.

1.1.2. Copy-Based Customization

Code copies are well-known for their disadvantages in the field of software engineering in general and software evolution in particular. Parnas [145] has discussed and criticized code duplication, what he calls the "Clone and Own" approach, already in 1976. However, copying and customizing existing products is a still widespread procedure, as recently studied by Dubinsky et al. [45]. They have identified three reasons why copying code is still used in practice [45, page 28]:

- "Efficiency"
- "Short-term Thinking"
- "Lack of Governance"

The first reason has been illustrated in the example described above for coping with the short time frame to realize the customizations. "Short-term thinking", exists according to Dubinsky et al. [45], when companies focus on delivering individual products and postpone activities for enabling reuse. As a third reason, they describe that a "Lack of Governance" exists when knowledge about and responsibility for reuse are rarely maintained by a company. The improved "Efficiency" as reason for copying has additionally been confirmed by the participants of our online survey (Section 8.5.3). The "Lack of Governance" was confirmed by the participants of the online survey and interviews we have performed (Section 8.5.1). Similarly, Rubin et al. [165, page 1] summarized the advantages of copy-based customization as "...the easiest and the fastest reuse mechanism, providing ... existing already tested code, while having the freedom and independence to make necessary modifications...".

However, Rubin et al. [165] and Dubinsky et al. [45] do not aim for the completeness of their lists, and even more reasons, such as unstable domains, intellectual properties, and organizational structures, force copying code instead of introducing variability in advance. Copy-based customization practices are not limited to copying products as a whole. It is applicable for

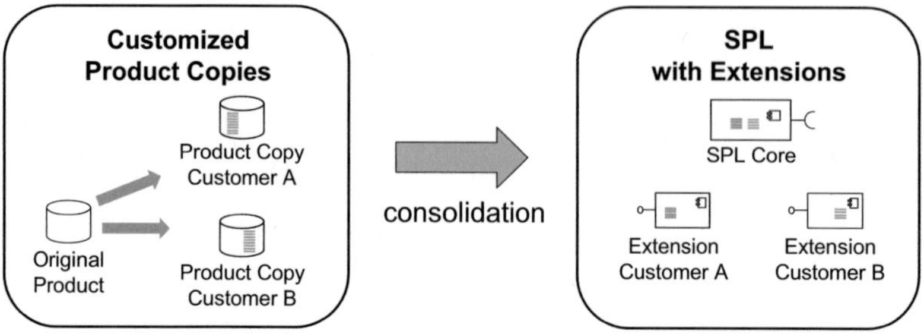

Figure 1.2.: Customized product copies (left) and derived SPL with core and extensions (right)

copies of complete products as well as for copies of extensions or components of a product as illustrated by the following two scenarios.

Customized Product Copies Figure 1.2 presents a typical customization scenario with the whole product being copied and modified to match the needs of customer A or customer B. It represents the traditional "Clown and Own" strategy discussed and criticized by Parnas [145]. This type of scenario is typical for introducing an SPL. It requires to design variation points and alternative variants for these points.

Grown Extension Repository Another application scenarios for consolidating customized copies are grown extension repositories. Figure 1.3 shows a software product that already implements an extension mechanism and appropriate extension points. Extension points are a certain type of variability realization mechanism. Extension points allow for flexibly adding new extending components according to a defined Application Programming Interface (API) as described by Klatt and Krogmann [98].

In practice, there are often grown extension repositories containing many extensions serving the same functionality but modified or adapted to customer-specific needs. To keep such extension repositories manageable and simplify the selection and reuse of extensions, the existing extensions must be reviewed and consolidated on a regular basis.

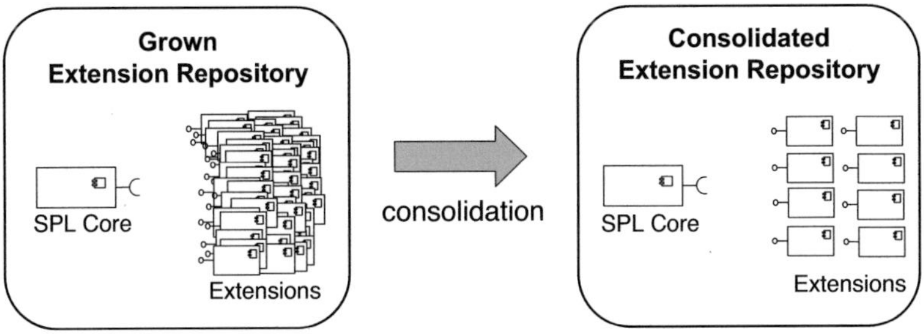

Figure 1.3.: Grown extension repository (left) and repository with consolidated and flexible extensions (right)

1.1.3. Advantages of Software Product Lines

Reuse is one of the major goals since the early years of software engineering (Jacobson et al. [88]). It is expected to shorten the time-to-market, reduce maintenance costs, and lead to an improved quality as a result of more often tested components. About a decade ago, the Software Product Line approach has been introduced as a concept of explicitly managed variability (Clements and Northrop [33]). Meanwhile, the approach has proven as a valuable concept to reach the goal of software reuse by achieving an "improved time-to-market and quality, reduced portfolio size, engineering costs and more" (Rubin and Chechik [164] referencing to Clements and Northrop [33] and Gomaa [67]).

1.1.4. Consolidation Challenges

Consolidating customized product copies is a typically challenging and expensive task. Especially, understanding the customizations from one copy to another is not obvious by nature. A possibly large amount of differences, irrelevant modifications (e.g., comments), relationships between those modifications, individual preferences on the future SPL and the need for a long-term manageable variability design, lead to challenges specific for consolidation activities.

Difference granularity and amount Independently customized product copies allow for flexible adaptations without any restrictions. As described by Alves et al. [4, page 4], tools for analyzing the differences between those copies provide many details one has to handle. Especially when text-based or line-based difference analyses approaches are used, their sensitivity to reformatting further complicates this challenge as described by Baxter et al. [12] and Hunt and Tichy [84, page 2].

Related differences When merging code bases, one has to identify related differences to improve the merging or prevent conflicts due to renaming as described by Hunt and Tichy [84]. Not only merging code bases but introducing variability at the same time further extends the challenge of identifying related differences. Developers need to find related differences scattered to many locations and must decide which of them contribute to the same variable feature, as described by Rubin and Chechik [163], Eyal-Salman et al. [57], Alves et al. [4] and Koschke et al. [108].

Individual goals As described by Bosch [21], Software Product Lines can exist in different shapes such as deploying different sets of components or multi-tenant systems adapting their behavior to the current user. Depending on the individual goals of a company, one shape is preferable over the other. However, besides the general shape of an SPL, individual points of variability require different types of variability. For example, even if multi-tenant systems allow for deciding about variability features at run time, there will be some variable features configured at system start up time anyway (e.g., the type of database server to use). Such decisions are influenced by technical as well as product management requirements and need to involve the according stakeholders.

In addition to the shape of the intended SPL, a company can have different quality goals when deciding for a consolidation, such as reducing code complexity or redundancy as described by Rubin and Chechik [164]. Thus, individual goals of a consolidation should be considered to achieve a valuable SPL at the end of a consolidation.

Uniformity of variability implementation As a general finding in software engineering, similar challenges should be handled in a similar manner for many reasons such as comprehensibility and effort reduction. Batory et al. [11] have stated the according *Principle of Uniformity* and in Apel et al. [7, page 60] adopted this principle for the context of variability and feature-oriented SPL development, stating that introducing variability in similar artifacts should be done in a similar manner.

1.2. Problem Statements

In accordance with the motivation described above, customized product copies cannot always be prevented but must be consolidated to benefit from an SPL approach in the long-term. Today, these consolidations are done in fully manual fashion and generic comparison tools are used that produce too much information that must be further interpreted by developers. Furthermore, how to refactor customized copies into a single code base is decided in an ad hoc manner with the risk of inappropriate and inconsistent implementations, not involving all stakeholders at the right time and leading to withdrawing implementations more often than necessary. Existing approaches for reactive SPL development focus on feature extraction from a single product to make them optional (Apel et al. [7, page 203]).

Based on the challenges of consolidating customized product copies and the lack of existing approaches to target them, this thesis is motivated by two problem statements:

> **Problem Statement I:** Today, the manual effort for consolidating customized copies is too high.
>
> **Problem Statement II:** Unstructured consolidation processes require unnecessary iterations and lead to inconsistent implementations.

1.3. Hypotheses

To approach the problems stated above, this thesis draws the following hypotheses which are targeted and evaluated in the following.

Hypothesis I: Consolidation Support It is possible to create automation for reducing developers' manual effort in consolidating customized product copies into a Software Product Line with explicit variability.

Hypothesis I.I: Difference Analysis It is possible to create a fully automated difference analysis that considers consolidation-specific requirements and improves information presented to developers.

Hypothesis I.II: Variability Design It is possible to recommend reasonable variability design decisions by analyzing relationships between code differences and thereby reducing manual efforts for inspecting the original copies.

Hypothesis I.III: Consolidation Refactoring It is possible to derive reasonable refactoring instructions from a variability design to guide developers in refactoring the code base.

Hypothesis II: Consolidation Process It is possible to specify a structured and industrially applicable consolidation process providing guidance for stakeholder involvement and reducing overheads for coordination and withdrawn implementations.

1.4. Contributions

This thesis proposes a novel approach to support the consolidation of customized product copies named SPLEVO ("**S**oftware **P**roduct **L**ine **evo**lution").

The contributions of this thesis are integrated in the SPLEVO approach as well as an evaluation of the contributions including studies of different analysis adaptions to gain insight into their individual value.

Difference Analysis for consolidating customized product copies A difference analysis has been developed that allows for a fully automated analysis of the differences between source code of customized product copies and allows for ignoring irrelevant differences. It is able to consider copy-based customization-specific practices to filter irrelevant differences and by that improves the results of the analysis (e.g., copies referencing their origin). In addition, the difference analysis allows for automatically deriving a variation point model for iteratively designing variability to introduce as part of a consolidation process.

Program analyses for designing variability Copy-specific features are typically implemented at many different code locations. To identify differences which are related to the same copy-specific feature, an analysis has been developed to identify relationships between such locations by exploiting and adapting existing software analysis approaches. Furthermore, recommendations to design the variability of the future SPL are derived from the detected relationships.

Specification concept and recommendation system for consolidation refactorings A concept for specifying refactorings aware of consolidating code and introducing variability at the same time has been developed. This allows for consistently implemented variability at multiple locations of a SPL, such that similar variability is realized in the same technical way. Furthermore, based on this specification concept, a recommendation system relieves developers of manually selecting the most appropriate variability mechanism for individual points of variability and thus reduces manual effort and promotes consistent selections.

Structured consolidation process A semi-automatic process which guides developers during a consolidation has been developed. An SPL Profile was developed to capture individual requirements on the future SPL and, thus, to allow for further automating the process. The process structures the consolidation into a fully automated difference analysis, a semi-automated design phase with a coordinated involvement of further stakeholders, and the initialization of a guided refactoring to implement the future SPL.

Evaluation and analysis study The contributions of the SPLEVO approach have been evaluated in case studies with variants of an open source software design tool as well as in an industrial case study. Within the case study, multiple relationship analyses with different optimization settings have been investigated to gain insight on their individual value for consolidating customized product copies. Furthermore, interviews and an online survey have been performed to show the validity of assumptions and concepts of the contributions for real-world scenarios.

1.5. Structure of this Thesis

This thesis is structured in three main parts: Customized Product Copies (Part I),The SPLevo Approach (Part II), and Outlook and Conclusion (Part III).

Part I: Customized Product Copies The first part of this thesis introduces the research topic and describes the motivation and hypotheses of this thesis in Chapter 1. The following Chapter 2 introduces the foundations of this thesis.

Part II: The SPLevo Approach The second part of this thesis presents the SPLEVO approach and details its contributions. In particular, Chapter 3 provides an overview of the approach in total. Following, Chapter 4 presents the proposed consolidation process for developer guidance. The process' individual steps are explained in the following chapters. Next, Chapter 5 presents the difference analysis specific for consolidating customized copies. Then, Chapter 6 describes the different aspects, activities, and analyses proposed to design the variability of the future SPL. Afterwards, Chapter 7 presents the proposed concept for specifying variability-aware refactorings as well as the support for variability realization and related activities. Chapter 8 describes the evaluation performed including the overall evaluation concepts and the different types of evaluations to prove the hypotheses of this thesis. At the end of the second part of this thesis, Chapter 9 summarizes the assumptions and identified limitations of the presented approach.

Part III: Outlook and Conclusion The third part concludes and summarizes this thesis. First, Chapter 10 presents approaches related to the contributions of this thesis. Next, Chapter 11 presents identified directions for future work. Finally, Chapter 12 summarizes this thesis and concludes the gained insight.

2. Foundations

This chapter presents the foundations this thesis builds upon. It makes use of contributions, approaches, and practices from an abundance of topics in the context of software engineering and beyond. The following sections introduce these foundations categorized in Model Driven Software Development (MDSD), Software Product Line (SPL), Variability, Software Maintenance, and Reengineering. In addition, Section 2.5 introduces techniques and concepts used during the evaluation.

2.1. Model Driven Software Development (MDSD)

The contributions of the SPLEVO approach make extensive use of techniques from the field of Model Driven Software Development.

2.1.1. "Model Driven Engineering" Approaches

Brambilla et al. [24, page 9] have classified different types of software engineering approaches in the field of MDSD according to the role of the models:

- Model Driven Development (MDD): The implementation of the software is (semi-) automatically generated from the models.
- Model Driven Architecture (MDA): A subset of MDD with models and languages standardized by the Object Management Group (OMG).

- Model Driven Engineering (MDE): A superset of MDD with models used in the engineering process not limited to pure development but also for analysis purposes (e.g., model-based evolution or reengineering legacy systems).
- Model Based Engineering (MBE): A softer version of MDE, where models are also used for software planning and design but implementation is done manually afterwards.

According to this classification, the SPLEVO approach is a Model Driven Engineering process. In case of an automated refactoring at the end of its process, some aspects of the Model Driven Development are covered as well. However, the approach itself is in the category of Model Driven Engineering (MDE) and, thus, the foundations cover only specific parts of the field of MDSD.

2.1.2. Modeling Levels

The OMG has specified different abstraction levels of modeling concepts [140]. Figure 2.1 shows the layers and the dependencies between them as published by Völter et al. [188].

On the lowest level (M0), actual object instances reside, such as data objects instantiated by a program at run time. On the second level (M1), models exist that describe classes of those objects. For example, data types are specified on this level. Hence, models can be defined by explicit modeling or general programming languages. The dotted line represents a boarder of abstraction that software developers do not pass in traditional non-MDSD software engineering. Above this border, on the third level (M2), metamodels are defined providing modeling languages to create specific models. Accordingly, a model is an instance of a metamodel. For example, the Unified Modeling Language (UML) is a popular metamodel (M2) for creating models (M1) when designing software systems. On the uppermost layer (M3), meta-metamodels exist. They provide an infrastructure for creating metamodels and are sometimes referred to as a language for creating modeling languages. The Meta Object Facility (MOF) standard provided by the OMG represents such a meta-metamodel.

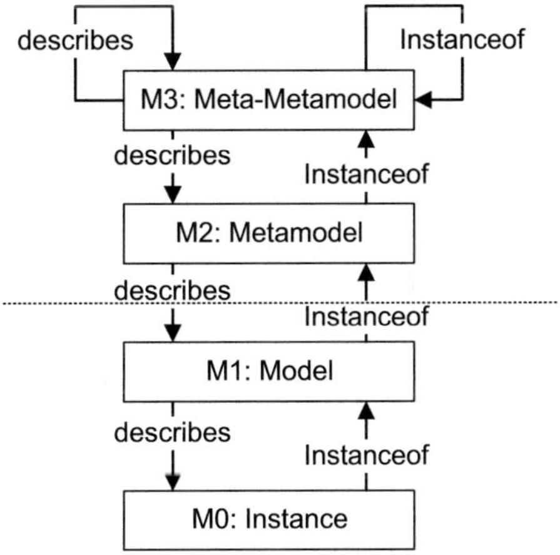

Figure 2.1.: Model abstraction levels (Völter et al. [188])

However, in the past, with version one of the MOF standard, the OMG proposed exactly four layers of model abstraction. Meanwhile, it is common sense that the number of layers is not fixed. Additional layers can be added or existing ones can be removed or merged (i.e., a minimum of two layers is declared as necessary in the MOF specification version 2 [140, page 17]).

2.1.3. Meta Object Facility (MOF)

As mentioned in the last section, the Meta Object Facility (MOF) is a specification for developing metamodels in a structured and standardized way. It is standardized by the OMG and meanwhile exists in its second version. Important changes of this revision are the explicitly not fixed number of layers and the formalization of the MOF infrastructure to be able to describe itself in a recursive way (see Figure 2.1).

EMOF The Essential Meta Object Facility (EMOF) metamodel infrastructure provided as part of the MOF specification provides essential facilities to "model object-oriented systems" [140, page 25]. Beside others, this includes classes, enumerations, data types, attributes, references as well as literals, operations and properties.

Ecore and the Eclipse Modeling Project The Eclipse Modeling Framework [50] provided by the Eclipse [48] community offers infrastructure for MDSD. This infrastructure includes the Ecore metamodel as a dialect of the UML. It is aligned to the EMOF specification while not covering it to its full extent.

The SPLEVO approach uses the EMOF standard to specify the proposed metamodels and the Ecore infrastructure to implement them within the SPLEVO prototype. Diagrams of the metamodels provided in this thesis have been generated from the Ecore-based metamodel implementations as well.

2.1.4. Object Constraint Language (OCL)

In addition to the MOF specification, the OMG has standardized the Object Constraint Language (OCL) [141] as formal language to express further constraints on object-oriented models with a predicate logic. It allows for expressing constraints such as pre- and post-conditions or invariants for any kind of operations and model validations. The Object Constraint Language (OCL) specification provides an abstract and a concrete syntax. The former defines the language concepts themselves, the latter defines a textual representation for OCL constraints.

Abstract syntax The abstract syntax [141, page 37] defines the concepts of the language itself. It contains a type package providing data types (e.g., BooleanType), collection types (e.g., OrderedSetType), as well as abstract types for checking type conformance (e.g., AnyType, VoidType). In addition, it contains an expression package providing several types of expressions to specify the predicates themselves. The expression package contains, for example, conditional and literal expressions. Furthermore, the package provides expressions that allow for operation on collections and navigating on objects.

Concrete syntax The concrete syntax [141, page 69] provides a standardized grammar for textual notation for OCL constraints. Thus, it prevents varying representations of OCL expressions as a reference for tool builders.

The SPLEVO approach uses OCL constraints to specify additional constraints that cannot be unambiguously expressed with EMOF only. This thesis sticks to the concrete syntax defined for OCL.

2.2. Software Product Lines

The Software Product Line (SPL) approach has been introduced more than a decade ago to provide managed reuse within families of similar products [33, 191]. Its core idea is to a have common base for a family of products and derive specific products with differing sets from it. The SPL approach has proven to be valuable for achieving goals such as cost reduction, improved time-to-market, and quality attributes [33, 67].

Definitions and aspects Many definitions of what constitutes product lines have been proposed according to the context they are used in. For example, the IEEE Systems and Software Engineering Vocabulary contains two different definitions covering products and services on one side, and systems with a common domain architecture on the other side [85, p 273]. However, reuse and variability are always the core aspects in context of Software Product Lines. Similarly, many different aspects to consider for SPL development have been identified. The following sections introduce the concepts, characteristics, and aspects relevant for the SPLEVO approach.

2.2.1. Assignment to General Concepts

To structure the development of SPLs, several concepts have been developed to cover different aspects. The following subsections describe the concepts related to this thesis and classifies the SPLEVO approach to them.

2.2.1.1. SPL Scoping

Developing an SPL requires to define the scope of what is covered by the product line and what is not. This is always a tradeoff between the flexibility and the complexity of an SPL as well as the effort to develop it. Three types of scoping have been established (e.g., [170, 18]):

Product Portfolio Scoping Product Portfolio Scoping is a high level view on the products that should be targeted by the SPL. This is mainly related to the product management of a company and facilitates approaches of marketing and strategic business development.

Domain Scoping Domain Scoping is about deriving the feature set and domains to be included in a specific SPL. Approaches to develop an SPL scoping such as the one described by Schmid [170], often describe a two-phase process. First, they identify related sub-domains of the overall product portfolio. Afterwards, they analyze these sub-domains about their re-usability potentials.

Asset Scoping Asset Scoping is about the implementation of the SPL artifacts. While the first two levels are more about the feature definition, this type of scoping is focused on how to design and implement the reusable components. It includes the definition and assignment of features to the reusable components. This type of scoping has a high impact on the economics of the SPL. Nevertheless, there are only a few approaches specific to identify reusable components. The most traditional approaches are more about cost-benefit analysis of already existing components.

Scoping in the context of the SPLEVO approach The SPLEVO approach assumes valid and satisfying product copies as an input for a consolidation. Thus, the scope of the intended SPL is defined by the capabilities of those copies. Related to the types of scoping proposed by Schmid, the SPLEVO approach relates to Asset Scoping at most. The "Domain Scoping" is touched only if the copies have been customized for different domains.

However, even in this case, the domains are defined by the copies to be consolidated.

2.2.1.2. Problem vs. Solution Space

Czarnecki and Eisenecker [38] introduced the distinction between a problem space and a solution space in the context of generative programming. The problem space relates to the requirements and needs of a domain and describes the features provided by SPL from a customer perspective. The solution space relates to the implementation of an SPL and describes the variability in the program from the perspective of the developers.

Berg et al. [15, page 114] mapped requirements and domain analysis to the problem space. Furthermore, they mapped the architecture, component design, and source code to the solution space. They propose to consider variability in an overarching manner, thus it can be traced between the two spaces.

The SPLEVO approach conforms to this perspective. The copies to be consolidated reside in the solution space. During the consolidation process, they are merged and variability is introduced in the solution space. However, the problem space is considered during the variability design. Finally, the variability design is used to move over to the problem space and keep the trace to the variability in the solution space.

2.2.1.3. Domain Engineering and Application Engineering

Weiss and Lai [191] proposed the distinction between Domain Engineering and Application Engineering. They describe two phases of an SPL engineering process. During Domain Engineering, the common SPL is developed and all development activities are covered (i.e., requirements engineering, design, and implementation). During Application Engineering, a specific product is derived from an SPL (i.e., an application). Application Engineering covers all development activities as well. However, depending on the type of SPL and the requirements of the concrete application, the activities are covered to different extent. For example, if an SPL allows for implementing product-specific features, all activities will be involved.

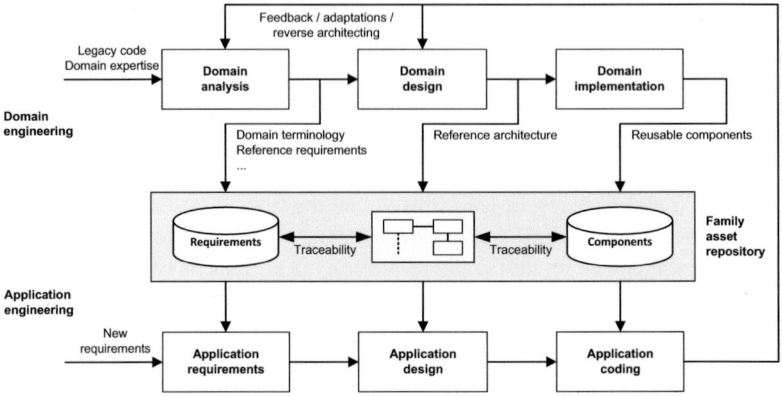

Figure 2.2.: SPL reference process by Van der Linden [186]

The distinction between Domain and Application Engineering has been adopted by others, such as, for the SPL development reference process, proposed by Van der Linden [186], shown in Figure 2.2. This process allows for creating new features during both engineering phases.

However, it is a critical decision to implement a new feature in the SPL or for an individual product only. Making the wrong decision may either result in an expensive and unnecessary variability or in a non-reusable asset which requires additional effort to transfer it to the overall SPL [18].

The SPLEVO approach targets the challenges of transferring application level features to SPL features. However, it is focused on independently customized product copies and initializing a complete new SPL. Extending the approach to support degenerated SPLs is a direction for future work (Section 11).

2.2.2. SPL Adoption Paths

Bosch [21] describes two different approaches for adopting an SPL approach: revolutionary and evolutionary SPL adoption. In the revolutionary approach, a company starts with a new SPL that designed as a superset of potential SPL members and further members that are predicted for the future. It allows

Project Type	Evolutionary	Revolutionary
Existing set of products	Develop vision for SPL based on family members. Develop one SPL component at a time (possibly for a subset of SPL members) by evolving existing components	SPL components are developed based on supersets of SPL member requirements and predicted future requirements
New SPL	SPL components evolve with the requirements posed by new SPL members	SPL components are developed to match requirements of all expected SPL members

Table 2.1.: Dimensions of product line initiation by Bosch [21]

taking future product variants into account and planning for a broader scope of the SPL. In contrast, in the evolutionary approach, the SPL is derived from existing products or concrete requirements reported by intended members of the SPL. It allows for a more focused and less complex adoption of the SPL approach. Table 2.1 summarizes the two different approaches in context of a set of existing products to integrate and in context of introducing an SPL from scratch.

The major benefit of evolutionary SPLs is the shortened time-to-market for new products or product variations. Especially small and medium-sized companies often rely on this strategy as they are not able to make big upfront investments as required by a revolutionary SPL approach (e.g., [130, 129]).

Krueger [113, page 5] has refined this concept into proactive, extractive, and reactive approaches. Apel et al. [7, page 203] summarize these approaches as:

- "The extractive approach starts with a collection of existing products and incrementally refactors them to form a product line."
- "The proactive approach develops a product line from scratch by carefully using analysis and design methods."

- "The reactive approach begins with a small, easy to handle product line (possibly consisting only of a single product) and is extended incrementally with new features and implementation artifacts, thus extending the product line's scope."

Especially larger companies spend an up-front investment to plan and build SPLs in a proactive and revolutionary approach (e.g., Bosch et al. [22] and Clements and Northrop [33]). Smaller and medium-sized enterprises are often not able to make such an investment before delivering the first new product or a customization. This leads to a more reactive and evolutionary SPL approach (e.g., Meister [129]). Dubinsky et al. [45] surveyed further reasons for product level customizations, such as lack of governance and efficiency. Moreover, evolving legacy systems into SPLs can improve the re-usability and maintainability of such systems (e.g., Koziolek et al. [109]) and require extractive or reactive SPL development by nature. Finally, a recent survey by Berger et al. [16, page 3] confirmed that extractive and reactive adoption strategies are most frequently used in practice.

The SPLEVO approach relates to evolutionary SPL approaches and supports scenarios of intended or unintended extractive SPL developments.

2.2.3. Features and Software Variability

The concept of features and the definition of their variability is well-known in the area of requirements- and SPL-engineering.

Variability exists on different abstraction levels as specified by the "Variability Pyramid" proposed by Pohl et al. [149, page 72], shown in Figure 2.3. They describe a relationship between those levels and a clear increase in the amount of variability as well as different types of artifacts that contain the variability when moving down to lower abstraction levels.

However, people rarely distinguish between the variability on the different abstraction levels. For example, people often tend to mix-up the variability of requirements, software entities, or even configurations in a single model without any differentiation when using feature trees as proposed by Kang et al. [90].

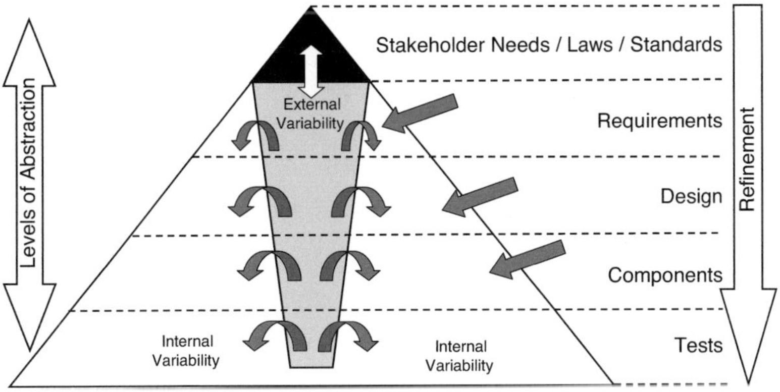

Figure 2.3.: Variability Pyramid by Pohl et al. [149]

In contrast, Bosch [20] and Svahnberg et al. [183] clearly differentiate between features and software variability. Features resist on a capability-level and relate to requirements management. Software variability is described as variation points and resists on the level of software design and architecture. The following subsections explain this differentiation in more detail.

2.2.3.1. Features

According to Bosch [20, page 194], "features are logical units of behavior specified by a set of functional and quality requirements". This implies features on the same level as requirements, and there is a many-to-many relationship between features and requirements. For example, an online banking feature relates to the requirements of a secure log-in and an account view. In contrast, the requirement of a secure data connection can be related to an online banking feature as well as to an online car rental feature. Because of the many-to-many relationship between features, variation points, and implementation, Svahnberg et al. [183, page 7] state that a "feature typically manifests itself as a set of variation points and may be implemented as a set of collaborating components". Features can combine multiple software requirements and can represent cross-cutting concerns of a software system (e.g., security infrastructure). Thus, they are implemented by one or more variation points realizing the variability in the implementation itself.

2.2.3.2. Software Variability

Svahnberg et al. [183, page 2] define software variability as "the ability of a software system or artifact to be efficiently extended, changed, customized, or configured for use in a particular context". The SPLEVO approach uses the same definition because it relates variability to the software design-level that describes the implementation of a software system. The variability in a software system is realized at variation points.

Svahnberg et al. [183] developed a classification of realization techniques based on characteristics, such as when, how, and by whom a specific variant is chosen for a variation point.

2.2.4. SPL Maturity Levels

Bosch [21] used the classification of variability realization techniques defined by Svahnberg et al. [183] to define different SPL maturity levels. These levels do not relate to the SPL itself, but to the company who is developing the SPL. Depending on the organizational structure and the available developer knowledge, different maturity levels should be adopted.

Figure 2.4 presents the identified levels and their dependencies. While independent products consist of copies of the same product, the configurable product base represents the most mature level, where people can select specific variants during application start or even at run time.

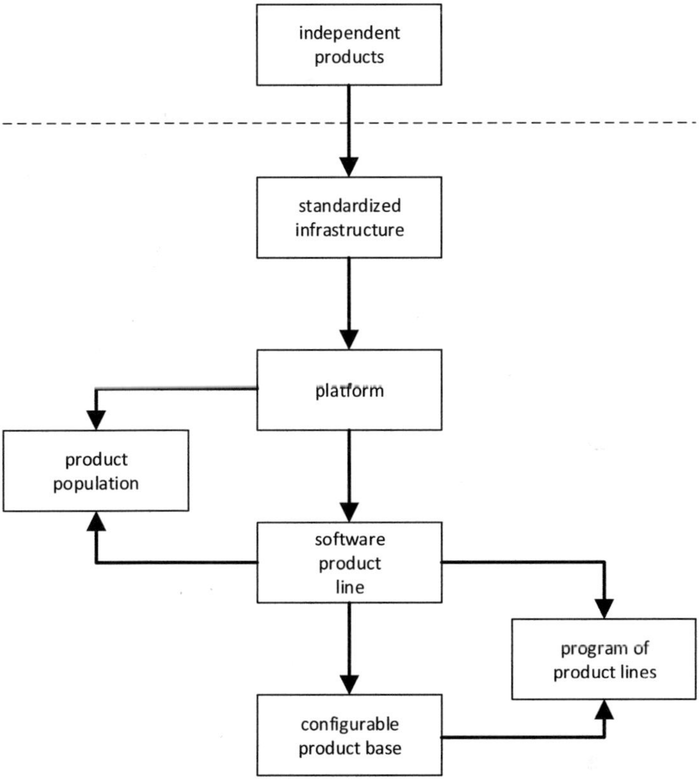

Figure 2.4.: Software Product Line maturity levels by Bosch [21]

2.2.5. SPL Quality Characteristics

Svahnberg et al. [183] and Rubin and Chechik [164] described quality characteristics one should consider when designing the variability of an SPL: The amount of variation points and the tradeoff between code quantity and code complexity. While the former relates to the structure of variability, the latter relates to its implementation.

2.2.5.1. Variation Point Amount

The amount of variation points in an SPL is tightly related to the possible range of products that can be derived. While it is desirable to cover a broad range of products with an SPL, variation points always imply additional complexity for the software design.

Svahnberg et al. [183, page 7] identified advantages of reducing the number of variation points as much as possible to improve the manageability and the complexity of the software itself. As a result, they propose to continuously revise variation points in an SPL. A few approaches for SPL evolution have been developed, such as by Alves et al. [3], who have developed an approach for variability-aware SPL refactoring. Additionally, Loesch and Ploedereder [122] present an approach to identify obsolete variation points.

This awareness is relevant for the variation point design as part of the SPLEVO approach discussed in Section 6.1.4.1.

2.2.5.2. Code Quantity vs. Complexity

Rubin and Chechik [164] describe code quantity and code complexity as two contrary quality goals when realizing variability. Code quantity means to reduce the total amount of code and prevent redundant code fragments. This quality goal corresponds to the idea that less duplicate code means less code to maintain. In contrast, code complexity means to reduce the number of variability mechanisms and reduce the execution paths, indirections, and identifiers. This quality goal corresponds to the idea that less complex code is more intuitive and easier to maintain.

Rubin and Chechik [164] propose to quantify those quality goals in terms of the size of the resulting code and the number of variation points. Especially the latter corresponds to the quality characteristic of Svahnberg et al. [183] described before.

2.2.6. SPL Management Tools

SPLs aim for an improved time-to-market and reduced maintenance costs. To permanently ensure these goals, SPL management tools have been developed to simplify product instantiations and track existing configurations and used variants.

Such tools use an internal representation of the variability (e.g., a Variability Model as described in Section 2.3.2) and a mapping to its implementation. Furthermore, they use an internal configuration model to describe the features selected for a concrete product instance.

Typical examples of such management tools are pure::variants [66] and Gears [112] as commercial solutions, as well as FeatureMapper [79] and FeatureIDE [91] as representatives from the academic community.

2.3. Software Variability

Variability in software systems can be designed and realized in many different manners. The following subsections introduce characteristics, models, and implementation strategies proposed for variability in the field of SPL research and considered by the SPLEVO approach.

2.3.1. Variability Characteristics

Variability characteristics describe aspects and capabilities of variability. They influence how variability can be configured, realized, and maintained within an SPL.

2.3.1.1. Variability Types

The variability type describes how many alternatives can or must be chosen for a specific variability to achieve a valid product configuration. Different sets of combinations of optional, alternative, and mandatory have been proposed in the literature. Svahnberg et al. [183] defined a set with three types OPTIONAL, XOR, and OR, as summarized in Table 2.2. Patzke and Muthig [146] extended this set with two additional types, combining the existing ones OPTIONAL & XOR and OPTIONAL & OR to express variability with more than one variant, but none has to be selected. The SPLEVO approach uses a subset of the variability types of Patzke and Muthig [146] as described in Section 3.2.2.4.

Variability Type		
Svahnberg et al.	**Patzke and Muthig**	**Cardinality**
OPTIONAL	OPTIONAL	0..1 out of 1
XOR	XOR	1 out of n
OR	OR	1..m out of n
	OPTIONAL & XOR:	0..1 out of n
	OPTIONAL & OR:	0..1 out of n

Table 2.2.: Variability types defined by Patzke and Muthig [146] and Svahnberg et al. [183]

2.3.1.2. Binding Time

The binding time of a variation point specifies the least possible point in time when a variant or combination of variants must be selected. Different classifications of binding times have been proposed according to different phases of the software life cycle.

Pohl et al. [149, page 250] distinguished five binding times aligned with development activities as shown in Table 2.3. Svahnberg et al. [183, page 10] proposed a slightly different set of binding times with an explicit architecture derivation. Furthermore, they describe linking as technology-dependent binding time that might happen right after compilation, at system start or even at run time. Finally, Apel et al. [7, page 48] distinguish only three binding times as presented in Table 2.3 as well: Compile Time, Load Time, Run Time. They remark that others distinguish between more binding times, but argue that those types are sufficient to decide how to realize variability. Apel et al. [7] summarize their proposed binding times as:

- **Compile Time:** "Variability is decided before or at compile time."
- **Load Time:** "Variability is decided after compilation when the program is started."
- **Run Time:** "Variability is decided and changed during program execution."

Binding Time			
Pohl et al.	**Svahnberg et al.**	**Apel et al.**	**Example**
Before Compilation	Architecture Derivation		Code generation, Aspect-oriented programming
Compile Time	Compilation	Compile Time	Pre-compiler
Link Time	Linking		Make files
Load Time		Load Time	Config. files
Run Time	Run Time	Run Time	Registry

Table 2.3.: Binding times by Pohl et al. [149], Svahnberg et al. [183] and Apel et al. [7]

2.3.1.3. Extensibility

The extensibility characteristic of variability defines who is able to populate new variants. Svahnberg et al. [183, page 9] describe this characteristic as who is allowed to extend the set of available variants. They explicitly distinguish between Domain Engineer (i.e., responsible for the SPL), Application Engineer (i.e., responsible for a specific product variant), and the End User (i.e., using a product instance). They claim that "one cannot expect end users to edit and compile source code", but "there is an increasing trend to provide variability to end users", for example based on plug-in mechanisms.

In particular, variability is designed to be extensible when it allows adding additional variants during application engineering (i.e., providing an extension point as described by Klatt and Krogmann [98]). In contrast, it is not extensible when only variants can be used that are already included in the SPL.

Extensibility comes with additional maintenance effort for ensuring compatibility with existing extensions. Furthermore, the extension mechanism has to be chosen carefully to not accidentally influence the products' quality attributes.

The extensibility characteristic is closely related to the classification of Positive and Negative variability. Gacek and Anastasopoules [64, page 2] refer to Sharp [174] as the one who has postulated this differentiation. They describe that "Positive Variability" allows for adding functionality to an SPL to achieve a concrete product. In contrast, "Negative Variability" allows for removing –or disabling– unwanted functionality from a set of functionality that is included in an SPL.

2.3.2. Variability Models

Diversity of variability models SPLs propose to provide an explicitly managed variability. To describe, design, and manage this variability, a broad range of different models has been proposed for many different purposes. Sinnema and Deelstra [176] studied and classified six representative variability modeling techniques according to their modeling capabilities and tool support. They also noticed the broad range of variability model types and purposes. Berger et al. [16] surveyed the use of variability modeling in practice. They report a variety of open source, commercial, and home-grown domain-specific solutions ranging from spread sheets to code annotations and explicit variability models.

Hence, there is no established standard for modeling variability and available models strongly depend on the purpose they are used for. The OMG is working on a future, not yet finished standard called Common Variability Language (CVL) [76].

Integrated and separate models In general, variability models can be distinguished into two groups: integrated models and independent models.

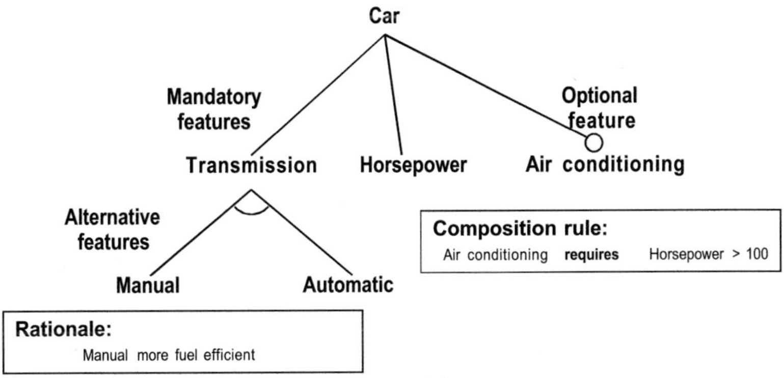

Figure 2.5.: FODA feature model example by Kang et al. [90, page 36]
(No legend provided with the original figure.)

The former are extensions of existing models, such as the UML extensions proposed by Gomaa [67] or Atkinson et al. [9]. As summarized by Pohl et al. [149, page 75], the latter are independently defined models that can exist on their own and probably reference elements of other models, such as feature models proposed by Kang et al. [90].

Feature Models Feature models as proposed by Kang et al. [90] in context of the Feature Oriented Domain Analysis (FODA) approach propose a hierarchical structure of parent and child features and a graphical notation as shown in Figure 2.5. Child features represent additional features that are included in a parent feature or represent variable options to choose from. Parent-child-relationships can be used to express different variability types (Section 2.3.1.1). In the graphical notation of Kang et al. [90], the variability type is expressed by arcs and circles added to the ends of parent-child-relationship connectors. Feature models provide a lightweight and flexible approach for describing variability. Thus, they are widely used in practice, as shown by the survey of Berger et al. [16, page 4].

Many SPL management tools use a variant of the feature model proposed by Kang et al. [90]. Especially the unlimited hierarchical structure allows for flexibly expressing a product management point of view. Similarly, feature models are facilitated for software development approaches as well. For example, Czarnecki and Eisenecker [38] propose the use of feature models to specify variability in context of generative programming. They use it for specifying which parts of a program can be generated and the options to choose from.

There is no standardized format of feature models and many proprietary variants exist. Independent from a specific tooling, the Eclipse Modeling Framework [50] provides the EMF Feature Model [51] as an Ecore-based specification and implementation. In addition, the EMF Feature Model provides a graphical editor aligned with the graphical notation proposed by Czarnecki and Eisenecker [38].

Orthogonal Variability Model Pohl et al. [149, page 75] defined an Orthogonal Variability Model as shown in Figure 2.6. They specify a variation point according to Jacobson et al. [88] as a point of variability within a software. Such a variation point can be represented by an arbitrary number of development artifacts. In contrast to Jacobson et al. [88] and according to the name of their model, Pohl et al. [149, page 83] do not limit the type of artifacts to realization artifacts and propose variation points to reference requirements, design, realization, and test artifacts. Furthermore, variation points reference their variants as either mandatory or optional according to the variability types defined by Svahnberg et al. [183] (Section 2.3.1.1).

OMG Common Variability Language (CVL) The OMG is working on a standard for variability modeling, which currently exists in a revised submission [76].

The main purpose of this standard is to specify a variability model to annotate existing base models and to derive adapted instances (i.e., Resolved Models) of such base models using model transformations (i.e., Resolution Models). This concept is aligned with the Model Driven Architecture (MDA) concept proposed by the OMG. However, the model infrastructure is intended to cover conceptual variability modeling as well as realization aspects in terms of variation points.

Until now, it is not clear when the Common Variability Language (CVL) will be finished, and it has not been evolved during the last two years.

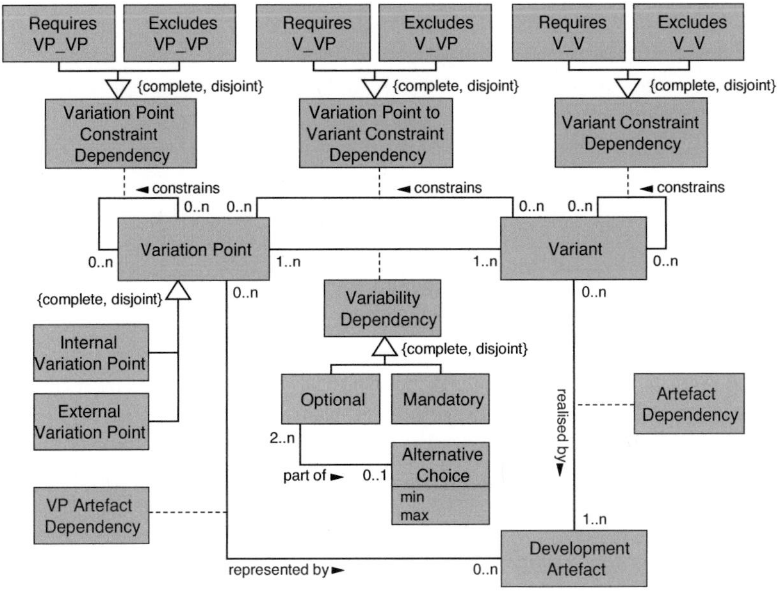

Figure 2.6.: Orthogonal Variability Model by Pohl et al. [149]

2.3.3. Variability Implementation

In any software technology, different approaches for realizing variability have been established. Which one is the best depends on the requirements of the intended SPL in general and the variation points to implement in specific. For example, if the available amount of storage is limited in the environment to operate the software in, it might be preferred to generate or compose a concrete product at development time. This would allow for installing only required code and to prevent any run time configuration processing. In contrast, a multi-tenant system requires to have all potential features in place and to select a variant at run time depending on the user currently interacting with the system.

Variability Realization Technique vs. Variability Mechanism In the literature, the terms "Variability Realization Technique" [183, 72] and "Variability Mechanism" [22, 171, 68] are used to describe concepts of how to implement variability. These terms are not clearly distinguished in the literature. For example, Clements and Northrop [33, page 69] refer to the "techniques" defined by Jacobson et al. [88, page 102] and repeated by Svahnberg and Bosch [182, page 150] as "Mechanisms for achieving variability". However, the former is used more frequently for concrete variability implementations, while the latter often describes more general concepts of software engineering such as "inheritance" or "generation" (e.g., Jacobson et al. [88, page 102]).

Within the SPLEVO approach, the terms are explicitly distinguished according to Definitions 1 and 2. In this thesis, the term `Variability Realization Technique` is used for general software engineering techniques or concepts and the term `Variability Mechanism` for concrete forms of variability implementation.

Definition 1 (Variability Realization Technique) *A* Variability Realization Technique *is a general software engineering technique or concept capable of implementing variability. Examples for Variability Realization Techniques are "inheritance", "code generation", or "dependency injection".*

Definition 2 (Variability Mechanism) *A* Variability Mechanism *is a concrete way to realize variability. It is technology-specific and, for example, uses programming-language capabilities to evaluate a configuration and decide for a variant to execute. Examples for Variability Mechanisms are If-Else conditional statements in Java [70, page 372] or dependency injections with Google Guice [187].*

In the field of object-oriented languages, different techniques and mechanisms exist to implement variability as described below.

2.3.3.1. Variability Techniques

Many different classifications for structuring the field of variability techniques in context of software reuse and SPL have been proposed. The most widely used classification was proposed by Jacobson et al. [88, page 102] in the context of software reuse and is presented in Table 2.4. Others such as Svahnberg and Bosch [182, page 150] and Clements and Northrop [33, page 69] reused this classification in context of software product lines.

This classification of variability techniques has been designed to cover and structure variability implementation with a top-down approach. It aims for supporting decisions about the general software engineering technique to be used for implementing variability. However, it does not provide guidance for developers and architects to choose a concrete variability mechanism to implement a specific variation point, such as how to realize a concrete configuration mechanism. As identified by the descriptions included in Table 2.4, the categories of this classifications are abstract and each of them identifies a variety of mechanisms.

2.3.3.2. Variability Mechanisms

Variability mechanisms provide guidelines how to implement variability. For example, a variability mechanism can be about implementing a conditional execution in a Java method with an IF-statement that evaluates a property of a Java properties file. Thus, variability mechanisms are specifications of variability techniques.

A variability mechanism defines how a variant is chosen as well as how the according configuration is evaluated. Thus, variability mechanisms cover generic as well as custom mechanisms. For example, the Java example above can be used in any Java-based application. In contrast, a company might have defined a custom license mechanism to be evaluated at run time. This requires a custom variability mechanism as well.

Thus, there is a theoretically unlimited amount of variability mechanisms and there is no general classification of mechanisms available. However, context-specific descriptions of concrete variability mechanisms exist, such as provided by Schnieders and Puhlmann [171].

Technique	Time of Specialization	Description
Inheritance	At class definition time	Inheritance is used when the variation point is a method that needs to be implemented for every application, or when an application needs to extend a type with additional functionality.
Extension	At requirements time	One use of a system can be defined by adding to the definition of another use.
Uses	At requirements time	One use of a system can be defined by including the functionality of another use.
Configuration	Previous to run time	A separate resource, such as a file, is used to specialize the component.
Parameters	At component implementation time	A functional definition is written in terms of unbound elements that are supplied when actual use is made of the definition.
Template Instantiation	At component implementation time	A type specification is written in terms of unbound elements that are supplied when actual use is made of the definition.
Generation	Before or during run time	A tool produces definitions from user input.

Table 2.4.: Classification of variability techniques proposed by Jacobson et al. [88, page 102] and summarized by Clements and Northrop [33, page 88]

2.3.3.3. Limitations of Variability Techniques and Mechanisms

In addition to provided variability characteristics, individual variability techniques and mechanisms come with technical limitations. Developers and architects must consider those limitations when deciding how to implement variability.

For example, Kästner et al. [92, 93] report limitations of Aspect Oriented Programming (AOP) they have identified within a case study. They describe difficulties with statements in the middle of methods and accessing local variables. They mention that some limitations result from AspectJ as a concrete technology used for AOP, but some limitations relate to AOP in general. In addition, Gacek and Anastasopoules [64, page 5] report about the shortcoming of AOP to not support run time variability.

2.3.3.4. Granularity

Variability techniques and mechanisms can exist on different levels of granularity in terms of software elements. Apel et al. [7, page 59] distinguish three levels of granularity: coarse, medium and fine-grained (Table 2.5). While the first two are not ordered and can be referenced explicitly, variability on a fine-grained level is more difficult to handle but allows for significant code reduction. Apel et al. [7] also refer to Kästner et al. [93] and Liebig et al. [118], who stated "that feature implementations take place at all levels of granularity".

Granularity	Description
Coarse Grained	Classes and above such as new files
Medium Grained	Members (e.g., fields and methods)
Fine-Grained	Statements and below

Table 2.5.: Variability granularity types defined by Apel et al. [7]

2.3.3.5. Delta-Oriented Programming

In addition to the feature-oriented programming approach for implementing variability, Schaefer et al. [167] propose an approach named delta-oriented programming.

Feature-oriented programming focuses on the features to be realized and exists as additive and subtractive strategies which relate to positive and negative variability described in Section 2.3.1.3.

In contrast, delta-oriented programming focuses on the differences between the core of the SPL and the concrete products. A delta-oriented approach uses transformations to modify the SPL core to achieve the intended product instance. Thus, the application engineering phase (Section 2.2.1.3) is realized in a transformation-driven manner.

2.4. Software Maintenance and Evolution

Software maintenance and evolution are major topics in the field of software engineering since several decades (Bennett and Rajlich [14]). Thus, a lot of research has been done in these topics and many different approaches have been proposed to cope with the according challenges. The following subsections introduce approaches and techniques used and considered in this thesis.

2.4.1. Software Configuration Management (SCM)

Software Configuration Management (SCM) is a process for managing the complete life cycle of a software system with a focus on coordinating software acquirer and suppliers. It is defined by the ISO/IEC TR 15846:1998 standard [86]. Beside others, this process covers the management of requirements, error reports, and according development activities.

To cope with these activities, two types of systems have been introduced and are meanwhile widely accepted in the field of software engineering: Version Control Systems and Issue Tracking and Management. The former focuses on artifacts, such as code, models, and documents, the latter is used for managing activities related within the software development process (e.g., implementing requirements or fixing errors).

2.4.1.1. Version Control System (VCS)

A Version Control System (VCS) tracks changes of artifacts compared to an initial baseline. According to the IEEE Vocabulary [85], version control and change control in general are used for "identifying, documenting, approving or rejecting, and controlling changes to the project baselines".

In software development, version control systems, such as the Revision Control System (RCS) presented by Tichy [184], are used to keep track of changes in software artifacts. Meanwhile, a range of systems such as CVS, Subversion, and git has been developed, with varying features and concepts. However, all of these systems provide a version history for the artifacts under version control as well as messages provided by a user when he stores new versions of artifacts (i.e., commit messages).

2.4.1.2. Issue Tracking and Management

As described by Bertram et al. [17], issue trackers are used by software development teams and stakeholders participating in the software life cycle. They define an issue tracker as a database for tracking bugs, features, and inquiries. Furthermore, they note the role of an issue tracker as a "focal point for communication and coordination".

Thus, in the context of SCM, an issue tracker is not limited to development teams but used by all stakeholders including support teams and project managers to coordinate their activities and issues.

State of the art issue tracking and management systems, such as provided by Jira or Team Foundation Server, allow for integration with the Version Control System (VCS) solutions to build traces between code changes and issues they belong to.

2.4.2. Coding Guidelines

The quality of a software system, especially in terms of comprehensibility, is critical for its maintainability, as described by Grubb and Takang [71, page 51]. Seng et al. [173] further describe the importance of the code quality as a key factor for the long-term success of software products.

An important factor for code comprehensibility is a common coding style. Meanwhile, it is common sense to use documentation and formatting guidelines, and even guidelines for efficient usage of coding guidelines are proposed, as done by Martin [128].

Furthermore, some technology specifications propose naming conventions to be used for a better comprehensible code, such as the Java Beans [73] or .Net [132] specifications.

2.4.3. Maintenance Types

Bennett and Rajlich [14] refer to Lientz and Swanson [119] as the ones who proposed to classify maintenance activities into adaptive, perfective, corrective, and preventive changes. They describe adaptive activities as adaptations to "changes in the software environment". Perfective activities are described as to realize "new user requirements". Corrective activities are about "fixing errors". And preventive activities are performed to "prevent problems in the future". Lientz and Swanson [119] report from an industrial study that 50% of maintenance effort is spent for perfective activities.

The ISO/IEC 14764 standard [37] categorizes these activities according to correction and enhancement. In the Guide to the Software Engineering Body of Knowledge [23, page 6-3], they are further categorized into proactive and reactive activities, as shown in Table 2.6. Consolidations as targeted in this thesis are perfective maintenance activities according to these definitions.

	Correction	Enhancement
Proactive	Preventive	Perfective
Reactive	Corrective	Adaptive

Table 2.6.: Software maintenance categories in Guide to the Software Engineering Body of Knowledge [23, page 6-3]

2.4.4. Software Metrics

Software metrics are widely used in the area of software maintenance in general and perfective and corrective maintenance tasks. They are typically used to capture characteristics of a system or to identify potential problems and quality issues, as described by Seng et al. [173].

In context of this thesis size metrics are used to classify the software systems used in the case studies. Therefore, we refer to the number of lines of code in a software system. This metric is influenced in terms of calculation and meaning by a couple of factors. Most important, the number of lines is a pure quantitative measure and does not respect the complexity of a line of code. Furthermore, depending on how it is calculated, individual programming styles can have a big impact on the metric (e.g., entering a line break before the next curly bracket in Java). However, different types of the Source Lines of Code (SLOC) software metric have been proposed to improve this situation:

Source Lines of Code (SLOC) The number of Source Lines of Code is the general software metric and exists in different variants such as Physical Lines of Code (PLOC) and Logical Lines of Code (LLOC).

Physical Lines of Code (PLOC) The number of Physical Lines of Code is calculated by the lines of code containing at least one character which is not white space or a comment. The PLOC count is typically used as software metric for the size of an implementation.

Logical Lines of Code (LLOC) The number of Logical Lines of Code is normalized in a way that relevant software elements are located on individual lines (e.g., no combined statements on one line). The LLOC count requires more effort to be calculated but allows for better comparison between different software systems due to its normalization step.

2.4.5. Reengineering

Reengineering is an essential activity in software engineering to prevent software systems to turn into legacy systems and losing value over time, as described by Demeyer [41]. Reengineering itself is defined by Chikofsky and Cross [32] as a combination of reverse engineering and forward engineering, as illustrated in Figure 2.7. According to their definition, reverse engineering allows for identifying components of a system and creating representations in another form or at a higher level of abstraction, such as design or requirements. As indicated in Figure 2.7, reverse engineering is not limited to the implementation level, but can be applied on the design level to reverse engineer requirements as well. Forward engineering is used when requirements, design, or both have been restructured and should be implemented in the design, respectively in the implementation.

Reengineering is an important aspect in context of the SPL reference process proposed by Van der Linden [186] and the consolidation of customized product copies. First, product-specific features developed during application engineering must be reverse engineered. Then, a forward engineering has to be performed to adapt the existing SPL respectively build a new one.

2.4.6. Software Model Extraction

An important part for the reverse engineering is the extraction of software models. A software model provides the representation on a higher level of abstraction, as mentioned by Chikofsky and Cross [32, page 15]. Extracting a model representation of a software implementation in general is a very common task and done by every compiler. However, these models are typically optimized for program compilation. In the context of this thesis, software models are used for the purpose of program comprehension and analysis.

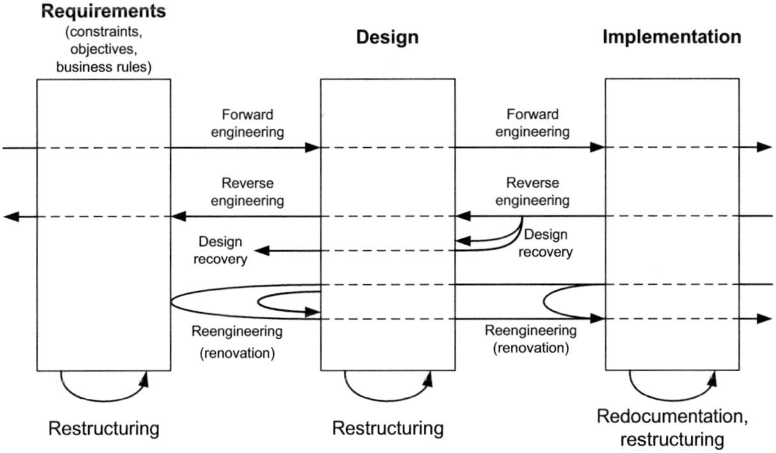

Figure 2.7.: Reengineering overview by Chikofsky and Cross [32]

Thus, the following subsections introduce software model extraction with a focus on models related to this purpose.

2.4.6.1. Parsing and Resolving

To analyze a software to its full extent, an extraction requires two phases: parsing and resolving. These phases are the same if software models are extracted by a compiler or for program comprehension and analysis.

Parsing Parsing extracts software elements from a textual representation. First, a lexer is used to identify sequences of characters that form a lexical unit representing a token defined in a grammar. Afterwards, a parser is applied to build the actual elements of a software model. At this point in process, containment relationships between these elements can be detected if they are defined in the grammar. Thus, the parsing phase provides a model of the software elements represented in the source code.

Resolving The resolving is done when the parsing is finished. Resolving is the process of identifying references between software elements other than containment relationships defined in the grammar (i.e., cross references). Resolving such references typically requires to evaluate the scope of an element and thus technology-specific logic. For example, in the Java programming language, resolving the reference to a variable requires to take the current context of the variable identifier, such as a method body or conditional statement, into account. Accordingly, resolving requires more processing effort than the parsing before.

Partial Program Analysis To cope with the processing effort, Dagenais and Hendren [39] proposed Partial Program Analysis as a technique to analyze parts of a program without resolving all dependencies. Especially, they propose not only a lazy resolving strategy, but to cope with not clearly resolvable bindings. Whether this technique can be applied depends on the individual analysis.

2.4.6.2. Software Models

Software models as used in this thesis conform to traditionally Abstract Syntax Tree (AST) models. For a consistent use of models throughout the SPLEVO approach, software models conforming to the EMOF/Ecore specifications 2.1.3 are used. Existing solutions for such Ecore-based models are designed in three different ways, as summarized in Table 2.7.

OMG KDM standardization initiative The OMG Architecture-Driven Modernization Task Force has developed the KDM standard for software reverse engineering [139]. The KDM standard includes a metamodel for Abstract Syntax Tree Models [138]. As shown in Figure 2.8, the OMG defined a metamodel system to represent language independent ASTs (i.e., Generic Abstract Syntax Tree Model - GAST), language specific ASTs (i.e., Specific Abstract Syntax Tree Model - SAST), and proprietary ASTs (i.e., Proprietary Abstract Syntax Tree Model - PAST). Table 2.8 of the specification [138, page 10] summarizes the purpose of these different metamodels.

Approach	Description	Example
Top Down	The model is designed first. The textual syntax is either derived or the extraction needs to translate between them.	OMG KDM [139, 138]
Bottom Up	Parser oriented. The textual syntax exists first and the model is designed according to the grammar of the language.	JaMoPP [78]
IDE Oriented	The model is derived from the internal model used within an IDE and neither aligned to a grammar or the purpose of the model.	MoDisco [26]

Table 2.7.: Ecore software model design approaches

Available implementations The OMG provided the specification for the metamodels only. However, they refer to the Eclipse MoDisco project [26] as the de facto reference implementation of the OMG KDM specification [139].

The MoDisco project provides an Ecore-based implementation of the overarching KDM metamodel. However, this model is not integrated with the AST model provided by the MoDisco model extractor. As shown in Table 2.7, the model extracted by MoDisco is aligned to the IDE internal model (i.e., Eclipse JDT AST) and does not conform to the OMG AST metamodel. Thus, there is no implementation according to the OMG AST specification available yet.

Name	Title	Description
GASTM	Generic AST Model	A generic set of language modeling elements common across numerous languages establishes a common core for language modeling, called the Generic Abstract Syntax Trees. In this specification, the GASTM model elements are expressed as UML class diagrams.
SASTM	Language Specific AST Models	Metamodels for particular languages such as Ada, C, Fortran, Java, etc. are modeled in Meta Object Facility (MOF) or MOF compatible forms and expressed as the GASTM along with modeling element extensions sufficient to capture the language.
PASTM	Proprietary AST Models	Metamodels that express ASTs for languages such as Ada, C, COBOL, etc. modeled in formats that are not consistent with MOF, the GSATM, or SASTM. For such proprietary AST, this specification defines the minimum conformance specifications needed to support model interchange.

Table 2.8.: AST Models of the OMG AST specification [138, page 10]

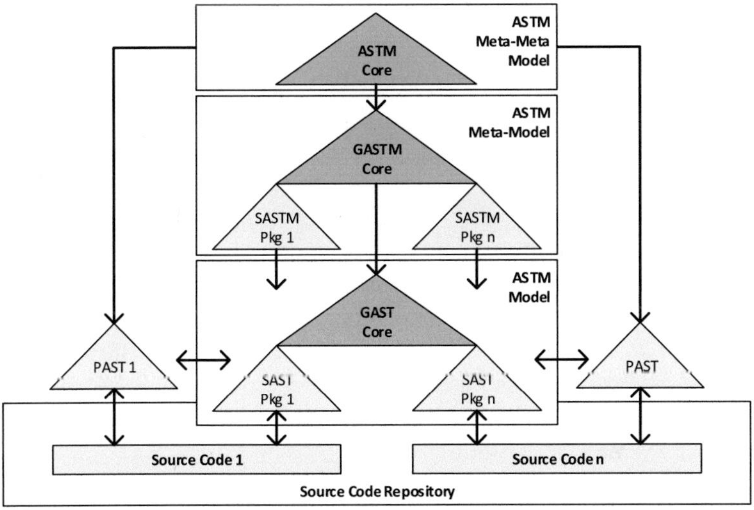

Figure 2.8.: OMG AST metamodel structure [138]

2.4.7. Difference Analysis

To analyze the differences between software implementations, two general approaches exist: text-based and model-based difference analysis. Figure 2.9 illustrates their different approaches.

Text-based analysis Text-based difference analysis first performs a comparison of the software artifacts' textual representations. The results are differing textual areas in matched files (e.g., `.java` compilation units.) or completely added or deleted files of the compared code copies. Next, the differing textual areas are interpreted to identify the modified software elements. The latter is a challenging task because the differing textual areas may not correspond to syntactic software elements in the source code. For example, a differing area can start in the body of a method and reach up to the body of another method while crossing other elements such as field declarations or static initializations. According to Baxter et al. [12] and Malpohl et al. [126], the text-based approach is too sensitive, e.g., because of too many false positives due to changes in formatting or missing differentiation between code and comments.

Model-based analysis Model-based difference analysis first extracts syntactic model representations of the software copies. In a second step, it compares the models instead of the textual representations. Due to this, the comparison can use additional semantic and syntactic information gained during the extraction. For example, only software elements of the same type are compared with each other. Furthermore, differences identified by this approach are aligned with the software elements by nature. Baxter et al. [12] propose this approach because of the additional semantics in sense of types, methods and others gained by interpreting the code based on the programming language's grammar.

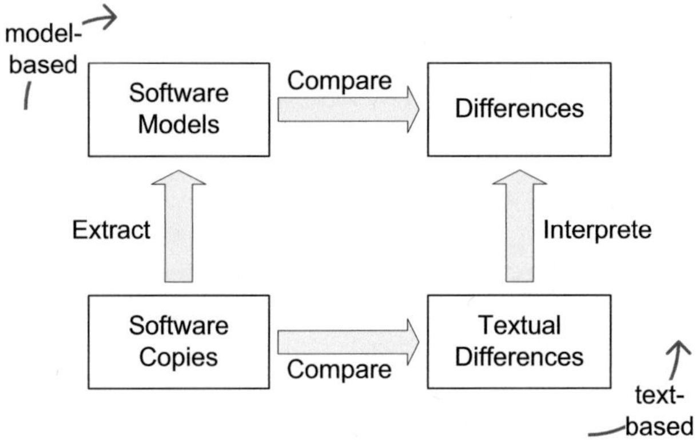

Figure 2.9.: Model- vs. text-based difference analysis

2.4.7.1. General Model Comparison

In MDSD, model comparison is the general term for analyzing differences between model instances. Xing and Stroulia [195] proposed a two-phase model comparison process with the phases "Matching" and "Diffing". Based on this approach, Kehrer et al. [95] propose a Post-Processing phase to enhance the semantics of the identified differences. Both approaches propose to describe the results of a model-based comparison as a model as well. Thus, the resulting difference model can reference elements of the input models. Furthermore, they are focused on comparing two models at the same time.

Matching phase In the matching phase, the models to compare are traversed to identify their corresponding elements. The result of this phase is a match model that references elements matched between the input models as well as elements without a correspondence in the other model.

Diffing phase In the diffing phase, the match model is traversed to identify elements without a match as well as matched elements with differing attributes or references. For each of these differences, a difference is recognized and an element describing this difference is created and stored in the result model. Depending on the concrete comparison used, the difference element can be stored within the match model or separately.

Post-Processing Kehrer et al. [95] propose a post-processing for an activity they refer to as a "semantic lift". The goal of a semantic lift is to analyze the generic fine-grained differences and derive more valuable types of differences representing the real semantics of changes specific to the metamodels of the compared models. In Yazdi et al. [196], they have applied their post-processing approach to the field of software model comparison with a simplified model of the Java programming language.

EMF Compare As part of the Eclipse Modeling Framework, the EMF Compare [25] project provides infrastructure for comparing Ecore-based models. This infrastructure is aligned with the approach proposed by Xing and Stroulia [195]. In addition, version 2 of EMF Compare provides post-processing phases not only after the diffing phase but also after the matching phase before the diffing is started. However, there is nothing performed within these post-processing phases by default. They provide extension points to add custom processing, such as a semantic-lift proposed by Kehrer et al. [95].

2.4.7.2. Optimization Strategies

Analyzing the differences between software implementations typically produces many findings. Even with a model-based approach that is insensitive to formatting changes, each refactoring and code change is reported. To cope with this amount of differences, several strategies have been developed to ignore irrelevant changes.

Semantic differences Jackson and Ladd [87] studied the external behavior of methods to focus on semantic differences only. They considered the input and output of methods to identify if their semantics has changed. With a similar intention, Apiwattanapong et al. [8] studied the Control Flow Graphs (CFGs) of methods to identify changes in their behavior. The intention of both approaches is to filter semantically irrelevant differences.

Change types Fluri and Gall [61] propose a set of change types to study the impact of individual changes on other software elements. Based on the type of changes, they classify changes and couplings of changes as functional-modifying and function-preserving. Similar to approaches for detecting semantic differences, their intention is to focus on functional-modifying differences. Furthermore, their approach is not limited to methods but considers other types of software elements as well. Fluri and Gall [61] use a model comparison strategy similar to those proposed by Chawathe et al. [30] and Neamtiu et al. [136] based on hierarchical software models such as ASTs.

Renaming detection Malpohl et al. [126] proposed an approach for detecting identifier renaming between different versions of a software system. They propose a language-aware approach and facilitate type and identifier references to detect renaming even if they cover several files. When detecting renaming, they allow for filtering all corresponding code changes to focus the user on other, relevant changes.

AST tree matching and name stability Neamtiu et al. [136] propose an AST based matching approach for difference analysis. They report about their observation of "relatively stable function names" over time for C programs. Their case study on reasonable systems such as the Linux Kernel and Apache confirmed this observation, except for early versions of Apache (i.e. only 3% of the changes respectively 30% - Neamtiu et al. [136, page 3]). Based on this observation, their tree matching could be optimized by matching methods with similar names.

2.4.7.3. Merging

As Perry et al. [147] observed in a case study, developers need to modify resources in parallel to scale software development. Furthermore, they report the need for merging parallel changes later on to allow for optimistic resource handling. To cope with this need, modern Software Configuration Management (SCM) systems and Version Control System (VCS) tightly integrate difference analysis and merging capabilities. Mens [131] has performed a survey on existing merging approaches and identified four different types of approaches: textual, operational, structural, and semantic. Additionally, combinations of those types exist such as the language-aware merging proposed by Hunt and Tichy [84].

Textual merging Today, in practice, merging is typically done on a textual level and integrated with tools such as GNUDiff [124] or WinMerge [42].

Operational merging Lippe and Oosterom [121] proposed tracking the editing operations of developers and derive merge operations for this information instead of interpreting differences.

Structural merging Buffenbarger [27] and Westfechtel [192] both use structural information gained from programming language syntax to improve merges proposed to developers. Westfechtel [192] further enhance the use of structural information with a lightweight tracking of developers' editing operations.

Semantic merging Finally, semantic approaches such as the one proposed by Horwitz et al. [80] gain further information from program slices and others to propose reasonable merges and reduce merge conflicts.

Language-aware merging Language-aware merging is an approach proposed by Hunt and Tichy [84] to produce more reasonable merging compared to textual merges and more efficient merging compared to existing structural and semantic approaches. They use techniques such as Partial Program Analysis to improve software processing and renaming detections to reduce sets of differences to handle explicitly.

2.4.8. Clone Detection

Baxter et al. [12] define "clones" as a program fragment that is identical to another, and "near miss clones" as one that is nearly identical to another. With a reference to Baxter et al. [12], Roy et al. [159] give a definition of "code clones are code fragments which are similar by a given definition of similarity". From a software maintenance point of view, code clones represent redundant code that makes code comprehension more difficult because developers need to understand why a code exists twice if they recognize this similarity at all. In addition, the pure amount of code leads to increased maintenance efforts. Roy et al. [159] surveyed existing approaches for clone detection and classified them according to different types of clones they are able to detect.

Clone types Roy et al. [159] described different types of clones that reach from exact textual copies to code sections that perform the same computation but have different implementations. Accordingly, they specified four types of clones (type 0 added for completeness):

- (Type 0: Exact clones)
- Type 1: Code Layout & Comments
- Type 2: Literals Changed
- Type 3: Added, Changed, or Removed Statements

- Type 4: Same Computation but other Implementation

In a recent study performed by Bellon et al. [13], the AST-based clone detection of Baxter et al. [12] was identified as one of the best performing algorithms. However, selecting a clone detection algorithm is a trade-off between performance, detected clone type, and the purpose for detecting clones.

2.4.9. Program Comprehension

Program comprehension has been identified as one of the most critical tasks in software maintenance. Pigoski and April [148, page 6-4] compared several studies on maintenance efforts and summarized that developers spend 40%–60% of their maintenance effort on program comprehension.

Internal and external information Program comprehension requires to consider internal and external information about a software. The former relates to the implementation of the software itself. The latter refers to documentation, design artifacts, and process documentation. A broad variety of different approaches has been proposed in these areas.

The following subsections introduce approaches for program comprehension relevant in context of this thesis.

2.4.9.1. Program dependencies

Program dependencies are studied for many different purposes in the context of program comprehension, such as change impact analyses (e.g., Lehnert [117] and Klatt et al. [105]) or feature location (e.g., Dit et al. [43]). Wilde [193, page 4] has classified program dependencies according to the type of elements dependencies can exist between:

- Data Item Dependencies
- Data Type Dependencies
- Subprogram Dependencies
- Source File Dependencies
- Source Location Relationships

In addition, he has described strategies to identify dependencies between those items:

- Textual Search
- Cross-Referencing
- Tracing Indirect Dependencies
- Data Flow Methods

Wilde [193] has defined this classification independent from the purpose the dependencies are used for. The following subsections describe applications of program dependencies relevant to the context of this thesis.

2.4.9.2. Program Slicing

Weiser [189] introduce the concept of program slices and described their usefulness for people who need to understand a program. Weiser [190] provides the results of a study showing that programmers use program slices intuitively for debugging and understanding programs. A program slice represents a sequence of software elements involved in a program execution. For example, a variable declaration, its subsequent usages (i.e., a forward slice), as well as the previous calculation of its initial value (i.e., a backward slice).

Approaches for program slicing Tip [185] surveyed that many approaches for program slices have been proposed and differentiates them into static and dynamic slices. While the former builds slices based on the program structure only, the latter takes aspects of a program execution such as concrete inputs into account. Two important techniques used for building program slices are Program Dependency Graphs and Program Execution Traces detailed in the following.

Program Dependency Graphs (PDG) Program Dependency Graph (PDG) were introduced by Ottenstein and Ottenstein [144] and provide a graph representation of dependencies in a software program (e.g., a statement reading a variable). Many approaches analyzing PDGs exist for different purposes, such as change impact analysis as surveyed by Lehnert [117] and feature location as surveyed by Dit et al. [43] and Rubin and Chechik [161]. Accordingly, PDGs exist in many different flavors, such as the extension for higher program structures proposed by Horwitz et al. [81]. Software models with resolved-cross references as described in Section 2.4.6 contain PDGs as sub-graphs. However, to analyze PDGs, these sub-graphs must be identified explicitly.

Program Execution Traces (PET) Agrawal and Horgan [2] propose the use of execution histories (i.e. Program Execution Traces) to build more reliable program slices. Program execution traces represent program execution flows monitored during the execution of one or more specific features. They can be gathered from instrumenting the program code before its execution. Alternatively, a profiler can be used that returns information about the dynamic behavior of the software, such as method invocations or object instantiations. Program execution traces and according program slices are used for several purposes, such as identifying features within programs as done by Chen and Rajlich [31] and Cornelissen et al. [35].

2.4.9.3. Feature Location Techniques

Locating the software elements implementing a feature within a software implementation is necessary for various tasks in the context of software maintenance. Extending an existing functionality and fixing errors are only two examples. Dit et al. [43] and Rubin and Chechik [161] recently published surveys about existing approaches in general respectively with a focus on SPL engineering.

General Dit et al. [43] refer to Rajlich and Gosavi [154] and argue for feature location as being one of the most frequent tasks in software maintenance. Beside other attributes, they classified existing techniques according to the types of "Static analysis" based on source code analysis, "Dynamic analysis" based on information from program execution, "Textual approaches" based on natural language processing, and "Historical analysis" based on information from software repositories. They report a trend for textual and dynamic feature location techniques as well as combining several types of techniques.

SPL engineering Rubin focused on feature location techniques in context of transitions to SPLs such as done by Alves et al. [4] to encapsulate features using AOP. They identified the shortcomings of existing approaches in this context. They distinguished static and dynamic as well as plain and guided approaches according to the considered input respectively the required user interaction.

2.4.9.4. Concern Graphs using Program Dependencies

Concern graphs are closely related to feature location techniques but concerns can include several features.

Robillard and Murphy [158] proposed a static code analysis approach to identify code locations implementing a common concern. Starting with a seed (i.e., a class, method or field), they collect incoming and outgoing references to other elements. They assume users to provide reasonable seeds to use their approach and recommend techniques such as lexical searches for types and members to identify such seeds.

Considered elements and references With classes (C), fields (F), and methods (M) as elements under study, they investigate the references between specific pairs of these elements, identified as (M,M), (M,F), (M,C), (C,C), (C,M), and (C,F) and summarized in Table 2.9.

Robillard and Murphy propose an iterative creation of concern graphs based on these references. Each iteration starts with a set of seeds and collects all elements identified by the references under study. The new elements identified by an iteration can be used as seeds for the next one. In this way, users can iteratively build up a concern graph until they reach a satisfying coverage or no further references are found.

2.4.10. Natural Language Program Analysis (NLPA)

Pollock et al. [150] introduce the term Natural Language Program Analysis (NLPA) as the application of natural language analysis to further extend the analysis of program structure and semantics. Natural language analysis is a subtopic in the field of computer linguistics (e.g., Carstensen et al. [29]). Kuhn et al. [114] describe that developers often introduce linguistic semantics by the terms they use in comments as well as in the names of their variables, methods, and classes. Such linguistic semantics can support program comprehension in addition to programming language structures and semantics (e.g., Pollock et al. [150, page 2]). For example, Kuhn et al. [114] use semantic code clustering techniques to find clusters of related code in software products.

Reference	Description
(calls,m1,m2)	The body of method m1 contains a call that can bind (statically or dynamically) to m2.
(reads,m,f)	The body of method m contains an instruction that reads (uses) a value from field f.
(writes,m,f)	The body of method m contains an instruction that writes (defines) a value to field f.
(checks,m,c)	The body of method m checks the class of an object, or casts an object to c.
(creates,m,c)	The body of method m creates an object of class c.
(declares,c,m|f)	Class c declares method m or declares field f.
(superclass,c1,c2)	Class c1 is the superclass of c2.

Table 2.9.: Program dependencies investigated by Robillard and Murphy [158, page 3]

Language processing Spek et al. [177, Page 2] describe the need for processing terms extracted from software programs to improve their analysis. They propose to apply splitting and filtering steps that have been proven to be valuable in the context of natural language processing in general:

- Splitting: Separate strings into individual terms (e.g., "getProductCopies" to {"get", "Product", "Copies"}).
- Filtering: Removing useless words (e.g., {"get", "Product", "Copies"} to {"Product", "Copies"}).

Stemming is another processing typically used in context of natural language processing:

- Stemming: Transform a term to the stem of a word (e.g., {"Product", "Copies"} to {"Product", "Copy"}).

Infrastructure Computer Linguistics in general is used for many different purposes such as speech recognition and information retrieval (e.g. Carstensen et al. [29]). Among others, the success of search engines for information retrieval through the internet and within companies has produced several mature infrastructures that can be reused in the Natural Language Program Analysis (NLPA) as well. Thus, many commercial and open source software solutions have been developed. The Lucene project [75] is one of the major representatives for open source solutions and provides implementations for language processing (e.g., Splitting, Filtering, and Stemming) and efficient storage and query (e.g., inverted indexes as described by Carstensen et al. [29, page 588]).

Stemming Stemming is a language processing step to transform terms to the stem of a word. This is used to normalize different variants of a word such as standardizing plural and singular or different forms of verbs (e.g., "Copies" to "Copy" and "creates" to "create"). Stemming approaches are distinguished between lexical and algorithmic approaches. A component processing terms by applying a stemming algorithm to them is typically referred to as "Stemmer".

Lexical Lexical stemming approaches use a dictionary or a database with predefined normalizations. This allows for handling special cases such as verbs that cannot be normalized according to a given rules, such as "mice" and "mouse". An example of such a stemmer is the PlingStemmer [180] proposed by Suchanek et al. [181]. This stemmer is based on the WordNet lexical database for English introduced by Fellbaum [58] and continuously maintained at the Princeton University [153].

Algorithmic Algorithmic stemming approaches reduce letters or syllables until a known term in a specific language is found. Depending on the algorithm used, slightly different results are returned by the individual stemmers. Typical examples of stemming algorithms are the Porter [152] algorithm and its revised version Snowball Porter [151] algorithm, both proposed by Porter. Other often used examples are the KStem algorithm proposed by Krovetz [111] and the suffixing algorithm proposed by Harman [74]. All of these stemming algorithms are implemented as Stemmer components by the Lucene project (e.g., Porter Stemmer, Snowball Porter Stemmer, KStem-Stemmer, and S-Stemmer).

Typical terms used in Java The vocabulary used by programmers is one of the topics investigated in the context of NLPA. Natural language analysis in general has identified that standardized vocabularies support comprehension and reliable communication. For example, the aviation industry has standardized a vocabulary for their domain [55].

Caprile and Tonella [28, page 8] published the twenty most frequently used verbs extracted from a set of ten procedural programs developed with the C programming language: "get print set expand make copy list delete init search add write read put do parse free send find handle".

Similarly, Høst and Østvold [83] analyzed Java programs with regard to the used terms and their intention. They have published a list of verbs used by programmers and explained what people can expect from a method with such a verb in its name. For example, they describe the verb "init" by:

> "**init:** Methods named init very often manipulate state. Furthermore, they often return void, create objects and have no parameters, and rarely call methods of the same name."

2.4.11. Refactoring

Refactoring describes the task of changing the source code of a program to improve its internal quality. Chikofsky and Cross [32] describe refactoring as one task to perform in context of reengineering (Section 2.4.5). However, they also state that refactoring is often done within a smaller context to continuously improve the quality of a software system.

Code refactoring defined by Fowler Fowler et al. [63] has established the clear definition of refactoring as improving the internal structure of a software system without changing its external behavior. He has published a catalog of recommendable refactorings and used a template to specify refactorings in the same style. The templates contain a name to identify a refactoring and a summary when a refactoring is reasonable and what benefits to expect by applying it. A motivation describes why to apply a refactoring as well as conditions when it is not a must. Additionally, the template provides for a definition of mechanics how to precisely perform a refactoring. At the end, an example section is used to provide an idea of the code before and after a refactoring is applied.

SPL Refactoring Alves et al. [3, page 2] described refactorings of feature models that improve the configurability and further qualities of an existing SPL. They defined the term "Product Line Refactoring" as not modifying the observable behavior, as done by Fowler et al. [63] for refactorings in general. In contrast to Fowler et al. [63], they put this behavior protection in the context of the original configured products and not to the overall configuration space of the SPL.

Role-based model refactorings In the context of MDSD, several refactoring approaches have been proposed based on transformations and pattern matching. Reimann et al. [156] proposed a role-based refactoring specification concept. They explicitly separate the roles involved in a refactoring, the transformations to apply to these roles, and a mapping between the roles and concrete metamodels. The separation allows for specifying refactorings independent from a concrete metamodel. Accordingly, refactorings can be reused by creating a mapping model between the role model and a concrete metamodel only.

2.5. Evaluation

To evaluate the contributions of this thesis, an evaluation concept proposed by Basili and Weiss [10] is used. Furthermore, the performed validations are related to the concept of validation levels proposed by Böhme and Reussner [19]. Both of them are introduced in the following subsections.

2.5.1. Goal Question Metric (GQM)

Basili and Weiss [10] have proposed the Goal Question Metric (GQM) approach as a structured concept for evaluations. They propose to first define a goal of what should be evaluated. Next, questions are defined in a way that answering them provides a statement if the goal is reached or not. Finally, metrics have to be defined to quantify the answers for the questions and, thus, make them reproducible.

Basili and Weiss [10] developed this approach in context of evaluating software engineering methods. However, the concept itself is not limited to this field and can be used for evaluation in other fields as well.

2.5.2. Validation Levels

Böhme and Reussner [19, page 15] defined four levels of validation of prediction models. These levels can be applied to the area of software analysis in general and consolidation approaches in specific as well.

Level 0: Implementation Validity This level is about the possibility to implement the approach under study. As Böhme and Reussner [19] describe, level 0 is obviously validated in context of the other levels, as a prototype is required to perform any other level of validation. This also applies for the area of software analysis in general and consolidation support in specific.

Level 1: Result Validation This level is about a qualitative comparing of the results of the approach with the reality. Additionally, this can include a comparison with other, similar approaches to show an improvement compared to the state-of-the-art.

Level 2: Applicability Validation This level is about validating that an approach can be applied in reality. It includes the availability of necessary input and conditions in appropriate scenarios to apply the approach. Especially if input is obtained by humans, experiments or case studies are necessary to validate the applicability.

Level 3: Benefit Validation This level is about validating the improvement compared to existing approaches or practices. Depending on an approach's motivation, this can require extensive studies and it might be hard to convince companies to participate. Especially validating approaches involving human participants and considering process aspects requires parallel studies, and coping with threats to their validity is challenging.

Part II.

The SPLevo Approach

3. Approach Overview

This chapter introduces the approach proposed by this thesis and relates the contributions of this thesis to each other.

To cope with the challenges of consolidating customized product copies into a Software Product Line (SPL), a novel approach named SPLEVO has been developed providing i) a structured consolidation process and ii) novel software analyses, both leading to less manual effort for copy comprehension and variability design and to more consistent variability implementations in the future SPL.

The following sections provide an overview of the overall SPLEVO approach, followed by subsequent chapters discussing the individual contributions in detail.

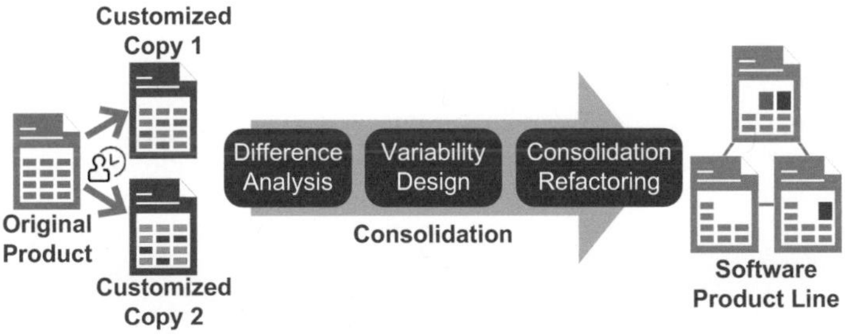

Figure 3.1.: Main consolidation phases

3.1. Main Consolidation Phases

Figure 3.1 illustrates the three main phases of the SPLEVO approach to consolidate customized product copies into an SPL: Difference Analysis, Variability Design, and Consolidation Refactoring. This section provides an overview of the main phases of the SPLEVO approach. The details of the process and the other contributions are described in the following chapters. In the first phase, the differences between the product copies must be identified. In the second phase, a variability design (i.e., the structure and characteristics of the future variability) must be created to specify how to reflect related differences as variability in the future SPL. Finally, in the third phase, the copies' implementations must be transformed into a single code base containing the implementation of the SPL core and included features, according to the previously created variability design. All these phases are integrated based on a Variation Point Model as a common data model (Section 3.2). In addition to the main phases, pre- and post-processing phases exist to setup the consolidation process and to handover the resulting SPL to the continuous maintenance (not presented in Figure 3.1 for the sake of brevity).

Focus on Difference Analysis and Variability Design According to Pigoski and April [148, page 6–4], developers spend 40%–60% of their maintenance effort on program comprehension (Section 2.4.9). Thus, one can argue that Difference Analysis and Variability Design are reasonable phases to investigate support for. Furthermore, many approaches exist in the field of refactoring (Section 2.4.11) providing infrastructure that can be reused in the Consolidation Refactoring phase. Thus, the main focus of the SPLEVO approach is on the Difference Analysis and Variability Design phases. The Consolidation Refactoring is supported in the direction of ensuring consistent variability implementations, which is not covered by existing approaches, today.

Leading and Integration Copies Before starting the consolidation, SPL Consolidation Developers select one of the copies to consolidate as the *Leading Copy*. During the consolidation, this copy will be transformed into the final SPL instead of building a new separate code base. This procedure allows benefiting from development infrastructures, such as Version Control Systems (Section 7). Furthermore, consolidation activities can use the Leading Copy as a fixture for their processing. For example, the Difference Analysis can use it as reference for normalizing renaming. All other product copies to be integrated into the Leading Copy are called *Integration Copies*.

Definition 3 (Leading Copy) *A* Leading Copy *is one of the copies to consolidate what was selected as the main code base for the resulting SPL. It is used as reference code base throughout the consolidation process. Furthermore, the accepted variants of all other copies will be merged into the Leading Copy's code base during the refactoring. The Leading Copy is selected as part of the process configuration activity.*

Definition 4 (Integration Copy) *An* Integration Copy *is any of the copies to consolidate what was not selected as Leading Copy.*

The following subsections briefly introduce the main phases of the consolidation, their challenges, and the contributions of the SPLEVO approach to cope with. Section 4 discusses the activities in detail.

3.1.1. Difference Analysis Phase

Phase summary Understanding the customizations from one copy to another starts with identifying the differences of their implementations in place. The Difference Analysis consumes the copies' implementations and produces an initial model of the future SPL's variability design representing the individual differences. This phase is crucial for the overall process as the downstream phases' qualities and processing strongly depend on this output.

Challenges In general, a Difference Analysis phase is challenging due to a possibly large amount of differences, irrelevant modifications (e.g., comments), preferred variability mechanisms, and copying practices (e.g., naming conventions or Derived Copies referencing their origin).

Related contributions The contribution of the SPLEVO approach to support developers in the Difference Analysis phase is a fully automated difference detection as described in Section 5. In addition, the SPLEVO process specification identifies stakeholders and information sources to incorporate to gain export knowledge to be considered (e.g., applied company guidelines for copy-based customization).

3.1.2. Variability Design Phase

Phase summary Designing variability in a consolidation process means to identify copy-specific code contributing to the same copy-specific feature and to decide about its representation as variability in the future SPL (e.g., run time or compile time configuration). The variability design must ensure a consistent configuration of variable code locations related to each other as well as the necessary flexibility for instantiating reasonable products from the future SPL. Thus, the differences returned by the Difference Analysis must be related to each other and it must be decided how to reflect them in the future SPL.

Challenges Designing the variability of an SPL is affected by many factors. Technical constraints between the differences (i.e., code dependencies) and logical relationships (e.g., a copy-specific functionality which makes no sense without another one) must be identified and soft factors, such as organizational reasons or product management decisions [33], must be respected to achieve a satisfying variability design. Reviewing the differences and deriving reasonable design decisions is tedious because of the amount of differences, their potential relationships, and the degrees of freedom in deciding about their combination and characteristics. In particular, the soft factors eliminate the chance for a fully automated consolidation and require involving different stakeholders.

Related contributions The contributions of the SPLEVO approach to cope with this challenges are i) a novel software analysis providing variability design recommendations, ii) a definition of explicit design activities to reduce wasted efforts, and iii) an SPL requirements specification (i.e., SPL

Profile) to guide consistent design decisions. The software analysis allows for identifying technical dependencies as well as similar and simultaneous modifications as indicators for relationships in the copy-specific code to automatically derive refinement recommendations for the variability design. The consolidation process specified in the SPLEVO approach distinguishes several explicit design activities and identifies sources of information to consider as well as stakeholders to involve for achieving consistent and prevent redundant and reverted design decisions. Third, an SPL Profile is specified to define guidelines for choosing variability characteristics as part of the variability design in a more consistent way.

3.1.3. Consolidation Refactoring Phase

Phase summary In the final Consolidation Refactoring phase, the copies' implementations are transformed into a single code base, and appropriate variability mechanisms (e.g., conditional execution based on configuration files or user information) are introduced at the same time to switch between the available variants. Based on the copies' implementations and the variability design created before, the implementation of the SPL core and the included features have to be created. This requires deciding which mechanisms to implement for the variability specified in the variability design and to refactor the implementations themselves.

Challenges Deciding for appropriate variability mechanisms is challenging as many different techniques and mechanisms are available (Section 2.3.3) to choose from. Furthermore, ensuring a consistent implementation even for the same type of variability mechanisms is tedious as developers have to agree on an implementation style and manually ensure its consistent realization. Mature refactoring solutions exist, but not for introducing variability mechanisms as part of consolidating code from several code bases. Accordingly, there is no automation to be used here.

Related contributions The contributions of the SPLEVO approach to support the Consolidation Refactoring phase are i) a specification concept for consolidation refactorings, ii) an automated variability mechanism recommendation, and iii) support for selecting intended variability mechanisms when defining SPL guidelines. The specification concept allows for describing refactorings for introducing variability mechanisms including their supported characteristics (e.g., binding time) in a structured manner, enabling automation. Furthermore, it includes a specification of how to implement the mechanism for different types of software elements. The SPLEVO approach includes a recommendation system automatically assigning the most appropriate variability mechanism to a variation point. The recommendation evaluates the characteristics and implementing elements of a Variation Point (VP), the specifications of the available refactorings, and the list of intended variability mechanisms defined in the SPL guidelines. When specifying these guidelines, the selection of reasonable mechanisms is supported by automatically recommending available mechanisms based on the characteristics chosen before.

3.2. Variation Point Model

To enable the consolidation process, a Variation Point Model (VPM) has been developed that allows for iteratively designing variability in the SPL solution space, referencing involved software elements (e.g., classes, methods, and statements) in several code bases, and integrating all process phases as well as their activities.

3.2.1. Model Concept

Similar to Svahnberg et al. [183], the SPLEVO VPM distinguishes features on the product management level and VPs on the software design level as described in Klatt et al. [97] and illustrated in Figure 3.2.

Variation Points, Groups, and Variants Similar to Jacobson et al. [88] and Pohl et al. [149], the SPLEVO VPM defines a VP as a location of variability. In contrast to them, an SPLEVO VP focuses on a single location, and a Variation Point Group (VPG) contains related VPs contributing to the same feature. Finally, a Variant (V) is an available implementation for a VP. For example, if methods in two classes have been added for the same feature, Jacobson et al. [88] use a single VP referencing both classes with variant elements referencing the methods. In the SPLEVO VPM, two VPs are used, each referencing one of the classes, and their variant elements reference the according methods. Furthermore, a VPG contains the two VPs to indicate their unity.

Integration with feature models To integrate with the product management level, VPGs can reference features implemented by their VPs, and Variants can reference child features as the available alternatives. Furthermore, a VP's location and a Variant's implementation are specified by *Software-Elements* as wrappers for referencing elements of concrete software models, such as nodes of an Abstract Syntax Tree (AST).

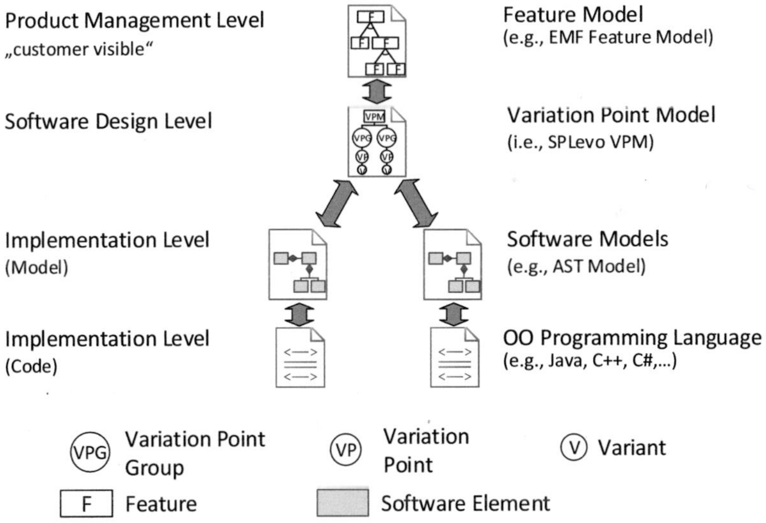

Figure 3.2.: SPLEVO VPM model concept

Reuse of existing models The feature model and software model reuses mature models satisfying the SPLEVO approach's requirements [51, 78, 77]. The SPLEVO VPM allows for integrating such existing feature and software models for i) enabling an export to existing SPL management tools (e.g., pure::variants [66] or FeatureMapper [79]) without being limited to a specific model and ii) reusing existing solutions for software model extraction to allow for adding support of additional technologies.

Link from solution to problem space For a well-structured consolidation process, the SPLEVO VPM is designed to bridge the gap between features on an SPL's problem space and software models on an SPL's solution space. It enables an integrated consolidation process starting with the extracted software models and building VPGs representing the implemented features on the lowest granularity level of a feature model. On one side, software models can be reverse engineered from the existing software implementations and need to provide enough detail to support comparison and refactoring later on. On the other side, feature models must be abstract and focused on the SPL's problem space to describe variable features for stakeholders interested in software capabilities, such as product managers or customers.

Variability design Within the SPLEVO approach, variability design is defined in two directions and accordingly supported by the VPM: The *Variation Point Structure Design* and the *Variation Point Characteristics Design*.

Definition 5 (Variation Point Structure Design) *In the overall variability design, the* Variation Point Structure *identifies locations of variability (i.e., VPs), alternatives available at these locations (i.e., Variants and their implementing SoftwareElements), and clusters of related locations of variability (i.e., VPGs). Designing the structure means:*

1. *Assigning VPs to the same VPG, if they are identified as contributing to the same feature and, thus, need to be configured in a consistent way later on.*

2. *Clustering co-located and related VPs into coarse grain ones, if their variants can and should be implemented with a single variability mechanism in the future SPL.*

Definition 6 (Variation Point Characteristics Design) *In variability design, the* Variation Point Characteristics *specify the capabilities of the variability reflecting a VP in the future SPL. More specific, the characteristics selected for a VP specify the requirements on the variability mechanism implemented during the consolidation refactoring.*

3.2.2. Metamodel

The SPLEVO Variation Point Model is specified as an Essential Meta Object Facility (EMOF) metamodel [140, page 25]. Figure 3.3 provides a class diagram of the types of the metamodel and their relationships (attributes omitted for clarity).

The VPM's base structure is similar to the one specified by Svahnberg et al. [183, page 7] in how Variation Points, Variants, Features and Software-Elements (i.e., Software Entities in their terminology) are linked to each other. However, because of the need to group related VPs, define their characteristics and access the related copies' implementations, additional model elements such as VPGs, characteristics and source locations have been introduced in the SPLEVO VPM metamodel.

Furthermore, the SPLEVO VPM metamodel specifies wrapper elements for technology-specific elements (i.e., SoftwareElement). They exist to define a technology-independent VPM allowing for links to technology-specific software models and even allow for different software models for the same technology (e.g., different models for the Java technology). This enables a generic consolidation approach providing adaptation points for improvements facilitating technology-specific information. Further details about this adaptation concept are described in Section 3.4.2.

The following subsections describe the metamodel elements in detail.

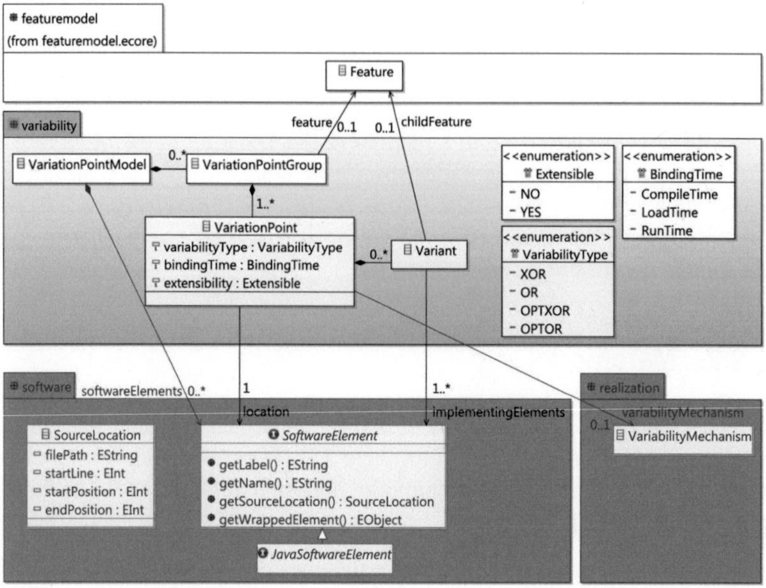

Figure 3.3.: SPLEvo VPM metamodel
(attributes partly omitted for simplicity but provided in the according sections)

3.2.2.1. VariationPoint

Figure 3.4 represents the VariationPoint element and its direct context. The *VariationPoint* itself represents a location at which variability resides between the copies' implementations. The location of a VP is represented by a referenced *SoftwareElement* (e.g., a class or method). Typically, the location is a SoftwareElement of the Leading Copy to integrate the variability in. However, if a new software element was created in an Integration Copy not contained by any other SoftwareElement (e.g., an added file resource), there might be no corresponding location in the Leading Copy. In such a case, the location references the new top-level SoftwareElement in the software model of the Integration Copy it results from.

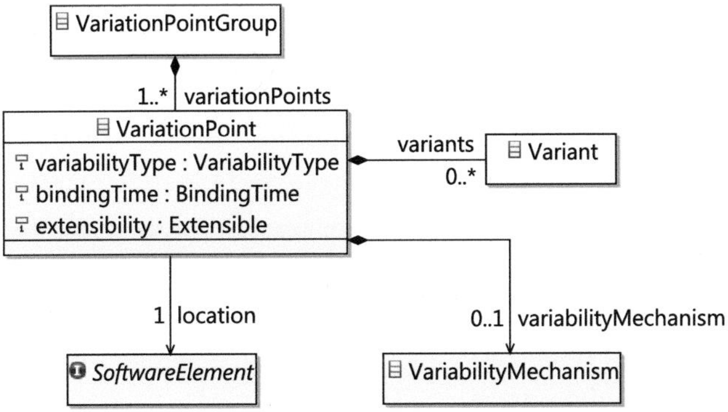

Figure 3.4.: VariationPoint

The options available at a VP are represented by Variant elements which are further described below.

In addition to its location and variants, a VP has variability characteristics (Section 3.2.2.4) to describe its required or intended variability. The variability characteristics are adjusted as part of the Variability Design phase (Section 4.2.6).

Finally, a VP allows specifying a Variability Mechanism that describes how the VP should be implemented as well as the VPG referencing all VPs it relates to.

A VP can reference zero, one, or more variants (i.e., customer-specific changes). One or many means there is at least one customized product copy providing code for this location and at least one variant will be part of the SPL. Zero means there is no variant to include in the SPL itself but there should be variability allowing to add product-specific variants at this location (i.e., an extension point). To declare a valid extension point, the "extensible" characteristic of VPs with no variant assigned must be set to YES as defined by the OCL constraint in Listing 1. However, it is not intended to create extension points during a consolidation process and the configuration option results from provided degrees of freedom in the metamodel. Furthermore, extensibility comes with maintenance challenges in general, which developers and architects must be aware of (Section 2.3.1.3).

```
context VariationPoint
inv PureExtensionPoint : variants->size()
                  = 0 implies extensibility = Extensible::YES
```

Listing 1: Pure extension point constraint

However, the goal of the SPLEVO approach is to consolidate the existing implementations. Thus, specifying a VP without any Variant element is not further investigated in this thesis.

3.2.2.2. VariationPointGroup

A VP in the SPLEVO VPM represents a single variability location only. This slightly differs from definitions such as the one of Jacobson et al. [88]: "A variation point identifies one or more locations at which the variation will occur". In the SPLEVO VPM, a VPG is specified as an entity which contains all VPs contributing to the same implemented feature – for example, several code locations modified to change a temperature calculation from Celsius to Fahrenheit. This is done to have VPs explicitly identify individual locations of variability and distinguish them from logical dependencies between several VPs. Additionally, the VPGs allow for a more flexible clustering within the consolidation process as they can provide additional information and can be changed without changing the VPs themselves.

As shown in Figure 3.5, a VPG has an id attribute as identifier. It further references all VPs contributing to the same feature. To identify this feature when the consolidated SPL is handed over to product management, the VPG can optionally reference a feature element. As a representative, the feature element of the standardized EMF Feature Model [51] is used here.

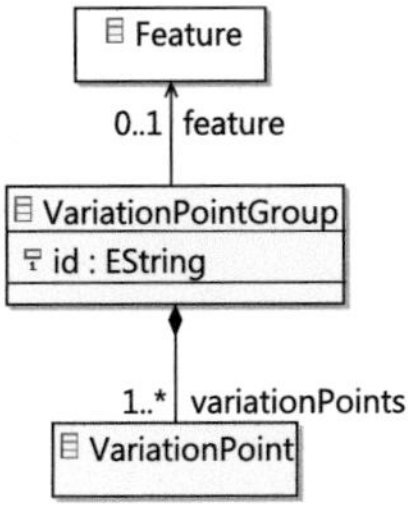

Figure 3.5.: VariationPointGroup

3.2.2.3. Variant

The alternatives available for a *VariationPoint* are described by Variant elements. As shown in Figure 3.6, each Variant references one or more implementing elements. These elements are SoftwareElements of one of the consolidated copy's software models. At the beginning of and during the consolidation process, the implementing elements ("implementingElements") of a Variant originate from any of the consolidated copies, but always the same for one variant. When the refactoring into a single code base is done, all Variant elements refer to implementing elements in the single code base of the SPL.

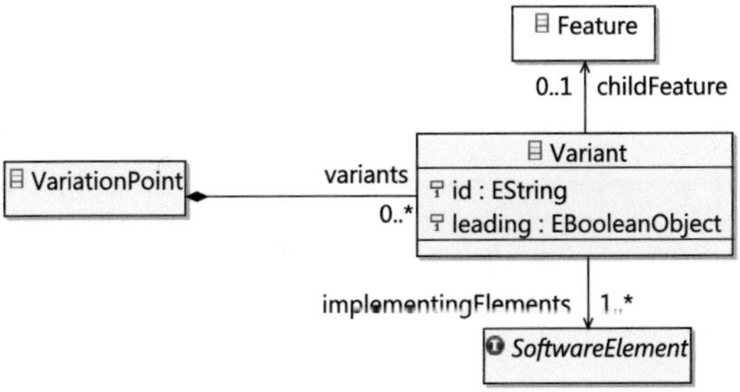

Figure 3.6.: Variant

The Variant element's "leading" attribute identifies if its implementing elements originate from the Leading Copy. This attribute allows for identifying variants of a Leading Copy without the need for loading and analyzing the SoftwareElements themselves.

The id attribute identifies the represented option for a VP. If multiple VPs contribute to the same variable feature, their Variant elements contributing to the same option have the same id.

Clarification of the term Variant The term "Variant" is used in two different manners in the field of variability and SPL engineering: a product configuration and an alternative of a VP. The former uses the term "Variant" for a configuration of a product derived from an SPL. The latter uses the term "Variant" to refer to an option of a VP within a VPM. The SPLEVO approach uses the term according to the latter.

3.2.2.4. Variability Characteristics

The VPM allows for specifying variability characteristics for a VP. Many different types of characteristics have been proposed in context of SPLs (Section 2.3.1). The SPLEVO approach uses a specific set of characteristics supporting the selection of a variability mechanism during the consolidation refactoring. Figure 3.7 presents the set of characteristics and their options which are explained below.

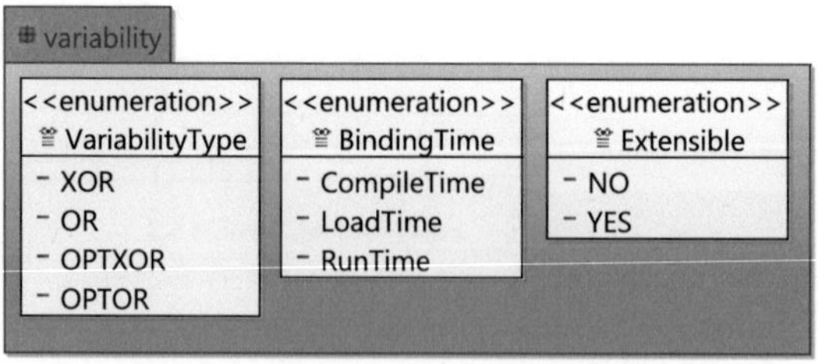

Figure 3.7.: Variability characteristics

Variability Type For each VP, a variability type can be defined, describing how many variants can and must be selected for a concrete product. Table 3.1 summarizes the available options specified in the VPM. “XOR” means the variability mechanism respectively its configuration has to ensure that one but not more than one variant can be used. “OR” means that at least one but also more variants can be chosen. “OPTXOR” and “OPTOR” are extensions of the regular “XOR” and “OR” also allowing explicit selection of no variant.

The types are aligned with the “basic” and “merged” types defined by Patzke and Muthig [146] (Section 2.3.1.1), except for not using the basic type “optional”, which can be expressed with the other types as well.

Variability Type	Cardinality of a Variation Point	Cardinality ($m \leq n$)
XOR	Exactly one of the available variants must be selected.	1 out of n
OR	One or more of the available variants must be selected.	1..m out of n
OPTXOR	None or one of the available variants must be selected.	0..1 out of n
OPTOR	None, one, or more of the available variants must be selected.	0..m out of n

Table 3.1.: VariationPoint characteristic: Variability Type

Binding Time The binding time of a VP specifies the latest point in time when a specific variant to be used can be chosen (Section 2.3.1.2). Table 3.2 summarizes the options defined in the VPM, which are aligned with the binding times defined by Apel et al. [7]. Each of them means a variant can be selected at this point in time or even before.

Binding Time	Description	Benefit
Compile Time	Variability decided during implementation or compilation.	Allows for deploying required code only.
Load Time	Variability decided when program is started.	Saves processing time for variability examination.
Run Time	Variability decided and changed when program is executed.	Offers highest flexibility.

Table 3.2.: VariationPoint characteristic: Binding Time

"Compile Time" means variants must be chosen before compiling the source code of the product. This is typically used to reduce the amount of code deployed in production and to prevent evaluating configurations at load or run time. However, it is less flexible in serving different customers compared to the other options and requires more effort for maintaining the customer-specific installations.

"Load Time" requires having the configuration in place before the application is started. Compared to compile time binding, this allows for more consistent installations in production and, thus, system support is simplified. In the mean, the processing effort for evaluating the configuration is lower compared to run time binding.

"Run Time" means the product's configuration can be adapted in operation. Typically, run time binding is used to adapt the product's behavior according to the user or client interacting with it. This allows for using the same product installation for different feature configurations.

Extensible The "Extensible" characteristic of VPs describes if all variants to choose from are part of the SPL or product-specific ones can be added later on. Whether a VP is extensible, or not is a boolean decision as shown in Table 3.3. However, the alternatives are modeled explicitly for the sake of conformity to the other characteristics. The characteristic also relates to the definition of population roles described by Svahnberg et al. [183], except that it does not distinguish whether a product developer or an end user adds a new variant.

Extensible	Description
NO	All available variants are included in the SPL.
YES	New variants can be added for a concrete product.

Table 3.3.: VariationPoint characteristic: Extensible

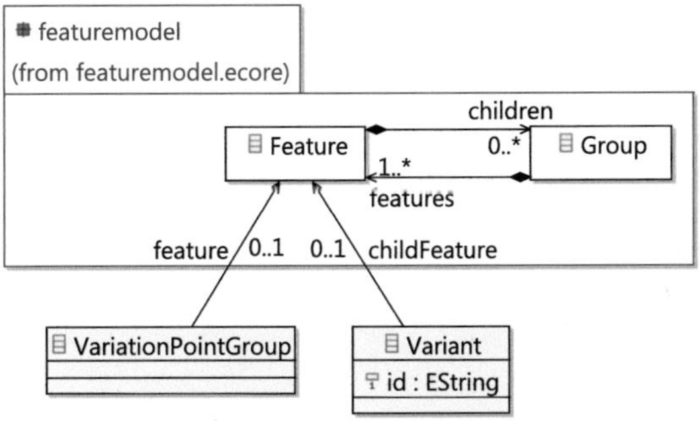

Figure 3.8.: Feature

3.2.2.5. Feature

The Feature element allows for connecting the software design VPM with a feature model used by product management. The Feature element used here is derived from the EMF Feature Model [51]. Feature models are structured in a hierarchical manner, which is realized with Group elements in the EMF Feature Model as shown in Figure 3.8. A Feature has child features representing its available options. In feature models, the parent-child hierarchy is not limited in any way.

As a VPG contains all VPs contributing to the same feature, the VPG references the feature they realize. Similarly, the Variants of these VPs represent the available options for this feature and, thus, reference the according child feature. Which variants must link the same feature is indicated by the Variants' ids.

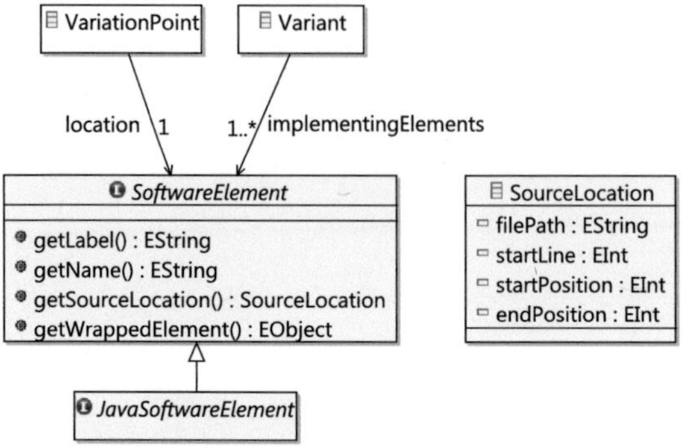

Figure 3.9.: SoftwareElement

3.2.2.6. SoftwareElement

The VPM *SoftwareElement* is a wrapper element that allows for referencing SoftwareElements of technology-specific software models in a uniform manner. The similar names of the two metamodel classes are intended as they identify the same element in a copy's implementation. They are used in the same manner during the consolidation and will be generically referenced as "SoftwareElement" only throughout this thesis, as long as it is not required to reference a software element of a specific metamodel. The VPM SoftwareElement provides a uniform interface for information required by the consolidation process. As shown in Figure 3.9, the VP and Variant elements reference the SoftwareElement instead of referencing elements of a concrete software model. This allows for adapting the overall SPLEVO approach for different technologies, as further described in Section 3.4.2.

Sub-interfaces allow further typifying the SoftwareElement for concrete technologies and provide specific utilities, such as opening Java Elements in a Java Editor. The technology-specific sub-interfaces allow for reusing such utilities with different software models and extractors for the same technology (e.g., JaMoPP or MoDisco for Java, Section 2.4.6). The operations specified by the SoftwareElement interface must be implemented in a technology-specific manner by the concrete wrappers. On the one hand, technical information (e.g., source locations) can be retrieved in a technology-specific manner only. On the other hand, labels and names should match presentations developers are used to (e.g., identifier names differ between technologies such as "`myObjectAttribute`" in Java and "`my.object.attributes`" in properties files).

3.2.2.7. SourceLocation

A *SourceLocation* element identifies a software element in its textual representation (e.g., a method in a source code file). As shown in Figure 3.9, it identifies the software element's containing file resource by its file system path. In addition, attributes specify the software element's position within the file resource in terms of start and end character offsets.

3.3. Software Product Line Profile

All SPLs share common principles, such as explicitly managed variability. However, each SPL has individual characteristics, such as its maturity level. Furthermore, each vendor has different intentions to introduce an SPL, such as enabling a faster product derivation or configuring more product variants. Thus, software vendors raise different quality goals for their SPL implementation, such as code simplicity versus code reduction (Section 2.2). Those individual preferences influence the copy consolidation and must be considered.

We have developed a "Software Product Line Profile" ("SPL Profile") as part of the SPLEVO approach that allows for capturing the individual requirements for the future SPL. The main purposes of the SPL Profile are i) to improve the consolidation process's automation and ii) to support the involved stakeholders' design decisions to gain more consistent results. Thus, the SPL Profile's relevance for the consolidation process is similar to the relevance of architecture styles for general architecture development.

As shown in the class diagram presented in Figure 3.10 and according to its main purpose, the SPL Profile allows for specifying two types of guidelines:

1. SPL Style Guidelines
2. SPL Implementation Guidelines

The former allows for specifying the intention and goal of the SPL to introduce (e.g., characteristics and principle quality goals). The latter provides technical specifications to be considered during the consolidation (e.g., allowed variability mechanisms).

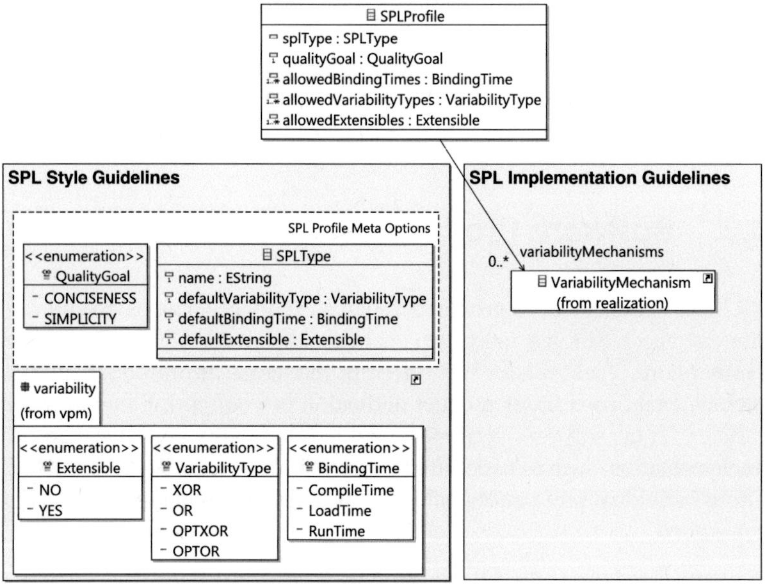

Figure 3.10.: SPL Profile metamodel

In the end, the SPL Profile is used to ensure a satisfying and consistently implemented SPL as consolidation result. Thus, its most critical content is the list of intended Variability Mechanisms for realizing the VPs. All other information is i) used for selecting variability mechanisms during the SPL Profile definition or ii) considered by stakeholders during their manual decision making. According to the purpose of the SPL Profile, it must be specified before starting the consolidation. However, if guidelines are not sufficient to perform a concrete consolidation, such as when the variability mechanisms are too limited, this becomes perceptible to SPL Consolidation Developers and Software Architects. Without such an indicator, variability might be implemented in an unintended manner.

The following subsections describe the SPL Profile attributes presented in the class diagram in Figure 3.10 in detail.

3.3.1. SPL Style Guidelines

SPL style guidelines represent general rules to consider during the consolidation. For example, targeting a multi-tenant system requires to have run time adaptable tenant-specific behavior. But, it does not forbid to have other VPs that are configured before the system is loaded (i.e., load time).

3.3.1.1. SPL Type

A fundamental decision is the type of SPL targeted by the consolidation. There is no standardized classification of SPL types available. As summarized in Table 3.4, we have defined three types of SPLs primarily aligned to their typical binding time according to the goal of the SPL Profile to support further decisions. The types are strongly influenced by the maturity levels identified by Bosch [21] but are no exact matches. The maturity types of Bosh et al. focus on the development maturity of the software vendor. In contrast, our SPL Types are defined according to the characteristics of the SPL itself.

The SPLEVO approach uses SPL types to i) pre-configure the appropriate settings in SPL Profiles and ii) adjust the default characteristics of VPs created during the consolidation. The defined types of SPLs differ in their default variability type, binding time, and extensibility. Accordingly, each SPL Type is a triple of a default variability type, a default binding time, and a default extensible setting identified by a name. However, none of them is restricted to be implemented with these default characteristics only.

SPL Type	Description	Default Characteristics		
		VT	*BT*	*EX*
Multi-Tenant System	A single installation can serve different users by adapting to the current user's context or characteristics. Adding tenant-specific extensions is possible in general but not the regular case.	XOR	run	NO
Configurable Product Base	Products are individually configured per installation. Product-specific extensions are used more often.	XOR	load	NO
Adaptable Code Base	Products are assembled from the SPL code base before compilation and installation. Product-specific extensions can be done in the most flexible manner.	XOR	compile	NO

Table 3.4.: SPL Profile: SPL Types (*VT = Variability Type, BT = Binding Time, EX = Extensible*)

The SPL types define a normative guideline for the VP settings and require their default variability characteristics to be allowed in the SPL Profile for designing an according future SPL. For example, targeting a multi-tenant system but not allowing for run time variability binding and not providing any run time capable variability mechanism contradicts the intention of a multi-tenant system. In contrast, even an “Adaptable Code Base” SPL can have VPs with configurations evaluated at load time. However, if no VP provides a compile time binding time, this does not match the goal of building an “Adaptable Code Base”.

Quality Goal	Description
Conciseness	Prefer variability implementations leading to less redundant code while accepting more execution paths or indirections.
Simplicity	Prefer variability implementations leading to code that is as easy to understand and find as possible.

Table 3.5.: SPL Profile: Quality Goals

3.3.1.2. Quality Goals

The overall consolidation goal of better code maintainability and faster product instantiation can exist in different flavors. As described in Section 2.2.5, one can prefer either less complex or less redundant code. Thus, the quality goal is a decision between "Simplicity" (i.e., less complex code) and "Conciseness" (i.e., less redundant code). The preferred goal provides a hint for implementing variability. For example, on the one side, more coarse grain variation points and variability implementations (e.g., variants encapsulated into separate methods or classes) require less execution paths in the code. On the other side, they require more redundant code compared to fine-grained variation points and variability mechanisms (e.g., conditional executions within the same method).

3.3.1.3. Allowed Variability Characteristics

By default, all Variability Characteristics considered in the SPLEVO approach and supported by the VPM (Section 3.2.2.4) can be assigned to VPs. However, sometimes specific characteristics are not wanted and thus should not be available during variability design. For example, one might not want to have extensible VPs and does not allow for compile time variability to ensure the same code base for all installations.

By default, all options of all Variability Characteristics are selected in the "Allowed Variability Characteristics" setting of the SPL Profile. Those not wanted can be deselected except for the characteristics mandatory for the chosen SPL type, which make no sense to be deselected.

3.3.2. SPL Implementation Guidelines

During the consolidation, concrete variability mechanisms are assigned to the VPs to instruct the refactoring in how to realize the according variability in the SPL. The Variability Mechanisms part of the SPL Profile specifies the Variability Mechanisms allowed to be used. They are defined as an ordered list with the more preferred mechanisms at the top.

The available variability mechanisms to choose from depend on the current setup of the SPLEVO approach. To cope with the requirement to support custom variability mechanisms (Section 2.3.3.2), the SPLEVO approach allows for working with an adaptable set of variability mechanisms. They are specified as part of a Consolidation Refactoring Specification, because, at the end, for each mechanism assigned to a VP, it must be clear how it should be realized in the refactoring phase. To support the complete consolidation process, the developed Consolidation Refactoring Specification concept specifies for each refactoring i) the offered variability mechanism including its variability characteristics, ii) the quality goal by trend of its implementation, iii) the SoftwareElements that can be refactored, and iv) the procedure of the refactoring itself to implement the variability. Section 7.1 describes the Consolidation Refactoring Specification concept in detail.

3.3.3. SPL Profile Definition Support

Figure 3.11 shows an example of a configuration form to specify an SPL Profile. The configuration of the SPL Profile, and especially the allowed variability mechanisms, is supported by i) recommending reasonable mechanisms and ii) validating already selected ones. As illustrated by the SPL Profile evaluation concept in Figure 3.12, this is done based on the overall settings in the SPL Profile. Each SPL Type requires allowing specific variability characteristics. In addition to those required ones, additional characteristics can be added to the allowed set. The complete set is then used to filter the total list of available variability mechanisms. On the other side, already selected variability mechanisms can be validated and reported if they realize any characteristic that is not allowed. Finally, the quality goals and the selected SPL Type's required characteristics influence the prioritization of the variability mechanisms. Variability mechanisms providing the selec-

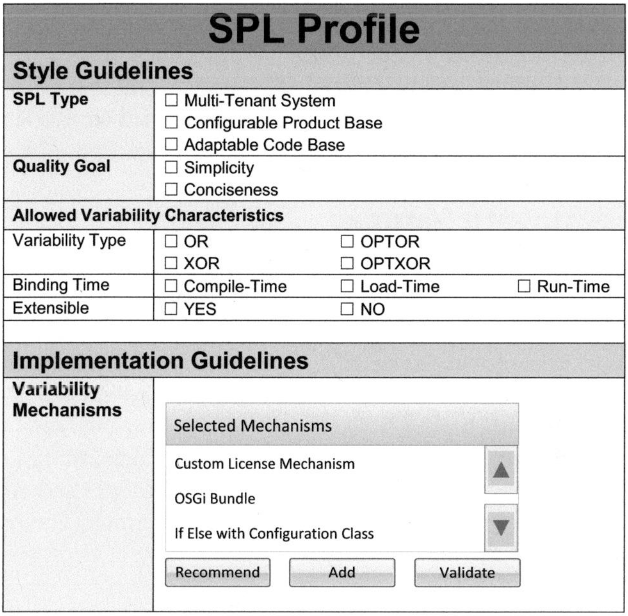

Figure 3.11.: SPL Profile example
(selected mechanisms are illustrating examples only)

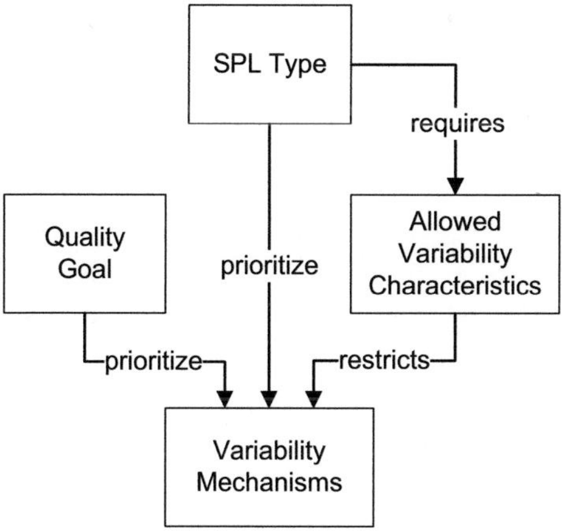

Figure 3.12.: SPL Profile evaluation concept

ted SPL Type's required characteristics and tending to support the preferred quality goal are prioritized higher than the other ones. This prioritization is used i) to order the recommended list of mechanisms and ii) to provide feedback for improving the order of the already selected mechanisms.

3.4. Software Models

The SPLEVO approach provides a model-based integration for software comprehension, design, and refactoring. To enable this, the implementations of the product copies under study must be accessible as model representations as well (i.e., software models). The SPLEVO approach is not limited to a specific technology (e.g., a programming language such as Java), but allows for processing any artifacts that can be represented as a model conforming to SPLEVO's definition of a Software Model and allows for technology-specific adaptations for process optimizations. The following Subsection 3.4.1 defines the assumed minimal structure of a software model, and Subsection 3.4.2 provides an overview of the concept of the SPLEVO approach for technology-specific adaptations.

3.4.1. Software Model Structure

The SPLEVO approach supports software models for any technology if they conform to SPLEVO's minimal definition of a Software Model (Definition 7).

Definition 7 (Software Model) *A* Software Model *describes all resources contributing to a software implementation. Each resource contains a tree of SoftwareElements with a single root element. All elements contained in a SoftwareModel are arranged as a tree based on containment relationships which are unique, directed and free of cycles.*

Figure 3.13 shows a class diagram of a metamodel (i.e., the software model structure) confirming to SPLEVO's minimal software model definition. A `SoftwareModel` has a containment reference to zero or more `Resource` elements. Each `Resource` contains one `SoftwareElement` referenced as `root`. Exactly one root `SoftwareElement` is required, as this might represent an empty container inside the resource (e.g., an empty text file with an encoding defined by its container). Each `SoftwareElement` contains at least other `SoftwareElements` referenced as `childElements`. In this thesis, algorithms and descriptions which do not refer to a specific technology make use of the terminology of the metamodel. The terminology overlap of the `SoftwareElement` with the VPM metamodel's SoftwareElement is intended. The former is a wrapper element for the latter and abstraction for `SoftwareElements` of specific software models (e.g., a class `SoftwareElement` of the JaMoPP Java model [78]). However, if a specific one of those two is meant, it will be explicitly stated, if not clear from the context.

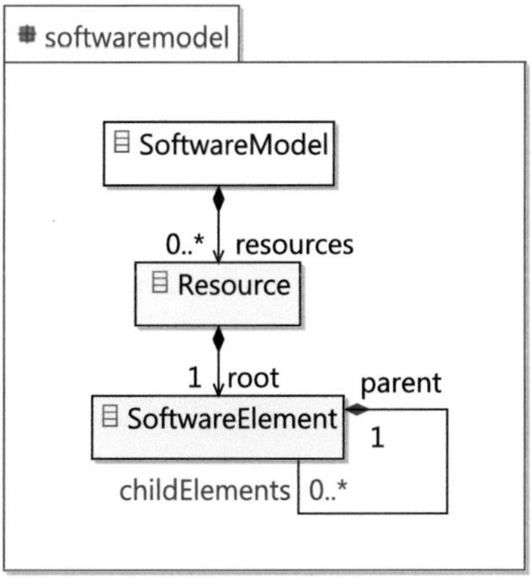

Figure 3.13.: SPLEVO software model definition

This minimal assumed structure of a software model is an arguable assumption, as standardized coresponding AST models exist (e.g., OMG's GAST specification [138]) and existing model extraction infrastructures are able to provide corresponding models (e.g., xText [54], EMFText [78] and the EMFText Syntax Zoo [44]).

3.4.2. Technology Adaptations

The general SPLEVO approach treats software implementations in a unified manner in terms of software models specified in this section. However, on one side, considering specifics of concrete technologies is required to make valuable decisions on how to treat differences between product copies and even to identify those differences. On the other side, technology specifics can be used to improve the consolidation process by providing additional relationships between SoftwareElements compared to completely generic treatment (e.g., program dependencies such as method calls).

The SPLEVO approach in general is not limited to a specific technology to cope with the diversity of software artifacts used in software systems today. Moreover, it specifies several adaptation points to consider technology specifics and provide better analyses by considering aspects such as concrete types and typical development habits.

However, in this thesis, adaptations for the Java technology have been implemented. Java has been chosen as it is a representative for object-oriented languages and widely used in modern software development. In addition, the case study systems used in the evaluation are implemented with the Java technology, too (Section 8).

Several parts of the SPLEVO approach provide technology adaptation points. The Difference Analysis allows for technology-specific software model extractors, provides adaptation points for technology-specific comparison logic, and allows for technology-specific SoftwareElement wrapper creation during the VPM initialization. The Variability Design support provides adaptation points for technology-specific VP analyses and refinement recommendation logic. The refactoring specification concept defined by the Consolidation Refactoring supports technology specifics, as nearly all refactorings require considering the underlying technologies. Further details about those adaptation capabilities are provided in the according sections of this thesis.

4. Consolidation Process

This chapter introduces the structured consolidation process proposed as part of the SPLEVO approach for considering all stakeholders, reducing overheads, and achieving a consistent variability design and implementation. The consolidation process is aligned with the main consolidation phases introduced in Section 3.1: Difference Analysis, Variability Design, and Consolidation Refactoring. These phases are refined into individual activities and assigned to roles responsible for them. The activities allow for a reproducible and guided consolidation. The SPLEVO consolidation process has been designed to be applicable in practice and even by companies without experience in consolidating customized product copies. As confirmed by our online survey, companies are aware of the advantages and disadvantages of customized product copies, but rarely experienced in consolidating them (Section 8.5.3.1).

Consolidation process overview Figure 4.1 shows an activity diagram of the detailed activities refining the three main consolidation phases. Furthermore, the diagram allocates the activities to the responsible stakeholder roles. The header of the diagram shows the responsible roles, and the columns identify the activities they are responsible for (i.e., activity swim lanes). The first two activities *SPL Profile Definition* (Section 4.2.1) and *Process Configuration* (Section 4.2.2) are preparations performed by different stakeholders in a pre-processing phase. The third activity *Difference Analysis* (Section 4.2.3) implements the corresponding first main phase of the consolidation and identifies differences between the copies and derives the initial variability design. The Variability Design phase splits into the activities: *Relationship Analysis* (Section 4.2.4), *Variation Point Structure Design* (Section 4.2.5), and *Variation Point Characteristic Definition* (Section 4.2.6) as well as the *Design Review* activity (Section 4.2.7). These activities produce the variability design for the future Software Product Line

(SPL). The Consolidation Refactoring phase manifests itself in the *Variability Realization Decision* (Section 4.2.8) and the *Consolidation Refactoring* (Section 4.2.9) activities for the actual transformation of the copies' implementations. Finally, the last activity *SPL Export* is an optional transfer of the resulting SPL to tools for continuous SPL management (Section 4.2.10). The following subsections describe roles representing stakeholders that are directly or indirectly involved in the process. In addition, the subsections discuss the individual process activities in context of the responsible roles.

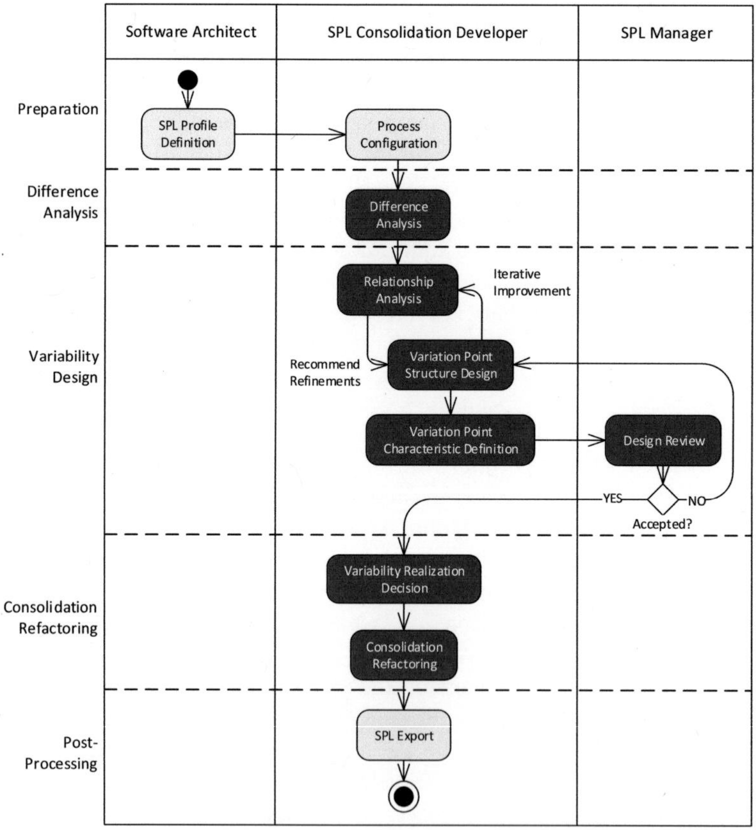

Figure 4.1.: Activities of the SPLevo consolidation process

4.1. Stakeholders

The SPLEVO approach defines six stakeholders participating in the consolidation, as summarized in Table 4.1.

The stakeholders are classified according to their process involvement, which identifies the necessity to support their activities for an improved consolidation. The classification defines three stakeholder groups:

- **Primary Stakeholders** are actively involved in the process and either provide information, make decisions, or trigger activities.
- **Supporting Stakeholders** enable or support the consolidation process and somehow help the primary stakeholders.
- **Affected Stakeholders** are influenced by the result of the consolidation and the decisions made by primary stakeholders.

This classification does not cover stakeholders without a relationship to the process in terms of content. For example, stakeholders funding a consolidation or end users of the products are not covered because we assume valid product copies, which are already decided to get consolidated, as input, and roles responsible for the future SPL and products derived from it, which also represent the end user needs.

Stakeholder	Responsibility	Involvement
Software Architect	Define SPL guidelines	Primary
SPL Consolidation Developer	Perform consolidation	Primary
SPL Manager	Long-term SPL management	Primary
SPL Consolidation Consultant	Adapt consolidation support	Supporting
Product Manager	Product variant management	Affected
Software Developer	Long-term SPL & variant development	Affected

Table 4.1.: SPLEVO consolidation process: Considered stakeholders

Stakeholder: Software Architect
Involvement: Primary
Responsibility: Define SPL guidelines
Software Architects are responsible for defining the overarching goal and style of the future SPL. They have to specify intended technical solutions and provide guidance for design and realization decisions. Thus, they are responsible for defining the SPL Profile that is considered within a concrete consolidation.

Stakeholder: SPL Consolidation Developer
Involvement: Primary
Responsibility: Perform consolidation
SPL Consolidation Developers perform the actual consolidation process. They trigger process activities, involve other stakeholders, review analysis results, and drive variability design decisions as well as the refactoring. Thus, they are the stakeholders with the highest effort, and their activities are primarily targeted by the SPLEVO consolidation support. During the process, they interact with Software Architects to set up the process and with SPL Managers to verify design decisions.

Stakeholder: SPL Manager
Involvement: Primary
Responsibility: Long-term SPL management
SPL Managers are responsible for the target SPL from a product management perspective, in the long-term. Thus, they have to account for the implemented variability from a feature point of view in the SPL problem space (Section 2.2.1.2). During the consolidation, they review the variation point design and argue for adaptations if necessary.

Stakeholder: SPL Consolidation Consultant
Involvement: Supporting
Responsibility: Adapt consolidation support
SPL Consolidation Consultants implement extensions for the SPLEVO approach. They are familiar with the SPLEVO approach's extension and adaptation points to adapt the process to company or project specific conditions.

For example, they are able to extend the analysis to process a company's specific code documentation or enable support of new technologies (Section 3.4.2). Furthermore, they are able to add support for new general or company-specific variability mechanisms.

Stakeholder: Product Manager
Involvement: Affected
Responsibility: Product variant management
Product Managers are responsible for a specific product instantiated from the future SPL that was possibly represented as a product copy before. They are affected by the resulting SPL, and their efficiency is strongly influenced by the provided flexibility and characteristics. They are not involved in the consolidation, but SPL Managers have to take care of Product Managers' requirements as part of their activities.

Stakeholder: Software Developer
Involvement: Affected
Responsibility: Long-term SPL and variant development
Software Developers are responsible for the long-term SPL maintenance and evolution. This covers the SPL core, the included features, as well as product-specific extensions. Their work is influenced by the flexibility of the variability design as well as the implemented variability mechanisms. Thus, SPL Managers and SPL Consolidation Developers must consider Software Developers' requirements concerning the target SPL.

4.2. Process Activities

As shown in Figure 4.1, the SPLEVO consolidation process is structured into ten activities. The activities have been defined according to their goals, actions, responsible stakeholders, as well as their inputs and outputs. The following subsections describe each activity, including a table summarizing the respective main attributes.

Figure 4.2 provides an overview on the activities and the artifacts they either produce or update. The first two activities define the SPL Profile and the configuration for the overall consolidation process. The Difference Analysis produces the initial Variation Point Model (VPM). Afterwards, the Relationship Analysis produces recommendations for design improvements.

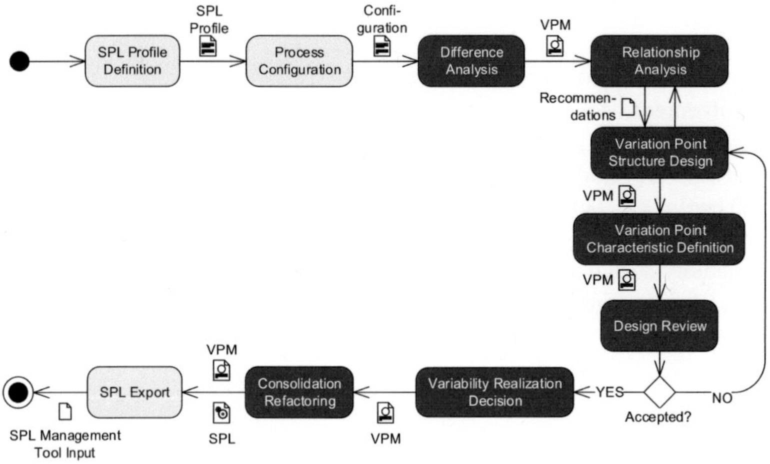

Figure 4.2.: Consolidation process activities with artifacts produced or modified

Next, the Variation Point Structure Design produces a VPM with an accepted Variation Point (VP) structure, which is further enhanced by the Variation Point Characteristic Definition, deciding about the individual variability characteristics of the VPs. If the design represented in the VPM is accepted in the Design Review, the Variability Realization Decision further enhances the VPM by assigning variability mechanisms to the VPs matching their variability characteristics and software elements. Finally, the Consolidation Refactoring produces the resulting SPL and a VPM describing the VPs of this SPL.

4.2.1. SPL Profile Definition

ACTIVITY	SPL Profile Definition
GOAL	Defining guidelines for variability design and realization of future SPLs
ROLE	Software Architect
INPUT	/
OUTPUT	SPL Profile
ACTIONS	Configure or select SPL Profile
SPLEVO Support	Automated SPL Profile recommendations and validation (Section 3.3)

During the *SPL Profile Definition* activity at the beginning of the process, the Software Architect defines the guidelines how to implement the SPL. Such guidelines might be reused between several consolidations within the same company or project. This initial preparing activity does not need any input. The output will be the configured SPL Profile to be used in the downstream consolidation according to the SPL Profile data model described in Section 3.3. The activity is supported in the SPLEVO approach with an automation to recommend and validate settings of the SPL Profile as described in Section 3.3.

4.2.2. Process Configuration

In the *Process Configuration* activity, SPL Consolidation Developers provide configurations for the concrete copies to consolidate. On one side, the source projects to analyze are configured. On the other side, available expert knowledge about the copies, such as renaming conventions applied during customization, are captured in the configuration. The latter covers information to improve the downstream consolidation, such as restricting the copies' parts to consider or providing company-specific practices for copy-based customizations. Which expert knowledge can be considered, is described in detail in the appropriate sections (i.e., Sections 5, 6, and 7). Similar to the first preparing activity, the Process Configuration does not expect any input and provides the configuration itself as output. To improve the configuration activity, the prototype implementation of the SPLEVO approach provides a wizard to guide SPL Consolidation Developers as described in Section 8.3.

ACTIVITY	**Process Configuration**
GOAL	Consolidation-specific process configuration
ROLE	SPL Consolidation Developer
INPUT	/
OUTPUT	Process Configuration
ACTIONS	Define copies to consolidate and capture export knowledge
SPLEVO Support	Configuration wizard as part of the prototype (Section 8.3)

4.2.3. Difference Analysis

ACTIVITY	**Difference Analysis**
GOAL	Detecting differences between product copies
ROLE	SPL Consolidation Developer
INPUT	Copy implementations, process configuration, and SPL Profile
OUTPUT	Fine-grained VPM initialized from differences
ACTIONS	Trigger automatic process
SPLEVO Support	SPLEVO Difference Analysis (Section 5)

In the *Difference Analysis* activity, SPL Consolidation Developers identify the differences between the copies to consolidate. The result of the activity is a fine-grained VPM with each VP identifying a separate difference between the copies. To enable the VPM initialization, differences must identify changed software elements. As part of the Difference Analysis activity, the expert knowledge captured during the Process Configuration activity is used to improve the difference analysis. For example, naming conventions are used to better match software elements or reduce the amount of differences to be processed later on. Furthermore, each VP is initialized with the variability characteristics required by the SPL Type selected in the SPL Profile. The SPLEVO approach provides a consolidation-specific difference analysis to fully automate this activity as described in Section 5.

4.2.4. Relationship Analysis

ACTIVITY	**Relationship Analysis**
GOAL	Identify VP relationships and reasonable aggregations
ROLE	SPL Consolidation Developer
INPUT	SPL Profile and process configuration
OUTPUT	Refinement recommendations
ACTIONS	Choose and start the analysis
SPLEVO Support	SPLEVO Variability Analysis (Section 6)

During the *Relationship Analysis* activity, the SPL Consolidation Developers analyze the VPs in the current VPM to enable educated decisions on refining the VPs' structure as part of the variability design. The activity's output is a list of sets of related VPs representing candidates for being aggregated. While today developers analyze those relationships manually in an ad hoc manner and with a limited scope, one of the main contributions of the SPLEVO approach is to automate them and allow to consider further relationship types across complete implementations. SPL Consolidation Developers start such an automated analysis to receive the aggregation candidates. Details about the analysis are documented in Section 6.

4.2.5. Variation Point Structure Design

ACTIVITY	Variation Point Structure Design
GOAL	Shape variability coverage and localization
ROLE	SPL Consolidation Developer
INPUT	VPM and VPM refinement recommendations
OUTPUT	Refined VPM
ACTIONS	Review recommendations and apply appropriate ones
SPLEVO Support	UI facilities in the prototype (Section 8.3)

In the *Variation Point Structure Design* activity, the SPL Consolidation Developers refine the VPM until all VPs contributing to the same feature from a technical perspective are connected to each other. To do this, they refine the current VPM by reviewing the candidates provided by the relationship analysis or manually editing the VPM. If they are satisfied with the VPM structure, they can continue with the Variation Point Characteristic Definition. Otherwise, they can choose to perform another relationship analysis to receive further recommendations. To support the SPL Consolidation Developers in this activity, the User Interface (UI) provided with the SPLEVO prototype allows for according tasks (Section 8.3).

4.2.6. Variation Point Characteristic Definition

ACTIVITY	Variation Point Characteristic Definition
GOAL	Define intended variability properties
ROLE	SPL Consolidation Developer
INPUT	VPM with approved VP characteristics
OUTPUT	VPM representing a technically satisfying design
ACTIONS	Change default characteristics where appropriate
SPLEVO Support	VP initializing & UI facilities in the prototype (Section 8.3)

At this point of the process, a variation point structure has been designed, representing an appropriate degree of variability for the future SPL by grouped and merged VPs. During the Difference Analysis, each VP was initialized with the default variability characteristics derived from the SPL Profile. In the *Variation Point Characteristic Definition* activity, the SPL Consolidation Developers adapt them according to their technical requirements (e.g., when to choose a variant of a variation point). VPs located in and realized by the same type of software elements can be realized with different variability characteristics (e.g., being extensible for product-specific variants). This is a matter of individual variation point design and cannot be automated. The result of the activity is a VPM representing a variability design which is satisfying from the technical perspective of the SPL Consolidation Developers. While this activity is about manual decisions only, the user interface of the SPLEVO approach's prototype provides utilities for accessing and configuring the VPs (Section 8.3).

4.2.7. Design Review

ACTIVITY	**Design Review**
GOAL	Considering product management perspective in the SPL design
ROLE	SPL Manager
INPUT	VPM representing a technically satisfying design
OUTPUT	Required VPM adaptations
ACTIONS	Identify VPs to be restructured or reconfigured
SPLEVO Support	UI facilities in the prototype (Section 8.3)

During the *Design Review* activity, SPL Managers prove the variability design represented in the current VPM for possible improvements from a product management perspective. For example, the flexibility to derive products from the future SPL might be adapted to individual product strategies by requiring another binding time for variation points. The output of the activity are required adaptations of the VPM. If the VPM is accepted as it is, the process can continue with the Consolidation Refactoring phase. If possible improvements, such as further aggregating variation points, were found, the required adaptations are communicated to the SPL Consolidation Developers. In this case, the process goes back to the Variation Point

Structure Design activity, as SPL Consolidation Developers must decide if restructurings are necessary or defining other characteristics is sufficient. The review activity is performed manually and guided by utilities in the UI of the SPLEVO prototype implementation (Section 8.3).

4.2.8. Variability Realization Decision

ACTIVITY	Variability Realization Decision
GOAL	Decide how to implement VPs
ROLE	SPL Consolidation Developer
INPUT	VPM with approved VP design and SPL Profile
OUTPUT	VPM with assigned variability mechanisms
ACTIONS	Choose variability mechanism per VP
SPLEVO Support	Variability mechanism recommender engine (Section 7.2.1)

In the *Variability Realization Decision* activity, SPL Consolidation Developers must decide how to reflect each VP's implementation in the future SPL (e.g., by conditional statements or dynamically loaded components). This is done by assigning a variability mechanism to each of them. Based on the SPL Profile and the contained prioritized set of variability mechanisms, SPL Consolidation Developers can choose the highest ranked mechanism providing the characteristics defined for a specific VP. Due to the implementation guidelines, no additional interaction with other stakeholders for each of the VPs is necessary, except for the need to add new variability mechanisms to support not yet covered combinations of characteristics. The output of the activity is a VPM with a variability mechanism for each VP and forming a valid input for the downstream refactoring. The SPLEVO approach provides a variability mechanism recommender engine to support this task as described in Section 7.2.1.

4.2.9. Consolidation Refactoring

During the *Consolidation Refactoring* activity, each VP is refactored according to its assigned variability mechanism. The implementations of each VP's

ACTIVITY	Consolidation Refactoring
GOAL	Change implementation to a single code base SPL
ROLE	SPL Consolidation Developer
INPUT	VPM with assigned variability mechanisms
OUTPUT	Consolidated code and/or manual task list and according VPM
ACTIONS	Apply refactorings to implement variability mechanisms and merge code basis
SPLEVO Support	Refactoring specification and extensible infrastructure for automation (Section 7.3)

variants and the code for the assigned variability mechanism are combined and implemented in the product copy chosen as the leading one. How the refactoring is performed depends on the variability-mechanism-specific refactoring's degree of automation as described in Section 7.3. Depending on the degree of automation, the result of the activity is either a ready to use single code base SPL, a list of refactoring tasks, or a mix of both. In addition, an evolved VPM with updated VPs referencing the changed code base is produced. Beside a refactoring specification concept, the SPLEVO approach defines an extensible infrastructure to automate refactorings as described in Section 7.3.

4.2.10. SPL Export

ACTIVITY	SPL Export
GOAL	Provide input for tools to manage the future SPL
ROLE	SPL Consolidation Developer
INPUT	VPM linked with refactored code base
OUTPUT	Input for SPL management tool
ACTIONS	Trigger export to send information to SPL management tool
SPLEVO Support	Export interface and implementation for standardized feature model

For a continuous management of the created SPL, SPL Consolidation Developers export the results to an SPL management tool in the *SPL Export* activity. Such an export includes the implementation of the SPL as well as a model of the variability referencing the according variation points. The SPLEVO approach defines an interface for implementing automated exports based on the VPM representing the single code base SPL as described in Section 7.4.

5. Difference Analysis

This chapter describes the SPLEVO difference analysis developed for the context of consolidating customized product copies. As shown in Figure 5.1, the Difference Analysis is the first activity performed when the SPLEVO consolidation process configuration is done. Its purpose is to provide the necessary input for the downstream variability design. The goal of the analysis is to allow for fully automatically detecting differences and deriving an initial Variation Point Model (VPM) without any user interaction. In addition, consolidation-specifics should be considered to improve the analysis results.

The chapter is structured as follows: The consolidation-specific requirements are described in Section 5.1 and the model-based approach in Section 5.2. The difference analysis algorithm is detailed in Section 5.3 and the initialization of a VPM is described in Section 5.4, followed by a concept for analyzing more than two copies in Section 5.5.

Variation Point Model as analysis result The result of the SPLEVO Difference Analysis is a VPM initialized from the differences detected. It describes varying code locations between the copies as Variation Points (VPs). Each VP references a code location containing one of the differences, and at each VP, the code alternatives of the difference are referenced by variant elements. This allows for providing the developer with a single, uniform view for understanding the differences between the copies and designing the intended variability. Section 5.4 describes the details of this initialization.

Reliable difference analysis results To enable the initialization of a VPM, it is important to identify the software elements (e.g., classes, methods, or statements) that have been modified and must be reflected as variability in the future Software Product Line (SPL). This requires to not miss any differences to consider (e.g., due to heuristics for interpreting coupled change operations). Furthermore, the SPLEVO approach aims to support independently developed copies and, thus, there has been no restriction for possible modification. Accordingly, many differences between the copies do not need to be reflected as variability (e.g., modified comments) and should be concealed from SPL Consolidation Developers.

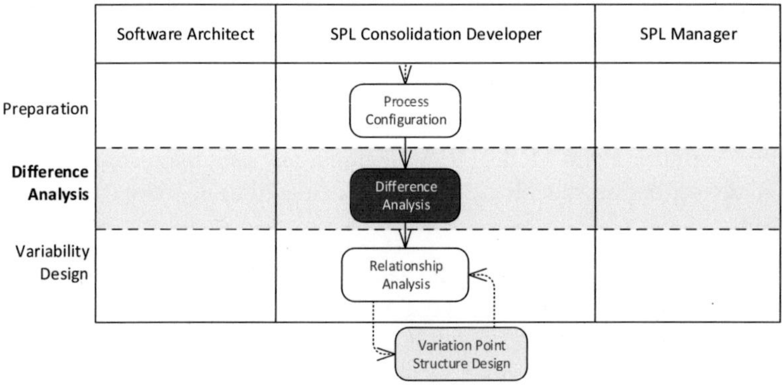

Figure 5.1.: SPLEVO process: Difference Analysis

Difference algorithm for consolidation conditions As part of the SPLEVO approach, a model-based difference detection algorithm for consolidation scenarios was developed to cope with limitations of existing approaches. For example, it allows for considering conventions on copy-based customization, such as introducing reuse dependencies between copies and their origin, to reduce the amount of copied code (i.e., Derived Copies). Furthermore, it supports aligning the granularity of differences with the variability mechanisms planned to be implemented as specified in the SPL Profile, ignoring differences outside a defined consolidation scope, associating differences to software elements, and analyzing complete source directories without any preconditions, such as code repositories providing change history information for the copies. In total, we have identified eight requirements on a difference analysis specific for consolidation processes such as the SPLEVO approach. They are documented in Section 5.1.

5.1. Specific Requirements of Copy Consolidation Scenarios

The following eight requirements have been derived from the overarching consolidation processes and industrial consolidation scenarios in the KoPL research project [107]. We do not claim for completeness, but elaborate on the value of each requirement to support SPL Consolidation Developers.

R1: Support Independent and Derived Copies Copy-based customization in object-oriented systems occurs in two manners: *Independent* and *Derived Copies*. *Independent Copies* are created by a pure "copy" action as illustrated for `MyClass` and `MyClassCustom` in Figure 5.2. Both classes have no dependency on each other and the copy can be modified fully independently at the cost of losing the original relation between them. *Derived Copies* are created by a copy action and by introducing an inheritance relationship between the copy and the original class. In Figure 5.2, this is shown for `BaseClass` and `BaseClassCustom`. Here, `method1()` was copied to the sub class and modified to override the super class's behavior. In such a case, the difference analysis must not report `method2()` as deleted in class `BaseClassCustom`, as it is still accessible. In a similar way, fields and imports must not be reported as deleted if they are still accessible, respectively not being required by the deriving class. Derived Copies are often used when some but not all methods of a class must be customized, but the class neither provides sufficient extension capabilities (e.g., hook methods to override) nor the code design allows for a reuse-by-delegation approach. Derived Copies are not limited to classes. They can occur for any type of container with some kind of "use" relationship to other containers of a compatible type. For example, a component is copied and a "requires"-dependency is created from the copied to the existing one. The copied component is able to access everything published by the original one. Hence, the copied component must not duplicate published parts that need no modification.

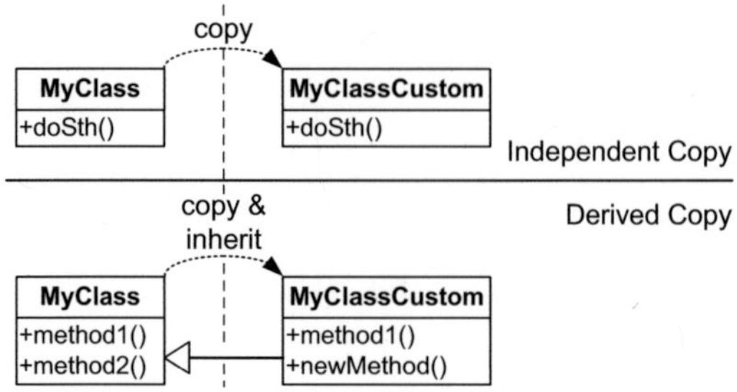

Figure 5.2.: Copy-based customization procedures in object-oriented technologies

Definition 8 (Independent Copy) *An* Independent Copy *is a copied software element without any relationship to its origin and, thus, any kind of modification might have been performed on it.*

Definition 9 (Derived Copy) *A* Derived Copy *is a copied software element for which the following rules apply:*

1. *It is of a type supporting inheritance relationships to other elements of the same type.*
2. *An inheritance relationship was introduced to the copy, referencing the original element.*
3. *The original software element is still present in or accessible by the copy and, thus, a renaming or namespace change was applied to the copy.*

R2: Consider Copy Renaming Conventions Many developers use a common renaming during copy-based customization, either intuitively or according to their coding guidelines. Typical renaming is done by pre- or suffixing of named code elements (e.g., classes) with a customer or customization identifying term (e.g., the term “Custom” in Figure 5.2). In languages supporting namespaces, those namespaces may also be enhanced with customization fragments. For example, a Java package `org.company.product` may be renamed to `org.company.customer.product`. If a convention for such a structured renaming is available, this can be considered by the difference analysis to improve the matching between original and copied artifacts.

However, this is not about an algorithmic detection of renaming because the overall goal of a fully automated difference analysis must not be missed due to invalid or unclear renaming detections.

R3: Support Intended Variability Mechanisms A broad range of mechanisms exists to implement variability on different levels of software element granularity (e.g., statements, classes, components) in SPLs [168, 7, 146]. According to the individual requirements for the targeted SPL, a reasonable set of mechanisms should be defined to prevent divergent implementations of the same type of variability. This set also specifies the "minimum granularity level" variability should be implemented at, which also determines the minimum granularity level differences must be identified for. For example, allowing preprocessor annotations, variability can be implemented even within expressions, but using conditional program execution, the minimum granularity to implement variability are statements. The difference analysis needs to take the minimum granularity level of the intended variability mechanisms into account. Otherwise, many fine-grained differences are reported where fewer coarse grain ones are sufficient.

R4: Allow for Configuration of Analysis Scope A consolidation of customized copies typically does not affect all components of a software system. For example, only some of the customizations are intended to become part of the SPL. All other parts and also third party code can be excluded from the difference analysis. Hence, the required processing and the information presented to SPL Consolidation Developers can be reduced. If a scope is defined (e.g., Java packages to exclude), this should be used to optimize the difference analysis. If it is not, the analysis must still return a valid result.

R5: Analyze Independent Source Directories Customized copies are often developed by different developers and cannot be assumed to be maintained in a common code base, repository, or with a coupled change history. Thus, the difference analysis must be able to handle complete and independent source directories without any existing mapping between the contained compilation units.

R6: Favor False Positives over False Negatives Due to the possibly large amount of differences, developers should not be confronted with more information than necessary. However, it is important to not miss any differences in order to provide them with reliable input for the downstream consolidation process. Otherwise, this could lead to wrong variability design decisions, which is inferior to confronting developers with irrelevant differences they have to ignore. Thus, in the context of a consolidation, false positive differences must be favored over false negative ones.

R7: Provide Binary Decision Similar to providing all relevant differences, software elements should be clearly classified as changed or not. All software elements not identified as similar must be reviewed by developers anyway. That means, even if a software element would be classified as "maybe changed", developers have to investigate this element. Thus, the differentiation between "changed" and "potentially changed" does not help but leads to additional confusion and therefore is omitted.

R8: Support Heterogeneous Software Artifacts Modifications between customized code copies can be performed on all types of artifacts in addition to their source code. For example, component descriptors or configuration files can be adapted. To allow for a comprehensive difference analysis, extensibility for additional artifacts is necessary.

5.2. Model-Based Difference Analysis Approach

The SPLEVO difference analysis follows a model-based approach as an overarching strategy to analyze the differences between the product copies under study. As shown in Figure 5.3, first, model representations of the code copies are extracted. Next, matching elements are identified to derive a match model. Following, the Diffing derives a Diff Model from the identified differences in the matches. Afterwards, a Post-Processing optimizes the Diff Model before a VPM is initialized. To enable the last step, references to the original software model elements are continuously tracked throughout the difference analysis. When the VPM is initialized, all other models can be cleaned up.

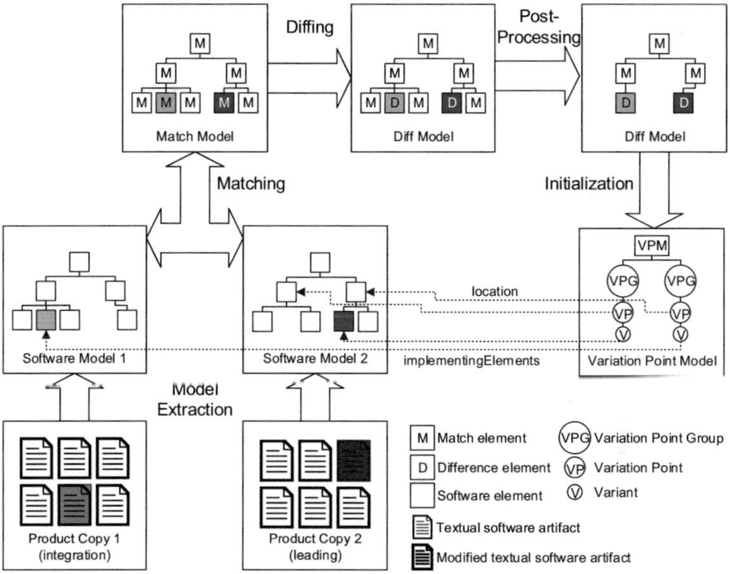

Figure 5.3.: Difference analysis concept

Reasoning for the model-based approach Such an approach respects software structures (e.g., methods, blocks, classes) by design, and the analysis benefits from syntactical information gained during extraction (e.g., by comparing only elements of the same type), as described in Section 2.4.7. Extracting models first requires an initial overhead compared to textual comparisons. However, textual comparison requires additional effort for interpretation of the findings afterwards and the initial extraction effort is acceptable as the models are required in the downstream consolidation process anyway. In addition, reference resolving requires the most effort but can be cached to considerably improve the overall consolidation process. During the consolidation process, the customized copies are not changed. Thus, the cache must not be invalidated.

Infrastructure for model extraction Today, extracting software models is well supported by many different approaches, as described in Section 2.4.6. For the SPLEVO difference analysis, software models must align with the software model structure specified by Definition 7 in Section 3.4.1. Furthermore, the SPLEVO approach uses Ecore respectively EMOF based models. The Ecore modeling infrastructure is not a limitation of the difference analysis but supports the integration in the overall SPLEVO consolidation process. The Ecore infrastructure is well supported by existing model extraction facilities (Section 2.4.6). The model-based approach in general, and the hierarchical structure of software models (Section 3.4) in specific, allow for specifying an abstract difference algorithm and enabling technology-specific adaptations to improve the analysis.

5.3. Difference Algorithm

The SPLEVO model comparison itself is structured in two main phases – Matching and Diffing – and a post-processing phase as a third. They build a difference model which itself is used for initializing the VPM afterwards (see difference analysis steps in Figure 5.3). The separation of matching and diffing is a typical approach in model-based difference analysis as proposed by Xing and Stroulia [195]. The post-processing is done to improve and clean-up results as proposed by Kehrer et al. [95].

Metamodel All models involved in this process are based on the Ecore infrastructure according to the EMOF specification as used for the software models as well. This allows for continuously linking the elements of the original software models and creating the SoftwareElement references when initializing a VPM. Figure 5.4 shows a class diagram of the SPLEVO difference metamodel that relates varying software elements of two or more copies (i.e., the metamodel of the Diff Model in Figure 5.3). The metamodel supports the matching model and the difference model, as the latter is not a completely new model but adds information to the former.

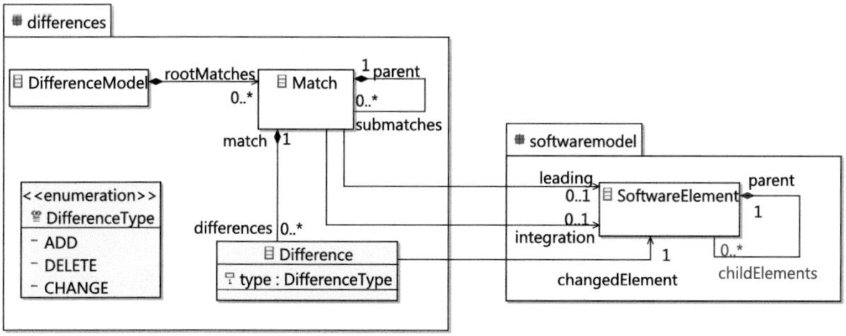

Figure 5.4.: SPLEVO difference metamodel

`Match` elements are organized in a tree structure according to their containment references to child `Match` elements (i.e., `submatches`). Furthermore, they provide references to the matched `SoftwareElements` identified as leading (i.e., from the Leading Copy's software model) and integration (i.e., origin from the Integration Copy's software model). Either leading, integration, or both references must be set as specified by the OCL constraint in Listing 2.

```
context Match
inv SufficientReferences: leading <> null or integration <> null;
```

Listing 2: Match element reference constraint

A `DifferenceModel` references the root elements of the `Match` element trees (i.e., reference `rootMatches`). Those root elements represent the top most elements of matched `Resources` in the software models under study. `Difference` elements identify the changed `SoftwareElement` and are contained by `Match` elements to identify their location (i.e., the `Match` element's references). A `Difference`'s `type` attribute describes the way a `Difference` was created during the copy-based customization (i.e., in which copy a `SoftwareElement` exists). The possible `DifferenceTypes` are:

- `ADD` identifying a `SoftwareElement` was added during customization and thus exists in the Integration Copy only.
- `DELETE` identifying a `SoftwareElement` was deleted during customization and thus exists in the Leading Copy only.
- `CHANGE` identifying a `SoftwareElement` was modified during customization and exists in both copies.

According to the SPLEVO SoftwareModel concept described in Section 3.4, the SoftwareElements referenced by the Differences can result from technology-specific software models. Furthermore, sub-classes of the Difference metamodel class can be used for typed references to technology-specific changed elements (e.g., a Java StatementDifference referencing a changed statement).

The metamodel is similar to the one proposed by EMF Compare [25], as `Difference` elements are contained by hierarchically organized `Match` elements. However, the SPLEVO `Difference` elements provide a reference to the changed software element, and `Match` elements do not reference arbitrary objects but `SoftwareElements` of the Leading or Integration Copy. This allows for type safety on the one side and adaptability for handling multi-programming language differences on the other side (e.g., support systems with a mix of Java and component frameworks). This allows for type safety on the one side and adaptability for handling multi-programming language differences on the other side (e.g., support systems with a mix of Java and component frameworks).

Matching During the matching phase, the software models of the copies are scanned for model elements representing the same software elements (e.g., a class existing in both copies). Match elements can be of two types according to their number of references: i) `Regular Match` (Definition 10) and ii) `Single Side Match` (Definition 11). The terminology is used to simplify the difference algorithm description and aligned with terminology proposed by [25]. The type itself is a derived attribute resulting from the number of referenced software elements.

Definition 10 (Regular Match) *A* Regular Match *represents SoftwareElements which exist in the software models of the Leading and the Integration Copies under study. The leading as well as the integration reference of the according* `Match` *element are set.*

```
context Match
inv RegularMatch: leading <> null and integration <> null;
```

Listing 3: Match constraint: Regular Match

Definition 11 (Single Side Match) *A* Single Side Match *represents an element which exist in either the Leading or the Integration Copies' software models but not in both. Either the leading or the integration reference of the according* `Match` *element are set, but not both at the same time.*

```
context Match
inv SingleSideMatch: leading <> null xor integration <> null;
```

Listing 4: Match constraint: Single Side Match

If software elements could be matched with each other in the matching phase, a *Regular Match* is created. The Regular Match element references the matched software elements in the software models they originate from. If an element from either the Leading or the Integration Copy could not be matched with an element of the other copy, a *Single Side Match* is created, referencing this individual element only.

Diffing and Post-Processing In the diffing phase, software elements added, deleted, and changed are derived from the matches, and according difference elements are created in the diff model. Finally, during the post-processing, the size of the diff model is reduced by removing dispensable match elements and by removing false positive differences. The latter must be done, as it requires all differences to be at hand to perform a pattern detection on this differences.

Algorithm structure Figure 5.5 provides an overview of the algorithm's main components assigned to the phases of the difference analysis they are executed in.

The *SoftwareModelMatching*, *BestMatchResource*, *ScopeFilter*, *Element-TypeFilter*, as well as *SubMatchTraversing* and *SimilarityCheck* are part of the matching phase (Section 5.3.1). The *Difference Derivation* creates the actual Difference elements in the diffing phase (Section 5.3.2). The *Derived Copy Cleanup* and the *Model Condensation* are performed as part of the post-processing phase (Section 5.3.3).

The SPLEVO Difference Analysis uses the Leading Copy (Definition 3) selected in the configuration of the consolidation process for structuring its traversing, as a reference for similarity checks on software elements, and for normalizations.

The following subsections describe the components and concepts of the SPLEVO model-based difference analysis in detail. Subsequently, Section 5.3.4 maps the difference analysis design decisions to the consolidation-specific requirements identified in Section 5.1.

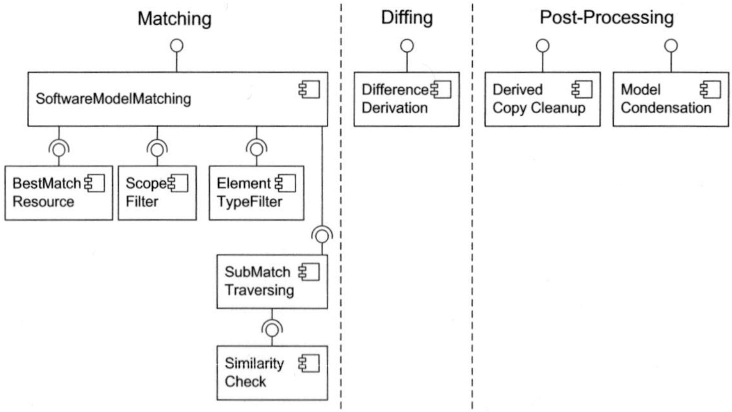

Figure 5.5.: Difference analysis algorithm components

5.3.1. Matching

The matching identifies elements of the software models representing the same software element in the copies' implementation – for example, a class declaration existing in all copies without any modifications. The result of the matching algorithm is a tree of match elements reflecting the sum of the input copies' software model trees.

During the matching phase, a depth-first traversing of the copies' software models is performed, following the structure of the Leading Copy's containment relationships. According to SPLEVO's definition of a SoftwareModel (Definition 7), the containment relationships are definite, terminated by SoftwareElements without further childElements, and free of cycles. Thus, the traversing according to these references will always terminate, as the number of elements in software models is finite. The match traversing algorithm is separated in two parts: First, the copies' SoftwareModels, respectively their contained Resources, are matched with each other (Algorithm 1). Following, for each matched leading and integration resource, their contained SoftwareElements are recursively matched with each other (Algorithm 2). The algorithm components for the matching are either involved in the traversing (i.e., SoftwareModelMatching, BestMatchResource, ScopeFilter, and ElementTypeFilter) or the SoftwareElement comparison (i.e., SimilarityCheck) and thus described in the following subsections.

5.3.1.1. Traversing

As shown in Algorithm 1, the matching takes the copies' SoftwareModels as input and returns a set of the root match elements to be stored in the DifferenceModel. Matches are structured in a hierarchy according to the hierarchies of the input models. Each match can reference matching elements of the two input models (i.e., a *Regular Match*), or only one if no match exists (i.e., a *Single Side Match*).

Filter At the beginning of the algorithm, *ScopeFilter* and *ElementTypeFilter* are applied on the SoftwareModels to filter elements that can be ignored by the rest of the difference analysis.

The *ScopeFilter* scans the model trees for Resources and SoftwareElements in scopes (e.g., namespaces) explicitly excluded in the process configuration. What a scope is, depends on the technology a software model relates to. For example, in Java, a scope can be defined by packages. In PHP or C++, namespaces can define a scope. According to the technology-specific nature of a scope, a *ScopeFilter* is technology-specific as well, and thus the specification of scopes to include as part of the process configuration also depends on the *ScopeFilter* used.

The *ElementTypeFilter* scans the model trees for Resources and Software-Elements of types not relevant for the copies' behavior. For example, comments or layout information might be modified but not relevant for the copies behavior. The concrete set of element types that can be ignored is technology-specific, as, for example, layout information can be relevant in some languages such as PHP. Thus, the *ElementTypeFilter* provides another point of technology-specific adaptation.

Resource matching When the filtering is done, the Resources of the resulting SoftwareModels are matched with each other. First, the resources of the Integration Copy's SoftwareModel are stored as a list of matching candidates.

Now, for each resource of the Leading Copy, the best matching candidate is identified by the BestMatchResource algorithm component. This identifies the best matching resource for the leading resource to match. A resource is identified by its Uniform Resource Identifier (URI), which is an identifier string consisting of several segments (i.e., strings between "/" characters). For example, a URI identifying a file of a Leading Copy in the file system might look like `file:/C:/project1/example/File.xyz`. In contrast, files of an Integration Copy might be placed in different folders or file systems. Thus, the URIs of a copy's files might start with a string such as `file:/C:/`**`project-copy/`**`...` or even **`file:/D:/copy/`**`...` To identify the best matching resource, it is not possible to simply match the full URI, as the algorithm does not know the base path of the resources. Furthermore, a copy can consist of several projects. To cope with this, segments of the URIs of the resources are compared. This is done from back to forth, as the front segments differ anyway because of different source directories used.

Now, the BestMatchResource algorithm identifies the resource of the matching candidates with the highest number of matching segments at the end of their URIs. As a cross check, the identified best matching resource from the Integration Copy is compared with all other not yet matched Leading Copy resources. Again, this is done by comparing their URI segments from back to front. If there is a pair of leading and integration resources with a higher number of similar segments at the end of their URIs, this is an even better match than the one identified before. Thus, the integration resource with the next lower number of matched segments will be used and the cross check will be done again. The BestMatchResource algorithm considers renaming patterns specified in the process configuration. If a renaming pattern influences the resources' URIs (e.g., renamed Java packages reflected in classes' file system paths), it will be used here to normalize the URIs before matching their segments.

If a best matching resource was detected, a new Match element is created for their root elements (i.e., `Match(`se_l`,`se_i`)`. Next, those root elements are used to recursively detect their matching child elements (i.e., by calling `SubMatchTraversing` recursively) and the resulting set of submatches is assigned to the newly created match element (i.e., Match: *m*). Afterwards, *m* is added to the list of detected rootMatches and the matched integration resource is removed from the candidates list. If no matching resource was found for a leading resource, a *Single Side Match* is created that references the leading resource's root SoftwareElement only. Finally, if there are resources remaining in the list of matchingCandidates, further *Single Side Match* elements are created and stored in the rootMatches set.

Software element matching The Sub Match Traversing (Algorithm 2) specifies how submatches are recursively detected for a pair of already matched software elements. A depth-first traversing according to the Leading Copy's software model containment hierarchy is performed.

During each recursion, first, the child elements of the Integration Copy's software element are used as matching candidates. Next, each child node of the Leading Copy's software element is checked for similarity with the matching candidates. If a candidate is identified to be similar, a *Regular Match* element is created and stored in the result list of detected submatches. The matched candidate is removed from the list of candidates, and the next child element of the Leading Copy is processed. If no similar candidate could be found for a Leading Copy's child element, a *Single Side Match* is created referencing this element only. When all child elements of the Leading Copy are checked, *Single Side Match* elements are created for each of the remaining Integration Copy's child elements. The child elements are checked in the order they are stored in the software model, as it represents their occurrence in the real implementation.

To decide about elements' similarity, an algorithm component named `SimilarityCheck` decides if two elements represent the same software element, as further described in Section 5.3.1.2. The strictly hierarchical traversing allows assuming matching locations for elements passed to the `SimilarityCheck`. Here, location relates to the elements' containing parent software elements.

The described algorithm for hierarchical match traversing is generic and can be applied to all software models with unique containment relationships. As mentioned above, the *ScopeFilter* and *ElementTypeFilter* provide adaptation points for technology-specific behavior. Furthermore, the *BestMatchResource* detection provides an adaptation point to consider renaming practices. Those three are straightforward checks of namespaces (e.g., packages) and element types or name mappings. In contrast, the `SimilarityCheck` used during the recursive traversing is more complex, depending on the type of software model under study and therefore further explained below.

5.3.1.2. Similarity Check

The purpose of the `SimilarityCheck` is to decide if software elements of the Leading and Integration Copies represent the same, unmodified element in their implementation. Three main characteristics of the elements must be considered for this decision:

- The elements' locations
- The elements' types
- The elements' identifying attributes

The matching algorithm's traversing strategy ensures the locations of the elements represented by their containing parent software elements are similar before the elements are passed to the `SimilarityCheck`. Thus, the `SimilarityCheck` can assume the elements' locations as similar and start with checking the elements' types. Here, types refer to the technology-specific SoftwareElement types such as a class, statement, expression or variable. If their types do not match exactly, the elements are immediately returned as being not similar. If the types are similar, next, the elements' identifying attributes are compared. Which attributes to consider, depends on the type of software model under study. However, during the prototype implementation and the case studies, we have identified typical attribute similarities of software elements in object-oriented programming languages. A certain type of software element can correspond to none or multiple of those identified generic attribute similarities. If a language-specific `SimilarityCheck` identifies a set of attributes to be identifying for a type of software elements, all values of these attributes must be equal to identify two elements of this type as similar. The generic attribute similarities are summarized in the following paragraphs:

Named Elements Software elements with a name attribute that is used for their identification (e.g., methods or fields). These attributes must be considered to check their similarity. If renaming conventions are available from the process configuration, they need to be considered here to decide about similarity (e.g., ignoring suffixes). Using names as identifying attributes conforms to the approach of Neamtiu et al. [136], who observed name stability over time for methods (Section 2.4.7.2). At the same time, they report performance improvement in their AST matching algorithm.

Referencing Elements Software elements representing a reference to another software element only (e.g., import declarations and method calls). To check the similarity of such elements, their referenced software elements must be checked. If the reference elements are similar, the referencing elements are similar, too. The `SimilarityCheck` component can be reused for this as long as the referenced elements' locations are ensured to be similar.

Parameterized Elements Software elements which can be declared multiple times in parallel with differing parameter sets (e.g., overload method declarations). To decide about the similarity of such elements, the type of their parameters must be checked as well. For example, changing a parameter of a method call to a more specific type can lead to calling a different method with a similar name.

Namespace-Aware Elements Software elements that are unique within a namespace only (e.g., classes and interfaces). To decide about the similarity of those software elements, their namespaces must be checked. In case of namespace-aware elements and available conventions for namespace renaming, the conventions must be considered here to improve the matching.

Leaf Elements Software elements without further containment references to (e.g., string literals). If such elements have value attributes representing a fixed value in the software implementation (e.g., a specific string), these attributes must be checked. Leaf elements without value attributes are always similar, as their similarity depends on their type and location only, which have been checked before.

Ordered Elements Software elements which are referenced by their containing parent element in an ordered manner because their position in the implementation matters for their behavior (e.g., Statements). Deciding about the similarity of such elements is challenging in the general case. For example, inserting a new statement at the beginning of a method's body influences the positions of all subsequent statements and potentially changes the overall processing. However, for consolidating customized code copies, the difference analysis and the similarity decision in specific are performed from a static point of view on the copies' implementations. Thus, it is sufficient to check an ordered element's direct neighbors (i.e., the predecessor and successor elements in the containment list). If both neighbors did not change, the element did not move in its context.

5.3.2. Diffing

When the matching is done, the resulting match model is further processed in the diffing phase to derive the actual differences from the match elements. This is done by the `Recursive Difference Derivation` (Algorithm 3) by traversing the match model's containment tree, identifying Single Side Matches, creating according *Difference* elements, and storing them into the same model. As specified in the DifferenceModel metamodel, three types of differences are possible: ADD, DELETE, and CHANGE. ADD and DELETE identify differences that exist in an Integration Copy or the Leading Copy only. CHANGE identifies differing elements existing in the Leading as well as in the Integration Copy, but elements on a level of granularity below a minimum granularity level (`minGranularity`, Definition 12) exist in only one or the other. The minimum granularity level depends on the variability mechanisms to be used for consolidating the customized copies (Section 5.1).

Definition 12 (Minimum Granularity) *The granularity of software elements is a partial order on the element types defined by the metamodel of certain software models under study. It corresponds to the containment references between element types and, thus, it is technology-specific. The* Minimum Granularity *is a set of software element types defining a border within this partial order. Elements of types below this border should not be reported as differing but lifted to CHANGE differences of a parent element with a type on or above this border.*

For example, in the Java programming language, expressions are child elements of statements and more fine-grained but not vice versa. Thus, using the statement type as minimum granularity level, differing expressions will be reported as changes of the enclosing statements.

For each of the top level Match elements (i.e., rootMatches), the function `CheckForDifferences` is called to recursively evaluate the elements as well as their submatches. Each match element is evaluated if it is a *Regular Match* or a *Single Side Match*. In case of a *Regular Match*, the function `CheckForDifferences` is called for each of its submatches. In case of a *Single Side Match*, the match element is further evaluated to decide which type of Difference to create. `BelowMinGranularity` checks if the software elements referenced by the match element are below the minimum granularity level specified in the process configuration. This is done to not report differences more detailed as necessary for the intended variability mechanisms. In case of differing but too fine-grained software elements, the Difference element is created with the type CHANGE and stored in the next parent match element that is coarse grain enough according to the minimum granularity level. `FindCoarseGrainEnoughParent` looks up the next sufficient parent match by traversing the parent match containment chain upwards, until the first match references a coarse grain enough Leading Copy's SoftwareElement. If the *Single Side Match* itself is coarse grain enough, it is checked if its leading or its integration reference is set, and an ADD respectively DELETE Difference is created.

5.3.3. Post-Processing

The SPLEVO difference algorithm's post-processing executes two algorithm components: The *Derived Copy Cleanup* to remove false positive differences resulting from copy-based customization practices, and the *Model Condensation* to reduce the size of the final difference model.

5.3.3.1. Derived Copy Cleanup

When the diffing phase is finished, a post-processing step is performed to detect and handle instances of the `Derived Copy` pattern. As described in Section 5.1, a Derived Copy introduces an inheritance relationship between the copy and its origin, granting the copy access to the original element's children of an appropriate accessibility. Such relationships are always technology-specific and cannot be specified or detected in a language-independent manner.

For example, using Java technology, copied classes can extend the original class and inherit all methods and fields that are not private. Thus, they must be treated as unmodified by the difference analysis as long as they are not overridden. The difference analysis itself identifies inherited fields, methods, and not re-declared imports as differences with type DELETE. However, those differences must not be reflected as variability in the future SPL. Accordingly, they are false positive differences from a consolidation perspective, and the results of the difference analysis can be improved by filtering them from the DifferenceModel.

Algorithm 4 specifies the `Derived Copy` detection and filtering algorithm for an object-oriented programming language with classes, fields, methods, and imports as defined by the Java technology. Each difference describing a deleted method, field or import is checked by the algorithm (i.e., function `TypeOf` provides the technology-specific type of a SoftwareElement). If such a difference is contained in a $class_l$ of the Leading Copy that is matched by a customized $class_i$ of the Integration Copy and $class_i$ extends $class_l$, the difference is detected as a false positive DELETE and removed from the difference result model.

Figure 5.6 provides an illustrating example of a Derived Copy pattern the algorithm detects. In the example, class MyClass is copied and extended by MyClassCustom. The difference algorithm detects a Difference of type DELETE for field1. The Derived Copy cleanup detects the field1 deletion and notices that the containing Match element references MyClassCustom and MyClass, with the former extending the latter and being able to access field1. Accordingly, the shown Difference element is removed from the DifferenceModel. Notice that a copy-based customization guideline to append the suffix "Custom" is assumed to be configured for the example, allowing to match MyClass and MyClassCustom with each other.

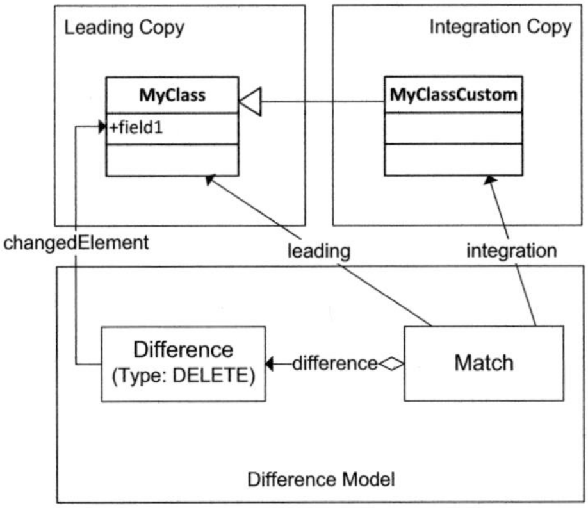

Figure 5.6.: Derived Copy example before cleanup

5.3.3.2. Model Condensation

The matching and diffing phases produce a DifferenceModel containing a tree of match elements that reflects the combined structures of the leading and integration software models under study. Matches and sub-matches exist in the difference model, whether they contain difference elements or not. As illustrated in Figure 5.3, an additional post-processing is performed to remove matches and their sub-trees to reduce the overall model's size if they contain no differences.

The Model Condensation algorithm (Algorithm 5) traverses the match element tree in a depth-first order. It removes match elements containing neither differences nor sub-matches in a bottom-up manner.

5.3.4. Explicit Support for Copy Consolidation

To cope with the consolidation-specific requirements on analyzing differences, which are presented in Section 5.1, the SPLEVO difference analysis algorithm has been designed to explicitly target these requirements as summarized in Table 5.1.

To target R1, the SPLEVO approach contains an explicit post-processing step presented in Section 5.3.3.1. R2 is explicitly considered by normalizing element names and namespaces during the matching phase. To support R3, the algorithm is not limited to any specific variability mechanism, but allows for a minimum granularity level aligned with the intended variability mechanisms to return appropriate differences (Section 5.3.2). To support R4, the match traversing (Section 5.3.1) ignores elements not in the configured scope (i.e., the ScopeFilter algorithm component). For the support of R5, the algorithm uses all resources contained in provided source directories, provides an automated application of renaming conventions, and does not require pre-matched compilation units. R6 and R7 are targeted by abstaining from any heuristics to guess matching elements which might not be a 100% clear match. Finally, for R8, the algorithm itself is specified for any type of software model with a hierarchical containment structure as assumed for the overall SPLEVO approach (Definition 7). However, explicit adaptation points for technology-specific software models are provided allowing for technology-aware algorithm improvements.

5.4. Variation Point Model Initialization

The SPLEVO difference analysis is embedded in the overall context of the consolidation process and designed as a fully automated activity. It does not involve SPL Consolidation Developers in its processing and completely hides the match and difference models from them. Instead, it provides them with an initialized VPM representing the individual differences identified between the consolidated copies. At this point, the differences are related to each other. Thus, in the initial VPM each difference is represented by a single VP contained in a separate Variation Point Group (VPG).

VP initialization algorithm The Variation Point initialization algorithm specifies the initialization of a VPM (Algorithm 7). For each difference, the function *CreateVariationPointGroup* creates a VPG and invokes *CreateVariationPoint* to create a containing VP. The id of the VPG is derived from the VP location's label as an initial, humanly readable value that can be refined by SPL Consolidation Developers later on. The Variant elements created for a VP depend on the type of the currently processed difference. Function *CreateVariants* returns single variants for DELETE and ADD differences, with implementing elements from the Leading or Integration Copy, and the leading attribute set to true or false appropriately. For CHANGE differences, two Variants are created, as the according element exists in the Leading and Integration Copies' software models. For CHANGE differences, the changed elements are received from the containing match element, as the Difference element is contained by the Match, identifying the differing SoftwareElements in both copies (Section 5.3.2). The location of the VP depends on the match element containing the currently processed difference. If the match references a leading SoftwareElement, this is preferred as a location. Only if no leading reference is available (i.e., for Integration Copies' SoftwareElements added at the top level, such as completely new resources), the integration reference is used. For the sake of brevity, in Algorithm 7 the software model elements are returned directly, but actually are first wrapped with a SoftwareElement of the Variation Point Model.

SPL Profile Impact The SPL Profile allows for choosing an intended SPL Type which comes with a set of default variability characteristics (i.e., Variability Type, Binding Time, and Extensible). When a VP is created by the VPM initialization process and an SPL Type was chosen in the SPL Profile, the VP's characteristics are set to the SPL Type's default characteristics. Alternatively, if no SPL Type was chosen, at least one option for each variability characteristic must have been defined in the SPL Profile anyway. For each characteristic, the first allowed option – in their natural order – will be used for the new VP's characteristics. The metamodels of the SPL Profile and the VPM are specified in Section 3.3 respectively Section 3.2.

The initialized VPM describes VPs on the most fine-grained level, each of them corresponding to a single difference. In the downstream consolidation process, those VPs are correlated to each other and transformed to more valued VPs in the variability design phase. To cope with the potentially high number of differences to review and refine, the SPLEVO approach's support for variability design reads the VPM and provides automation for comprehension and design decisions, as described in Section 6.

5.5. Multi Copy Difference Analysis

Comparing more than two copies at the same time is a challenging task. In particular, deciding about the similarity of more than two elements is not sufficiently done as a binary decision. For example, with three elements e_1, e_2, and e_3, there are five possible similarity results, as shown in Table 5.2. Similarity is a transitive relationship, thus either all elements are differing, all are similar, or only one pair is similar. A binary decision about all elements would return "true" for the last case only, with all elements being similar (i.e., column 5 in Table 5.2). However, there are three cases of partly similarity not covered by a binary decision about all elements' similarity (i.e., column 2–3 in Table 5.2).

Iterative element matching To cope with this challenge, the SPLEVO approach proposes to stick to a pairwise element matching of each Integration Copy with the Leading Copy and iteratively build up the match model in several, steps as illustrated in Figure 5.7. With each step, the match model is extended with further Regular Matches or Single Side Matches, and the final match model combines not only the SoftwareModel structures of two copies but of all copies analyzed. If a SoftwareElement cannot be matched with the Leading Copy, it will be compared to SoftwareElements of the previously compared Integration Copies. Here, only SoftwareElements will be compared that exist at the same location and did not match to the Leading Copy as well. This allows identifying similarities between the Integration Copies without a match to the Leading Copy.

Difference derivation Afterwards, the difference derivation still needs to check for Single Side Matches. In the context of multi-copy difference analysis, the definitions of Regular and Single Side Matches are still valid, but a Match element must now be able to reference more than one integration SoftwareElement (i.e., cardinality of the reference *Match.integration* must be changed from 0..1 to 0..∗). Thus, a Single Side Match now indicates a SoftwareElement exists in either the Leading Copy only or in one or more Integration Copies. Accordingly, if a Single Side Match refers to more than one Integration Copy, separate Difference elements of type ADD must be created for each referenced integration element. Similarly, for Regular Matches with a SoftwareElement existing in at least one but not all Integration Copies, Difference elements of type DELETE will be created for each of the integration copies not containing the element.

Model adaptations To realize this approach, the metamodel of the DifferenceModel requires an adaptation, as already mentioned above. Match elements must become able to reference more than one integration SoftwareElement, as the same element might be detected in more than one Integration Copy.

Conclusion The strategy presented above allows for comparing more than two product copies without the need of a full pairwise comparison between all copies. At the same time, the strategy allows for binary similarity decisions between pairs of elements to reduce the complexity of the similarity decisions and to enable more precise decisions, as exemplified in Table 5.2.

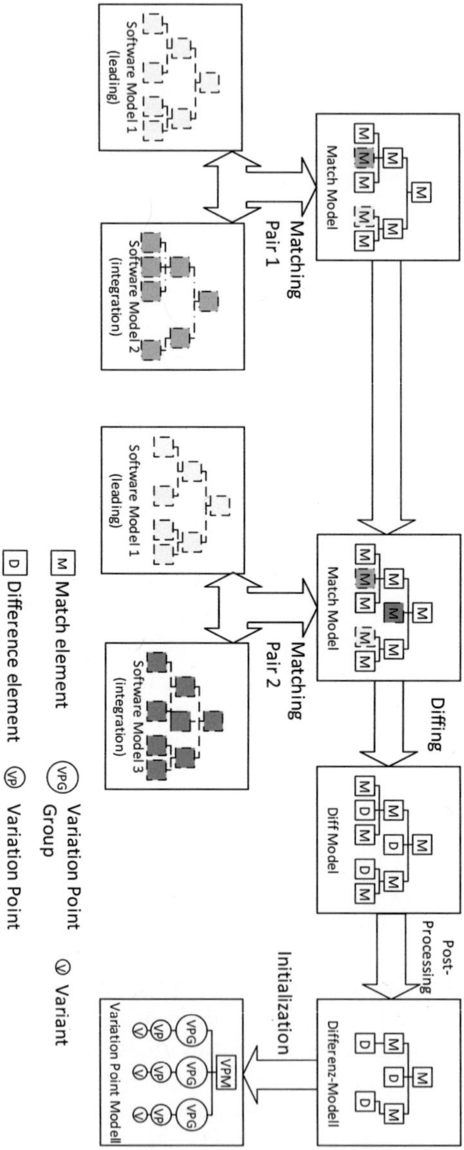

Figure 5.7.: Multi copy difference analysis concept
Software model extraction left out for the sake of brevity

Algorithm 1: Software Model Matching

```
input  : SoftwareModel: sm_l // of Leading Copy l
         SoftwareModel: sm_i // of Integration Copy i
output : Set&lt;Match&gt;: rootMatches ← ∅

ScopeFilter (sm_l)        // Filter resources and elements out of scope
ScopeFilter (sm_i)
ElementTypeFilter(sm_l)   // Filter behavior irrelevant elements
ElementTypeFilter(sm_i)
Set<Resource>: matchingCandidates ← sm_i.resources
foreach Resource: r_l ∈ sm_l.resources do
    Resource:
     r_i ← BestMatchResource(r_l, sm_l.resources, matchingCandidates)
    if r_i != null then
        SoftwareElement: se_l ← r_l.root
        SoftwareElement: se_i ← r_i.root
        Match: m ← Match(se_l, se_i)                      // Regular Match
        m.submatches ← SubMatchTraversing(se_l, se_i)    // Recursion
        rootMatches ← rootMatches ∪ m
        matchingCandidates ← matchingCandidates \ r_i
    else
        rootMatches ← rootMatches ∪ Match(se_l, null)    // Single Side Match
    end
end
foreach r_i ∈ matchingCandidates do                      // remaining candidates
    rootMatches ← rootMatches ∪ Match(null, r_i.root)    // Single Side Match
end
```

Algorithm 2: Sub Match Traversing

```
input  : SoftwareElement: se_l // of Leading Copy l
         SoftwareElement: se_i // of Integration Copy i
output : Set&lt;Match&gt;: submatches ← ∅

Set<SoftwareElement>: matchCandidates ← se_i.childElements
foreach SoftwareElement: ce_l in se_l.childElements do
    foreach SoftwareElement: ce_i in matchCandidates do
        if SimilarityCheck(ce_l,ce_i) == true then
            Match: m ← Match(ce_l,ce_i)                          // Regular Match
            m.submatches ←SubMatchTraversing(ce_l,ce_i)
             // Recursion
            submatches ← submatches ∪ m
            matchCandidates ← matchCandidates \ ce_i
            continue with next leading ce_l;
        end
    end
    submatches ← submatches ∪ Match(ce_l, null)   // Create Single
     Side Match
end
foreach ce_i in matchCandidates do                //remaining candidates
    submatches ← submatches ∪ Match(null, ce_i)   // Create Single
     Side Match
end
return submatches;
```

Algorithm 3: Recursive Difference Derivation

```
input  : DifferenceModel: dm // the match model
output : DifferenceModel: dm // the match model with difference
         elements

foreach Match: m ∈ dm.rootMatches do
    DetectDifferences(m)
end

Function DetectDifferences(m: match) is
    if m.leading != null AND m.integration != null then    // Regular Match
        foreach Match: m_sub ∈ m.submatches do
            DetectDifferences(m_sub)
        end
    else                                                     // Single Side Match
        if BelowMinGranularity (m) then
            Match: m_p ← FindCoarseGrainEnoughParent(m)
            Difference: d ← Difference(m_p.leading, CHANGE)
            m_p.differences ← m_p.differences ∪ d
        else if m.leading == null then
            Difference: d ← Difference(m.integration, ADD)
            Match: m_p ← m.parent
            if m_p == null then  m_p ← m
            m_p.differences ← m_p.differences ∪ d
        else if m.integration == null then
            Difference: d ← Difference(m.leading, DELETE)
            Match: m_p ← m.parent
            m_p.differences ← m_p.differences ∪ d
        end
    end
end
```

Algorithm 4: Derived Copy Cleanup (for Java technology)

```
input  : DifferenceModel: dm
output : DifferenceModel: dm // without Derived Copy false positives

foreach Difference : d ∈ dm do    // Collected by traversing the
 Match Element tree
    if d.type == DELETE AND
     TypeOf(d.changedElement) ∈ {Field, Method, Import} then
        Match: m ← d.match.parent
        if TypeOf(m.leading) ∈ {Class} then
            Class: class_l ← m.leading
            Class: class_i ← m.integration
            if class_i extends class_l then        // Java inheritance
                dm.differnces ← dm.differnces \ d
            end
        end
    end
end
```

Algorithm 5: Model Condensation

```
input  : DifferenceModel: dm
output : DifferenceModel: dm // reduced in size

foreach Match: m ∈ dm.rootMatches do
    CondenseMatch(m)
end

Function CondenseMatch(Match: m) is
    foreach Match: sm ∈ m.submatches do
        CondenseMatch(sm)
    end
    if m.submatches == ∅ ∧ m.differences == ∅ then
        Match: m_p ← m.parent
        m_p.submatches ← m_p.submatches \ m
    end
end
```

#	Requirement	Supported by	Section
R1	Support Independent and Derived Copies	Derived Copy Cleanup	5.3.3.1
R2	Consider Copy Renaming Conventions	Normalization during matching phase	5.3.1
R3	Support Intended Variability Mechanisms	Granularity level-aware difference derivation	5.3.2
R4	Allow for Configuration of Analysis Scope	ScopeFilter during matching	5.3.1
R5	Analyze Independent Source Directories	No assumptions except software model structure	5.3.1
R6	Favor False Positives over False Negatives	Strict hierarchical comparison	5.3.1.2
R7	Provide Binary Decision	Omit heuristics	5.3.1.2
R8	Support Heterogeneous Software Artifacts	Overall generic algorithm with explicit adaptation points	

Table 5.1.: SPLEVO Difference Analysis: Design decisions for consolidation requirements

Algorithm 6: Variation Point Initialization, part 1

```
input  : DifferenceModel: dm
output : VariationPointModel: vpm

foreach Difference: d ∈ dm do        // Collected by traversing the
 Match tree
    VariationPointGroup: vpg ← CreateVariationPointGroup(d)
    vpm.variationPointGroups ← vpm.variationPointGroups ∪ vpg
end

Function CreateVariationPointGroup(Difference: d) is
    VariationPointGroup: vpg
    VariationPoint: vp ← CreateVariationPoint(d)
    vpg.variationPoints ← vpg.variationPoints ∪ vp
    vpg.id ← vp.location.getLabel()
    return vpg
end

Function CreateVariationPoint(Difference: d) is
    VariationPoint: vp
    vp.variants ← CreateVariants(d)
    vp.location ← DetermineVariationPointLocation(d)
    return vp;
end
```

Algorithm 7: Variation Point Initialization, part 2

```
Function CreateVariants(Difference: d) is
    if d.type == ADD then
        Variant: v ← Variant(d.changedElement, leading = false)
        return ∅ ∪ v;
    else if d.type == DELETE then
        Variant: v ← Variant(d.changedElement, leading = true)
        return ∅ ∪ v;
    else if d.type == CHANGE then
        Variant: v_l ← Variant(d.match.leading, leading = true)
        Variant: v_i ← Variant(d.match.integration, leading = false)
        return ∅ ∪ v_l ∪ v_i
end

Function DetermineVariationPointLocation(Difference: d) is
    if d.match.leading! = null then        // prefer the Leading Copy's
     SoftwareElement
        return d.match.leading
    else
        return d.match.integration
end
```

Element Pairs	Possible Similarities				
	1	2	3	4	5
(e_1, e_2)	d	s	d	d	s
(e_2, e_3)	d	d	s	d	s
(e_1, e_3)	d	d	d	s	s

Table 5.2.: SPLEVO Difference Analysis:Similarity examples for three software elements
(e_n=software elements, d=different, s=similar)

6. Variability Design

This chapter describes the SPLEVO variability design phase and the contributions to support the design of variability of the future Software Product Line (SPL). As shown in Figure 6.1, the design phase follows the Difference Analysis and its purpose is to define the variation points to implement in the future SPL and the characteristics of variability to provide. The goal of the *Variability Design* phase is to create a Variation Point Model (VPM) describing a variability design in terms of structure (e.g., related variation points) and characteristics that is approved by SPL Consolidation Developers and SPL Managers. Therefore, the activities Relationship Analysis and Variation Point Structure Design are iteratively performed to receive and review refinement recommendations for the variation points. Next, during Variation Point Characteristic Definition, the characteristics are reviewed and defined from a technical perspective, and finally, in the Design Review, the variability design is proven from the product management perspective.

The chapter is structured as follows: First, it is explained how the variation point structure is designed, and the contributions to support these activities is detailed in Section 6.1. Next, the definition of the characteristics is presented in Section 6.2. Finally, the relationship analysis implemented in the SPLEVO approach are detailed in Section 6.3 and Section 6.4.

Satisfying variability design A variability design is specified by a VPM in terms of i) Variation Points (VPs) identifying where to implement variability, ii) Variants representing the available alternatives, iii) Variation Point Groups (VPGs) connecting VPs to be configured in a consistent manner, and iv) VP characteristics defining the requirements on the variability mechanism to implement (i.e., Definitions 5 and 6). A variability design can be considered "Satisfying" based on the decision of the SPL Consolidation Developers and SPL Managers. "Satisfying" means the design describes variability that is flexible enough to configure the intended product variants and provides a manageable amount of variation points. A "satisfying" variability design must reflect the demands of the SPL Consolidation Developers and SPL Managers to ensure the downstream Consolidation Refactoring will produce an SPL that meets their requirements (e.g., with manageable variation points and enough flexibility for reasonable product variants).

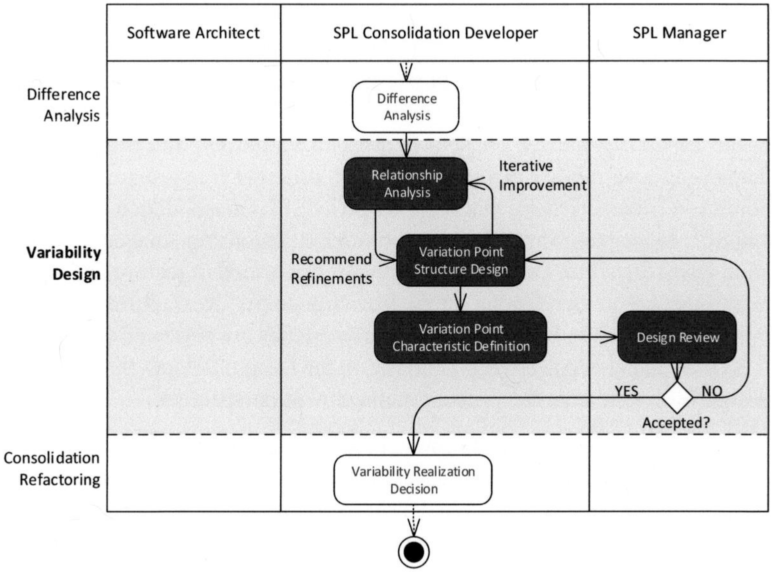

Figure 6.1.: SPLEVO process: Variability Design

Variation Point Model refinement As Klatt et al. introduced in [100], the initial VPM is derived from the differences between the product copies, representing all fine-grained differences in an unrelated manner. To achieve a manageable amount of variability in the resulting SPL, the VPM's initial structure must be refined. Manually analyzing all VPs to aggregate them into more coarse grained ones is tedious due to the typically high number of differences. The SPLEVO approach contributes a Variability Analyses to automatically identify related variation points and provide recommendations for their aggregation. In general, such aggregations cannot be decided in a fully automated fashion. Often, equivalent alternatives are possible and selected due to non-technical criteria, such as organizational reasons or personal preferences (e.g., product configuration responsibilities). To cope with this, the SPLEVO Variability Analysis returns recommendations only and SPL Consolidation Developers can accept, decline, or adapt them. Reasons for aggregating VPs range from technical constraints (e.g., program dependencies) up to hints for related modifications (e.g., terms used in the source code). To cover the variety of reasons for refinements and the amount of differences, the structure design can be done in an iterative manner.

Structure and characteristic decisions The SPLEVO consolidation process distinguishes between designing the structure (e.g., aggregations) and defining the characteristics (e.g., binding time and variability type) of the VPs and the VPMs. This enables SPL Consolidation Developers to first decide about the VPM structure. When they are satisfied, they choose variability characteristics for the refined VPs according to their required capabilities of the variability implementations later on. Thus, characteristic definitions do not need to be adapted several times because of still changing VPs during the iterative structure design.

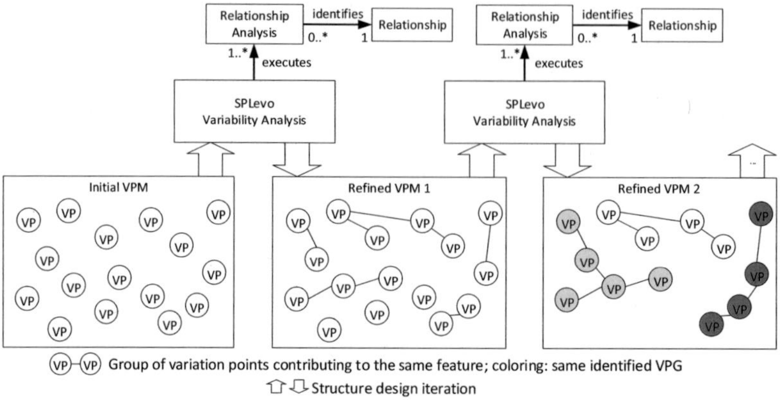

Figure 6.2.: Iterations to build coarse grain variation point structures

6.1. Variation Point Structure Design

According to Definition 5, the purpose of the VP structure design is to decide which VPGs, VPs, and Variants should be combined with each other or probably completely removed from the VPM. According to the difference analysis, the initial VPM reflects fine-grained differences between product copies but no relationships between them. Thus, the VPM needs to be refined to build more coarse grain structures, but there is no need to get even fine-grained ones. As illustrated in Figure 6.2, the initial model is iteratively refined to build such structures. In each iteration, different types of relationships between VPs are studied and, based on the findings, VPs are aggregated, as further described in Section 6.1.1. Furthermore, VPs can be filtered if they do not need to be reflected as variability in the future SPL. For example, if a VP represents a modification which is about code beautifying only, there is no need to introduce variability at this location. Details about the VP filtering are given in Section 6.1.2.

To cope with the challenging and tedious task of identifying related VPs, the SPLEVO approach defines a classification of relationship types to consider, as described in Section 6.1.3. In addition, an automated relationship analysis and refinement recommendation is proposed, as described in Section 6.1.4.

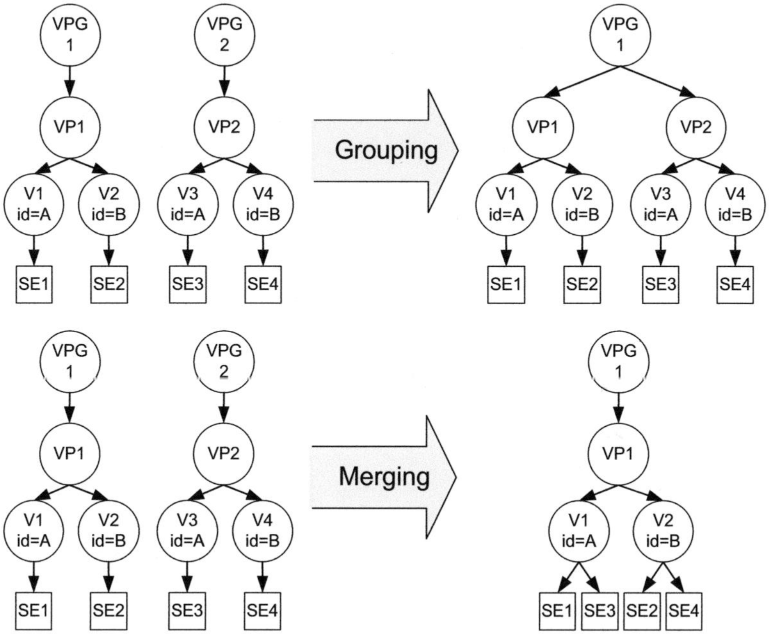

Figure 6.3.: Variation point aggregation operators

This automation also allows for adaptation to individual technologies and consolidation scenarios.

6.1.1. Variation Point Aggregation

A satisfying variability design is a trade-off between providing variability to configure as much feature combinations as possible and minimizing the number of VPs to manage. While the former obviously allows for providing more individual product variants, the latter is a recommendation with regard to SPL manageability, reported by Svahnberg et al. [183].

In the SPLEVO approach, the design phase starts with a fine-grained VPM on the level of individual and unrelated, differing SoftwareElements. To gain more coarse grain structures, the VPM's VPs must be aggregated. The

SPLEVO approach defines two aggregation operators for VPs: “merging” and “grouping”. The operators are specified for the VPM’s metamodel defined in Section 3.2 and detailed in the following subsections. The decision to execute those operators on a set of VPs, especially the decision if VPs should be merged or grouped, is assumed to be done in advance and is not part of the operators themselves.

6.1.1.1. Merging Variation Points Operator

The VP merging operator is based on the capability of *Variant* elements to reference one or more SoftwareElements they are implemented by. VPs are merged by combining their Variant elements and their implementing SoftwareElements in only one of the VPs.

Definition 13 (Variation Point Merging) *Merging two or more VPs means to aggregate them into a single VP. Variants as well as their implementing SoftwareElements are merged in the single, surviving VP. Variants with the same id are also merged into a single Variant element. All VPs except for the surviving one are removed.*

The VP merging operator reduces the number of VPs and is preferred in general as it improves the manageability of the SPL (Svahnberg et al. [183]). However, the merging operator comes with technical constraints as the VPs must be co-located and the SoftwareElements implementing their Variants must be mergeable. The decision whether SoftwareElements can be merged or not is technology-specific.

Algorithm 8 specifies the procedure of merging two or more VPs. First, one VP is selected to survive. Then, for all other VPs their contained Variant elements are checked. If a Variant with the same id exists in the surviving VP, all implementing elements of the current variant are moved to the already existing one. Otherwise, if no variant with the same id exists, the current Variant is completely moved to the surviving VP. Finally, when all Variants of a VP are processed, the VP is removed from the group it is contained in. In addition, if no more VPs exist in this VPG, the group itself is removed from the VPM.

6.1.1.2. Grouping Variation Points Operator

The VP grouping operator is based on the VPG's purpose to connect all VPs contributing to the same variable feature. Even if VPs reside at different locations of the implementation they can be contained in the same VPG. VPs are grouped by moving them into only one of their VPGs and removing now empty VPGs.

Definition 14 (Variation Point Grouping) *Grouping two or more VPs means to aggregate them into a single VPG (i.e., the surviving VPG) and removing the other empty VPGs. The VP grouping operator neither reduces the number of VPs nor modifies the VPs themselves. But it does reduce the number of VPGs and thus the number of variable features of the future SPL. Furthermore, it is a logical aggregation which can be applied to any VP.*

Algorithm 9 specifies the procedure of grouping two or more VPs. First, the VPG of one of the VPs to group is selected as the surviving VPG. Next, all other VPs are moved from their old VPG to this surviving one. Finally, if any of the old VPGs no longer contains any VPs, it is removed from the VPM.

6.1.2. Variation Point Filtering

Variation Point Filtering removes detected VPs from the VPM (e.g., irrelevant differences such as representing code beautifying) to increase the precision of subsequent relationship analyses. This section describes the Variation Point Filtering concept proposed as part of the SPLEVO approach to allow for reusing existing program analyses to identify candidates of VPs to be filtered. The concept has neither been implemented nor evaluated in the case studies as no corresponding variability-irrelevant modifications could be identified by reviewing the code. However, we argue for the value of such a filtering because of the reports on such modifications by the authors of the approaches proposed for reuse.

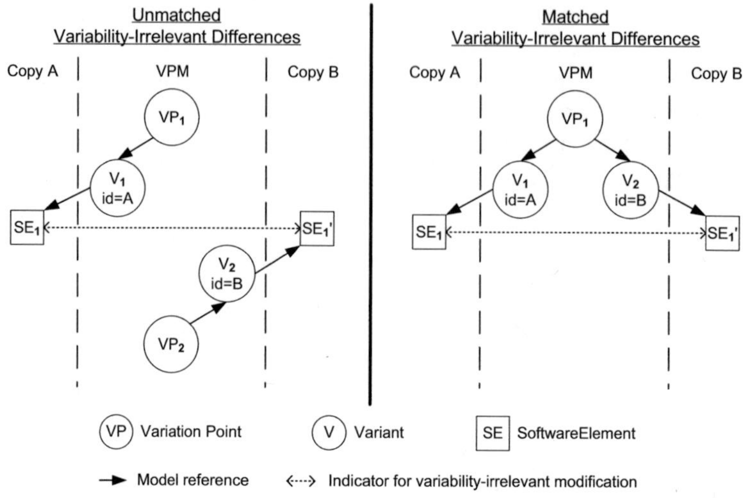

Figure 6.4.: Shapes of variability-irrelevant differences

Filtering variation points In addition to feature-specific modifications in the product copies, there are differences irrelevant for the variability of the future SPL. The SPLEVO Difference Analysis already filters formatting changes. Furthermore, code beautifying, such as renaming, is typically variability-irrelevant too. VPs identifying such variability-irrelevant differences can be removed from the VPM and, thus, no longer result in variability of the future SPL. However, such VPs are not automatically filtered because they might represent code optimization that must be reflected as variability (e.g., as professional or free option). Hence, a manual confirmation is necessary.

Variability-irrelevant differences As illustrated in Figure 6.4, two alternatives exist how variability-irrelevant differences can be reflected by VPs. If an identifying part of a SoftwareElement (e.g., its name) has been modified, the SPLEVO Difference Analysis does not match the origin and the copy of this element and reports two separate VPs (Section 5.3.1.2), for example if the name of an identifier was changed. As illustrated on the left side of Figure 6.4, an indicator for such an unmatched variability-irrelevant difference must relate two SoftwareElements with each other that originate in different copies and are identified by different VPs. In contrast, if a modification did not change an identifying part of an element, the matched variability-irrelevant differences are reflected as variants of a single VP, for example if the expression defining the initial value of a variable declaration has been simplified. As illustrated on the right side of Figure 6.4, an according indicator must relate two SoftwareElements with each other that originate in different copies and are identified by a single VP.

Proposal for reusing existing approaches The SPLEVO approach proposes to reuse existing approaches for identifying such indicators of variability-irrelevant differences. Existing approaches from the fields of clone detection, renaming detection, and change assessment provide mature strategies that can be applied in this context. However, these proposals have neither been implemented in the SPLEVO prototype nor evaluated as no corresponding modifications have been identified in the case studies.

Clone Detection In the field of clone detection, many approaches have been proposed to identify similar code, reaching from exact matches up to semantic equivalent computations (Section 10.3.3). The SPLEVO approach proposes to reuse existing approaches for clone detection to identify similar SoftwareElements implementing Variants from different copies for finding any variability-irrelevant differences of both shapes mentioned above. SoftwareElements moved to different locations represent similar code and thus clones of each other. Such moved elements can have been additionally modified, which requires to reuse a more mature type of clone detection. A reasonable candidate for being reused is the clone detection algorithm proposed by Baxter et al. [12]. Their Abstract Syntax Tree (AST)-based approach fits to the hierarchical structure of software models assumed by the SPLEVO approach (Definition 7). However, a clone-detection-based filtering has not been implemented and evaluated because no corresponding modific ations were identified in the case studies, as mentioned in the introduction of this section.

Renaming Detection Renaming means to change the identifier of a SoftwareElement. This leads to unmatched software elements and, thus, differences in the shape presented on the left side of Figure 6.4. Malpohl et al. [126] propose an algorithm for detecting renaming operations in the field of software difference analysis. They use programming language-specific structures to compare SoftwareElements while ignoring formatting information as well as identifier names. Thus, their approach can be compared to the AST-based clone detection of Baxter et al. [12] but operates on a linear representation of the parse tree for improved performance. However, applying their renaming detection to SoftwareElements implementing Variants from different product copies potentially allows for detecting renamed and thus unmatched variability-irrelevant differences. The SPLEVO approach proposes to reuse the renaming detection of Malpohl et al. [126]. However, a renaming-detection-based-filtering has not been implemented and evaluated because no corresponding modifications were identified in the case studies, as mentioned in the introduction of this section.

Non-Essential Changes Kawrykow and Robillard [94] proposed an approach for detecting "non-essential changes" based on change history information. In addition to renaming, they aim for identifying "Trivial Type Updates", "Local Variable Extractions", and "Trivial Keyword Modifications". They propose to add type resolving to existing difference analyses and use similarity rules for detecting and filtering such potentially irrelevant changes. They facilitate Partial Program Analysis (PPA)-based type resolving due to the limitation of the difference sets their approach originates from. SPLEVO VPMs provide access to the software models of the product copies under study, providing already resolved types. Thus, the detection rules of Kawrykow and Robillard [94] are proposed for being reused but have not been implemented, as mentioned in the introduction of this section.

Necessity of manual confirmation The SPLEVO approach does not automatically remove VPs. Instead, identifying indicators as described above are recommended to be used to guide SPL Consolidation Developers to the appropriate candidates of variability-irrelevant differences. Hence, SPL Consolidation developers can actively decide to manually remove VPs from the model. This manual investigation is required as it is crucial to not lose any VPs unintentionally, and not all of the approaches mentioned above offer a 100% precision in their findings. For example, Kawrykow and

Robillard [94, page 352] report a precision of 98.8% in their overall findings. In addition, SPL Consolidation Developers might have preferences for a specific alternative due to improved naming or other reasons. However, to use an alternative that does not originate from the Leading Copy requires manual code adaptation later on. Such modifications are not explicitly targeted by the SPLEVO approach, as they represent regular software development tasks.

6.1.3. Variation Point Relationships

Variation Point Relationships link previously independent VPs with each other, based on relations extracted from the software models of the product copies. The SPLEVO approach assumes relationships between modified SoftwareElements to be indicators for VPs contributing to the same copy-specific feature. Thus, the SPLEVO approach proposes to study such relationships to identify VP candidates for aggregation.

As shown in Figure 6.5, in the SPLEVO approach, relationships are associated with one or two meanings and a type. The former describes the value of the information a relationship can provide to developers. The latter distinguishes relationships according to the type of modification that produced the analyzed information. Additionally, relationships are identified by a relationship analysis, as further described in Section 6.1.4.

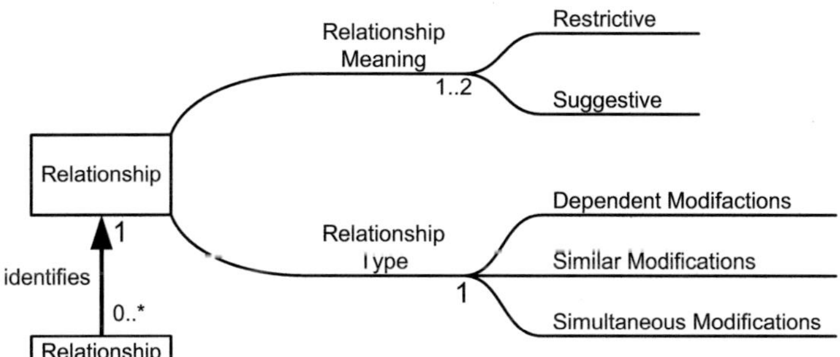

Figure 6.5.: Relationship meanings and types

Relationship Meanings The SPLEVO approach defines a range of relationship meanings providing a direction of a relationship's value as indicator for related VPs. As illustrated in Figure 6.6, the relationship meanings range from restrictive relationships (e.g., code modifications that must be considered as a bundle) to suggestive relationships (e.g., code modifications reasonable to consider as a bundle).

Definition 15 (Relationship Meaning: Restrictive) *A* Restrictive Relationship *is an indicator for the necessity to treat VPs in a common way. If two or more VPs are restrictively related to each other, all of their variants with the same id must be in place for compiling and/or executing the product copies. Accordingly, the representation of the relationship is interpreted by the compiler or by the execution environment and, thus, it is unique and allows for an automated detection and developers need only to review the recommendations.*

Definition 16 (Relationship Meaning: Suggestive) *A* Suggestive Relationship *is a hint to consider the related VPs for treating them in a common way. A suggestive relationship does not need to be reflected in the implementation. It can be represented by metadata on the product copies or by additional systems managing their implementations. A suggestive relationship results from the intention or context when the modification has been implemented. Such a relationship does not need to be unique and neither the compiler nor the execution environment must notice them. While they typically allow for automated analysis, interpretation of the results is typically necessary.*

As illustrated in Figure 6.6, restrictive and suggestive relationships are not distinct and relationships can belong to both meanings in different degrees. However, a relationship's tendency to one or the other type provides a direction of its value and applicability. Restrictive relationships can be studied in all consolidation scenarios but typically only for a specific technology (e.g., because of technology-specific structures). They are unique and allow for automated analysis. In contrast, suggestive relationships are more vague. While interpreting context, they typically come with more assumptions to be studied and need to be adjusted for specific consolidation scenarios (e.g., respecting individual development infrastructures or coding guidelines). Furthermore, suggestive relationships require a stricter manual reviewing of their results because of their ambiguity.

Figure 6.6.: Meanings of variation point relationships

Relationship Types Beside the range of relationship meanings the SPLEVO approach distinguishes relationship types according to the modification they reflect. This allows for guiding SPL Consolidation Developers' expectations when reviewing the recommendations derived from a relationship.

As presented in Figure 6.7, three types of relationships are distinguished according to analyzed aspects of modifications:

- Dependent Modifications ("What?")
- Similar Modifications ("How?")
- Simultaneous Modifications ("When?/Why?")

Rubin et al. [165] propose to study dependencies between code changes (i.e., Dependent Modifications) as well as information tracked in Change Management (CM) and Software Configuration Management (SCM) systems (i.e., Simultaneous Modifications). The SPLEVO relationship type classification extends their proposal by i) specifying more generally applicable categories and ii) defining an additional category of Similar Modifications which do not fit into the other categories.

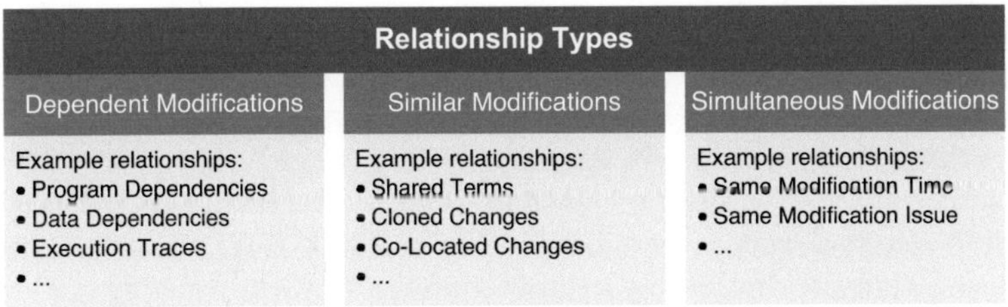

Figure 6.7.: Types of variation point relationships and examples

The following subsections provide further descriptions of the relationship categories as well as representative examples. The presented relationships and the given examples do not aim for completeness. Individual technologies, companies, and projects can allow for investigating further relationships according to their specific needs or infrastructures. For example, a company can have a specific guideline to enclose code modifications with markers identifying the issue of the modification. Similarly, markers at different locations provide a source for additional relationships to study in the category of simultaneous modifications. However, we argue for the validity of the examples given for each category. Each of them is motivated by existing research in the area of program comprehension. Furthermore, each of them was used before in a broader context of research on SPL evolution, variability, or feature location. Additionally, as representatives for the first two categories, Program Dependency and Shared Term VP analyses have been implemented as part of the SPLEVO approach (Sections 6.3 and 6.4). They have been applied in case studies to evaluate their benefits (Section 8.7). For the third category, no VP analysis was implemented as part of the SPLEVO approach because the available case studies did not provide the required data to analyze. However, we argue for the category's validity and the existence of appropriate scenarios providing the required data (Section 6.1.3.3).

6.1.3.1. Relationship Type: Dependent Modifications

Dependent modifications are two or more modifications on a copy's implementation (e.g., modified, added, or deleted SoftwareElements) with one modification depending on another. Relationships resulting from dependent modifications are typical examples for restrictive relationships according to Definition 15. They are unique and directly or indirectly represented in the implementation. In general software engineering, dependencies between SoftwareElements are studied for many reasons, such as impact analysis or bug detection (Section 2.4.9). Accordingly, they are gathered in many different manners, such as static or dynamic analyses. The SPLEVO approach is not limited to a specific set of dependency analyses. It is intended to reuse existing software dependency analysis concepts. However, existing analyses are typically not designed for analyzing relationships between differences of customized product copies. Thus, the individual concepts for studying dependencies must be adapted according to SPLEVO's concept of deriving VP relationships from SoftwareElement relationships.

Examples of relationships in the category of Dependent Modifications are: Program Dependencies, Data Dependencies, and Program Execution Traces.

Program Dependency Relationships Program dependencies are dependencies statically coded into software implementations. They can be implemented as a reference from one SoftwareElement to another based reference specified in a programming language (e.g., a method call). Alternatively, they can involve additional resources establishing a dependency indirectly when they are loaded (e.g., configuration files for wiring components). Figure 6.8 provides an example of a VP relationship due to a direct program dependency resulting from a statement calling a method.

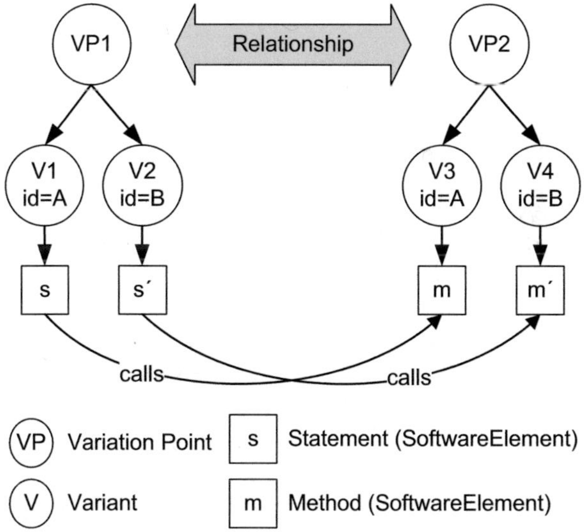

Figure 6.8.: Program dependency relationship example

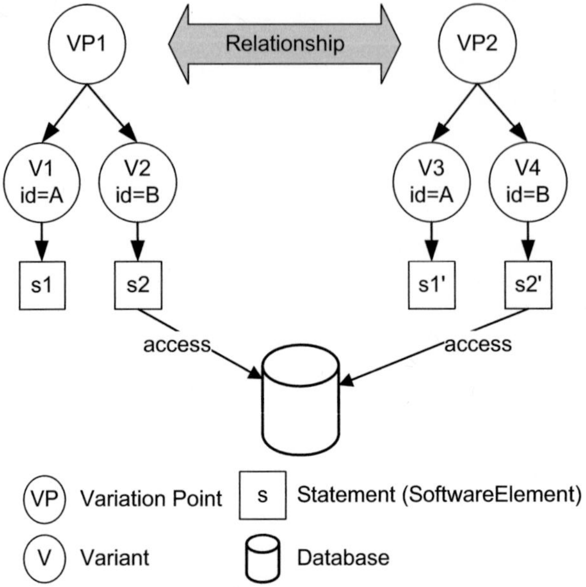

Figure 6.9.: Data dependency relationship example

Data Dependency Relationships Data dependency relationships between SoftwareElements exist when they potentially influence each other because of data objects they manipulate or access. Data objects cover program internal elements and external resources. The former includes variables and constants as well as results from method invocations and data initializations. The latter includes resources such as files, databases, or remote services. Data objects of both types can represent complex objects. The value of the identified relationships strongly depends on the precision of identifying the data within those complex objects accessed by the modified SoftwareElements. For example, the relationship resulting from access to the same database field provides more value than resulting from access to same database in total. Figure 6.9 provides an example of a VP relationship resulting from SoftwareElements accessing the same database.

Identifying data dependencies is more challenging compared to program dependencies. Accessed objects or resources are probably defined in a configuration file that must be processed in addition. This requires additional processing and probably adaptation of the analysis. Furthermore, it can influence the precision of the accessed data object identification.

Program Execution Trace Relationships A program execution trace-dependency between two SoftwareElements exists when both are involved in the execution of a single feature. A program execution trace is recorded at run time and describes a chain of SoftwareElements executed one after the other (e.g., the chain of methods or statements executed).

Identifying program execution trace relationships is challenging due to the necessity of executing a program in a realistic manner (e.g., during production). Recording a trace requires to balance between a low program influence and a high precision of the trace at the same time. Matching the recorded trace with the SoftwareElements represented in the software models is an additional challenge to overcome.

Figure 6.10 illustrates two modified statements being crossed by a program execution trace. This leads to identifying a relationship between the VPs containing the variants the statements are implementing.

6.1.3.2. Relationship Type: Similar Modifications

Similar Modifications are modifications of a copy's implementation done in a similar manner. This can range from exactly the same modifications performed at different locations (e.g., introducing the same lines of code) up to similar concepts implemented at different locations. Relationships resulting from similar modifications are both: restrictive and suggestive relationships. On one side, they typically allow for automated identification and are represented in the code. On the other side, depending on the type of studied similarity, they may be ambiguous and provide only vague indicators requiring a strict review.

Similar Modifications can be studied in many different manners as done in the field of program comprehension. For example, they are studied for concern or feature location, clone detection, and Natural Language Program

Analysis (NLPA) (Section 2.4.9). The SPLEVO approach is not limited in the relationships to study, but, proposes to reuse existing concepts. However, existing approaches need to be adapted for analyzing relationships between modified SoftwareElements respectively their containing VPs.

Typical examples of similar modifications are: Shared Terms, Cloned Changes, and Co-Located Changes.

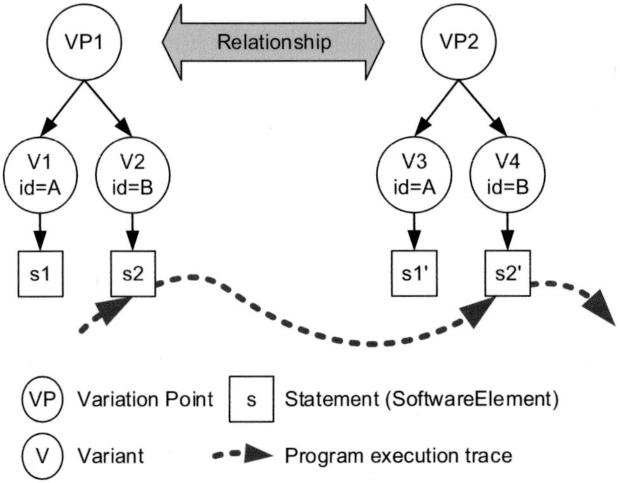

Figure 6.10.: Program execution trace relationship example

Shared Terms Relationships A software implementation includes terms pre-defined by a programming language's syntax and terms freely eligible by developers, such as identifiers or values. As identified in the field of NLPA, developers tend to express concepts and knowledge within those eligible terms. For example, when implementing a custom feature at several locations, the developer might use the same terms from the context of the feature at those locations. Which SoftwareElements define eligible terms depends on the technology used. For example, in object-oriented programming languages, such as Java, class and method names are typical places to use feature-specific terms.

Figure 6.11 provides an example of two VPs introducing a new class "ClassFoo" and a new method "doFoo" in variant B, with both SoftwareElements sharing the term "foo" being an indicator for a relationship between them. Subsequently, this is an indicator for a relationship between the VPs as well.

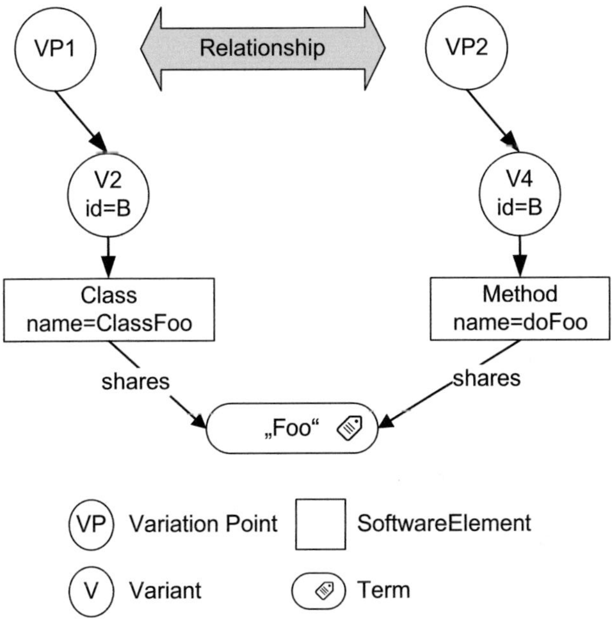

Figure 6.11.: Shared term relationship example

However, interpreting shared terms is challenging. Programmers use not only terms and texts representing concepts of the newly implemented features. They also introduce terms because of general programming concepts and programming habits. Section 6.4 describes the Shared Term Analysis developed as part of the SPLEVO approach and discusses strategies to cope with this challenge.

Cloned Changes Relationships Code clones in general identify similar code fragments according to a given definition of similarity (Roy et al. [159, page 471], Section 2.4.8). To identify relationships between VPs, the customized product copies can be investigated for cloned modifications at different locations. To do this, clone detection can be applied to the SoftwareElements implementing the variants of a set of VPs. If clones are identified, this is an indicator for a relationship between the enclosing VPs. The underlying assumption is that similar code changes are performed to implement the same feature.

As surveyed by Roy et al. [159], many approaches exist for clone detection with a divergent support of their described types of clones (Section 2.4.8). Especially, the more differing the implementations of clones are (i.e., in order from type 0 to type 4), the harder it is to detect those clones and the fewer approaches exist. However, clones of higher types are also more vague and less valuable indicators for detecting VP relationships.

In an evaluation performed by Bellon et al. [13], the AST-based clone detection of Baxter et al. [12] was identified as one of the best performing algorithms. The minimal structure of software models assumed by the SPLEVO approach (Definition 7) provides the necessary data structure to be analyzed by this algorithm.

Figure 6.12 illustrates an example of cloned changes. When the Software-Elements se_1 and se_2 have been copied, their implementations have been changed by introducing the same child elements. For example, at both locations the same conditional statement containing nested statements might have been introduced. This can be detected by sending all changed Software-Elements (e.g., se_1 and se_2) of the same variant (e.g., id=B) to a clone detection.

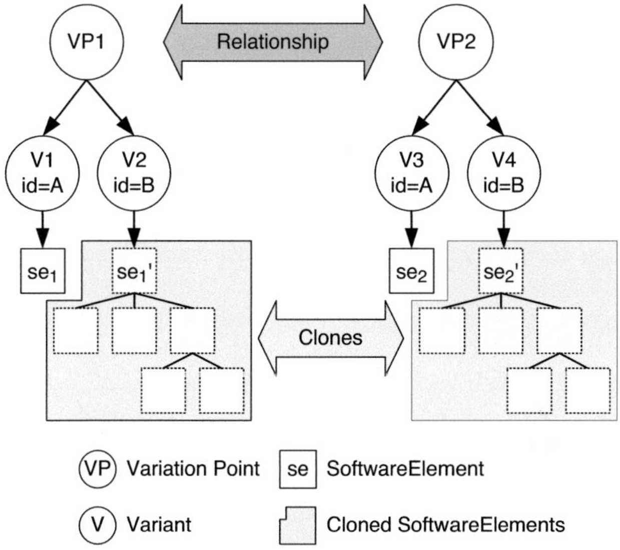

Figure 6.12.: Cloned changes relationship example

Co-Located Changes Relationships Co-located changes are modifications on a customized product copy performed at the same location. Examples for such relationships are modified statements in the same method and modified methods in the same class.

In software models as assumed by the SPLEVO approach, locations of SoftwareElements are expressed by containment references (i.e., a SoftwareElement is located in its containing parent SoftwareElement). If modifications are performed at the same location, this is an indicator for required adaptations of the same part of a software implementation. However, this type of relationship is ambiguous and requires strict reviews. For example, software programs always have central parts containing elements for several features (e.g., a class defining shared constants).

In a VPM, VPs identify the location of modifications. Accordingly, VPs with location references to the same SoftwareElement identify modifications at the same location. Figure 6.13 illustrates an example of co-located changes.

The two VPs VP1 and VP2 reference the same SoftwareElement as their locations. Thus, a relationship between them is derived.

Depending on the product copies under study, additional location information not stored in the software model might be available. For example, as published in Klatt and Küster [103], a component architecture might be provided as an existing component model or extracted with reverse engineering techniques. Such a component architecture can identify modified classes, interfaces, or compilation units located in the same component.

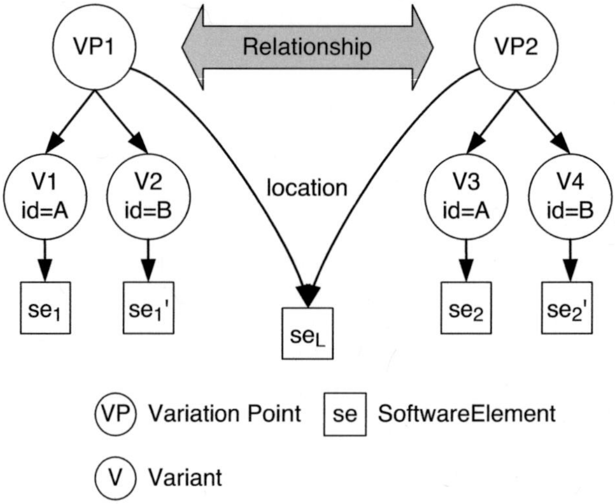

Figure 6.13.: Co-located changes relationship example

6.1.3.3. Relationship Type: Simultaneous Modifications

Simultaneous modification relationships represent modifications performed for the same intention. The intention is derived from the context the modifications have been performed in. This context can be defined either by the time span when a modification was done, or by an explicit context, such as a customer requirement to introduce a feature (i.e., an issue).

In the defined range of meanings of relationship types, the simultaneous modifications tend to the end of suggestive relationships. They typically allow for automation but require a strict review. This results from developers, who potentially implemented several custom features in the same time frame or a single issue includes several custom features at once.

The two directions of simultaneous modifications (i.e., same modification time and same modification issue) are general concepts of relationship types to study. In specific scenarios, the development processes, infrastructures, and guidelines vary a lot (e.g., different infrastructures for capturing issues and tracking implementation changes). The concrete information available and relationships to study vary in a similar manner. To cope with this variety, the SPLEVO approach is not limited to a specific set of information sources for simultaneous modifications. Instead, the following subsections describe details on how to derive such relationships between VPs independent from a specific infrastructure.

Same Modification Time Relationships When a feature is implemented in a product copy, the required modifications or at least parts of them are typically done at once. However, related modifications are often committed at once to a Version Control System (VCS), such as CVS, git or SVN (Section 2.4.1.1). The modification time stamp tracked by a VCS can be interpreted as the time of modification. In contrast to the last modification time tracked by a file system, all files committed to a VCS at once are automatically linked with the same commit. This further improves the detection of relationships between the modifications, as it is not necessary to handle slightly differing time stamps. Furthermore, when customized product copies are consolidated, the last modification time stamp of a file system will be neither available nor useful, as the files might have been changed several times in the meantime.

However, most VCSs track changed files or changed lines of code inside those files in a textual manner and do not provide any links to the according SoftwareElements. Thus, identifying relationships between SoftwareElements based on their modification time stamps requires to identify their textual representations in the file resources and to get their modification history from the VCS.

Figure 6.14 illustrates two VPs with variants implemented by SoftwareElements which are referenced by the same commit log entry of a VCS.

To further improve the identification of such relationships, not only the commit time stamps or identifiers can be considered but also the messages of the commits. If developers performed several modifications to implement a custom feature, those modifications might have been committed as multiple commits with the same commit message. Investigating in similar commit messages allows for identifying relationships between VPs resulting from modifications being part of several commits.

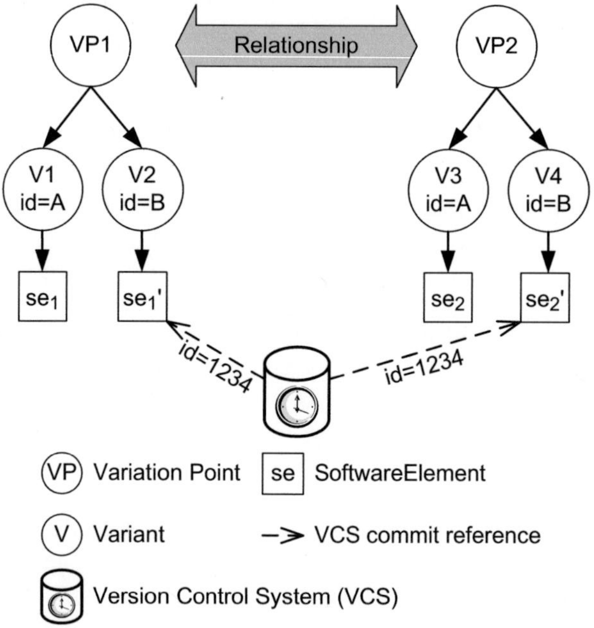

Figure 6.14.: Same modification time relationship example

Same Modification Issue Relationships With an issue tracking and management system in place, modifications of a product copy are planned as issues to be implemented by developers (Section 2.4.1.2). Such an issue defines a context in terms of content for all modifications done to implement the issue. Accordingly, identifying modifications to be performed for the same issue provides an indicator for a relationship between them.

The capabilities of issue tracking and management systems as well as their usage within companies and development teams vary a lot. Similarly, the ways to identify the issues for modifications vary as well. On the one side, mature systems which are used in a proper way allow for tracing commits performed to a VCS. Thus, they provide traces from the issue to the modifications performed, or at least to the resources modified. On the other side, some companies use coding conventions to add code markers identifying the code modified for an issue. Often, these markers include the unique id assigned to an issue by an issue tracking and management system. This id can be used to identify the issue a modification belongs to. The explicit tracing approach requires a continuous and proper use of the issue tracking and management system as well as the responsible creation of the traces throughout the development of the customized copies. In contrast, the marker approach does not require such a mature system but relies on developers' discipline to place code markers correctly.

To identify relationships in a VPM as mentioned above, the SoftwareElements implementing VPs' variants must be matched with the explicit external traces, or their software model contents (i.e., parent and sibling SoftwareElements) must be checked for according code markers.

Figure 6.15 illustrates an example with two VPs and according SoftwareElements (i.e., se_1' and se_2') referenced by the same issue (i.e., Issue ID=123). Because of the common issue, a relationship between the VPs is identified.

Compared to Similar Modification Time relationships, this strategy allows for considering context in terms of content. However, having an issue tracking and management system in place which is used in a proper way, is a strong assumption. This limits the scenarios Same Modification Issue relationships can be identified in.

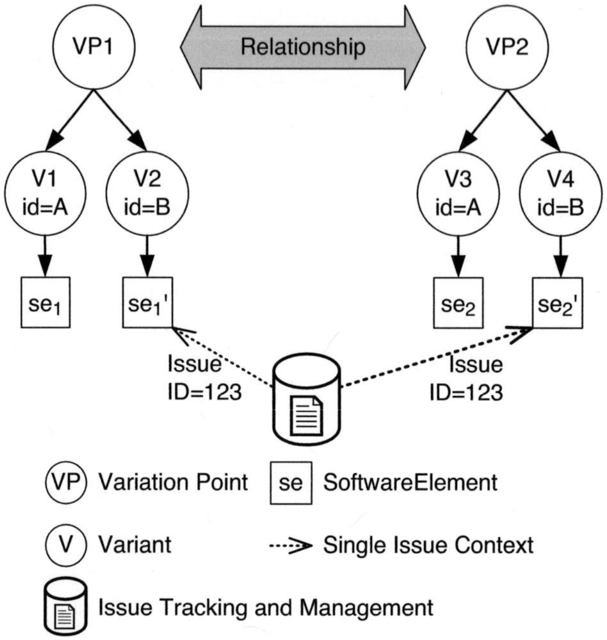

Figure 6.15.: Same modification issue relationship example

6.1.4. Variability Analysis

The SPLEVO approach provides a variability analysis to support SPL Consolidation Developers in aggregating VPs. As shown in Figure 6.16, the SPLEVO Variability Analysis receives the VPs of the current version n of the VPM (i.e., VPM_n), executes one or more relationship analyses, and returns recommendations for refining the VPM to derive version n+1 (i.e., VPM_{n+1}).

From SoftwareElement relationships to VP relationships As introduced in the last section, the variability analysis investigates relationships between implementing elements to derive relationships between the containing variation points.

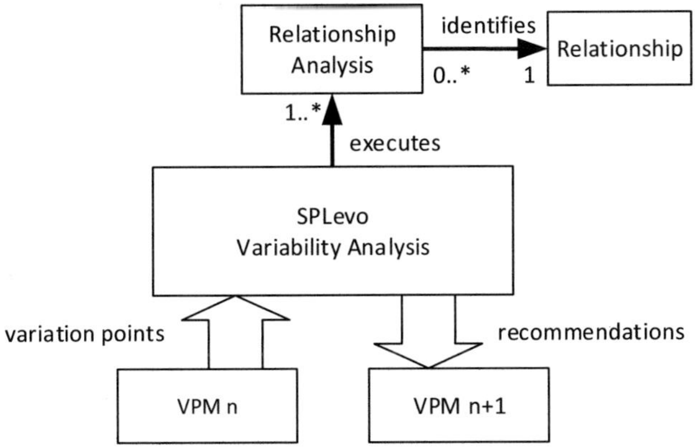

Figure 6.16.: SPLEVO Variability Analysis concept

Figure 6.17 illustrates this concept for two variation points (i.e., VP_1 and VP_2). The analysis identifies varying SoftwareElements in two copies under study (i.e., Copy A and Copy B). SoftwareElements SE_1 and SE_2 of Copy A have been modified in Copy B (i.e., SE_1' and SE_2'). Before the analysis starts, there are no relationships in the initial VPM (i.e., Step 0). First, relationships between the SoftwareElements are studied separately in each copy. This is done to identify related modifications for features present in only one or the other copy. Accordingly, in Step 1, relationships might be identified between SE_1 and SE_2 in Copy A (i.e., ser_{A1} and ser_{A2}), or between SE_1' and SE_2' in Copy B (i.e., sre_{B1} and ser_{B2}). Relationships are always directed, but, depending on the type of relationship studied, they might exist in one or both directions. Finally, in Step 2, if a relationship between SoftwareElements is identified, a relationship between the VPs containing the Variant elements implemented by related SoftwareElements is derived (i.e., vpr_{A1} and vpr_{A2}). The direction of the VP relationship depends on the SoftwareElement relationship it is derived from.

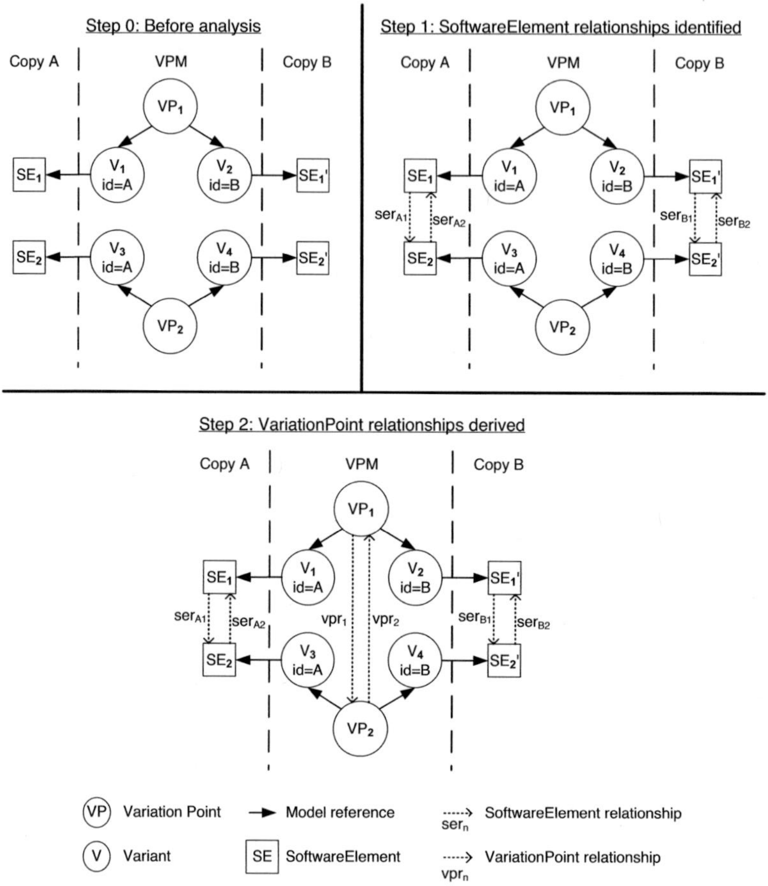

Figure 6.17.: Illustration of VP relationship identification steps

Framework for relationship analyses Furthermore, the SPLEVO Variability Analysis provides a framework for adding relationship analyses in a flexible manner. This allows for adaptation as there is no finite set of relationships to study. Additionally, all types of relationships identified in Section 6.1.3 can benefit from or even need adaptation to specific technologies and consolidation scenarios.

Recommendations to be reviewed by Developers The overall goal of the SPLEVO approach is to reduce the manual effort for SPL Consolidation Developers. Accordingly, the variability analysis does not only identify relationships, but also derives aggregations including the decision if a grouping or merging can be applied. However, the SPLEVO Variability Analysis returns recommendations only. This is done to cope with the need of SPL Consolidation Developers to finally decide about aggregating VPs or not. Developers can review and either accept, decline, or adapt the recommendations to their needs (Section 6.1.4.1).

Iterative and parallel analyses The SPLEVO Variability Analysis provides two alternatives for performing multiple relationship analyses: iteratively in a serial manner and simultaneously in a combined manner. The former allows for reviewing the results of the analyses separately (Section 6.1.4.3). Thus, SPL Consolidation Developers need to understand only one type of relationship at once. In contrast, the latter allows for running several analyses in parallel and combining their results (Section 6.1.4.4). Thus, only VPs sharing all analyzed relationships at the same time are recommended for aggregation.

The following subsections explain how recommendations are designed and which information they provide. Afterwards, the merge detection mechanism is explained, before the iterative and combined analysis options are described in detail.

6.1.4.1. Refinement Recommendation

Refinement recommendations are VP aggregations recommended to improve the structure of a VPM. They are automatically derived from VP relationships identified by an according analysis. Afterwards, they are presented to SPL Consolidation Developers to decide about their applicability. If recommendations are accepted, the according operators are executed on their referenced VPs, as explained in Section 6.1.1.

A refinement metamodel has been developed specifying a data structure for refinement recommendations and for providing access to information necessary for deciding about recommendations.

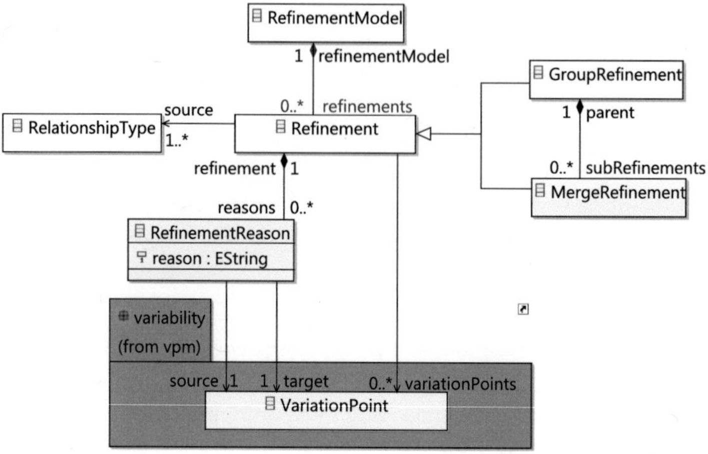

Figure 6.18.: Class diagram of the refinement metamodel

Figure 6.18 shows a class diagram of the refinement metamodel. A `RefinementModel` contains all `Refinements` resulting from an analysis. A `Refinement` references one or more `RelationshipTypes` representing the type of relationship(s) it was derived from. Thus, at least one `RelationshipType` must be set. In case of a combined relationship analysis, a `Refinement` can reference several types of relationships at once.

A single `Refinement` is created for all VPs transitively connected by the identified relationships. For the refinement itself, the directions of the VP relationships are not relevant, as the VP aggregation operations do not depend on them.

Two concrete types of `Refinements` exist: `GroupRefinement` as well as `MergeRefinement`. The former relates to the *Grouping Variation Point Operator*, the latter to the *Merging Variation Point Operator*.

Initially, all recommendations are created as `GroupRefinements`, as grouping can be applied to any set of VPs (Section 6.1.1.2). In a second step, each `GroupRefinement` is checked if its complete set of contained VPs, or at least a part of it, can be merged, as this is preferred to grouping. A containment relationship between `GroupRefinements` and `MergeRefinements` is designed for the case that only a part of the VPs can be merged. In such a case, new `MergeRefinements` are created for each set of VPs merging can be applied to. These new `MergeRefinements` are added to the set of sub-refinements of the original `GroupRefinement`. As a result, the surviving VPs of the `MergeRefinements` will still be grouped by the original `GroupRefinement`. As defined in the OCL constraint in Listing 5, a `GroupRefinement` must contain at least two elements being `MergeRefinements` or `VariationPoints` in a desired combination . Otherwise, a `GroupRefinement` does not represent a reasonable aggregation.

```
context GroupRefinement
inv GroupRefinementSignificance:
   variationPoints->size() + subRefinements->size() >= 2;
```

Listing 5: GroupRefinement significance constraint

Similarly, `MergeRefinements` must be contained either in a top level `RefinementModel` or in a set of `subRefinements` of a `GroupRefinement` (see OCL constraint in Listing 6).

```
context MergeRefinement
inv MergeRefinementLocation: refinementModel <> null
   or parent <> null;
```

Listing 6: MergeRefinement location constraint

Furthermore, as `MergeRefinements` cannot contain any sub-refinements, it has to reference at least two VPs for representing a reasonable aggregation, as defined in the OCL constraint in Listing 7.

```
context MergeRefinement
inv MergeRefinementSignificance: variationPoints->size() >= 2;
```

Listing 7: MergeRefinement significance constraint

A `Refinement` references zero, one, or more `RefinementReasons` providing additional information about the refinement's origin. To provide additional information about a `Refinement`, a `RefinementReason` references the source and target VPs of an identified relationship. For example, assuming a VP vp_A identifying a modified statement that calls a modified method identified by a VP vp_B. An according `RefinementReason` references vp_A as the source and vp_B as the target of the relationship. The reason attribute of the `RefinementReason` provides additional information about the relationship in a human-readable manner. It is filled when the `Refinement` is derived from the recognized relationships. For the example above, the reason would contain a description that it results from a method call between the modified statement and method.

A refinement model covers not only the types and reasons of relationships identified by an analysis. In addition, it allows for navigating the VPs to be refined as well as the SoftwareElements implementing their variants. Accordingly, all information required to decide about the refinement recommendations is accessible for SPL Consolidation Developers.

6.1.4.2. Merge Detection

As described in Section 6.1.1, the *Grouping VP Operator* can be applied to any combination of VPs, as it is a link only and the VPs remain untouched. In contrast, the *Merging VP Operator* comes with technical restrictions and requires additional effort to check if it can be applied. As published in Klatt et al. [100], the SPLEVO approach includes a merge detection improving recommended `GroupRefinements` by either fully or partially transforming them into `MergeRefinements` depending on the VPs' technical constraints. This detection relieves SPL Consolidation Developers from manual investigation into the VPs' ability for being merged. Partially means that if only a subset of a `GroupRefinement`'s VPs can be merged, an according sub-refinement will be created. The surviving VP of the partial merging operation will become part of the VPG produced by the original `GroupRefinement`.

Assuming that VP1, VP2, and VP3 in Listing 8 are VPs according to newly introduced Java statements, the program dependency analysis described in Section 6.3 will recognize relationships between VP3 and VP1 as well as between VP3 and VP2 because of their declared or referenced variables (i.e., var1 and var2). Accordingly, an initial `GroupRefinement` will be derived containing all of the three VPs. Now, the merge detection will recognize that the statements are direct siblings that can be merged.

```
BigInteger var1 = new BigInteger(1); //VP1
BigInteger var2 = new BigInteger(2); //VP2
BigInteger gcd = var1.gcd(var2); //VP3
```

Listing 8: Example for Mergeable Variation Points

As shown in the example above, the decision that two VPs can be merged is technology-specific. Thus, the SPLEVO approach defines a general *Merge Detection Operator* $m(vp_1, vp_2)$ that has to be adapted in a technology-specific manner (Definition 17). If no technology-specific *Merge Detection Operator* is provided, the analysis still returns valid results and recommends `GroupRefinements` only.

Definition 17 (Merge Detection Operator) *A* Merge Detection Operator *m maps two VPs on a Boolean value, identifying if the VPs can be merged or not.*

$$MergeDetectionOperator\ m : V \rightarrow \mathbb{B}$$
$$V = VariationPointxVariationPoint$$
$$\mathbb{B} = \{true, false\}$$

$$m(vp_1, vp_2) = \begin{cases} true & \text{if } vp_1 \text{ and } vp_2 \text{ can be merged with certainty} \\ false & \text{otherwise} \end{cases} \tag{6.1}$$

$$m(vp_1, vp_2) \wedge m(vp_2, vp_3) \implies m(vp_1, vp_3) \tag{6.2}$$

Certainty Characteristic (6.1) The *Merge Detection Operator* must return true only if VPs can be merged with certainty. Otherwise, it has to return false. A merge operation further improves a refinement compared to a group operation. But, as merging VPs which cannot be merged would result in invalid VPs, a *Merge Detection Operator* has to return false in case of uncertainty.

Transitive Characteristic (6.2) The VPs' ability to being merged is defined as a transitive characteristic and must be considered by technology-specific *Merge Detection Operators*. The transitive characteristic is required to ensure that several SoftwareElements which can be merged one by one can also be merged as a group. For example, this allows merging more than two VPs, and VPs with Variants being implemented by two or more SoftwareElements can be merged as well. The Merging VP Operator and the merge detection algorithm presented below are based on this characteristic.

For the Java example in Listing 8, the merge detection evaluates as follows:
$m(VP1, VP3) = true$
$m(VP2, VP3) = true$
$m(VP1, VP3) \wedge m(VP2, VP3) \implies m(VP1, VP2)$

MergeRefinement Detection Algorithm The SPLEVO approach specifies an algorithm for applying the merge detection on initially recommended GroupRefinements. The algorithm provides deterministic results independent from the order the contained VPs are processed in. The algorithm processes each GroupRefinement separately. Depending on the contained VPs, the algorithm either transforms a GroupRefinement to a MergeRefinement, improves it with MergeRefinements as sub-refinements, or leaves it as it is. In case of MergeRefinements as sub-refinements, the according VPs will be merged before the surviving VPs will be aggregated into a single VPG (Section 6.1.1). The algorithm facilitates technology-specific *Merge Detection Operators* by executing the function `MergeDetection`. This function triggers all available *Merge Detection Operators* one after another. If at least one of them returns true for the provided VPs, the `MergeDetection` function will return true in total.

As specified in Algorithm 10, the algorithm sorts all VPs that can be merged with each other into common buckets. Later on, VPs within the same bucket are combined into a MergeRefinement.

For each Grouping, the algorithm executes the `MergeDetection` function to all pairs of the contained VPs to check if they can be merged. If a pair can be merged, they are put into the same bucket. As specified by Algorithm 11, if both VPs are already contained in buckets, those buckets will be merged.

This is possible because of the transitive characteristic defined for merge detection operators. If only one of the VPs is contained in a bucket, the other one is added to the same bucket. If none of the VPs is contained in a bucket yet, a new bucket will be created for them.

When all pairs have been checked, the algorithm processes the buckets to derive MergeRefinements. In case that no bucket was created, no VPs can be merged and the GroupRefinement remains as it is. In case of a single bucket containing all VPs, the original GroupRefinement is replaced with a MergeRefinement. In any other case, the GroupRefinement is kept, and for each bucket a MergeRefinement is created to merge the contained VPs. Then, all merged VPs are removed from the GroupRefinement, and the MergeRefinement is added to the GroupRefinement's set of sub-refinements.

6.1.4.3. Iterative Analyses

To identify VPs contributing to the same copy-specific feature, different types of relationships can be studied, as discussed in Section 6.1.3. Relationships are indicators for VPs being candidates for aggregation. Reviewing the according recommendations is required to verify the candidates.

The SPLEVO approach proposes an iterative application of different relationship analyses. It is recommended to analyze less ambiguous relationships (i.e., restrictive relationships) first, as they are easier to review due to their degree of unambiguity. Furthermore, in general, it is recommended to analyze one relationship after the other to reduce the complexity of SPL Consolidation Developers' reviews.

A single iteration comprises of i) executing an analysis, ii) reviewing the resulting refinement recommendations, and iii) applying the accepted ones.

When SPL Consolidation Developers accept at least one of the recommendations, a new version of the VPM is created. The metamodel of the VPM does not change between different versions of a VPM. Thus, SPL Consolidation Developers can i) perform as many iterations as they like, and ii) go back to a VPM resulting from a previous iteration.

6.1.4.4. Combined Analyses

In addition to iteratively analyzing one type of relationship after the other, the SPLEVO approach allows for combining different analyses in a single iteration.

This can be used to i) analyze several types of relationships in parallel without the need of performing multiple iterations and ii) combine the results of several analyses. For example, if SPL Consolidation Developers are interested in VPs with program dependencies and sharing a similar term, the combined analysis concept enables them to perform a Program Dependency Analysis and a Shared Term Analysis in a combined manner.

As we have published in [104], the SPLEVO approach includes a graph-based analysis concept to combine the results of several relationship analyses. As shown in Figure 6.19, the total set of VPs in a VPM is considered as an undirected edge-labeled graph with no edges at the beginning. The analyses to combine are executed in parallel. For each identified relationship, an edge is created and labeled with the according type of the relationship. Furthermore, the related VPs are referenced as shown in Figure 6.20 (i.e., R1, R2, and R3 in Figure 6.19).

The results are merged into a single graph by combining the edge labels (e.g., "R1, R2"). Finally, a set of detection rules is applied to derive GroupRefinements from the relationship combinations SPL Consolidation Developers are interested in. Those GroupRefinements might be further improved by the merge detection, as described in Section 6.1.4.2, before they are returned.

Using an intermediate graph allows for executing the individual analyses in parallel, without the need of synchronizing edit operations on the VPM. As most analyses require a reasonable amount of processing resources, such a parallelization supports a better utilization of parallel processing resources on a top level.

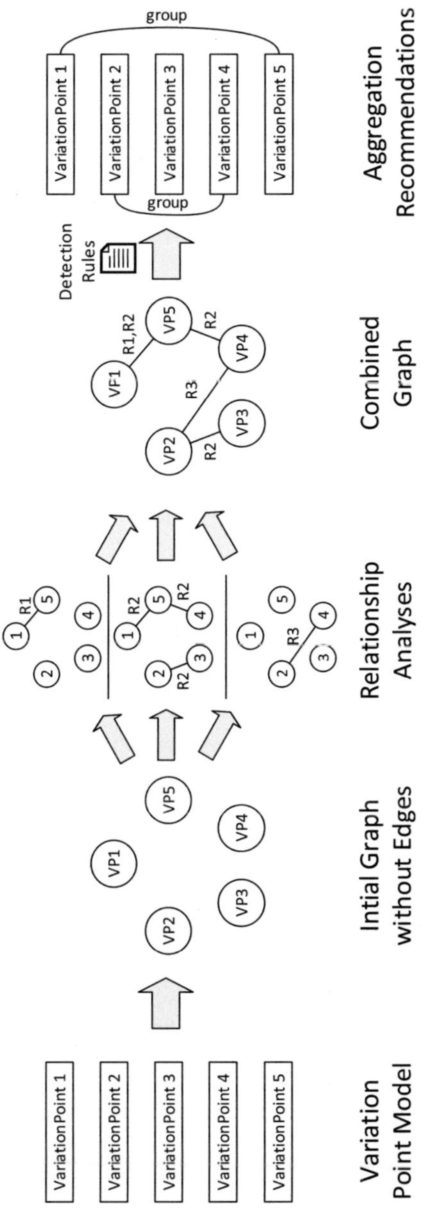

Figure 6.19.: Graph-based analyses composition

A detection rule is specified as a set of relationship types that must be matched by edges' labels to derive a relationship between two or more VPs and an according refinement recommendation (i.e., reference "types" in Figure 6.21).

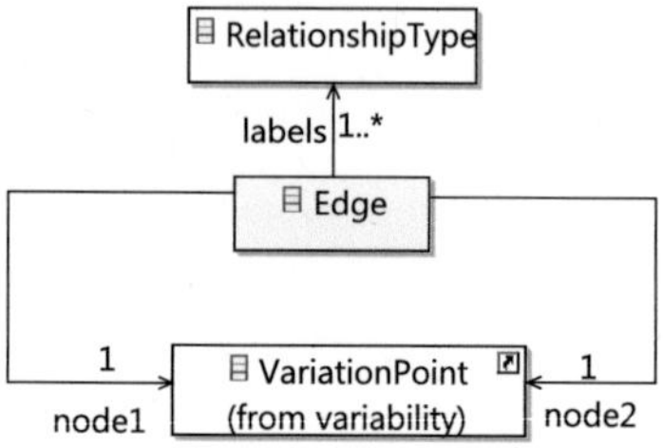

Figure 6.20.: Graph-based analysis edge

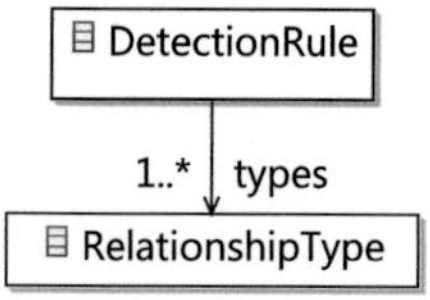

Figure 6.21.: Detection rule

To apply a detection rule, each of the graph's edges is checked against the rule, as specified in Algorithm 12. A match is detected if an edge's set of labels contains exactly the same relationship types as referenced by the detection rule. In this case, the two VPs represented by the matching edge's nodes are assigned to a common sub-graph. Three strategies for sub-graph assignment are used: If both VPs are already assigned to sub-graphs, the sub-graphs are merged. If only one VP is already assigned to a sub-graph, the other VP is assigned to the same one. If none of them was assigned to a sub-graph before, a new one is created and both VPs are assigned to it.

When all edges are processed, a GroupRefinement is created for each sub-graph. All VPs connected by the same sub-graph are assigned to the same GroupRefinement. In addition, the relationship types of the detection rule are added to the set of sources of the GroupRefinement.

Detection rules are always applied in a defined order. If edges are matched by a rule's condition, they are ignored by any rules applied later on to prevent conflicting recommendations. The set of rules to apply as well as their order depends on the individual scenario and the relationship analysis to perform.

As described in Section 6.1.4.3, the SPLEVO approach recommends analyzing one type of relationship after the other. Restrictive relationship types should be analyzed first to simplify SPL Consolidation Developers' review of the derived recommendations. However, analyzing a single relationship might result in recommending aggregations of too many VPs. In such a case, it is a reasonable approach to combine several analyses and to search for all their relationship types at once. As a result, VPs recommended for being aggregated must share all those types of relationships probably leading to more precise results. Furthermore, if SPL Consolidation Developers are used to apply different analyses, they can execute them all at once. To avoid searching for combined results, they can use individual detection rules for each of the analyzed relationship types. Thus, they will benefit from the parallel execution.

6.2. Variation Point Characteristics

A VP's characteristics include its variability characteristics and its naming. The former defines the capabilities of the according variability in the future SPL. The latter simplifies the discussion between SPL Consolidation Developers and SPL Managers. Both aspects are further discussed in the following subsections.

6.2.1. Variability Characteristics

The variability characteristics of a VP include the variability type, binding time, and extensibility, as defined by the VPM metamodel in Section 3.2.2.4. According to Definition 6, they "specify the capabilities of the variability reflecting a VP in the future SPL". Hence, they define the requirements on the VP's implementation and are used in the Consolidation Refactoring phase to select concrete variability realization mechanisms (Section 7.2). Accordingly, SPL Consolidation Developers must define appropriate variability characteristics to ensure the right type of variability will be available in the future SPL.

Initially, VPs are created with the default characteristics defined by the SPL Type chosen in the SPL Profile (Section 3.3.1.1). However, those characteristics are default settings only and, for example, a run time binding is not reasonable for all VPs in a multi-tenant system. Consolidation Developers must change the variability characteristics according to their preferences for working with the SPL in the future.

A VPM allows for navigating to the implementing SoftwareElements of a VP respectively of its Variants. This source of information can be used by SPL Consolidation Developers, for example to choose the same variability characteristics for all VPs located in the same type of SoftwareElements (e.g., load time binding for all classes with varying extend references).

6.2.2. Variation Point Group Naming

A VPG contains VPs that have been identified to contribute to the same variable feature. As part of the consolidation process, SPL Consolidation Developers and SPL Managers have to review the variability design described by a VPM.

To simplify their communication and review, VPGs provide an id attribute for identifying the group and the related variable feature, as specified by the VPM metamodel (Section 3.2.2.2).

The SPLEVO approach aims for supporting consolidations of customized copies, even without any documentation of the custom features or performed modifications. In addition to the need of reverse engineering the features themselves (i.e., VPGs), their names (i.e., VPG IDs) must be reverse engineered as well. It cannot be assumed to find obvious names in the feature-specific implementations.

The initial VPGs are created based on differences detected between the copies (Section 5.4). During the VPM initialization, each VPG contains only one VP. The id of the VPG is set to the label of the SoftwareElement representing the VP's location. This provides SPL Consolidation Developers with a first idea about the VPG.

The final decision of naming a feature is up to SPL Consolidation Developers and SPL Managers. However, their decision can be supported by extracting hints from i) the implementing SoftwareElements and ii) the relationships between the VPs contained in a VPG. Especially when the VPM structure is improved and the number of VPs contained in a VPG increases, further SoftwareElements and relationships to study are available.

6.2.2.1. Terms from SoftwareElements

Often, Software Developers implement semantics into their code when realizing a feature. For example, variables can be named according to the feature currently implemented. NLPA investigates in such semantics by extracting and analyzing terms used in identifiers, comments, or values (Section 2.4.10). Similar to the Shared Term Analysis (Section 6.4), first, the terms must be extracted from the implementing SoftwareElements. Next, they must be normalized, for example by splitting (e.g., separate terms with a dash in between) or stemming (e.g., using singular terms only). Then, non-essential terms (e.g., programming language syntax and short terms with less than three characters) are excluded.

The NLPA used for the SPLEVO Shared Term Analysis extracts the terms of each VP separately and tries to identify commonalities between them. In contrast, here, the common semantics of all SoftwareElements implementing all VPs of a VPG is investigated. Accordingly, also terms within comments are considered and term frequencies might provide additional sources of information.

To cope with the typically high amount of terms arising in such analyses, weights can be used to improve the ranking of the terms in addition to their frequency. For example, terms extracted from class names can get a higher weight compared to the name of a variable inside a method.

However, extracting terms and considering the SoftwareElements they are used in requires a technology-specific processing and an additional point for adaptation.

6.2.2.2. Terms from Relationships

If two or more VPs are contained in the same VPG, they share one or more relationships. Depending on the type of relationship, they can provide further hints for the ID of a VPG respectively the name of the according variable feature. For example, a shared term analysis might already have identified terms used by the VPs. Another example is a simultaneous modification relationship because of VPs implemented in the context of a single issue tracked in an SCM system. This issue would provide useful information about the feature realized by the VPs.

However, the names derived from either SoftwareElements or relationships represent only hints and cannot be expected to provide satisfying names from Product Managers' perspectives later on. Accordingly, manual investigation by SPL Consolidation Developers and SPL Managers is required.

6.3. SPLEVO Program Dependency Analysis

The SPLEVO Program Dependency Analysis extracts relationships between sets of software elements implementing the variants of VPs. These relationships are then used for deriving relationships between the containing variation points and for recommending aggregations. This analysis is implemented as a representative for the Relationship Type of Dependent Modifications (Section 6.1.3.1) and used to study their benefits. The analysis and results from the evaluation were also published in Klatt et al. [100].

Analyzing program dependencies Designing features of an SPL is affected by many soft factors, such as organizational reasons or product management decisions [33]. Thus, creating a reasonable design cannot be fully automated. However, when consolidating copies and their already implemented copy-specific features, there are given technical relationships between modifications (i.e., dependent modifications) one must consider to avoid implementing everything from scratch. Program dependencies are representatives for such restrictive relationships, and software developers are used to read them in general. However, as described in Section 6.1.3, the SPLEVO approach proposes to reuse existing dependency analysis concepts. But, at the same time, it mentions the need for adaption to use those analyses in the context of consolidating customized copies.

To cope with this challenge, the SPLEVO approach proposes a program dependency analysis specialized for dependencies between VPs. In particular, this includes i) considering code of more than one code base, ii) focusing on dependencies between modified SoftwareElements, and iii) supporting groups of SoftwareElements in case of previously merged VPs and SoftwareElements representing a larger sub-tree of a software model. Program dependencies exist in nearly every technology, but concrete dependencies to consider are technology-specific. All case studies conducted to evaluate the SPLEVO approach are implemented with Java technology. Hence, the program dependency analysis developed in the SPLEVO approach was implemented to support the Java programing language specifics as well.

The following subsections present the concept of the SPLEVO program dependency analysis. This covers the general analysis concept, the set of considered dependencies, and the algorithm to identify the dependencies between VPs, as well as the derivation of refinement recommendations as presented in Section 6.1.4.1.

6.3.1. Analysis Concept

The SPLEVO program dependency analysis is designed to cope with i) handling multiple code bases, ii) focusing on differences, and iii) supporting VPs with variants implemented by more than one SoftwareElement (e.g., a set of statements).

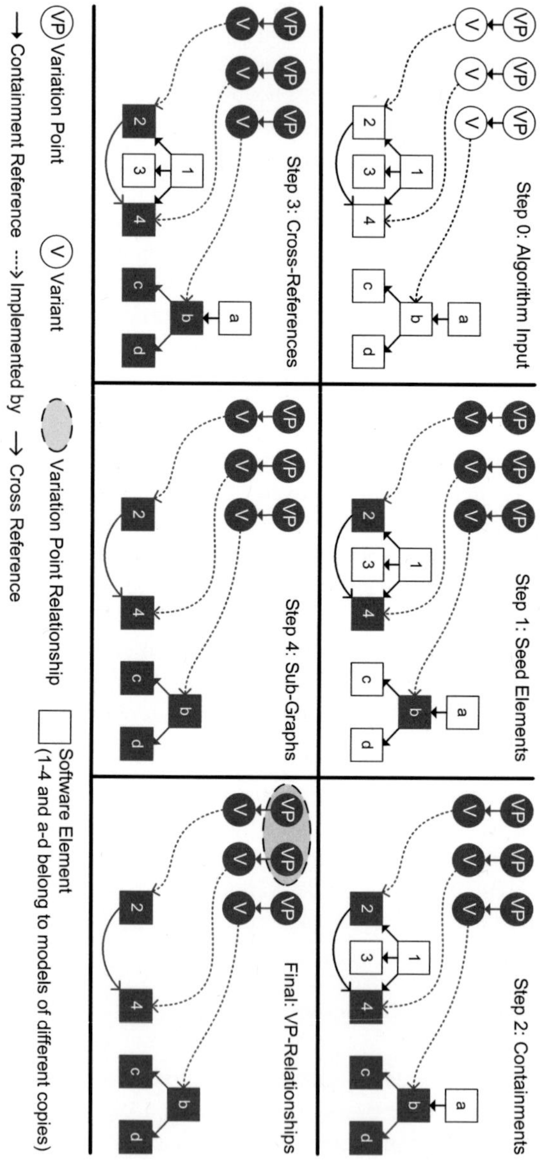

Figure 6.22.: Program dependency analysis graph-based algorithm concept

Figure 6.22 presents a diagram of the analysis concept. It receives a VPM respectively its VPs as input, which provides access to the complete software models of the copies' code bases (i.e. SoftwareElements 1..3 and *a..d* in the diagram). Those models are trees of SoftwareElements according to the elements' containment references (Definition 7). In addition to this minimal structure of supported software models, they can contain cross-references identifying dependencies between SoftwareElements that are not contained by each other. The dependencies studied by the SPLEVO analysis are represented as such cross-references. Furthermore, the VPs' variants reference their implementing SoftwareElements in the model trees, which are possibly root elements of complete sub-trees.

- In step 0, the analysis receives the VPMs to analyze, including references to the copies' software models.
- In step 1, the analysis marks sub-graphs consisting of the VPs, their variants, and the referenced implementing SoftwareElements.
- In step 2, the sub-graphs are extended to the SoftwareElements contained by the implementing elements.
- In step 3, the sub-graphs are further extended by the cross-references representing studied dependencies.
- Step 4 in Figure 6.22 illustrates the resulting sub-graphs.
- Finally, in step 5, all VPs included in the same sub-graph are considered as related to each other, and according relationships are derived.

6.3.2. Studied Program Dependencies

The SPLEVO program dependency analysis investigates in program dependencies typically represented in Program Dependency Graphs (PDGs) as proposed by Ottenstein and Ottenstein [144] and by cross-references in software models as described by Wilde [193]. In general, program dependencies are studied for many reasons and with different characteristics, such as for optimization (e.g., Ferrante et al. [59]), change impact analysis (e.g., Lehnert [117]), or feature location (e.g., Dit et al. [43] and Rubin and Chechik [161]).

Extension of the dependencies proposed by Robillard and Murphy [158] The SPLEVO program dependency analysis is based on a set of dependencies proposed by Robillard and Murphy [158] in the field of feature location. The analysis proposed by Robillard and Murphy [158] was also previously used by Alves et al. [3] in the context of refactoring SPL models. Furthermore, this base set of program dependencies has been chosen as it is already tailored for object-oriented programming languages. It was also used for the Java programming language as required for the case studies during the SPLEVO evaluation. Furthermore, the experience reported by Alves et al. [3] was rated as an indicator for a reasonable set to start with. However, it was necessary to extend this set. For example, it does not cover dependencies below the granularity of methods. But, for example, dependencies between statements are required in the context of the SPLEVO approach. Further details about the extension of the dependency set are described below.

Studied Java elements Robillard and Murphy [158] recommend studying dependencies between `Classes (C)`, `Fields (F)`, and `Methods`. The SPLEVO program dependency analysis refines the method handling proposed by Robillard and Murphy [158]. It distinguishes between `Method Signatures (M)` and `Statements (S)` implementing a method's body. Considering statements, as more detailed elements, allows for gaining more precise dependency results. Furthermore, the SPLEVO program analysis investigates in `Parameters (P)`, `Variables (V)`, `Interfaces (I)`, and `Enumerations (E)`. In the following, the term "type" is used if classes, interfaces, or enumerations are referred equally.

Studied dependencies between Java elements In addition to the types of elements to study, Robillard and Murphy [158] recommend a set of dependencies to consider: `superType` represents inheritance relationships. `calls` represents functional invocations, while `reads` means accessing the value of another element. `writes` means to replace the value of another element, and `creates` instantiates a new instance of a type.

Furthermore, Robillard and Murphy [158] define a `declares` dependency. This type of dependency is superfluous in the context of analyzing relationships between VPs as done in the SPLEVO approach. In the context of a Java software model conforming to SPLEVO's structure definition (Definition 7), this is similar to a containment relationship between the declaring and the declared elements. If a containing element differs between two product copies, its content is handled as differing as well and the according variant element of the VP references the containing SoftwareElement only. For example, if a new Java class has been introduced in a product copy, it will be referenced as implementing element by a variant. The fields declared by the new Java class are not referenced by separate variant elements. Instead, they are indirectly identified through a containment reference of the SoftwareElement representing the new Java class. Thus, analyzing declared relationships would not provide additional relationships between any of the VPs.

The SPLEVO program dependency analysis also proposes additional dependencies to consider. The `typed` dependency is identified if a SoftwareElement is declared with a specific type. Furthermore, the SPLEVO program dependency defines an `import` dependency between a SoftwareElement and an import declaration for a type required by the SoftwareElement. Finally, a `modifies` dependency is proposed. As described by Flanagan [60, page 86], Java uses a "pass by value" strategy and handles objects by reference. That means references are passed as values instead of the objects themselves. A `modifies` dependency indicates that a referenced object is manipulated but the reference itself remains unchanged. For example, assuming a variable references an object and a method is called on this object, this is treated as a `modifies` dependency between the method call statement and the variable. Such a modifies dependency is marked for line 2 in Listing 9. In contrast, a `writes` dependency completely changes the object referenced by a variable (e.g., line 3 in Listing 9).

```
1 MyClass a = new MyClass(); // declaration of a
2 a.doSth(); // statement modifies a
3 a = new MyClass(); // statement writes a
```

Listing 9: Examples of Modifies and Writes Dependencies

Overview of analyzed dependencies Table 6.1 summarizes the dependencies considered by the SPLEVO program dependency analysis. Each cell represents the dependency of the element in the column's header, linked by the dependency type in the row's leftmost column with the element in the row's second column. For example, the top right cell represents the dependency "Interface I is superType of Class C". Not all combinations are reasonable to consider, such as "Class superTypes Interface". Dependencies proposed by Robillard and Murphy [158] are marked with an R. Those added by the SPLEVO approach are marked with an SPL. All dependencies marked in the table are considered by the SPLEVO program dependency analysis (i.e., all cells marked with either an R or an SPL).

Two sets of Java-specific SoftwareElement types and one set of dependencies (i.e., references between SoftwareElements) are derived from the dependencies investigated by the SPLEVO program dependency analysis.

1. The set of types of source SoftwareElements referencing other SoftwareElements by a program dependency is referred as:
   $T_s : \{Class, Field, Method, Statement, Parameter, Interface\}$.
2. The set of types of target SoftwareElements referenced by source elements with a program dependency under study is referred as:
   $T_t : \{Class, Interface, Enumeration, Field, Method, Variable, Statement, Parameter\}$.
3. The dependencies from a source type $t_s \in T_s$ to a target type $t_t \in T_t$ as indicated by an R or S in Table 6.1. The dependencies are represented by triples:
   D: SET<$\{t_s, t_t, t_d\}$> with dependency type $t_d \in \{superTypes, calls, reads, writes, checks, creates, typed, import, modifies\}$.

6.3.3. Analysis Algorithm

As part of the SPLEVO program dependency analysis, an algorithm has been developed to realize its analysis concept. It uses an internal index to derive VP relationships with a single traversing of sub-trees of the software models.

Figure 6.23 illustrates an index-oriented view of how the algorithm realizes the graph-based concept described above. The illustration is also in line with the example code given in Listing 10.

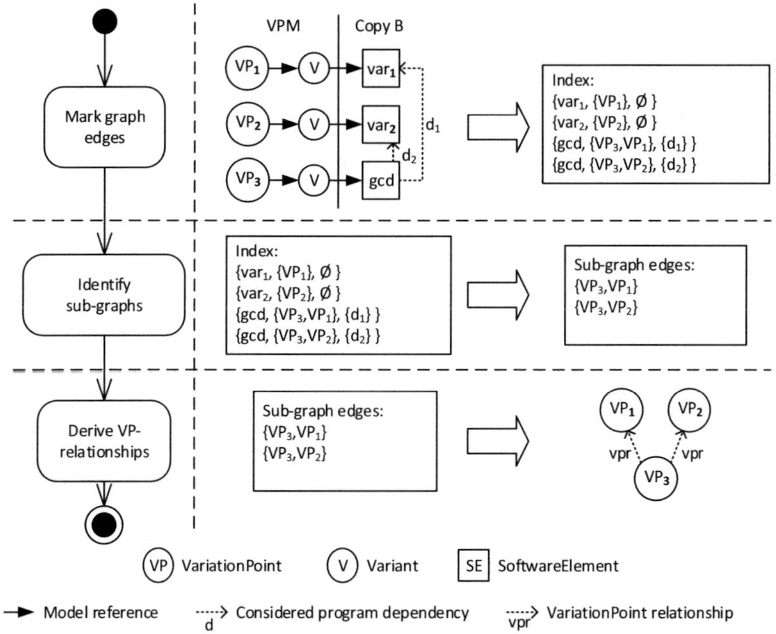

Figure 6.23.: SPLEVO Program Dependency Analysis: Algorithm illustrating example

```java
BigInteger var1 = new BigInteger(1); //VP1
BigInteger var2 = new BigInteger(2); //VP2
BigInteger gcd = var1.gcd(var2); //VP3
```

Listing 10: Code Example with Variation Points

Mark graph edges First, the algorithm marks graph edges for SoftwareElements that either implement a variant by themselves or are referenced by such an element with a cross-reference or a direct or indirect containment reference. During the indexing, only SoftwareElements of the studied element types (i.e., T_s respectively T_t) are considered. Similarly, only cross-references representing one of the studied dependencies are taken into account (i.e., D).

The index links each SoftwareElement with its own VP and VPs of the SoftwareElements it depends on. The type of the identified dependency is stored as well (i.e., d).

The example provided in Listing 10 contains three copy-specific statements marked as VariationPoints VP_1, VP_2, and VP_3. For the sake of brevity, the index illustrated in Figure 6.23 contains entries relevant for this example only. After VP_1's statement in line 1 is processed, the index contains three entries: i) the statement itself, ii) the type BigInteger, and iii) the variable var_1, all linked to VP1 (e.g., $\{var_1, \{VP_1\}, \emptyset\}$). When line 2 is processed, the index contains additional entries, again for the statements, the type BigInteger, and the second variable var_2, all referencing VP_2 (e.g., $\{var_2, \{VP_2\}, \emptyset\}$). Finally, when line 3 is processed, the index now contains entries for the dependencies from variable gcd to var_1 and var_2: $\{var_1\{VP_1\},\emptyset\},\{var_2, \{VP_2\}, \emptyset\},\{gcd, \{VP_3, VP_1\}, d_1\},\{gcd, \{VP_3, VP_2\}, d_2\}$.

Identify sub-graphs Next, the algorithm scans the index to identify sub-graphs. The index used by the algorithm does not repeat all references present in the original software models but detects pairs of VPs (i.e., sub-graph edges) connected by SoftwareElements covered in the index. For the example given above, VP_3 and VP_1 are detected because they are both referenced by the SoftwareElement gcd. Similarly, VP_1 and VP_2 are detected as both are referenced by the SoftwareElement gcd as well. The algorithm derives sub-graph edges from those references (i.e., $\{VP_3, VP_1\}$ and $\{VP_3, VP_2\}$).

Derive VP-Relationships Finally, the algorithm derives VP-relationships from the sub-graphs identified in the previous step. Those relationships will be used to recommend aggregations to SPL Consolidation Developers. For the example illustrated in Figure 6.23, an aggregation of VP_1, VP_2, and VP_3 will be recommended.

6.4. SPLEVO Shared Term Analysis

The SPLEVO Shared Term Analysis extracts terms from the software elements implementing the variants of VPs and identifies relationships between elements of different VPs if they share similar terms. These relationships are then used to derive relationships between the containing variation points and to recommend aggregations. This analysis is implemented as a representative for the Relationship Type of Similar Modifications (Section 6.1.3.2) and used to study ids benefits. As terms provide varying meanings, the identified relationships have suggestive meaning (Section 6.1.3).

Analyzing terms in source code As identified by Kuhn et al. [114] in the field of NLPA, developers express conceptual knowledge (e.g., about a specific feature) not only with the syntax of a programing language but also with linguistic information stored in identifiers (e.g., method or class names). As described in Section 6.1.3.2, terms present in modified SoftwareElements provide hints about VPs contributing to the same feature (i.e., shared term analysis).

Listing 11 provides an example of a term used at different modified code locations, assuming developers created a new class named *CreditCardPayment*, a new field named *creditCardField* in the class Dialog, and a new variable named *newCreditCardNumber* in the method save. The identifiers of all these SoftwareElements contain the term "credit card" in one or the other variation. Identifying this shared term provides a hint that all these SoftwareElements have been modified for the same "credit card" feature.

In the fields of general computer linguistics and information retrieval, many approaches exist to investigate terms used in documents or texts (Section 2.4.10). Research approaches in the field of NLPA apply such approaches to program analysis in general. The SPLEVO approach proposes to reuse these existing concepts, such as stemming to normalize slightly varying terms (e.g., conflating plural and singular variants of a term). However, the existing concepts must be adapted for finding relationships between modifications and non-semantic contexts of code in general.

```
public class CreditCardPayment {
  ...
}
```

```
public class Dialog {
  public Input creditCardField
          =...;
}
```

```
public void save() {
  String newCreditCardNumber
      = dialog.creditCardField.getValue();
  ...
}
```

Listing 11: Code example for shared term

To cope with this need for adaptation, the SPLEVO Shared Term Analysis is able to i) extract terms from SoftwareElements implementing specific variants, ii) support strategies to cope with useless terms, and iii) derive VP relationships from terms shared by SoftwareElements.

The following subsections describe the general concept of the SPLEVO Shared Term Analysis, which terms are studied, and details of its processing.

6.4.1. Analysis Concept

The SPLEVO Shared Term Analysis is designed to cope with the requirements of i) handling multiple code bases, ii) allowing for technology-specific term extraction, and iii) supporting different term processing strategies.

The first is required by the context of the consolidation. It is necessary to handle the code bases of the customized copies at once, which is not supported by general NLPA analyses. The term extraction is required if the analysis can be adapted for different technologies. This is necessary as only specific attributes of SoftwareElements can be used by developers for context related terms. Finally, different term processing strategies are required to cope with varying term quality and relevance, as described in the next section.

Figure 6.24 presents a diagram of the analysis concept. It receives a VPM as input, which provides access to the complete software models of the copies' code bases (i.e. SoftwareElements 1..3 and *a..d* in the diagram). Those models are trees of SoftwareElements according to the elements' containment references (Definition 7). The SoftwareElements in the models have attributes containing the terms chosen by developers. Furthermore, the VPs' variants reference their implementing SoftwareElements in the model trees, which are possibly root elements of complete sub-trees.

- In step 0, the analysis receives the VPMs to analyze and including references to the software models of the product copies.
- In step 1, the analysis marks sub-graphs of the VPs, their variants, and the referenced implementing SoftwareElements.
- In step 2, the sub-graphs are extended with the SoftwareElements contained by the implementing elements.
- In step 3, terms are extracted from the SoftwareElements (i.e., $t_{1..5}$).
- In step 4, the extracted terms are normalized to handle variations of the same term, such as plural and singular (i.e., $t_{n1..n2}$).
- Finally, in step 5, similar terms are connected with each other (i.e., t_{n1}).

In addition, VPs participating in the same sub-graph are considered as related to each other.

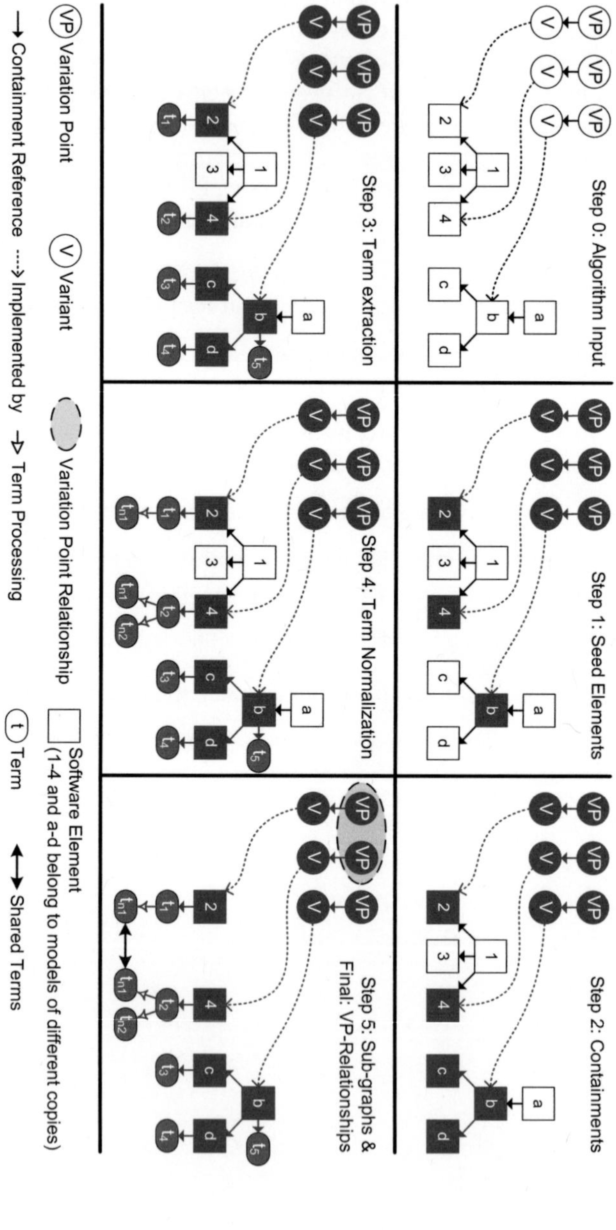

Figure 6.24.: Shared term analysis graph-based algorithm concept

6.4.2. Studied Terms

As published in Klatt et al. [99], the SPLEVO Shared Term Analysis analyzes terms stored in identifiers of the SoftwareElements. Identifiers provide a reasonable source of conceptual knowledge implemented by developers in a lexical manner [150, 114].

The analysis provides an adaption point to decide which attribute of a SoftwareElement represents an identifier according to the type of the SoftwareElement. This decision has to be done in a technology-specific manner because the type of a SoftwareElement and the attributes to consider depend on the concrete type of software model under study. However, deciding about the type of a SoftwareElement and its attributes is typically a straight forward decision. Programming languages and according software models specify which elements and attributes are to be considered as an identifier. For example, the JaMoPP [78] Java metamodel used in the SPLEVO prototype defines an explicit *NamedElement* as a super type of all identifiers and defining a *name* attribute.

The raw strings extracted from attributes of SoftwareElements are typically not sufficient to subsequently perform further analyses (e.g., Spek et al. [177]). To cope with this insufficiency, the SPLEVO Shared Term Analysis uses term processing to normalize the extracted strings and receive more valuable terms. The proposed processing includes splitting – also known as tokenization – (e.g., "MyIdentifier" to "My" and "Identifier"), stemming (e.g., "records" to "record"), and filtering (e.g., removing terms with less than three characters). These generic steps are in line with typical processing recommended by others (e.g., Spek et al. [177, page 2]). However, many different approaches and algorithms exist for each of these steps (Section 2.4.10).

As discovered in the case studies, the quality of VP relationships discovered by the shared term analysis strongly depends on the quality of the identifiers. This correlates with the findings of Kuhn et al. [114, page 240] by analyzing terms in context of semantic clustering of source code. For example, if developers adhere to guidelines such as the camel case separation of words recommended by the JavaBeans coding conventions [73], this provides structure to be automatically processed by the splitting operation.

The SPLEvo Shared Term Analysis denotes terms not relevant in the context of copy-specific features as Term Spam (Definition 18).

Definition 18 (Term Spam) Term Spam *is a set of terms that does not represent contextual knowledge introduced by implementing a copy-specific feature. From the perspective of the* SPLEvo *Shared Term Analysis, Term Spam leads to false indicators for VP relationships. Thus, Term Spam is undesired and needs to be either removed or faded out from the analysis.*

In contrast to Term Spam, there might be terms which are known to be relevant in the context customized features. The SPLEvo Shared Term Analysis allows for specifying relevant terms and using them to improve the analysis results. Such terms are referred to as "featured terms" (Definition 19).

Definition 19 (Featured Term) *A* Featured Term *is known to be relevant for identifying copy-specific features. Thus, the processing recognizes also slightly varying representations of a featured term and never splits it. Compound terms are often reasonable to be specified as featured terms. For example, developers tend to use different separators according to personal styles or types of identifiers the compound terms are used in (e.g., variables and constants).*

The SPLEvo approach does not assume to receive any featured terms as input, and the analysis can also be used without any of them. However, several parts of the analysis algorithm benefit from considering available featured terms, as described in Section 6.4.3. Furthermore, featured terms might not be available in advance to the consolidation process. The iterative analysis approach allows SPL Consolidation Developers to define featured terms before executing an analysis. They can run an analysis and review the results. If they recognize a new term to be featured, they can decline the current recommendations, add the new featured term, and execute the analysis again.

The SPLEvo Shared Term Analysis defines an adaptation point for processing extracted terms. This adaptation point allows for coping with varying identifier qualities and programmer habits to further improve the quality of the terms to analyze. Further details about the build-in processing strategies are documented in the following sections.

6.4.3. Analysis Algorithm

The SPLEVO approach makes use of common infrastructures for term processing and textual searches (Section 2.4.10). For example, an inverted index is used to link terms with VPs. A VP is linked if the term results from a SoftwareElement implementing one of the VP's variants. This index is filled during the analysis and finally considered to retrieve all VPs indexed for the same term (i.e., step 5 in Figure 6.24).

As mentioned in the last section, the analysis processes terms in three manners before they are stored by the index: Splitting, Stemming, and Filtering. The following subsections provide details about the specific implementations of the processing within the SPLEVO Shared Term Analysis.

6.4.3.1. Splitting

The SPLEVO Shared Term Analysis makes use of splitting rules proposed in the general field of computer linguistics and NLPA. It splits terms when the case of their characters changes (i.e., camel case notation) or white space and other non-alphabetic characters are found.

Furthermore, the splitting of the analysis takes featured terms (Definition 19) into account. If featured terms are defined, they are protected from splitting. They will not be split, even if they are used in a camel case style or when single non-alphabetic characters are used as part of them. In the latter case, those non-alphabetic characters will also be removed to clean up the featured term's occurrence.

For example, in the ArgoUML case study, the term "usecase" occurs in feature-specific code in the variations "UseCase", "Use_case", "useCase", "usecase", and "Usecase". Thus, providing "usecase" as featured term allows for treating all of these variations as the same shared term.

The splitting improvement based on featured terms allows for finding additional relationships between varying featured terms as shown in the example above.

6.4.3.2. Stemming

The SPLEVO Shared Term Analysis performs a stemming to normalize terms. For example, plural forms of terms are often used in identifiers referring to a list of elements (e.g., "dialogs"). Those identifiers are stemmed to their singular form (e.g., "dialog") as typically used in identifiers referring to a single object.

The SPLEVO Shared Term Analysis uses the algorithm-based Snowball variant of the Porter stemmer by default (Porter [151]). It has been chosen from a list of five publicly available approaches: Snowball Porter [151], Porter [152], KStem [111], S-Stemmer [74], and Pling [181]. For the first four, implementations provided by the Lucene project [75] have been used. For the last one, an implementation provided by Suchanek et al. [181] as part of the Yago project [180] has been used.

All stemmers show comparable results when applied in the case studies. Thus, all of them are supported by the SPLEVO algorithm. However, the Snowball Porter algorithm has been chosen as default because it provides satisfying and comprehensible stemming results. Compared to the initial Porter algorithm, it returns more comprehensible results for short terms (e.g., "use" instead of "us" or "xpos" instead of "xpo"). Compared to the KStem stemmer, it has shown better results for plural/singular terms. For example, the KStem stemmer does not stem "points" and "point" to the same term whereas the Snowball Porter stemmer does. The Pling stemmer uses a lexical approach based on general spoken language (Section 2.4.10). As identified by Høst and Østvold [82], developers use a more specific vocabulary than in general spoken languages. Thus, even if the case studies did not show notable differences, it is not clear what the impact of the differing languages on the stemming results is. Finally, the S-Stemmmer performs a basic plural to singular conversion only. For example, it is not capable to stem conjugation of verbs. "Order" and "isOrdered" are both about ordering (e.g., a book or anything else). Without being able to stem "ordered" to "order", these example terms cannot be matched. Similar to the lexical approach, the S-Stemmer lead to minor differences in the case studies only, but the general impact of its limitations is not clear. Stemming extracted terms allows for finding additional relationships between otherwise varying terms, such as for "points" and "point".

6.4.3.3. Filtering

Developers use not only terms representing contextual knowledge. They also use terms representing processing concepts (e.g., "load" or "create") or coding guidelines (e.g., get or set), as studied by Høst and Østvold [83], Sajaniemi and Prieto [166], and Caprile and Tonella [28].

The SPLEVO Shared Term Analysis uses a short term filter to remove terms with less than three characters. There is no fixed recommendation about the minimum length to use. However, in the case studies, we experienced that terms with a length of one or two characters often represent useless variable identifiers. Beside others, the terms "as", "bo", and "de" have been identified in the industrial case study and confirmed as meaningless variable identifiers by the developer participating in the case study. In contrast, terms with three characters have been identified that are possible, such as "txt", "pos", and "svg".

Beside the minimum term length filtering, four strategies for targeting Term Spam have been identified: term frequency, seed terms, stop word lists, and shared term clusters. Term frequency strategies increase or decrease the value of terms according to the number of their occurrences within a specific scope. Seed terms define a positive list of terms to search for. Either the value of seed terms is increased compared to the value of other terms, or they are the only terms considered by the analysis. Stop word lists define negative lists of terms which are filtered out before terms are stored in the inverted index. Shared term clusters restrict the groups of related VPs by requiring all VPs within a group to share the same set of terms.

Filtering stop words or short terms allows for reducing the number of false relationships and thus recommending fewer aggregations to be declined by SPL Consolidation Developers.

Term frequency Frequency based strategies are often used to evaluate the semantics of a text or set of terms. For example, to provide an idea about the concern of a source file, the most frequently used terms in the contained identifiers could be considered. A high frequency can be rated in both directions: Being an indicator for a term representative for a specific code location, or being an indicator for a term used in many locations and thus not representative for a specific location.

In the context of the SPLEVO Shared Term Analysis, none of these directions provides a reliable indicator for related SoftwareElements. On the one side, variant elements of VPs are often implemented by a few SoftwareElements only. Thus, they are providing a limited number of terms to analyze (e.g., a changed statement) with correspondingly similar frequencies. On the other side, even for larger copy-specific code (e.g., added compilation units), the frequency does not provide a good indicator for the relevance of a term. A relevant term might be used just once within a set of many terms (e.g., the name of a large and completely copy-specific class). But in other cases, a relevant term might be used quite often (e.g., the name of a field newly introduced in an existing class). Also, the frequency a term is used in different VPs is not convincing. If only one feature has been added to a copy, it is reasonable to have a single term used to implement variants of all VPs. In contrast, an arbitrary term recommended by programming guidelines might be used in all VPs as well, but without any relevance for a copy-specific feature.

However, the goal of the shared term analysis is to identify non-arbitrary terms used by several locations as an indicator for a relationship between those locations. This does not require discovering the real semantics of the code locations. Thus, other filtering approaches should be preferred over evaluating the frequency of extracted terms.

Seed Terms Seed terms are terms known to represent a copy-specific feature or at least assumed to be used for a feature's implementation. Based on a set of seed terms, all other terms can be filtered. This would remove any Term Spam at all. The drawback of this approach is the need to have good seed terms provided by SPL Consolidation Developers.

Often, SPL Consolidation Developers, SPL Managers, and Product Managers have an idea of the features implemented in specific copies. Terms or names of these features can be used to improve the shared term analysis. For example, as part of the ArgoUML case study (Section 8.4.1), names for the coarse grain features such as UseCase, Sequence, or Activity are known upfront and reasonable to be considered.

One source of seed terms can be featured terms as defined in the context of the SPLEVO Shared Term Analysis (Definition 19). However, the approach uses these terms to improve the analysis' results. It does not rely on them, as the list of seed terms might be incomplete and developers might have used a slightly differing vocabulary. Furthermore, in one of the case studies, developers were not even able to provide a list of seed terms (i.e., featured terms).

Seed terms are a possible strategy for filtering Term Spam as part of the SPLEVO Shared Term Analysis. Nevertheless, the strategy's limitations, such as the possibly incomplete list of terms, also limit the relationships that can be identified. Especially, filtering all terms other than the seed terms prevents identifying shared terms not expected in advance.

Stop Word Lists Stop word lists are used in natural language processing to filter irrelevant terms before executing an analysis (Section 2.4.10). To improve the results of the SPLEVO Shared Term Analysis, stop words are filtered from the set of extracted terms to reduce Term Spam.

During the term processing, stop words are filtered after stemming has been finished. The stop words are stemmed as well. In this way, stop words must be specified in one variant only and not for all of their variants present in the SoftwareElements. Additionally, the provided variant of a stop word is not required to match the stem of the word. Especially, depending on the facilitated stemmer, the stem of the word can be artificial and difficult to be defined by SPL Consolidation Developers. For example, the Snowball Porter stemmer produces stems such as "additi" for "addition" and "locat" for "location".

As published in Klatt et al. [99], there is no publicly available and generally applicable stop word list to be used for program analysis. For general spoken languages, many stop word lists exist and are publicly available (e.g., for the MySQL database [142]). However, as identified by Høst and Østvold [82], developers use a more specific vocabulary than in general spoken language. Accordingly, more specific stop words are required for filtering Term Spam in the context of the shared term analysis. They even depend on the domain, application type, developing company, and products to consolidate copies of.

The SPLEVO approach proposes a guideline for developing stop word lists for specific contexts. This guideline distinguishes different scopes of stop word lists (i.e., programming language, technology, and domain) and recommends sources to check for according terms. However, only terms clearly expected to be Term Spam must be added to a stop word list. To facilitate the creation of stop word lists, it is recommended to develop separate lists aligned with the different scopes. This allows for reusing more generally applicable lists, such as for a specific programming language. Furthermore, the context simplifies decisions about adding a term to a stop word list or not.

The **programming language scope** relates to the programming language used to develop the product copies. For each programming language, common sense naming conventions exist. For example, in Java, methods to access an attribute of an object should start with the term “get”. A stop word list for a programming language should reflect such terms. Common sense terms can be retrieved from coding guidelines (e.g., for Java [73] or .Net [132]). In addition, there are existing studies on programming habits and terms recommended to express program concepts. For example, Høst and Østvold [83], Sajaniemi and Prieto [166] and Caprile and Tonella [28] analyzed programs to identify frequently used terms expressing more technical and less feature related knowledge. Such terms are programming-language-specific and might be considered for being reused. Finally, design patterns as proposed by Gamma et al. [65] are often implemented by using terms identifying the role of a SoftwareElement within a pattern (e.g., Observer, View, Controller).

The **technology scope** relates to technologies and infrastructures, such as the type of products under study or frameworks they are built with. In each program, there are terms used because of the underlying technology and not because of a feature actually implemented. For example, developing OSGi components includes classes to control the life cycle of a component [143, page 109]. The identifier of such a class typically includes the term “Activator”, which might not relate to a copy-specific feature. In addition, Ratiu [155] has classified types of applications (e.g., graphical user interfaces or web applications) and typical terminologies used during their development (e.g., ”button” or “dialog”).

The **domain scope** relates to a business or product domain. In most domains, common sense terms exist. For example, in applications for library management, the term ISBN might be used quite frequently as a global identifier with low contribution to specific features. Specific industries, such as the aviation industry, have developed glossaries providing starting points for discovering terms to add to a stop word list. Finally, many companies have custom naming conventions for developing their products. For example, they can include terms to be used for identifiers of specific infrastructures or for instances of components from custom development libraries. Such conventions provide an additional source for stop words in the scope of a domain.

To conclude, filtering stop word lists are a reasonable approach to reduce Term Spam. However, stop word lists for program analyses, such as the SPLEVO Shared Term Analysis, strongly depend on the context they are applied in. For example, the term "Activator" is often used in context of OSGi bundles, as mentioned before. However, it is no Term Spam if an OSGi wrapper for an existing product has been developed as a copy-specific feature. Thus, there is a necessity to build or adapt stop word lists for the specific contexts. The guidelines presented above can be used for this. Nevertheless, the different scopes come with different sources, varying potential for being reused, as well as varying clarity for identifying Term Spam.

Shared Term Clusters VPs can share more than one term at the same time. Assuming three VPs VP_1, VP_2, and VP_3. VP_1 can share a term t_2 with VP_2 and another term t_3 with VP_3. If there is no further connection between VP_2 and VP_3, it is not clear if the group of all three of them is reasonable. Furthermore, deciding about such a group is difficult, as either relationships might be reasonable, only one of them, or even none.

To cope with this situation, the SPLEVO approach proposes to limit identified relationships to clusters of VPs all sharing the same terms with each other. For the example given above, if t_2 and t_3 would represent the same set of terms, they will be returned. Otherwise no relationship is recommended.

In addition, it is recommended to combine the shared term cluster strategy with the other strategies presented above. In particular, if seed terms are available, they should be used during the first analysis run.

Algorithm 8: VP Merging Operator

input : Set<VariationPoint>: $vps \leftarrow \{vp_1,..,vp_n\}$ // n > 1 variation points to be merged
VariationPointModel: vpm
output : VariationPoint: $vp_{surviving}$

```
VariationPoint: vp_surviving ← vp_1
Set<VariationPoint>: vps_remove ← vps \ vp_1
foreach VariationPoint: vp ∈ vps_remove do
    foreach Variant: v ∈ vp.variants do                         // VP Consolidation
        if (∃ Variant: v_surviving ∈ vp_surviving.variants|v_surviving.id == v.id)
         then
            vp_surviving.variants ← vp_surviving.variants ∪ v
        else
            Variant: v_surviving ← (Variant:
             v_s ∈ vp_surviving.variants|v_s.id == v.id)
            v_surviving.implementingElements ←
             v_surviving.implementingElements ∪ v.implementingElements
        end
    end
    VariationPointGroup: vpg ← vp.group                         // VP Removal
    vpg.variationPoints ← vpg.variationPoints \ vp
    if vpg.variationPoints == ∅ then
        vpm.variationPointGroups ← vpm.variationPointGroups \ vpg
    end
end
return vp_surviving
```

Algorithm 9: VP Grouping Operator

input : Set<VariationPoint>: vp_n // the n < 1 variation points to be grouped
VariationPointModel: vpm
output : VariationPointGroup: $vpg_{surviving}$

VariationPointGroup: $vpg_{surviving} \leftarrow vp_1.group$
Set<VariationPoint>: $vp_{move} \leftarrow vp_n \setminus vp_1$
foreach *VariationPoint:* $vp \in vp_{move}$ **do**
    VariationPointGroup: $vpg_{old} \leftarrow vp.group$
    $vpg_{old}.variationPoints \leftarrow vpg_{old}.variationPoints \setminus vp$
    $vpg_{surviving}.variationPoints \leftarrow vpg_{surviving}.variationPoints \cup vp$
    if $vpg_{old}.variationPoints == \emptyset$ **then**
        $vpm.variationPointGroups \leftarrow vpm.variationPointGroups \setminus vpg$
    end
end
$return\ vpg_{surviving}$

Algorithm 10: Detect and Build MergeRefinements Algorithm

input : GroupRefinement: *gr* // The group refinement check for mergeable VPs
output : Refinement: *improvedRefinement*

SET<SET<VariationPoint>>: $buckets \leftarrow \emptyset$ `// Buckets for mergeable VPs`
foreach *VariationPoint:* $vp_i \in gr.variationPoints$ **do**
  foreach *VariationPoint:* $vp_j \in gr.variationPoints \setminus vp_i$ **do**
    if `MergeDetection(`vp_i,vp_j`)` $==$ *true* **then**
      `PutIntoBucket(`$buckets$,vp_i,vp_j`)`
    end
  end
end
if $buckets == \emptyset$ **then**
  return gr `// No merge possible`
else if $|buckets| == 1 \wedge bucket_1 == gr.variationPoints$ **then**
  return $MergeRefinement(gr)$ `// All VPs mergeable`
else
  foreach *SET<VariationPoint>:* $bucket_i \in buckets$ **do**
    $gr.variationPoints \leftarrow gr.variationPoints \setminus bucket_i$ `// New sub-refinement`
    MergeRefinement: $r \leftarrow MergeRefinement()$
    $r.relationshipTypes \leftarrow gr.relationshipTypes$
    $r.variationPoints \leftarrow bucket_i$
    $r.reasons \leftarrow (rr \in gr.reasons | rr.source \in bucket_i \vee rr.target \in bucket_i)$
    $gr.subRefinements \leftarrow gr.subRefinements \cup r$
  end
  return gr
end

Algorithm 11: Order VPs into buckets algorithm (`PutIntoBucket`)

input : SET<SET<VariationPoint>>: *buckets* // set of VP buckets
VariationPoint: vp_i, vp_j // VPs to put into buckets

output :

SET<VariationPoint>: $bucket_i \leftarrow (b \in buckets | vp_i \in b)$
SET<VariationPoint>: $bucket_j \leftarrow (b \in buckets | vp_j \in b)$
if $bucket_i \neq \varnothing \wedge bucket_j \neq \varnothing$ **then**
| $bucket_i \leftarrow bucket_i \cup bucket_j$
else if $bucket_i \neq \varnothing$ **then**
| $bucket_i \leftarrow bucket_i \cup vp_j$
else if $bucket_j \neq \varnothing$ **then**
| $bucket_j \leftarrow bucket_j \cup vp_i$
else
| $buckets \leftarrow buckets \cup \{vp_i, vp_j\}$
end

Algorithm 12: Detection rule application

```
input  : SET<Edge>: edges // all edges in merged graph
         DetectionRule: d // Current detection rule to be applied
output : SET<GroupRefinement>: G ← ∅ // Derived refinements

SET<SET<VariationPoint>>: subgraphs ← ∅
foreach Edge: e ∈ edges do
    if e.labels ≡ d.types then                        // Detection Rule matched
        SET<VariationPoint>: sg1 ← (sg ∈ subgraphs | e.node1 ∈ sg)
        SET<VariationPoint>: sg2 ← (sg ∈ subgraphs | e.node2 ∈ sg)
        if sg1 ≠ ∅ ∧ sg2 ≠ ∅ then
            sg1 ← sg1 ∪ sg2
        else if sg1 ≠ ∅ then
            sg1 ← sg1 ∪ e.node1
        else if sg2 ≠ ∅ then
            sg2 ← sg2 ∪ e.node2
        else
            subgraphs ← subgraphs ∪ {sg1, sg2}
        end
    end
end
foreach SET<VariationPoint>: sg ∈ subgraphs do        // Derive
 refinements
    GroupRefinement: gr ← GroupRefinement(sg)         // Create
     GroupRefinement
    gr.source ← d.types
    G ← G ∪ gr
end
return G
```

		C	F	M	S	P	I
superType	**C**	R					SPL
	I						SPL
	E						SPL
calls	**M**		SPL		R		
reads	**F**		SPL		R		
	V				SPL		
writes	**F**		SPL		R		
	V				SPL		
checks	**C**				R		
	I				SPL		
	E				SPL		
creates	**C**		SPL		R		
typed	**C**		SPL	SPL	SPL	SPL	
	I		SPL	SPL	SPL	SPL	
	E		SPL	SPL	SPL	SPL	
import	**C**		SPL	SPL	SPL	SPL	
	I		SPL	SPL	SPL	SPL	
	E		SPL	SPL	SPL	SPL	
modifies	**F**				SPL		
	V				SPL		

Table 6.1.: SPLEVO Program Dependency Analysis: Studied program dependencies for the Java programming language
(R = Robillard and Murphy [158], SPL = additionally analyzed by SPLEVO
C = Class, I = Interface, E = Enumeration, M = Method Signature, F = Field, V = Variable, P = Parameter, S = Statement)

7. Consolidation Refactoring

This chapter describes the SPLEVO Consolidation Refactoring phase and the contributions to reduce the manual effort for initializing the refactoring and ensuring a consistent implementation of variability mechanisms. As shown in Figure 7.1, the refactoring phase follows the variability design phase to process an approved variability design. It is subdivided in two activities: deciding how to implement variability at the variation points (i.e., Variability Realization Decision) and the actual refactoring (i.e., Consolidation Refactoring). In a post-processing phase, an optional export to transfer the results to an SPL management tool can take place. The goal of the SPLEVO Consolidation Refactoring phase is to transform the product copies to the future Software Product Line (SPL) as illustrated in Figure 7.2.

The chapter is structured as follows: First, the specification concept for consolidation refactorings that allows for consistent implementation and support of realization decisions is presented in Section 7.1. Following, the support for variability realization decisions is explained in Section 7.2. Next, aspects of the consolidation refactoring activity are described in Section 7.3, before the SPL Export is explained in Section 7.4.

Refactoring overview The realization decision and actual refactoring are based on the Variation Point Model (VPM), the SPL Profile, and the software models representing the implementations of the product copies. The VPM provides the variability design approved by SPL Consolidation Developers and SPL Managers. Hence, it defines the variability to realize in the future SPL. The SPL Profile provides the guidelines how to implement variability in the SPL. It defines the variability mechanisms to choose from as selected by the Software Architects.

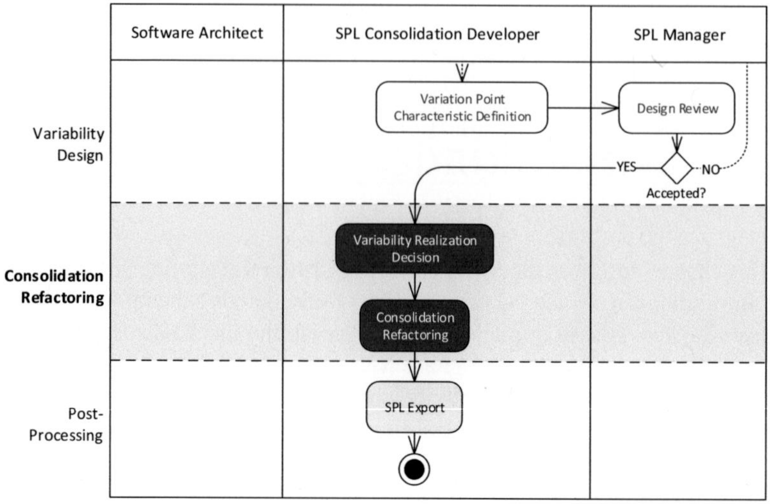

Figure 7.1.: SPLEVO process: Consolidation Refactoring

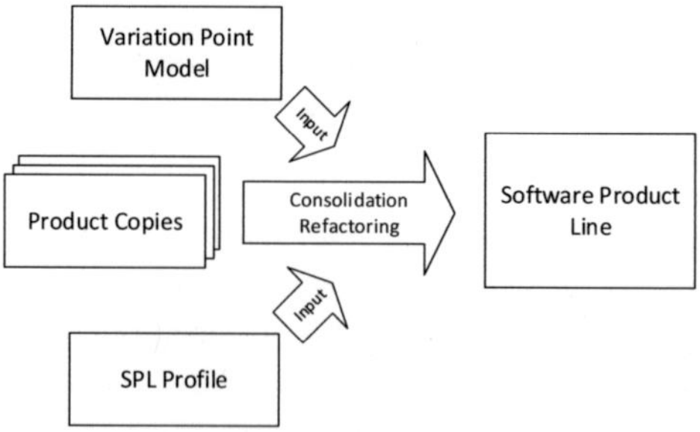

Figure 7.2.: Overview of the SPLEVO consolidation refactoring

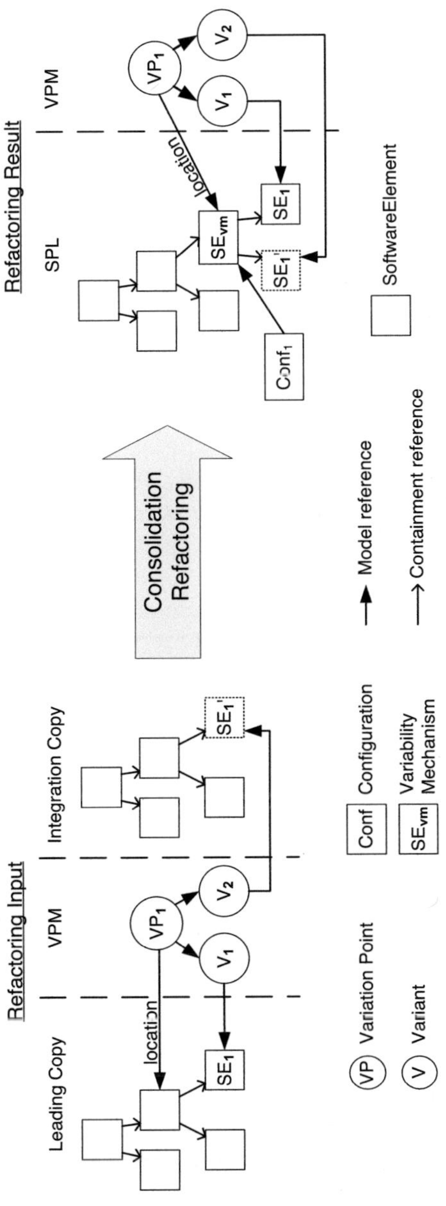

Figure 7.3.: Individual variation point refactoring

Implementation of variability mechanisms Considering an individual Variation Point (VP), the consolidation refactoring brings together the implementing SoftwareElements of its variants and a variability mechanism including a configuration to decide between the alternatives. Figure 7.3 illustrates the refactoring for VP VP_1. The product copy that was selected as Leading Copy serves as code base for the future SPL. The variants of the other product copies are integrated into this code base. A new SoftwareElement SE_{vm} represents the implementation of a variability mechanism and is inserted in the Leading Copy. The SoftwareElements of the product copies SE_1 and SE'_1 become child elements of the new SE_{vm} because they are now controlled by the variability mechanism. Additionally, a configuration element $Conf_1$ is added to decide which alternative should be activated by the variability mechanism represented by SE_{vm}.

Consolidation and traditional refactoring In respect to all product copies, the consolidation refactoring changes their implementations in order to improve their maintainability and configurability. It improves the internal structure of the overall set of product copies without changing the observable behavior from the perspective of a single product configuration (i.e., a product copy). Taking all copies, the resulting SPL, and the configuration into account, the "consolidation refactoring" conforms to the definition of a refactoring given by Fowler et al. [63, page 9].

Nevertheless, the consolidation refactoring comes with additional challenges compared to refactoring in the traditional manner. It has to combine code from several code bases while introducing a variability mechanism and configuration at the same time. In traditional refactoring, developers have to check the motivation of a concrete refactoring to decide if they should refactor at all. In the context of consolidation refactoring, a refactoring is unavoidable to receive an SPL. However, SPL Consolidation Developers still have to decide about the variability mechanism to introduce for a specific VP.

Reduction of manual refactoring effort The overall goal of the SPLEVO approach to reduce the manual effort of SPL Consolidation Developers and supporting a more consistent SPL realization also applies to the consolidation refactoring phase. According to this goal, the SPLEVO approach includes a specification concept to define and process consolidation refactorings (Section 7.1). Based on the refactoring specification concept, the SPLEVO approach provides automation for deciding about the variability mechanisms to use for individual VPs (Section 7.2). Furthermore, the refactoring specification concept is designed to support changing the implementation itself, which is denoted as "consolidation refactoring" (Section 7.3).

Not predetermined refactorings The SPLEVO approach does not include a predefined set of fixed refactoring specifications. The broad range of variability mechanisms, the varying shapes of similar mechanisms, and the varying company-specific requirements and preferences of implementing variability rarely allow for reusing the same set of refactorings in different consolidation scenarios. Instead, the refactoring specification concept allows for defining individual sets of refactorings to ensure consistency within a defined scope (e.g., a company).

Finally, the SPLEVO approach defines a concept to export the resulting SPL to SPL management tools for a continuous management.

7.1. Consolidation Refactoring Specification Concept

The SPLEVO approach designates Software Architects to specify a set of intended variability mechanisms with an SPL Profile (Section 3.3). Thus, SPL Consolidation Developers can choose from a consistent set of mechanisms.

To further ensure a consistent implementation of variability mechanisms, the SPLEVO approach provides a specification concept for specifying of consolidation refactorings. This concept allows for defining the variability mechanism introduced by a refactoring, the included configuration mechanism, and a description of how the consolidation refactoring must be performed. The variability mechanism is specified with its realized variability characteristics as well as additional descriptive information. This allows for supporting Software Architects in selecting mechanisms as part of the SPL Profile (Section 3.3.3). Furthermore, it allows for supporting

SPL Consolidation Developers in deciding which variability mechanism to use for an individual VPs. Finally, a detailed description of how to refactor different types of SoftwareElements allows for limiting the variety of shapes of the same variability mechanism.

The SPLEVO refactoring specification concept is derived from the refactoring specifications defined by Fowler et al. [63]. It provides descriptive information to support developers in deciding for a refactoring or not (e.g., motivations and short descriptions). Furthermore, it calls for mechanics that describe how to perform a refactoring without determining any automation.

The SPLEVO approach defines a data model for refactoring specifications allowing for standardized specifications and enabling automated utilization. Figure 7.4 presents a class diagram of the data model for refactoring specifications.

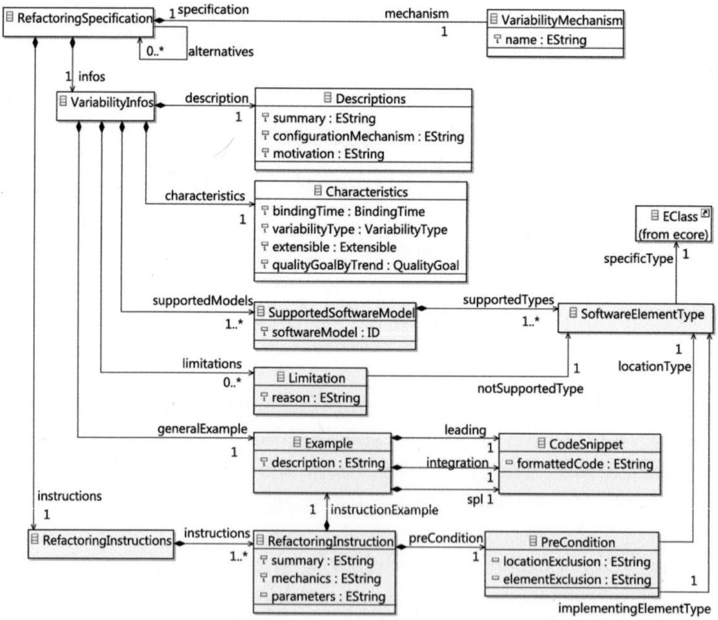

Figure 7.4.: Refactoring specification data model

A refactoring specification consists of the VariabilityMechanism it realizes. In addition, it contains two main parts: VariabilityInfos and RefactoringInstructions. The former provides information about the variability mechanism and the refactoring in general. The latter specifies how to refactor specific types of SoftwareElements.

7.1.1. Variability Infos

The VariabilityInfos contain descriptions such as a short summary, a description of the configuration mechanism that will be introduced, and the motivation when to use the specific refactoring. The latter describes the advantages and disadvantages of the implementation of the variability mechanism. The descriptions are informal and intended to give Software Architects and SPL Consolidation Developers an idea of the result.

In addition, the VariabilityInfos contain a set of characteristics supported by the variability mechanism introduced by the refactoring. The Binding Time, Variability Type, and Extensible definitions conform to those defined for VPs in a VPM and allowed characteristics in the SPL Profile. The quality goal by trend conforms to the quality goals of the SPL Profile. Accordingly, it is a subjective assessment of the person who specified the refactoring. Thus, it gives a direction only to decide about alternative refactorings providing the same characteristics.

Furthermore, the VariabilityInfos define the types of SoftwareElements supported by the specified refactoring. For each SoftwareModel supported in general, the supported types of SoftwareElements are defined. A supported software model is defined by a unique ID (e.g., its namespace URI). A type of SoftwareElements is defined by a reference to the according Ecore class. All types of SoftwareElements not explicitly defined as supported, cannot be handled by the refactoring. However, the specification concept and data model allow for providing reasons for types of SoftwareElements that are not supported (i.e., limitations).

Finally, the VariabilityInfos part provides a general example to give an idea about the refactoring respectively its variability mechanism. An example consists of a description and three CodeSnippets illustrating code of the Leading Copy, an Integration Copy, and their representations in the resulting

SPL. The CodeSnippets must not represent a complete and executable piece of code. Instead, they are intended to provide an intuitive illustration of the refactoring.

7.1.2. Refactoring Instructions

The second main part of the SPLEVO refactoring specification concept targets concrete refactoring instructions. For each supported type of SoftwareElement, a refactoring instruction must be specified according to the invariant "InstructionCompleteness" of the OCL constraint in Listing 12. There might be more than one refactoring instruction for the same supported SoftwareElementType. This is necessary because two instances of the same type of software element might require different refactoring mechanics due to their context or shape. For example, a Java statement in a method body requires different mechanics compared to a statement in a static field initialization.

```
context RefactoringSpecification
inv InstructionCompleteness :
  infos.supportedModels.supportedTypes->forAll( st |
    instructions.instructions->preCondition->
          implementingElementType->exists(rt | rt=st)
)
```

Listing 12: Refactoring instruction completeness constraint

A RefactoringInstruction provides mechanics describing how to perform a refactoring of the according type of SoftwareElement. Similar to Fowler et al. [63], mechanics must be detailed enough to verify a consistent implementation. In the best case, they should allow for automation. Details about different degrees and possibilities for automation are discussed in Section 7.3. However, Fowler et al. [63] specified refactorings for object-oriented languages in general. In contrast to their context, consolidation refactorings that confirm to the specification concept of the SPLEVO approach are defined for concrete software models (i.e., supportedModels). This allows for describing mechanics based on the concrete types and references defined in the metamodel of a software model.

As shown in Figure 7.4, each RefactoringInstruction contains a PreCondition element that identifies the types of software elements for the VariationPoint location (i.e., locationType) and the elements implementing the Variants (i.e., implementingElementType). Furthermore, the PreCondition element contains two attributes to describe exclusions for the location and implementing elements. For example, a refactoring instruction for variable declaration statement elements cannot be applied if the type of a declared variable has been modified. Such exclusions specify the cases when the refactoring cannot be applied.

The mechanics are not limited in their type and scope. Larger refactorings introducing new elements or new resources are possible, too. This allows for introducing even more complex variability mechanisms, such as exchangeable components. Furthermore, it allows for coping with limitations of individual variability mechanisms.

For example, using Aspect Oriented Programming (AOP) with AspectJ does not allow for varying statements in the middle of methods [93] (Section 2.3.3.3). Instead of excluding such types of elements, refactoring mechanics can be specified to extract a new method encapsulating the varying statements and to use AOP to varying the body of the method.

Finally, a RefactoringInstruction includes an example illustrating how SoftwareElements of the treated type are handled (i.e., instructionExample). RefactoringInstruction-specific examples are defined similar to general examples. They should provide CodeSnippets representing code of Leading and Integration Copies, as well as of the resulting SPL.

Figure 7.5 and Figure 7.6 present word processor templates to specify the VariabilityInfos part respectively individual instructions of a refactoring. An example application of this template for a concrete variability mechanism as well as concrete refactoring instructions are provided in Appendix A.1.

<table>
<tr><th colspan="4"><Name></th></tr>
<tr><td colspan="4">Summary</td></tr>
<tr><td colspan="4"><Abstract></td></tr>
<tr><td colspan="4">Configuration Mechanism</td></tr>
<tr><td colspan="4"><Description of the configuration mechanism></td></tr>
<tr><td colspan="4">Motivation</td></tr>
<tr><td colspan="4"><(Dis-)Advantages of using this refactoring></td></tr>
<tr><td colspan="2">Supported Characteristics</td><td colspan="2">Supported Elements</td></tr>
<tr><td>Binding Time</td><td><Selection></td><td colspan="2"><Concrete Software Model></td></tr>
<tr><td>Variability Type</td><td><Selection></td><td colspan="2" rowspan="2"><Supported types of SoftwareElements></td></tr>
<tr><td>Extensible</td><td><Selection></td></tr>
<tr><td colspan="2">Quality Goal by trend</td><td colspan="2"><Selection></td></tr>
<tr><td colspan="4">Limitations</td></tr>
<tr><td colspan="4"><Types of SoftwareElements not supported by the mechanism incl. a reason></td></tr>
<tr><td colspan="4">Alternatives</td></tr>
<tr><td colspan="4"><Alternative refactorings providing the same characteristics></td></tr>
<tr><td colspan="4">Example</td></tr>
<tr><td colspan="4"><Description of the example general example given below></td></tr>
<tr><td colspan="3">Leading</td><td>Integration</td></tr>
<tr><td colspan="3"><code><Code of the leading copy></code></td><td><code><Code of the integration copy></code></td></tr>
<tr><td colspan="4">Refactored SPL</td></tr>
<tr><td colspan="4"><code><Resulting SPL code including configuration></code></td></tr>
</table>

Figure 7.5.: Word processor template for refactoring specifications: Variability info part

Instruction: <SoftwareElementType>	
Summary	
<Abstract>	
Preconditions	
Location	
Element	<SoftwareElementType>
Exclusion	<Exclusion>
Implementing Elements	
Element	<SoftwareElementType>
Exclusion	<Exclusion>
Example	
<description of the general example given below>	
Leading	**Integration**
`<code of the leading copy>`	`<code of the integration copy>`
Refactored SPL	
`<resulting SPL code including configuration>`	
Additional Parameters	
<Type>: <Name>: <Description>	
Mechanics	
<Summary of the mechanics concept>	
`<pseudo code based on metamodel specifying the refactoring process>`	

Figure 7.6.: Word processor template for refactoring specifications: Refactoring instructions part

7.2. Variability Realization Decision

The first step of the Consolidation Refactoring phase of the SPLEVO process is to decide how to realize the variability of each VP. This is done by assigning a VariabilityMechanim to a VP according to the metamodel references shown in Figure 7.7.

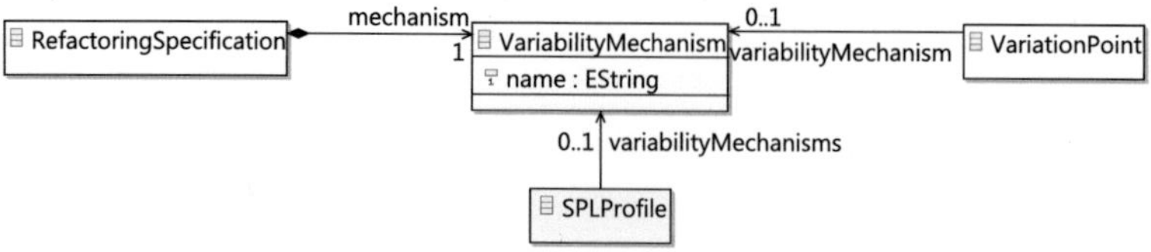

Figure 7.7.: Variability mechanism assignment

All VariabilityMechanisms assigned to VPs must have been specified in the SPL Profile. On the one side, this enables SPL Consolidation Developers to choose from a given set of mechanisms instead of finding mechanisms from scratch. On the other side, if no applicable mechanism has been defined in the SPL Profile, a communication with the Software Architects to improve the SPL guidelines is stimulated. Hence, unnoticed introductions of new VariabilityMechanisms are avoided. Listing 13 defines a constraint with an according invariant.

```
context VariationPoint
inv SPLProfileVariabilityMechanisms :
    variabilityMechanism <> null
     implies splProfile.variabilityMechanisms->
           exists(vm | vm=variabilityMechanism)
```

Listing 13: SPL Profile VariabilityMechanisms only constraint

Beside the need to respect the predefined set of VariabilityMechansisms, SPL Consolidation Developers have to take the required characteristics of a VP into account. The SPLEVO approach proposes automation for recommending Variability Mechanisms for individual VPs, as described in the following section. Afterwards, Section 7.2.2 describes strategies to handle VPs that could not be assigned with a VariabilityMechanism automatically.

7.2.1. Variability Mechanism Recommendation

The SPLEVO approach provides an automated recommendation of VariabilityMechanisms for VPs. This allows for releasing the SPL Consolidation Developers from manually checking VariabilityMechanisms whether they can be applied for the individual VPs.

Selecting VariabilityMechanisms requires to check several criteria for the individual VPs. On one side, all characteristics required by a VP have to be provided by a VariabilityMechanism. On the other side, the refactoring providing the VariabilityMechanism has to support all SoftwareElements implementing the Variants of the VP.

The SPLEVO approach defines a set of rules to evaluate those criteria. These rules are specified as invariants of the OCL constraint in Listing 14 and allow for automation. The automation is done by checking the VariabilityMechanisms defined in the SPL Profile for each VP a mechanism should be assigned to. The VariabilityMechanisms are checked in the order of their definition in the SPL Profile. For each pair of VP and VariabilityMechanism, the rules are evaluated until a VariabilityMechanism can be assigned. If all invariants are satisfied, the VariabilityMechanism is assigned to the VP. If at least one invariant is not satisfied, the evaluation stops and continues with the next VariabilityMechanism to check.

The minimum number of checks mentioned above is not reduced by those rules. Hence, the worst-case of the checks is that none of the VariabilityMechanisms is assignable to any of the VPs, but only the last invariant is not fulfilled for each of the mechanisms. The according worst-case computation complexity is $O(n) = n^2$ with the available VariabilityMechanisms and the VPs as input.

However, with the number of VPs to be expected in a consolidation scenario, this complexity is acceptable for automation, but it is not acceptable to be done manually in terms of effort and probability of human error.

```
context VariationPoint

inv Characteristics :
    variabilityMechanism <> null
      implies variabilityMechanism.specification.infos.
          characteristics.variabilityType = self.variabilityType
      and variabilityMechanism.specification.infos.characteristics.
          bindingTime = self.bindingTime
      and variabilityMechanism.specification.infos.characteristics.
          extensible = self.extensible

inv SupportedElementTypes :
    variabilityMechanism <> null
      implies variants.implementingElements.getWrappedElements()->
          forAll(ie | variabilityMechanism.specification.
        infos.supportedModels.supportedTypes->
          exists(t | ie.oclIsTypeOf(t.specificType)
        )
      )
```

Listing 14: Rules of the VariabilityMechanism applicability check

7.2.2. Manual Review and Refinement

The SPLEVO approach allows for manually reviewing the assigned VariabilityMechanisms. This can be necessary because of two reasons: adjustment to individual preferences and handling of VPs no VariabilityMechanism could be assigned to.

The necessity of an adjustment can result from SPL Consolidation Developers' expert knowledge about the use of the future product variants. For example, the Software Architects' guidelines and preferences might be satisfied by the auto assigned VariabilityMechanism. But, an alternative mechanism, providing the same characteristics, probably better fits to the knowledge of the Software Developers responsible to maintain specific VPs in the future.

In case of VPs that could not be assigned with a VariabilityMechanism, the set of mechanisms defined by Software Architects is not sufficient for the specific consolidation scenario. To solve such issues, SPL Consolidation

Developers can collaborate with Software Architects to extend the set of VariabilityMechanisms. Probably, an existing refactoring can be adapted to support the affected VPs as well, such as for the AspectJ example given in Section 7.1. If done, the auto recommendation can be used with the extended set of mechanisms, or the SPL Consolidation Developers can manually assign the not yet assigned VPs. As an alternative strategy, SPL Consolidation Developers can check the VPM for reasonable adaptations. Here, reasonable means to adapt the VP structures and characteristics to still represent a satisfying variability design, but allowing for using one of the previously defined VariabilityMechanisms. Thus, the set of VariabilityMechanisms must not be extended.

7.3. Consolidation Refactoring

The consolidation refactoring activity within the SPLEVO process is about the actual transformation of the implementations of the product copies to the future SPL. With reference to the SPLEVO refactoring specifications, this is about executing the mechanics specified by the refactoring specifications. The activity is denoted as "consolidation refactoring". This explicitly extends the traditional term "refactoring", as without a concrete configuration, no statement about changed or unchanged behavior can be given.

As described in Section 7.1, the specification of the mechanics must be detailed enough to transform the implementations with no significant variety (e.g., except for varying formatting). Such detailed mechanics are possible because the VPM resulting from the preceding process provides detailed references to the SoftwareElements to process. This further allows for different degrees of automation of the mechanics. The possible degrees include a full automated refactoring, completely manual refactoring, as well as a mixture of those two extremes. The degree of automation for a specific VariabilityMechanism depends on the mechanism itself and the preferences of SPL Consolidation Developers and Software Architects. For example, automating complex refactorings which are rarely applied might be out of proportion to the effort for building the automation. Nevertheless, other complex refactorings might be used frequently and justify a high effort for their automation.

7.3.1. Manual Refactoring

Manual refactoring product copies into the future SPL comes with the risk of differing implementations according to individual programming styles. Furthermore, the risk of manual faults and a higher manual effort are given by nature. Nevertheless, some developers reported their preference for manual refactoring to perform a code review while performing the refactorings (Section 8.5).

However, the SPLEVO approach provides the necessary information for generating task descriptions to support carrying out the specified mechanics manually. To reduce the risk of varying implementations, those descriptions must be as detailed as possible. In general, three levels of task descriptions can be generated based on the information provided by a VPM: issues descriptions, task contexts, and code annotations.

Issue tracking and management systems allow for describing tasks to perform and help to coordinate their resolution (Section 2.4.1.2). Such issues are typically more vague and provide an informal description of what has to be done (e.g., Anvik and Storey [6]).

In contrast, task-oriented software development approaches provide developers with task descriptions as well as a context to perform a task. Approaches such as Eclipse Mylyn [52] are able to provide developers with a context in terms of relevant resources and detailed software elements. However, a description is given for a complete Mylyn task and not on the level of individual SoftwareElements.

Finally, developers are used to document task descriptions within annotations and code comments (e.g., Storey et al. [179]). Depending on guidelines of a specific technology or company, developers use established comment markers to document tasks on the level of software elements. For example, code comments such as "`TODO: ...`" are established when developing with the Eclipse IDE [48], as observed by Storey et al. [179]. As an alternative, there are existing approaches proposing standardized annotations and infrastructures for their handling (e.g., TagSEA [178].

To this degree, generating fine-grained code comments and according entries in an issue tracking system conforms to an approach proposed by Anvik and Storey [6] for supporting manual implementation tasks.

7.3.2. Automated Refactoring

Automated refactorings represent tool supported executions of the mechanics specified as part of the RefactoringInstruction. From the perspective of the goal to reduce the manual effort, automated refactorings are preferred.

The model-based concept of the SPLEVO approach allows for two strategies for automation: model transformation and integration with traditional refactoring infrastructures.

The model transformation strategy facilitates the model-based representations of the implementations, manipulates them, and finally persists their textual representations (e.g., source code). Today, many different types of infrastructures for model transformation exist (Section 2.1). However, depending on the mechanics, an according infrastructure or even a general-purpose programming-language can be used for developing such transformations.

Facilitating traditional refactoring infrastructures is done by translating the mechanics into operations supported by a specific infrastructure. For example, the refactoring tools provided by the Eclipse JDT [49] provide a set of operations to be reused. Accordingly, the models processed within the SPLEVO consolidation approach are only input for controlling the existing refactoring tools. However, existing refactoring infrastructures cannot be assumed to provide all necessary operations and additional ones might need to be added.

7.4. SPL Export

To enable a continuous management of the future SPL, the SPLEVO approach proposes to export the variability design to existing mature SPL management tools (Section 2.2.6). Such tools typically support some kind of feature model and allow for building feature hierarchies to support product management needs. The Variation Point Groups (VPGs), VPs, and variants represent the lowest level of such feature models and are sufficient for an according export. The feature hierarchy for the product management perspective can be added on top of these features afterwards.

The VPM metamodel is already integrated with the EMF Feature Model metamodel (Section 2.3.2). Thus, the capability of exporting this model is given by design. Furthermore, the EMF Feature Model represents a public definition of a feature model and is supported by widely accepted tools, such as pure::variants [66].

Additionally, we successfully proved the compatibility with the metamodels of the FeatureMapper [79] as a representative for other SPL management tools using a proprietary feature model.

8. Evaluation

This chapter presents the evaluation of the approach presented in this thesis. The evaluation was performed aligned to the hypotheses advanced by this thesis. The following section provides an overview of the evaluation, introduces the evaluation concept, and explains the overall structure of this chapter.

8.1. Evaluation Overview

The SPLEVO approach was applied in open source and industrial case studies. Furthermore, interviews and a survey with industrial participants were performed to validate its contributions. This covers the results of the individual analyses as well as the applicability of the analyses and the overall process in practice.

Validated categories of contributions The SPLEVO approach aims for the categories of process-, people, and product-oriented contributions to the field of software engineering. First, following the proposed process and applying the analyses reduces the manual efforts and leads to more consistent consolidations. Second, due to the provided guidance of developers, it requires less decisions and knowledge by the individual roles. And third, the resulting products respectively the resulting Software Product Line (SPL) benefit not only from the advantages of an SPLs approach in general, but also from the more consistently realized variability. However, this evaluation focuses on the achievement of a consistent variability realization and not on the SPL advantages in general. The latter strongly depends on the variability mechanisms introduced and personal or organizational preferences.

Achieved levels of validation according to Böhme and Reussner Different levels of validation as defined by Böhme and Reussner [19] were achieved for the individual contributions (Section 2.5.2). A prototype was implemented for the approach (level 0) to validate the results of the difference and variability analyses (level 1). Validations of the applicability of the approach in practice (level 2) were performed by proving the availability of the necessary roles to provide the required input. The former was validated by interviews and a survey about the availability of roles providing required data and decisions in practice. The latter was validated by applying the prototype to realistic software systems. A study about the economic benefit (level 3) of the overall consolidation approach could not be performed due to the unavailability of an appropriate setup. However, the individual contributions were investigated with regard to the reduction of manual effort. According measurements were identified and industrial partners were asked for assessments where possible.

Section 8.2.3 provides an overview of the evaluation strategies used to answer each evaluation question and classifies them according to their respective level of validation. Table 8.1 summarizes the evaluation questions, used strategies, and achieved validation levels for each of them.

Summary of the overall results The evaluation corroborates the overall hypotheses from different points of view and based on case studies as well as interviews and surveys. Furthermore, insight into different analysis strategies and shapes of their optimizations was discovered. In total, the SPLEVO approach was satisfyingly validated and the expected values of the different analysis strategies were confirmed. In particular, the industrial applicability of the approach was shown.

Structure of the evaluation The presentation of the evaluation is structured as follows: The evaluation concept aligned with the research hypotheses is presented in Section 8.2. The SPLEVO prototype to evaluate the approach is described in Section 8.3. The case studies performed are introduced in Section 8.4 and an overview of the interviews and survey is provided in Section 8.5. Sections 8.6, 8.7, 8.8, and 8.9 present the details of the validations and are structured according to the hypotheses. Finally,

Section 8.10 discusses possible threats to the validity of the evaluation before Section 8.11 summarizes the results of the evaluation.

8.2. Evaluation Concept

An evaluation concept was developed to evaluate the SPLEVO approach. It is based on the claimed problem statements (Section 1.2) and the derived hypotheses (Section 1.3). The concept is inspired by the Goal Question Metric (GQM) approach proposed by Basili and Weiss [10]. The goal to achieve is to validate the hypotheses of this thesis based on the proposed SPLEVO approach.

Figure 8.1 presents the structure of the evaluation concept. Evaluation questions were defined for each hypothesis and metrics were identified to answer these questions in a traceable manner. For the sake of clarity, the diagram only indicates the metrics. Details about the metrics are presented in the according sections of the evaluation. The following subsections introduce the evaluation questions derived for each hypothesis.

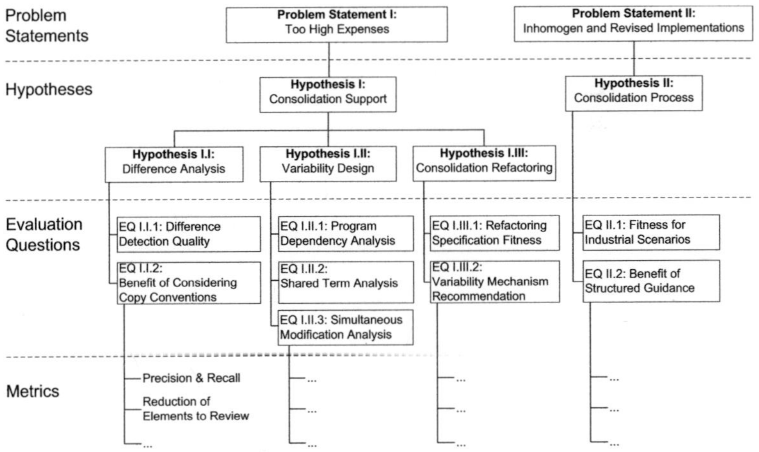

Figure 8.1.: Evaluation structure

8.2.1. Hypothesis I: Consolidation Support

Hypothesis I "Consolidation Support" splits into three sub-hypotheses and so do its evaluation questions. The according contributions must seamlessly integrate with each other to validate Hypothesis I based on the results of the sub-hypotheses. This integration is ensured by individual contributions building upon each other, and each sub-hypothesis is evaluated based on the results of its predecessors. Furthermore, the contributions seamlessly integrate on a technical level, as it is described for the prototype in Section 8.3. The following subsections describe the sub-hypotheses as well as the according evaluation questions.

8.2.1.1. Hypothesis I.I: Difference Analysis

Hypothesis I.I proposes that a consolidation process will benefit from a difference analysis adapted for consolidation scenarios. To corroborate this hypothesis, two aspects of the adapted difference analysis must be examined: its detection quality and its benefit. First, the quality of the difference detection must be proved to allow for a fully automated processing. Second, the benefit of considering copy-based customization conventions, such as detecting Derived Copy patterns, must be proven. These evaluation goals are refined into two evaluation questions:

> **Evaluation Question I.I.1: Difference Detection Quality**
> Does the difference analysis reliably detect differences between the customized product copies to allow for a fully automated process?
>
> **Evaluation Question I.I.2: Benefit of Considering Copy Conventions**
> To which degree does the consideration of copy-based customization conventions reduce false-positive differences?

8.2.1.2. Hypothesis I.II: Variability Design

Hypothesis I.II proposes that analyzing relationships between Variation Points (VPs) allows for supporting variability design decisions. This hypothesis can be assessed in context of concrete relationship analyses only, but general observations can be deduced from their results. Accordingly, evaluation questions for this hypothesis were elaborated for the concrete analyses studied in detail.

Evaluation Question I.II.1: Program Dependency Analysis
To which degree does the analysis of program dependencies help identifying related variation points?

Evaluation Question I.II.2: Shared Term Analysis
To which degree does the analysis of shared terms help identifying related variation points?

Evaluation Question I.II.3: Simultaneous Modification Analysis
To which degree does the analysis of commits and commit messages help identifying related variation points?

8.2.1.3. Hypothesis I.III: Consolidation Refactoring

Hypothesis I.III proposes that a refactoring specific for the consolidation of customized product copies allows for achieving consistent SPLs. The best evaluation question to corroborate this hypothesis would ask for the results of two parallel consolidation projects, one of them carried out with the SPLEVO approach and the other one without. However, such a level 3 validation could not be performed due to the unavailability of an appropriate setup. Instead, evaluation questions were raised about the fitness of the specification concept and the related recommendation system.

Evaluation Question I.III.1: Refactoring Specification Fitness
Is the refactoring specification formalism sufficient for specifying unambiguous refactorings?

Evaluation Question I.III.2: Variability Mechanism Recommendation
To which degree does the recommendation system reduce the manual effort for decision-making and the risk of inconsistent decisions?

8.2.2. Hypothesis II: Consolidation Process

Hypothesis II proposes that a structured consolidation process with clear roles and explicit activities enables consistent variability implementations and reduces coordination overheads. To corroborate this hypothesis, two evaluation questions were raised about the fitness of the process itself and the benefits to expect.

> **Evaluation Question II.1: Fitness for Industrial Scenarios**
> To which degree does the process fit into industrial scenarios?
>
> **Evaluation Question II.2: Benefit of Structured Guidance**
> Do consolidation projects benefit from the guidance provided by the explicit process?

8.2.3. Evaluation Strategies

The evaluation questions stated above are answered with different strategies. Table 8.1 provides an overview about which question was targeted with which type of strategy. Here, "Case Study" means that the SPLEVO prototype was applied to the according case studies and the evaluation question is answered based on metrics captured within the case study. Interviews (I) and Survey (S) means that the evaluation question is answered based on the answers given by the participants. Argumentation (A) means that a line of argumentation is used to answer the evaluation question.

Achieved levels of validation according to Böhme and Reussner In the cells of Table 8.1, the achieved validation levels according to Böhme and Reussner [19] are identified. The SPLEVO Difference Analysis and SPLEVO Variability Analysis were validated up to level 3 (benefit) by applying them in industrial and open source case studies, and measuring the benefit in terms of reduced elements to be review by developers. A comparing manual analysis performed by developers was not possible because of the unavailability of an unbiased control group.

Evaluation Question	**Case Study**		**I**	**S**	**A**
	ArgoUML	xRM			
I.I.1: Difference Detection Quality	3				
I.I.2: Benefit of Considering Copy Conventions		3			
I.II.1: Program Dependency Analysis	3	3			
I.II.2: Shared Term Analysis	3	3			
I.II.3: Simultaneous Modification Analysis					2
I.III.1: Refactoring Specification Fitness	2		2		2
I.III.2: Variability Mechanism Recommendation					2
II.1: Fitness for Industrial Scenarios			2	2	
II.2: Benefit of Structured Guidance			2		2

Table 8.1.: Evaluation questions, strategies, validation levels
(I = Interviews, S = Survey, A = Argumentation; 0-3 = level of validation;
ArgoUML = open source case study, xRM = industrial case study)

The contributions for achieving a consistent refactoring and the proposed overarching consolidation process were validated up to level 2 (industrial applicability) by a survey and interviews with industrial participants.

The simultaneous modification analysis could not be validated in a case study because of the unavailability of input data. Thus, we could only argue about it is meaningful and refer to reports of others about the availability of the required input data in other scenarios.

8.2.4. Execution Times

Performance ratios in terms of execution times are provided for the analyses. They provide a dimension of the individual execution times and were measured during the evaluation. They typically result from single executions and have not been studied in extensive performance experiments without impacts from other processes. Nevertheless, developers typically run several applications in parallel in their development environment. Thus, the presented execution times provide valid estimations for applying the analyses in practice.

8.3. SPLevo Prototype

To evaluate the SPLEVO approach, a prototype of the approach was implemented. It is designed to perform the case studies and allows for observing details of the results and the processing. The individual activities were implemented and connected to each other to prove their integration according to the proposed process. Furthermore, the prototype provides a user interface integrated in the widely used Eclipse [48] development environment. The integrated user interface was included to involve industrial stakeholders in the industrial case study.

The prototype reflects the technology-independent approach as well as the adaptability for technology-specific improvements. The product copies investigated in the case studies are realized with Java technology. Thus, an adaptation for the Java technology was developed as well. The prototype and the technology adaptation are publicly available at GitHub [96].

The following subsections introduce the architecture of the prototype, summarize integrated external components, and describe the user interface to provide input and present results.

8.3.1. Prototype Architecture

The SPLEVO prototype was designed with a component architecture providing the technology-independent infrastructure and process as well as extension points for technology-specific components. The Java-specific adaptation was developed according to these extension points and based on the JaMoPP [78] infrastructure for handling Java source code.

Main Components Figure 8.2 shows a component diagram of the main components of the prototype. The SPLEVO *UI* component realizes the integration in the Eclipse Integrated Development Environment (IDE) and the user interface for providing input, accessing results, and controlling the process. The components *Extraction*, *Diffing*, and *VPM Initialization* are technical components realizing the actions performed as part of the difference analysis (Section 5). The *VPM Analysis* component provides infrastructure for realizing relationship analyses and tracing details of the results of an analysis (Section 6.1.4). The *VPM Refinement* component is responsible for deriving the refinement recommendations from the results of relationship analyses (Section 6.1.4.2). The *Consolidation Refactoring* component includes infrastructure for specifying, recommending, and applying consolidation refactorings (Section 7).

Types of component interfaces The *SPL Export* component defines the interface and an extension point for SPL management tool-specific exports. The *VPM* component is a central component encapsulating the Variation Point Model (VPM) metamodel and editing infrastructure. In addition to standard interfaces to assemble components, several components are defined with interfaces for technology-specific (i.e., blue-colored sockets in Figure 8.2) and scenario-specific (i.e., green-colored sockets in Figure 8.2) adaptations. In this context, "technology-specific" relates to any adaptation to support a concrete technology. "Scenario-specific" relates to any other adaptation in terms of content. Thus, "scenario-specific" adaptations can be created for a single consolidation project or reused in several ones.

Included technology and scenario adaptations For example, the *JaMoPP Java Cartridge* component provides Java-specific adaptations of interfaces for technology-specific adaptations. In addition, the *Shared Term Analyzer* and the *JaMoPP Program Dependency Analyzer* represent scenario-specific adaptations. The *JaMoPP Program Dependency Analyzer* is also related to a specific technology. However, its main purpose is to provide an extension in terms of content not in terms of technology. Additionally, the *Shared Term Analyzer* can be adapted by a technology-specific extension again. Similarly, the *FeatureMapper Connector* and the *EMF FM Connector* components realize scenario-specific adaptations to export the future SPL into the according models.

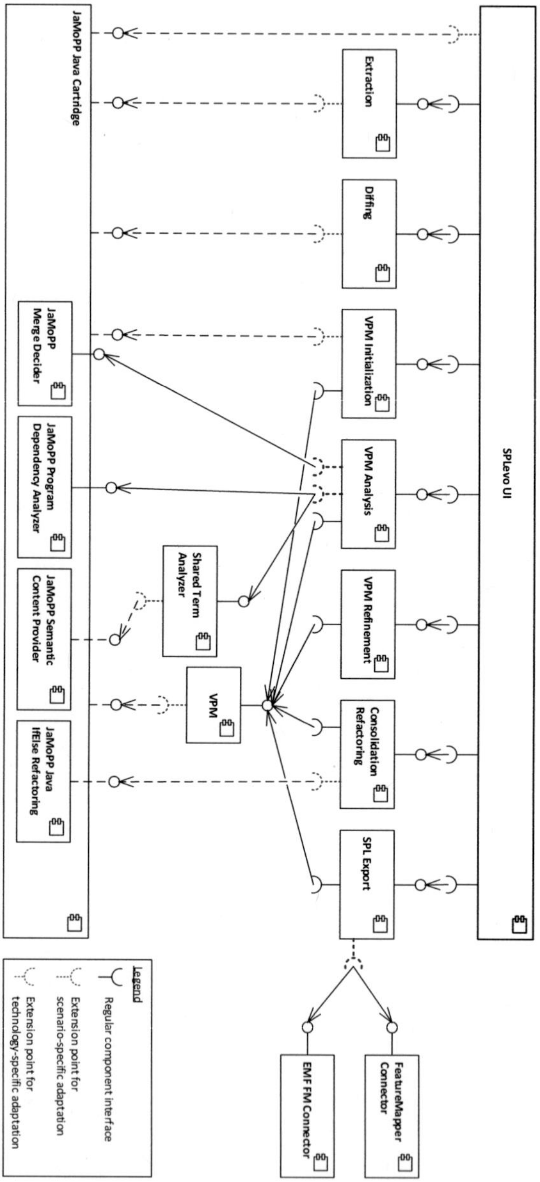

Figure 8.2.: SPLEVO prototype component architecture

Eclipse / OSGi platform The SPLEVO prototype was developed with Java technology and is based on the Eclipse platform. The prototype integrates not only with the Eclipse IDE but also with the Eclipse platform as an extensible component framework according to the OSGi specification [143]. The OSGi platform is used to realize the components described as part of the architecture above. Furthermore, the adaptability of the SPLEVO prototype is realized with the Eclipse plug-in infrastructure.

8.3.2. Integrated Components

The prototype reuses infrastructure provided by several external components. The most important ones are described below.

Eclipse MDSD Infrastructure The prototype reuses the infrastructure for metamodel definition and model processing of the Eclipse Modeling Framework (EMF) (Section 2.1). Several infrastructures of EMF, such as code generation at development time, model resource handling at run time, and EMF Compare for model comparison, are reused.

In particular for EMF Compare, the prototype reuses infrastructure for difference model realization but does not use any of the EMF Compare comparison algorithms. The latter are too generic and imply too many heuristics to be used for a fully automated difference detection as targeted by the SPLEVO approach.

Model Extraction The SPLEVO prototype reuses the EMFText [77] infrastructure to gain EMF-based model representations of textual artifacts. Models extracted by this infrastructure conform to the structure of software models defined and supported by the SPLEVO approach in general (Definition 7). The Java Model Parser and Printer (JaMoPP [78]) is used to extract EMF-based software models from Java source code. It is built on top of EMFText and provides Java-specific reference resolving and utilities for model processing.

The SPLEVO prototype adds a cache for reference resolving on top of the JaMoPP extraction infrastructure. This allows for coping with the challenge of time-consuming reference resolving when it comes to software model extraction and downstream model accesses (Section 2.4.6). If an element reference was resolved considering the Java-specific resolving strategies (e.g., respecting the scope of a variable reference), it is captured by the cache. The next time this reference must be resolved, it is directly provided by the cache without the need of evaluating the resolving strategies again.

Language Analysis The Shared Term Analysis realized as part of the prototype reuses infrastructure of the Lucene [75] project (Section 2.4.10). Lucene provides infrastructure such as the inverted index and either extends or reuses algorithms for splitting, stemming, and filtering (Section 6.4.3).

User Interface The user interface is primarily built upon infrastructure provided by the Eclipse IDE. In addition, components such as the ZEST framework [53] for graph visualization are reused from the Eclipse Modeling Framework.

8.3.3. User Interface for Input and Results

The prototype integrates in the Eclipse user interface to allow for controlling the process, providing input, and reviewing results. The product copies to consolidate can be provided as Eclipse projects within the Eclipse workspace. Figure 8.3 shows a screenshot of the main perspective of the prototype.

Basic UI components The SPLEVO dashboard is shown in the lower right corner of the screenshot. It includes tabs for the different configurations and buttons to start process activities. In the left margin, a resource tree presents the VPs per resource (i.e., a resource-oriented view on VPs). In the lower left corner, the feature outline presents the Variation Point Groups (VPGs). Each of the VPGs can be expanded to show its containing VPs that contribute to the same feature (i.e., a feature-oriented view on VPs). On the right of the feature outline, the properties view allows for configuring the variability characteristics of a selected VP.

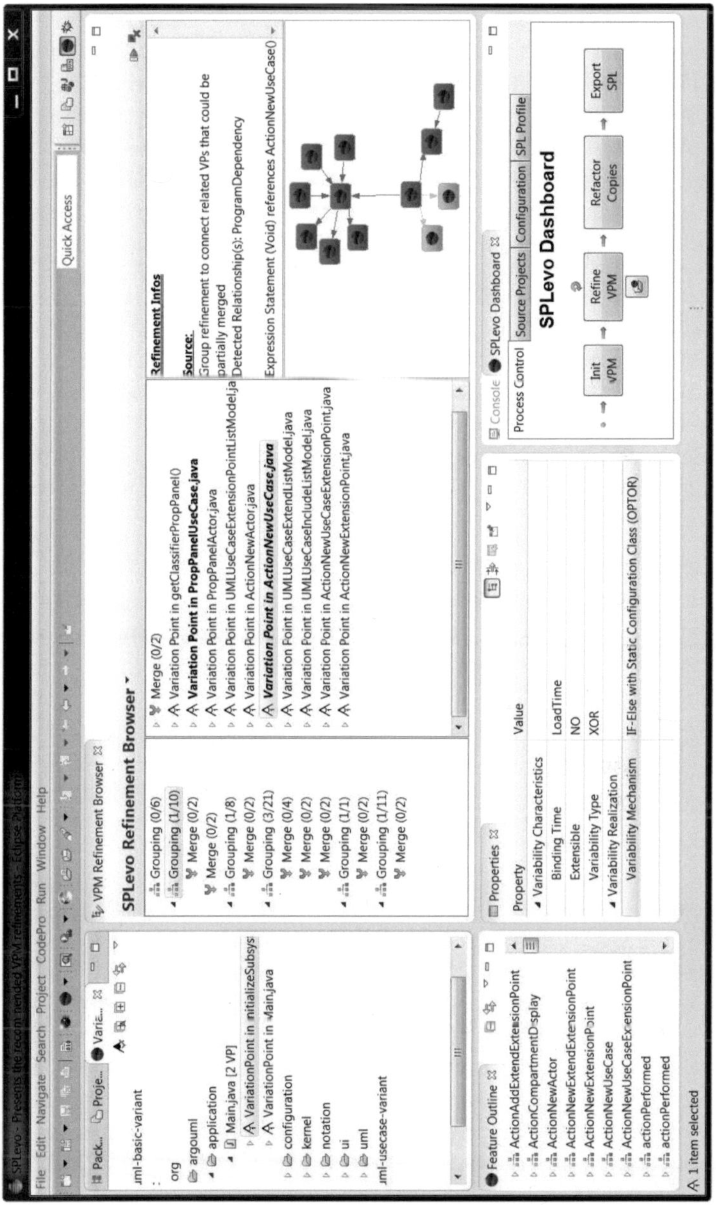

Figure 8.3.: SPLevo prototype screenshot

Refinement browser Finally, in the main area, the refinement browser shows refinement recommendations resulting from an analysis. The first column presents the actual refinement recommendations. The second column shows the VPs and sub-refinements of the recommended refinement selected in the first column. Finally, the third column provides additional information about the relationships of the currently selected refinement as well as a graph visualization of the related VPs. The latter simplifies the identification of VPs with many relationships. Such VPs are typically a reasonable starting point to decide about accepting a recommended refinement.

Data access (Input and Output) The prototype distinguishes between two types of data access: for stakeholders and for evaluation purposes. Any data accessed by stakeholders is available or editable through the prototype User Interface (UI). Data to perform the evaluation of the approach, such as intermediate results or traces of the analyzers, is available through data sensors and log files.

Configurations for the overall process are provided through the dashboard or an initialization wizard for starting a new consolidation. Configurations during the process are done through according wizards and forms (e.g., configuring an analysis to execute).

8.4. Case Study Systems

The SPLEVO approach was evaluated in two case studies on systems with different characteristics. First, the open source Unified Modeling Language (UML) modeling tool ArgoUML is used, which once gained industrial acceptance. It is of reasonable size and available with feature-specific annotated code. These annotations provide a benchmark for the evaluation of the feature-specific code. Second, customized copies of components of a commercial software system provided by an industrial partner were studied. The copies were created over several years under real-life conditions and with copy-based customization guidelines in place. The copies neither provide pre-documented feature-specific code nor have been consolidated before. However, a developer of the company was available throughout the case study to assess the quality of the findings from a stakeholder's perspective.

8.4.1. ArgoUML Modeling Tool

ArgoUML is an open source UML modeling tool that was widely used until 2011 (e.g., more than 250,000 downloads in 2005 [34]). Meanwhile, a commercial fork and many free alternative tools caused the ArgoUML development to nearly stop. However, one can argue that the modeling tool was accepted by the industry and evolved for a reasonable time.

Feature-specific code documented by Couto et al. Couto et al. [36] reviewed the ArgoUML implementation and identified feature-specific source code that could be encapsulated and made optional. Figure 8.4 shows a feature tree representing the eight variable features they have identified. Table 8.2 maps these features to acronyms used throughout this evaluation for the sake of brevity. As an ArgoUML sub-project, Couto et al. [36] marked the feature-specific code with preprocessor annotations. These annotations allow for deriving variants of ArgoUML with individual sets of these optional features.

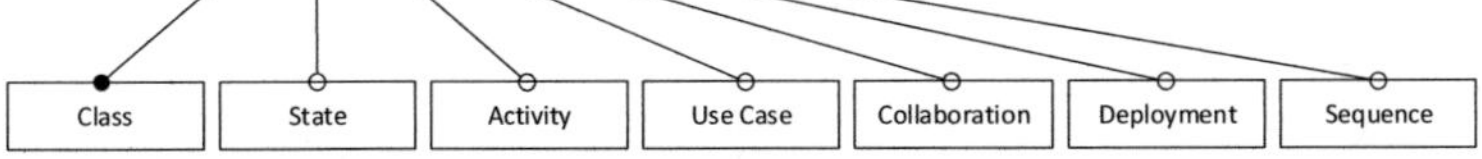

Figure 8.4.: ArgoUML case study: Feature tree [36]

ArgoUML implementation facts According to Couto et al. [36], the original ArgoUML code had 120,348 Source Lines of Code (SLOC). An analysis with CodePro Analytix [69] reported 151,700 SLOC for a variant generated with all optional features enabled and 113,823 SLOC for a variant with all features disabled. We cannot state a reason for the different numbers because Couto et al. [36] have not documented which version of ArgoUML they have used. Furthermore, it is not clear how they counted the lines of code (e.g., Logical Lines of Code (LLOC), Physical Lines of Code (PLOC), or including comments). The metrics we used represent the PLOC according to the documentation of CodePro Analytix: "This is a count of the number of lines in the target elements that contain characters other than white space and comments". Furthermore, revision 155 of the ArgoUML-SPL SVN repository was used throughout the SPLEVO evaluation.

Feature	Token	Feature	Token
Activity	ACT	Logging	LOG
Cognitive	COG	State	STA
Collaboration	COL	Sequence	SEQ
Deployment	DEP	Use Case	USE

Table 8.2.: ArgoUML case study: Features and acronyms

Characteristics of feature-specific code Couto et al. [36] have documented characteristics of the feature-specific code, such as its scattering or the granularity type of modified software elements. These characteristics include numbers of feature-specific code locations for each type of granularity as well. Furthermore, the different features come with different characteristics that can be studied.

Feature-specific code annotations In the code itself, these locations are marked with preprocessor annotations. Additionally, Couto et al. [36] added code comments to the annotations providing further information about the type of modification. Listing 15 shows an example of such a feature-specific code location. The code comments *//#if defined(USECASEDIAGRAM)* and *//#endif* are preprocessor annotations. The format is defined by the Java Preprocessor JavaPP [110] used by Couto et al. [36]. The code comment *//@#$LPS-USECASEDIAGRAM:GranularityType:Statement* identifies that the code belongs to the "UseCase Diagram" feature and has a granularity level of a statement. Couto et al. [36] placed the feature-specific comments inside the preprocessor annotations. Thus, they remain in the code only if the particular feature is activated. This allows for identifying the origin of a feature-specific code during the evaluation.

```
//#if defined(USECASEDIAGRAM)
//@#$LPS-USECASEDIAGRAM:GranularityType:Statement
SubsystemUtility.initSubsystem(new InitUseCaseDiagram());
//#endif
```

Listing 15: ArgoUML feature-specific code annotation example

However, a manual code review identified differences between the annotations in the code and the numbers provided by Couto et al. [36]. Furthermore, the review discovered annotations which were not mentioned in the paper at all (e.g., feature-specific import declarations). Accordingly, we use the annotations found in the code to evaluate the SPLEVO approach instead of the numbers documented in the paper.

ArgoUML variants for evaluation We have used the preprocessor annotations to generate several variants of ArgoUML, each with different features enabled. We applied the SPLEVO approach to these variants and validated the findings with the feature-specific code locations marked by Couto et al. [36]. This evaluation strategy assumes that each feature-specific code is similar to the modifications a developer would have performed to implement this feature in a basic variant of ArgoUML without any of the features enabled.

We applied the SPLEVO approach to pairs of these variants with two strategies. On one side, we analyzed variants with a single feature activated compared to a basic variant with neither of the optional features. By this, we studied the approach focused on the characteristics of the modifications performed for a specific feature (e.g., its scattering in the implementation). On the other side, we applied the SPLEVO approach on a variant with all features activated compared to a basic variant with no features enabled. By this, we studied the approach in a use case with several features implemented in the same product copy.

8.4.2. Industrial Software System

In a second case study, the SPLEVO approach was evaluated with a commercial relationship management software system (referred throughout this thesis as "industrial case study"). The system is approximately ten years old, has a client-server-architecture, and uses Java [70] as fundamental technology and OSGi [143] bundles as component infrastructure. The vendor provides this system to different markets, domains, and customers. To cope with this, the vendor has partly copied and customized the system for several customers. Here, partly means that individual components (i.e., OSGi bundles) were copied and customized.

Components under study For the case study, the vendor provided customized components that were copied and adapted for a specific customer since 2009. Thus, the copies were approximately five years old and evolved when the case study was performed. From the overall set of copied components, developers of the vendor identified two of the components (`Sales` and `Address`) as representative in terms of size and types of modification. The two components were analyzed in the case study compared to their original counterparts. The current versions of the original components were used including any modifications performed on them.

Table 8.3 presents the main characteristics of the components.

Component	SLOC		Classes		Interfaces	
	Orig.	Copy	Orig.	Copy	Orig.	Copy
Sales	3,126	2,919	88	88	1	0
Address	13,113	18,258	306	455	5	4

Table 8.3.: Industrial case study: Component facts

Copy-based customization practices to study The company has defined coding guidelines for copy-based customization containing three rules:

1. When copying a class, append a customization identifier to its name.

2. When copying a class or package, add a customization identifier to the package path between product and module segments.
3. When copying a class, introduce an extends relationship to the original class, if the copy should replace the original at run time.

The two former rules define renaming conventions. The third rule defines the copying practice we call Derived Copies, keeping a reference back to the original implementation. Both components investigated in the case study have dependencies to their original copies. Thus, they are candidates for containing instances of the Derived Copy pattern used in copy-based customization (Section 5.1).

Assessment of the findings The vendor did not document the code modifications performed on the copies and did not provide a change history of the modifications. Furthermore, the vendor has not performed any consolidation of the copies before. Thus, there is no benchmark to assess the findings of the SPLEVO prototype. Additionally, the developers who have customized the copies are either no longer employed by the vendor or were at least not available for the case study. However, a member of the development team of the core product participated in the case study to review and assess the findings. He is familiar with the original code and the architecture and infrastructure of the product in general.

A list of the custom features was not available for the case study. Nevertheless, from our perspective, the lack of information about the performed customizations is not a special case but results from typical constraints in customization projects.

8.4.3. Execution Environment

The case studies were performed on a regular laptop (Dell Latitude E6420), with a Samsung SSD hard drive, 8GB physical RAM, and an Intel i7-2760QM Quad-Core CPU. The laptop runs a Windows 7 64bit operating system. We have installed the SPLEVO prototype in an Eclipse Kepler service release 2 modeling package. Furthermore, we used a Java 1.7 virtual machine and configured the Eclipse installation to use a maximum of 2GB RAM and a heap space maximum of 1GB.

8.5. Interviews and Survey

We performed two types of interviews as well as an online survey to prove the fitness of the SPLEVO approach for industrial application. For the first type of interviews, we used a face-to-face workshop with employees of the vendor of the industrial case study. It was focused on capturing the current situation within the company as well as the employees' expectations in relation to a consolidation process. For the second type of interviews, we designed an online interview to ask four developers to provide feedback about the comprehensibility of the SPLEVO refactoring specification concept. Those developers were not involved in any of the case studies. As a third, we performed an anonymous online survey with 18 participants. The online survey captured feedback about the current situation in the working environment of the participants and about roles defined in the SPLEVO process.

8.5.1. Interview Workshop

The interview workshop took place in the office of the vendor of the industrial case study product and was performed within one day.

8.5.1.1. Participants

Four employees of the vendor were interviewed. They were informed about the general topic of copy consolidation in advance, but they were not provided with any further information about the approach. Two of the employees described their position within the company as developers (i.e., Participant 1 and Participant 2). One described his position as a mixture of an architect and a project manager (i.e., Participant 3). And one participant described his position as a mixture of a developer and an architect (i.e., Participant 4). In addition to the interviewed employees, two employees of the research department of the vendor, two employees of the FZI, and two employees of the DevBoost GmbH as an independent software consultancy participated in the workshop to capture the answers and evaluate the results later on.

8.5.1.2. Process

The workshop was moderated by an employee of the DevBoost GmbH. This was done to reduce the risk of accidentally influencing the interviewed employees with either knowledge of another employee of the vendor or knowledge or expectations from the perspective of the SPLEVO approach.

The workshop was started by first providing a short motivation for the topic of consolidating product copies. Next, an example of the limitations of the Eclipse Java Development Tools [49] as a representative for state-of-the-art tooling was given. Finally, the goal of the SPLEVO approach was introduced to provide the context of the workshop. The introduction took approximately 30 minutes and all interviewed employees participated. Afterwards, individual interviews with the employees were performed. Each of the individual interviews took approximately 30 to 40 minutes.

8.5.1.3. Questions

The interviewed employees were asked six motivating questions. An open formulation of the questions was used to promote extensive answers. This format allowed for answers not related to the SPLEVO approach. However, this was intended to capture results from other perspectives compared to the more guided format of the online survey. The following questions were asked:

1. How do you implement variability today?
2. How do you decide for a way to implement variability?
3. Imagine you have to consolidate a copied and customized component into a variable software product line. What would you do?
4. How would you like to see the differences and what are you interested in?
5. When working with code structures, which level of granularity do you expect to be useful?
6. What else would you like to have or is important for you in the context of a consolidation?

Summaries of the given answers are contained in Appendix B.2. The evaluation of these answers is discussed in context of the appropriate evaluation questions in the corresponding sections.

8.5.2. Interview Refactoring Specification

We have interviewed four developers to evaluate the comprehensibility of the refactoring specification concept. In the interviews, they answered a questionnaire about their experience, read an example specification, and answered questions about this example to prove their comprehension.

8.5.2.1. Participants

The focus of the interview was to assess the comprehensibility of the refactoring specification concept and not of a concrete specification. We selected four participants already familiar with the concrete software model used in the example specification (i.e., JaMoPP) as well as the general topics of refactoring and Model Driven Software Development (MDSD). Thus, we reduced the influences on the feedback about the specification concept because of missing knowledge on the topic in general. All participants reported several years of experience in software development. Furthermore, all of them declared to have either experienced or professional skills in the topics of refactoring, MDSD, and JaMoPP.

8.5.2.2. Process

The interviews were performed remotely with all participants located in different offices. We sent them one page with instructions on how to perform the interview and a four page questionnaire, both provided in Appendix B.4. The questionnaire was about the experience and an excerpt of the concrete consolidation refactoring specification provided in Appendix A.1. After completion, participants sent their answers via email. Three of four participants answered on the same day. One participant answered one day later.

8.5.2.3. Questions

The questionnaire was split into two parts. In the first part, the participants declared their experience with software development in general and their skills on refactoring, MDSD, and JaMoPP. For the last three of the answers, the participants could choose between options none, basic, experienced, and professional. The questions about the excerpt of the refactoring specification covered two types of question. The first type of question proved that the participants understood critical aspects of the specification, such as when the refactoring can be applied. The second type of questions asked for their assessment of the usefulness of specific information provided, such as examples given with the refactoring. Finally, they had the opportunity to list information they might have missed.

The presented excerpt of the concrete refactoring specification included the variability information part of the refactoring. In addition, the refactoring instructions for the Import and Method software element types were provided. The refactoring instructions for these types of software elements do not include the actual variability mechanism. However, the reduced complexity of the mechanics allowed to focus the interview on the comprehensibility of the specification concept and not of the mechanics.

Appendix B.4 contains the questionnaire and the captured data. The results are interpreted in the sections of the according evaluation questions.

8.5.3. Online Survey on Industrial Applicability

In addition to the interviews, an online survey was performed. The primary goal of the survey was to validate the industrial applicability of the proposed consolidation process. The secondary goal was to gain an impression of the participants' experience with product copies and SPLs in general as well as their experience with consolidation processes in specific.

8.5.3.1. Participants

The survey was sent out to 30 business contacts with a relationship to software product development. Furthermore, it was posted in the LinkedIn and

Xing networks. The recipients were asked to participate in the survey and to forward the link to further reasonable contacts.

In total, 68 people opened the first page and 26 people opened at least page 2. 18 of the 26 completed the survey. The other 8 stopped between page 2 and 9. Their breaking offs were distributed in a way that no reason could be identified. Thus, only the 18 complete data sets were included in the evaluation.

Participant characteristics Table 8.4 summarizes the positions declared by the participants. They were allowed to select more than one position. 15 participants declared at least one management position. 13 participants declared at least one development position. 2 participants declared a research position in combination with one of the other positions. Most of the participants work in medium to large size companies: 14 of 18 participants work in companies with 100 to 1,000 employees (Appendix, Table B.4). All of the participants declared to have experience with industrial software development (Appendix, Table B.3: min=1year, max=20years, average=8.6years). 15 of 18 also declared to have experience with open source or research software development (min=1year, max=20years, average=5.6years). One can conclude to having 18 industrial participants with balanced backgrounds in the fields of management and development.

Position	#	at least one selected
Management (Project)	10	
Management (Product)	6	
Management (Company)	10	15
Development (Product)	9	
Development (Solution) / Consulting	10	13
Research & Teaching (Employee)	2	
Research & Teaching (Student)	0	2

Table 8.4.: Survey participants: Distribution of positions (18 in total, multiple selections allowed)

Experience with product copies In the questionnaire the participants were asked for their agreement or disagreement to statements about product copies. The answers are summarized in Table B.5 (Appendix). Most of the participants agreed to the flexibility provided by customer-specific product copies and their ability to cope with project pressure. Only two of them slightly agreed to create copies as a well-directed development strategy. But at the same time, most participants agreed to accept copies when needed. Most of the participants agreed to the challenges of product copies and some declared to more or less actively fight against them.

Experience with SPL and Consolidation In addition to the questions about product copies, the participants were asked about their agreement to statements about SPLs and consolidation processes. The answers are summarized in Table B.5, too. Most of the participants have at least heard about SPLs, some had already made personal experience, but only a few are currently working with them. Only a minority declared to have experience with or observed any consolidation activities.

To conclude, the participants can be described as to be aware of the advantages and disadvantages of customized product copies, understand the concept of SPLs, but have only minor to no experience with consolidation activities.

8.5.3.2. Process

The online survey was performed in an anonymous manner. First, a pretest was performed to improve the questionnaire's quality. Four employees of the FZI and one industrial software developer participated in this pretest. Afterwards, the questionnaire was sent to the participants and published.

8.5.3.3. Questions

The questionnaire consists of two parts. The first part includes questions about the participants themselves to capture their position, experience, and working environment. The second part includes questions about the individual roles defined in the SPLEVO approach (Section 4.1). At the beginning of the second part, an overview of the roles in total is given. Afterwards, each role is sketched including its activities, responsibilities, and required skills. For each role, participants had to answer a set of questions about the applicability of the role in their working environment (e.g., the own company or a company they advise as a consultant).

The facts about the participants respectively their environment were asked as quantitative inputs or selections. The questions about experiences and roles were designed according to the scale proposed by Likert [120]. A Likert scale with six options was used to require the participants to decide at least for a tendency of their agreement. For the individual roles, an additional text field was provided to declare current positions of potential employees who could own this role.

Appendix B.3 provides the original questionnaire and the captured data. The results are interpreted in the sections of the according evaluation questions.

8.6. Evaluation I.I: Difference Detection

The SPLEVO difference analysis was implemented in the prototype to apply and evaluate it in both case studies. The results showed a satisfying difference detection, and its precision of 100% allows for a fully automated difference analysis. Furthermore, considering the coding conventions for copy-based customizations in the industrial case study showed a reasonable benefit by filtering irrelevant differences and, thus, reducing manual effort. The metrics used and the results are detailed in the following subsections.

8.6.1. Evaluation Question I.I.1: Difference Detection Quality

To decide about the overall quality of the difference analysis we have studied its recall and precision. We defined these metrics as:

1. **Recall**: Can we find all differences?
2. **Precision**: How many false positives do we produce?

According to the consolidation-specific requirements on a difference analysis, a recall of 100% is a necessity for a fully automated analysis. In addition, a precision below 100% does not invalidate the analysis, but the higher it is, the lower is the manual effort for processing the resulting irrelevant differences.

8.6.1.1. Metric capturing

We captured the precision and recall in the ArgoUML case study. The system is of a reasonable size and the annotations provided by Couto et al. [36] provide a benchmark to assess the findings of the analysis. Couto et al. [36] identified different characteristics for the code of each feature (e.g., its scattering across the software or the number of differences involved). Thus, we have generated single-feature variants of ArgoUML with only one feature activated and applied the difference analysis to each of them compared to a basic variant with none of these features. Afterwards, we assessed our findings with the feature-specific code locations annotated by Couto et al. [36].

8.6.1.2. Types of granularity

Couto et al. [36] documented the granularity of the software elements representing the feature-specific code. Table 8.5 presents the 17 types of granularity they have defined and maps them to the seven types of granularity used in the SPLEVO approach (i.e., SPLEVO Change Types).

Neither Interface nor Variable markers occur in the ArgoUML implementation at all. They are included in Table 8.5 for completeness only. Furthermore, Couto et al. [36] used StaticInitialization markers for changed field initializations (StaticInit$_f$), respectively changed variable initializations (StaticInit$_s$). We have mapped them to field respectively statement differences according to their granularity in terms of software elements. MethodBody, MethodCall, and Expression markers identify changed Statements and provide additional information, such as "all statements of a method are changed". In a similar way, the change types Package and Class both identify feature-specific compilation units, but Package identifies that all compilation units of a Java package are affected.

Couto Markers	SPLevo Change Types
Package	CompilationUnit
Class	
Import	Import
ClassSignature	Class
Enumeration	Enumeration
Field	Field
StaticInit_f	
Method	Method
InterfaceMethod	
MethodSignature	
Statement	Statement
MethodBody	
MethodCall	
Expression	
StaticInit_s	

Table 8.5.: ArgoUML case study: Granularity type mapping between Couto Markers and SPLEVO Change Types

8.6.1.3. Marker normalization

In addition to mapping the granularity types used by Couto et al. [36], we normalized the marker counts for comparability. Normalization was necessary because of three reasons: i) grouped, needless, and wrong code markers, ii) unmatched elements, and iii) hidden changes.

Grouped, needless, and wrong code markers Couto et al. [36] use single markers to document blocks of nearby changes (e.g., nearby imports). To assess the real number of differing software elements, we counted each of these nearby software elements separately. In addition, we identified markers that are not needed, respectively hidden by other markers. For example, assume an import is marked as specific to feature *a* and contained by a compilation unit that is marked as specific to feature *a* as well. In such a case, we count the outer marker only because all contained software elements are changed obviously. Furthermore, we identified several wrong markers, with an annotation documenting another feature than the code is about (e.g., Listing 16). In such cases, we counted the real number of affected elements.

```
//#if defined(SEQUENCEDIAGRAM)
//@#$LPS-ACTIVITYDIAGRAM:GranularityType:Import
import org.argouml.uml.diagram.sequence.ui.UMLSequenceDiagram;
//#endif
```

Listing 16: ArgoUML case study: Wrong code marker example

Unmatched elements Unmatched elements are an additional reason requiring normalization. They occur because of changes of identifying characteristics of elements (e.g., the parameter of a method signature). Couto et al. [36] marked them as single change in a few cases. However, as the identity of the enclosing element is changed, separate adds and deletes must be counted instead of a single change. This is required as a fully automated difference analysis must report such changes and should not automatically try to match them with the risk of false matches.

Hidden changes Hidden changes occur if several differing software elements are located in sub-trees of each other. For example, if the conditions of several else-if-branches are changed, the first differing condition potentially influences the logic of the complete sub-tree. In such a case, this complete sub-tree must be considered as changed. Thus, such hidden changes must be counted as a single comprehensive difference.

8.6.1.4. Analysis Results

Data Columns The SPLEVO difference analysis was applied to the eight single-feature variants of ArgoUML, each of them compared to a basic variant with no optional feature activated. The results are presented in Table 8.6 with three columns per variant: Column C presents the raw counts of the markers in the code. Column C_N contains the number of markers normalized according to the rules described above. The results of the analysis were compared to the numbers in column C_N and the deviation is documented in column A_Δ.

Findings The results show that the SPLEVO detection analysis successfully detected all 2,282 relevant differences. Furthermore, it identified eight differences in addition to the normalized markers. A review of these findings identified that all of them are false positive differences. They are all detected because of unchanged statements enclosed by real differences. This behavior results from the SPLEVO difference analysis identifying statements not only by their content, but also by their position related to other statements. This is done by design to prevent wrong matches of similar statements, as described in Section 5.3.1.2.

Metrics In total, our analysis achieved a precision of 99.65% and recall of 100% summarized over all variants as shown in Table 8.7. This represents a satisfying detection quality according to the goal of a fully automated detection analysis with an acceptable amount of false positives. Furthermore, the false positives identified are typical examples that will be identified by the SPLEVO VP filtering described in Section 6.1.2.

Change Type	ACT			COG			COL		
	C	C_N	A_Δ	C	C_N	A_Δ	C	C_N	A_Δ
Comp.Unit	33	33	*0*	199	199	*0*	18	18	*0*
Import	15	20	*0*	34	91	*0*	13	16	*0*
Class	0	0	*0*	2	2	*0*	0	0	*0*
Enumeration	1	1	*0*	0	0	*0*	1	1	*0*
Field	2	2	*0*	7	7	*0*	1	1	*0*
Method	8	8	*0*	14	19	*0*	2	2	*0*
Statement	67	109	*0*	65	112	*0*	41	62	2
Σ	**126**	**173**	***0***	**321**	**430**	***0***	**76**	**100**	**2**

Change Type	DEP			LOG			STA		
	C	C_N	A_Δ	C	C_N	A_Δ	C	C_N	A_Δ
Comp.Unit	20	20	*0*	0	0	*0*	51	51	*0*
Import	10	18	*0*	186	189	*0*	24	45	*0*
Class	0	0	*0*	0	0	*0*	0	0	*0*
Enumeration	1	1	*0*	0	0	*0*	1	1	*0*
Field	1	1	*0*	190	191	*0*	2	2	*0*
Method	0	0	*0*	3	3	*0*	6	6	*0*
Statement	11	15	*0*	700	727	*4*	65	112	2
Σ	**43**	**55**	***0***	**1079**	**1110**	***4***	**149**	**217**	**2**

Change Type	SEQ			USE		
	C	C_N	A_Δ	C	C_N	A_Δ
Comp.Unit	52	52	*0*	37	37	*0*
Import	10	10	*0*	11	18	*0*
Class	0	0	*0*	0	0	*0*
Enumeration	1	1	*0*	1	1	*0*
Field	1	1	*0*	2	2	*0*
Method	1	1	*0*	1	1	*0*
Statement	36	50	*0*	20	31	*0*
Σ	**101**	**115**	***0***	**72**	**90**	***0***

Table 8.6.: SPLEVO Difference Analysis: Results ArgoUML case study (C = Raw Markers, C_N = Normalized Markers, A_Δ = Analysis Deviation)

Detected Differences $\sum_{(C_N+A_\Delta)}$	2,290
False Positives $\sum_{A_\Delta}$	8
Relevant Differences $\sum_{C_N}$	2,282
Precision	99.65%
Recall	100%

Table 8.7.: SPLEVO Difference Analysis: Summarized quality

8.6.1.5. Execution Times

The execution time of the difference analysis was measured for the fully automated difference analysis activity including the actions: software model extraction, difference analysis, and VPM initialization.

Reference cache influence When extracting software models, the most time-consuming part is the resolving of references (Section 2.4.6). To cope with this, the SPLEVO prototype contains a reference resolving cache (Section 8.3.2). Accordingly, there is a significant difference in the observed execution times, depending on whether the reference cache is populated or not.

Caching	ACT	COG	COL	DEP		
Without (sec)	3,022	3,543	2,805	3,062		
With (sec)	133	149	178	134		
Δ (%)	96	96	94	96		
Caching	**LOG**	**STA**	**USE**	**SEQ**	**∅**	**Complete**
Without (sec)	3,350	3,471	3,023	3,738	3,252	4,534
With (sec)	130	145	141	157	146	177
Δ (%)	96	96	95	96	96	96

Table 8.8.: SPLEVO Difference Analysis: Execution times ArgoUML case study

Table 8.8 summarizes the measured execution times for the ArgoUML variants. As shown, the caching achieves an improvement of approximately 96% on average without a significant deviation for the different variants.

8.6.2. Evaluation Question I.I.2: Benefit of Considering Copy Conventions

Evaluating the benefit of considering conventions for copy-based customization requires to evaluate the detection quality as well as the benefit itself. Accordingly, we have defined the following three metrics:

1. **Recall**: Can we find all Derived Copies?
2. **Precision**: How many false positive Derived Copies do we detect?
3. **Benefit**: To which degree does the detection reduce the manual effort?

The first two metrics assess the quality of the SPLEVO difference analysis in detecting Derived Copies and the third evaluates the benefit itself. To quantify the reduction of manual effort, we measured the number of software elements that would have been detected as differing by default but could be filtered because of the Derived Copy detection.

In contrast to the difference analysis itself, the Derived Copy detection is used for filtering previously detected but irrelevant differences. To still allow for a fully automated difference analysis, such a filtering must filter differences only in case of absolute certainty. Accordingly, a precision of 100% is necessary for a valid detection. A recall below 100% is acceptable as it does not invalidate the filter and lowers the benefit only.

8.6.2.1. Metric capturing

The metrics were captured in the industrial case study, as the ArgoUML case study does not provide any instances of the Derived Copy practice. We have performed a manual code review to identify instances of the Derived Copy pattern according to the provided conventions for copy-based customization. Our manual findings were reviewed and confirmed by the developer participating in the case study. The resulting list of five Derived Copies in the Sales component and twelve Derived Copies in the Address component forms the benchmark to assess the findings of the difference analysis. We applied the SPLEVO difference analysis on each of the copied components compared to its counterpart in the product core.

8.6.2.2. Analysis Result: Detection Quality

Table 8.9 presents the results of the difference analysis in comparison to the manually identified Derived Copies. All instances were identified and the resulting precision and recall of 100% indicate a satisfying detection result.

Component	Manually Identified	Analysis Detected	Analysis Precision	Analysis Recall
Sales	5	5	100%	100%
Address	12	12	100%	100%

Table 8.9.: SPLEVO Difference Analysis: Derived Copy detection industrial case study

8.6.2.3. Analysis Result: Detection Benefit

The benefit of the Derived Copy detection is measured by the number of filtered differences that must not be reviewed by developers anymore. However, a benefit exists only if the filtering is reliable. To prove the validity of the filtering, the developer of the vendor participating in the case study reviewed and confirmed the appropriateness of filtering these elements.

To quantify the reduction, we compared the number of filtered software elements to the total number of elements of the same type in the original class. We did this comparison for all types of software elements that are reasonable to be filtered (i.e., imports, fields, and methods). This evaluation strategy was chosen because developers have to review all of these elements with existing difference analysis approaches as they do not consider the inheritance relationships. We count all software elements in an untyped manner for a lower bound of effort reduction. For example, field initializations and method implementations typically vary in their complexity and potentially lead to additional effort for comprehension. In practice, this can lead to even higher reductions than presented here.

Data columns Table 8.10 summarizes the evaluation results of the benefit of detecting Derived Copies. For each type of software element, the column "Total" provides the number of elements in the original classes of the Derived Copy instances. The column "Filtered" provides the number of differing elements that could be filtered. The Column "Reduction" (R) provides the resulting percentage of the filtered elements compared to the total number of elements. This reduction also represents the reduction in developers' manual effort for reviewing differences.

Element	Sales		
	Total	Filtered	R
Import	210	122	58%
Fields	8	2	25%
Methods	69	44	64%
Σ	287	168	59%
Element	**Address**		
	Total	Filtered	R
Import	378	252	67%
Fields	16	1	6%
Methods	124	72	58%
Σ	518	325	63%
Element	**Combined**		
	Total	Filtered	R
Import	588	374	64%
Fields	24	3	13%
Methods	193	116	60%
Σ	805	493	61%

Table 8.10.: SPLEVO Difference Analysis: Derived Copy detection effort reduction (R = Reduction of differing elements to review)

Results As a result, considering the Derived Copy instances allowed for filtering 61% of the differing elements in total for both components under study, This is a satisfying result and validates the application of such an improved difference analysis. Considering all differences for all types of software elements, the number of differences was reduced from 2,790 to 2,297. Thus, the reduction in relation to all types of differences is about 18%.

Applicability To give a note about the applicability: The detection algorithm requires the availability of rules for customization that can be evaluated. If not available as conventions for copy-based customization, a review for according indicators can be done with a justifiable amount of effort. The manual code review has shown that identifying inheritance relationships between the copied and the original component can be done within minutes. However, even without any of such rules, the difference analysis can be applied, provides valid results, and allows for a fully automated analysis.

8.6.2.4. Execution Times

To provide an estimation of the execution time required for analyzing the customized components, each of them was analyzed four times: with and without caching, respectively with and without activating the Derived Copy detection. The difference analysis was measured in terms of the fully automated difference analysis activity including the actions: software model extraction, difference analysis, and VPM initialization. Table 8.11 provides the times required by the analyses according to the different settings. As shown, a significant improvement of 91% could be achieved if the cache for resolving references is used and filled.

8.7. Evaluation I.II: Variability Design

The evaluation questions for Hypothesis I.II are focused on gaining insight into the values of the analyses for identifying relationships between VPs.

	Derived Copy Detection				
	Off		On		
Caching	Sales	Address	Sales	Address	∅
Without (sec)	36	440	37	443	239
With (sec)	14	29	15	30	22
Improvement (%)	61%	93%	59%	93%	91%

Table 8.11.: SPLEVO Difference Analysis: Execution times industrial case study

8.7.1. Evaluation Question I.II.1: Program Dependency Analysis

As published in Klatt et al. [100], we have implemented the SPLEVO Program Dependency Analysis (Section 6.3) in the SPLEVO prototype and applied it in the ArgoUML as well as in the industrial case studies. We have studied four metrics to assess the value of analyzing dependent modification:

- **Recall**: To which degree can we aggregate code modifications contributing to the same feature?
- **Precision**: Do all recommended aggregations belong to the same feature?
- **Benefit**: To which degree can we reduce developers' manual effort in terms of VPGs to review about possible connections?
- **Industrial Applicability**: Can the approach be applied in industrial scenarios and provide reasonable results for copies evolved for several years?

The first three metrics were captured in the ArgoUML case study, and feature-specific annotations by Couto et al. [36] were used as a benchmark to assess the findings. The fourth metric was studied in the industrial case study. However, the industrial case study does not provide a benchmark in terms of documented modifications or existing consolidation results. Thus, the findings of the analysis were manually reviewed by the developer of the vendor participating in the case study.

8.7.1.1. Metric capturing

In the ArgoUML case study, two strategies were used to assess the precision and recall of the program dependency detection for identifying related VPs.

Recall First, to assess the **recall** of the analysis, single-feature variants, with only one distinct ArgoUML feature activated, were generated as already done for evaluating the difference detection. We applied the SPLEVO Program Dependency analysis on each of them compared to a basic variant with no features enabled. Accordingly, all initial VPs (i.e., differences) are known to belong to a single feature. We define the recall as the number of VPs the analysis was able to aggregate with each other. We performed the analysis both for the set of dependencies proposed by Robillard and Murphy [158] and for our extended set of dependencies (Section 6.3.2).

Precision Second, to assess the **precision** of the analysis, we have applied it on a complete variant of ArgoUML with all features activated compared to a basic variant with none feature enabled. Thus, if the analysis detects a relationship between VPs that belong to different features, this was recognized as an invalid relationship. Couto et al. [36] identified feature-specific code that is shared by multiple features by intention (i.e., tangling features). Hence, if the analysis returns a relationship for such tangling features, this is registered as a valid relationship. Accordingly, we used the code markers provided by Couto et al. [36] as a benchmark for this evaluation, too. We measured the precision as the ratio between valid relationships and the total number of relationships returned.

Benefit The benefit of the SPLEVO Program Dependency Analysis is measured as the reduction of VP clusters (i.e., VPGs) developers must prove for relationships to each other. For example, in case of two VPGs with VPs contributing to the same feature, developers must identify their relationships and aggregate them. If the analysis is capable to aggregate those two VPGs, the resulting benefit is 100% according to the achieved reduction. Those 100% are the result of having two VPGs before and only one VPG afterwards. Thus, developers must no longer review any VPGs to find relationships between them.

Industrial applicability The industrial applicability is measured by i) proving that the approach can be applied in the industrial case study and ii) the developer of the vendor assessing the detected relationships. There are no finally decided features respectively VPGs representing a benchmark to measure the recall in the industrial case study. Thus, only the precision of the analysis could be measured in this case study.

8.7.1.2. Analysis Results

Recall As shown in Table 8.12, the analysis achieved a recall of 80% on average when analyzing the extended set of types of dependencies proposed as part of the SPLEVO approach. In contrast, analyzing only dependencies included in the set, as proposed by Robillard and Murphy [158], resulted in a lower recall of 33% on average.

Precision When analyzing the ArgoUML variant with all features enabled, 216 aggregations are identified in total. A review of those findings discovered three invalid aggregations containing VPGs which contain VPs that neither belong to a distinct feature nor to tangling features identified by Couto et al. [36]. Accordingly, only 213 of the 216 aggregations are valid and the resulting precision is 99%. A review of the three invalid aggregations revealed that all invalid relationships result from modifications of different conditions of if-else chains. Such modifications are possible with preprocessor statements but are cascaded in software-model-based difference analyses as performed in the SPLEVO approach.

Benefit To assess the benefit, we analyzed the reduction of VPGs developers have to review manually. Table 8.12 provides the total number of initial VPGs. The row "Resulting VPGs" presents the number of VPGs when the analysis was performed and all returned recommendations were accepted. The row "Reduction" represents the difference between the initial and the resulting VPGs in percentage. The average reduction over all experiments and the resulting benefit is approximately 72% for the extended set of types of program dependencies proposed by the SPLEVO approach. In comparison, analyzing only the dependencies proposed by Robillard and Murphy [158] achieved a lower reduction of only 39%.

Feature	ACT	COG	COL	DEP	LOG	STA	USE	SEQ	⌀
Initial VPG	174	431	101	56	1,110	218	91	116	
Robillard set of dependencies									
VP Aggreg.	66	294	30	32	16	85	53	61	
Recall (%)	38	68	30	57	1	39	58	53	43
#VPGs	113	141	77	26	1,100	146	44	60	
Reduct. (%)	35	67	24	54	1	33	52	48	39
SPLevo extended set of dependencies									
VP Aggreg.	112	386	69	49	1,091	154	75	88	
Recall (%)	64	90	68	88	98	71	82	76	80
#VPGs	71	49	45	9	204	76	23	40	
Reduct. (%)	59	89	55	84	82	65	75	66	72

Table 8.12.: SPLEVO Program Dependency Analysis: Aggregation results ArgoUML case study

Figure 8.5 provides a chart visualizing the initial number of VPGs and the numbers resulting from analyzing the two sets of program dependencies. Especially for the Logging variant (LOG), the number of VPGs was significantly reduced by the extended set of program dependencies.

Industrial applicability The SPLEVO Program Dependency Analysis could be applied to both copied components of the industrial case study without any limitations. The identified relationships were reviewed by a developer of the software vendor, who justified all of them as reasonable relationships. Thus, the program dependency analysis achieved a precision of 100%, as all aggregated VPs were related to each other. The recall could not be calculated, as the copies have not been consolidated by the company yet and the valid design decisions are not available for comparison. However, as shown in Table 8.13 and visualized in Figure 8.6, the resulting benefit, measured in terms of reduced VPGs to be reviewed by developers, is about 75% on average for the components under study (23% when analyzing the set of dependencies proposed by Robillard and Murphy [158]). In total, the high precision and execution times confirmed the industrial applicability of the analysis.

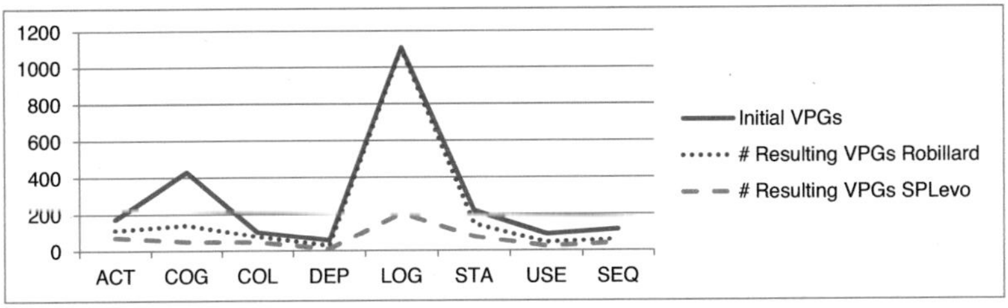

Figure 8.5.: SPLEVO Program Dependency Analysis: VPG reduction ArgoUML case study

	Sales	Address	∅
Initial VPG	569	1,758	
Robillard set of dependencies			
Resulting VPGs	449	1,310	
Reduction (%)	21	25	23
SPLevo extended set of dependencies			
Resulting VPGs	160	399	
Reduction (%)	72	77	75

Table 8.13.: SPLEVO Program Dependency Analysis: Aggregation results industrial case study

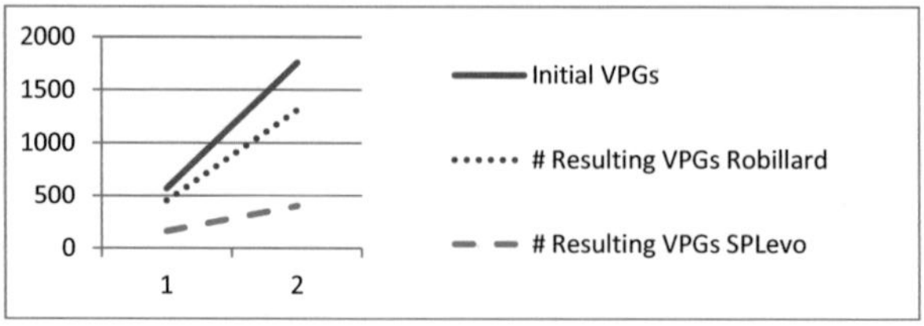

Figure 8.6.: SPLEVO Program Dependency Analysis: VPG reduction industrial case study

Dependencies	ACT	COG	COL	DEP	LOG	STA	USE	SEQ	∅
Rob (sec)	14	15	10	8	23	13	14	9	13
SPLEVO (sec)	21	22	18	11	40	21	17	15	20
Dependencies	Complete	Sales	Address						
Rob (sec)	51	3	16						
SPLEVO (sec)	82	5	40						

Table 8.14.: SPLEVO Program Dependency Analysis: Execution times all case studies (R = Set of Robillard and Murphy [158], S = Set of SPLEVO approach)

8.7.1.3. Execution Times

Analyzing the single-feature variants of ArgoUML took 20 seconds on average when analyzing the extended set of dependencies proposed in the SPLEVO approach. Performing the analyses with the set proposed by Robillard and Murphy [158] it took 13 seconds on average. For the complete variant of ArgoUML, the SPLEVO set of dependencies required 82 and the set proposed by Robillard and Murphy [158] 51 seconds. In the industrial case study, the program dependency analysis took five respectively 40 seconds for the Sales and Address component considering the SPLEVO set, and 3 respectively 16 seconds using the set proposed by Robillard and Murphy [158]. In total, analyzing the extended set proposed by the SPLEVO approach requires slightly more time, which is acceptable because of the improved findings.

8.7.2. Evaluation Question I.II.2: Shared Term Analysis

We have implemented the SPLEVO Shared Term Analysis (Section 6.4) in the SPLEVO prototype and applied it in the ArgoUML as well as in the industrial case studies. We have studied the same four metrics as done for the SPLEVO Program Dependency Analysis to assess the value of analyzing dependent modifications:

- **Recall**: To which degree can we aggregate code modifications contributing to the same feature?
- **Precision**: Do all recommended aggregations belong to the same feature?
- **Benefit**: To which degree can we reduce developers' manual effort in terms of VPGs to review about possible connections?
- **Industrial Applicability**: Can the approach be applied in industrial scenarios and provide reasonable results for copies evolved for several years?

Similar to the program dependency analyzer, we evaluated the first three metrics in the ArgoUML case study with the annotations of Couto et al. [36] as a benchmark to assess the findings. And, we used the industrial case study to prove the industrial applicability of the SPLEVO Shared Term Analysis.

8.7.2.1. Metric capturing

We have captured the metrics in the same way as done for the SPLEVO Program Dependency Analysis (Section 8.7.1.1). However, the results of the shared term analysis are influenced by terms irrelevant for detecting feature-specific code (i.e., Term Spam according to Definition 18). Thus, we captured the metrics using the Snowball Porter stemmer (Section 6.4.3.2), excluding comments and terms shorter than three characters while applying the term splitting but no Term Spam filter.

8.7.2.2. Analysis Results

Recall As shown in Table 8.15, analyzing the VPs for shared terms achieved a recall of 42% on average.

Precision Analyzing the complete variant of ArgoUML with all optional features in place returned a single aggregation of 755 VPs. These VPs represent modifications of all features and thus must not be aggregated. A review of the relationships has shown that they result from many shared terms irrelevant for the copy-specific features, such as "argouml", "item", and "design" (i.e., Term Spam according to Definition 18). Accordingly, there is only one false aggregation leading to a precision of 0%.

Benefit and Industrial Applicability The shared term analysis used with the base settings does not provide any benefit because of the unsatisfying precision. The reliability of the recommendations is too low to reduce the SPL Consolidation Developers' manual effort for reviewing the VPGs. Without any benefit, the analysis is not applicable in industrial scenarios as well.

The reason for the insufficient precision is the high amount of Term Spam in the identifiers. Section 6.4.3.3 describes several strategies to cope with the challenge of Term Spam. To prove the proposed strategies, we performed further analyses on the ArgoUML complete variant as described in the following subsections.

Feature	ACT	COG	COL	DEP	LOG	STA	USE	SEQ	∅
Initial VPG	174	431	101	56	1,110	218	91	116	
VP Aggreg.	76	255	33	23	198	91	44	68	
Recall (%)	44	59	33	41	18	42	47	59	43
#VPGs	99	177	69	34	913	128	48	49	
Reduct. (%)	43	59	32	39	18	41	47	58	42

Table 8.15.: SPLEVO Shared Term Analysis: Aggregation results ArgoUML case study

8.7.2.3. Term Frequency

We have reviewed the terms indexed during the analysis to evaluate their frequency as indicator for Term Spam. Table 8.16 provides four examples of indexed terms with different frequencies and validity to indicate relevant relationships. These findings show that the frequency of a term needs not to relate to its relevance to indicate validate relationships. Thus, the frequency is not a reliable indicator for filtering Term Spam.

Stemmed Term	VP Frequency	Valid Aggregation
caller	2	yes
feme	2	no
critic	143	yes
diagram	146	no

Table 8.16.: Example terms indicating uselessness of frequency (ArgoUML case study)

8.7.2.4. Seed Terms

Seed terms represent an exclusive list of terms to analyze as shared terms. We used the names of the eight features identified by Couto et al. [36] as seed terms to evaluate their value. We used the feature names in lowercase and concatenated compound terms: “activity”, “cognitive”, “collaboration”, “deployment”, “logging”, “state”, “usecase”, “sequence”.

Results Applying the seed term strategy when analyzing the ArgoUML complete variant, a single aggregation of 313 VPs is returned. This is less than half of the VPs aggregated by the unfiltered analysis. However, the precision is 0% as well and, thus, there is no benefit for developers. Analyzing the complete variant ArgoUML took about 46 seconds.

Source for low precision A review of the VPs has identified several code locations that include more than one of the featured terms. For example, Listing 17 shows fields declared by the class UMLStateDiagram. The class was introduced for the state feature but the term “sequence” is used as well without any relationship to the sequence feature.

```
  private Action actionStubState;
  private Action actionState;
...
  private Action actionActionSequence;
```

Listing 17: UMLStateDiagram class as example for mixed seed terms

Availability of seed terms Beside the results presented above, seed terms cannot be assumed to be available in each scenario. For example, in the industrial case study, the vendor was not able to provide us with either a list of customer-specific features implemented in recent years or a list of relevant seed terms in general.

Sensitivity of terms During the analysis of the seed terms provided for the ArgoUML case study, we observed a sensitivity to the quality of the terms. In particular, providing compound terms as seed terms allowed for relating several variants of their concatenations. For example, we identified five different types of writing for the term “use case” in the ArgoUML case study: “UseCase”, “Use_case”, “useCase”, “usecase”, and “Usecase”. At least the first three variants were split by default.

8.7.2.5. Stop Word Lists

To evaluate the benefit of filtering stop words, we performed analyses with two publicly available lists. The first stop word list includes the terms of the programmer vocabulary proposed by Høst and Østvold [82]. This list was used as a representative for programming language-specific stop word lists. The second stop word list corresponds to the stop word list implemented in the MySQL database server for full text searches [142]. It was used as a representative for natural language stop words. Furthermore, we proved the industrial applicability of developing custom stop word lists in the industrial case study.

Results with programmer vocabulary (Høst filter) Filtering terms proposed by the programming vocabulary resulted in a single aggregation, too. The aggregation contains 721 VPs, which is 34 less VPs than without any filtering. However, the precision is also 0% and, thus, filtering this stop word list does not improve the precision of the analysis. For completeness, the according stop word list is provided in Appendix B.1.1. Analyzing the complete variant of ArgoUML took about 235 seconds.

Results with MySQL stop word list Before performing the analysis itself, we prepared the MySQL stop word list in two steps. In the first step, we split the terms in the stop word list containing apostrophe characters (e.g., "aren t" instead of "aren't"). The Java programming language bars for using apostrophes in identifiers, thus they are useless in the analysis. In the second step, we removed all stop words with less than three characters, because these short terms will be filtered by the analysis already. The resulting stop word list is provided in Appendix B.1.2.

However, filtering terms with the prepared MySQL stop word list resulted in a single aggregation, too. The single aggregation contains 725 VPs, which is 30 less VPs than without any filtering and four VPs more than when filtering the programmer vocabulary. Accordingly, the precision is again 0% and, thus, filtering this stop word list does not improve the precision of the analysis, either. Analyzing the complete variant of ArgoUML took about 76 seconds.

Developing custom stop word lists Section 6.4.3.3 describes sources and concepts to develop custom stop word lists. We have investigated in developing such a stop word list in the industrial case study, as published in Klatt et al. [99]. We first asked two developers of the vendor to provide a stop word list without any preparations. As developing stop word lists is not a typical task in software development, they were not able to provide such a list because of the uncertainty how to do this. Next, we extracted all terms from the case study components. We presented the terms to the developers and asked for selecting terms that possibly relate to customer-specific features. Our intention was to filter all terms as stop words which have not been identified. However, again, it was not possible to clearly decide about the relevance of the terms. Further investigation in such a custom stop word list was not possible due to timing restrictions (i.e., a one-person day of effort). As a conclusion, developing a custom stop word list for a specific scenario is a challenging task and the benefit of the resulting list is unclear. Note: The list of terms is not included in this thesis due to legal restrictions.

8.7.2.6. Shared Term Clusters

To evaluate the improvement achieved by the shared term cluster strategy described in Section 6.4.3.3, we have performed several analyses to study it separately as well as combined with other strategies.

Precision Table 8.17 summarizes the precision measured with the ArgoUML complete variant. The columns "Valid" and "Invalid" contain the numbers of valid respectively invalid aggregations identified by the analysis. The column "Precision" represents the resulting precision for each configuration. Finally, the column "Execution Time" provides the time it tool to execute the analyses.

Configuration	Recommendations		Prec.	Exec. Time
	Valid	Invalid		(sec)
Cluster detection only	14	2	88%	73
Seed terms	7	0	100%	42
Høst stop words	13	2	87%	72
MySQL stop words	14	2	88%	79

Table 8.17.: Shared term cluster strategy: Precision in ArgoUML case study

As shown, the shared term cluster strategy leads to significantly higher precisions as the other strategies. Filtering stop words did not result in a significant difference in the results compared to applying the shared term cluster strategy only. In contrast, using seed terms resulted in a precision of 100% and, thus, provided fully reliable results. However, seed terms cannot be assumed to be available, as confirmed in the industrial case study. Furthermore, reviewing the recommended aggregations identified that the seed term variant missed an extensive aggregation of VPs related to the logging feature. This miss happened because the term "log" is used in the code, but the seed term is "logging". Also none of the stemming algorithms transformed "logging" to "log" and, thus, the seed term strategy prevented detecting this valid aggregation.

Recall We further evaluated the recall of the shared term cluster strategy. Table 8.18 summarizes the findings for the strategy alone and in combination with the other strategies as studied before. The best result on average is achieved by combining the shared term cluster and the seed term strategies with a recall of 22%. The results of the other alternatives did not vary a lot between each other.

Considering both recall and precision, the best alternative is to combine a seed term and shared term cluster strategy. However, if seed terms are not available, executing only the shared term clustering provides a good alternative. The differences of the execution times can be neglected.

Industrial applicability We applied the SPLEVO Shared Term Analysis with the shared term cluster strategy in the industrial use case twice: with and without the Høst programmer vocabulary as stop word list. With both settings, the analysis returned the same result, with slightly lower execution times when using the stop word list (i.e., 3 and 16 seconds instead of 8 and 19 seconds). As presented in Table 8.19, the precision in the industrial case study was 0% respectively 50%, which is not a satisfying result. The shared terms identified were "description", "log", and "attributes". The first two implicated invalid recommendations. The third one resulted from independently created return values in different conditional executions of the same method. Thus, it would not be found by the Program Dependency Analysis. However, it must be classified as detected by chance by the Shared Term Analysis as well. Furthermore, the absolute number of detected relationships does not provide a notifiable benefit in terms of reducing the manual effort of developers.

8.7.2.7. Execution Time

As shown in Table 8.20, the execution times for analyzing the ArgoUML variants with the default shared term analysis vary between 5 and 36 seconds.

Feature	ACT	COG	COL	DEP	LOG	STA	USE	SEQ	∅
Initial VPG	174	431	101	56	1,110	218	91	116	
Shared term clusters only									
VP Aggregated	28	180	2	0	196	5	0	2	
Recall (%)	16	42	2	0	18	2	0	2	10
Resulting VPGs	154	252	100	56	917	215	91	115	
Reduction (%)	11	42	1	0	17	1	0	1	9
Exec.-Time (sec)	13	17	5	10	34	13	11	6	14
Shared term clusters & seed terms									
VP Aggregated	34	179	13	20	0	44	37	8	
Recall (%)	20	42	13	36	0	20	41	7	22
Resulting VPGs	142	253	89	37	1,110	175	55	110	
Reduction (%)	18	41	12	34	0	20	40	5	21
Exec.-Time (sec)	10	19	6	4	19	6	7	9	10
Shared term clusters & Høst stop word filter									
VP Aggregated	30	19	2	2	196	12	0	0	
Recall (%)	17	4	2	4	18	6	0	0	6
Resulting VPGs	151	416	100	55	917	209	91	116	
Reduction (%)	13	3	1	2	17	4	0	0	5
Exec.-Time (sec)	7	15	6	4	36	12	6	8	12
Shared term clusters & MySQL stop word filter									
VP Aggregated	27	19	2	0	194	7	0	2	
Recall (%)	16	4	2	0	17	3	0	2	6
Resulting VPGs	155	417	100	56	918	214	91	115	
Reduction (%)	11	3	1	0	17	2	0	1	4
Exec.-Time (sec)		17	5	6	36	8	8	6	12

Table 8.18.: Shared term cluster strategy: Recall in ArgoUML case study

Configuration	Recommendations		Precision	Execution Time (seconds)
	Valid	Invalid		(Cluster only / Høst)
Sales	0	1	0%	8/3
Address	1	1	50%	19/16

Table 8.19.: Shared term cluster strategy: Precision in industrial case study

Feature	ACT	COG	COL	DEP	LOG	STA	USE	SEQ	∅
Execution time (sec)	13	21	5	6	36	8	10	14	14

Table 8.20.: Shared term analysis: Execution time in ArgoUML case study

The average execution time for all variants was about 14 seconds. Analyzing the complete variant with all optional features activated took about 208 seconds. In the industrial case study, the shared term analysis required 8 seconds for the sales and 36 seconds for the address component.

If the SPLEVO Shared Term Analysis is performed with additional strategies, such as shared term cluster strategies, the execution time is even shorter, as presented in the according subsections. As shown in Table 8.17, the execution times for the complete ArgoUML variant varied approximately between 40 and 80 seconds.

8.7.3. Evaluation Question I.II.3: Simultaneous Modification Analysis

To decide about the benefit of analyzing modifications committed at the same time or with a link to the same issue, it would be necessary to analyze precision, recall, and effort reduction as done for the other types of analysis.

None of the case studies provided the required data for such analyses. However, as Software Configuration Management (SCM) systems are used by many companies today, and the idea of a commit is to save modifications performed in a similar context, we argue that such an analysis can provide a benefit to identify related differences. Furthermore, others such as Rubin et al. [165] and Nunes et al. [137] propose a similar direction.

Nevertheless, also if such data is available, the quality of the analysis strongly depends on the discipline of the developers when committing their modifications. For example, threats to the validity of the analysis exist because of large commits containing modifications for several features, forgotten commit messages, or issues that describe several features at once.

To conclude about the benefit of analyzing simultaneous modifications: This type of analysis did not provide any benefit in the case studies due to the lack of according data. But, this result cannot be generalized except for cases which do not provide an SCM as well.

8.8. Evaluation I.III: Consolidation Refactoring

8.8.1. Evaluation Question I.III.1: Refactoring Specification Fitness

To evaluate the fitness of the concept for consolidation refactoring specifications, a case study with a concrete consolidation refactoring was performed. The refactoring used in the case study relates to Java technology and implements a variability mechanism using conditional statements. The configuration is provided by a static Java class which is introduced by the refactoring as well. A student studying computer science at the Karlsruhe Institute of Technology (KIT) specified this refactoring as part of his master thesis [40]. This allowed to prove the applicability of the concept from the perspective of the person specifying the refactoring. Furthermore, a student writing a master thesis is assumed to have typical software engineering skills similar to those available in practice. The resulting specification is provided in Appendix A.1.

To decide about the fitness of the specification concept, the following metrics were studied:

- **Unambiguity**: Can the refactoring be specified without ambiguity for a human reader?
- **Completeness**: Can all necessary code transformations be specified?
- **Automation**: To which degree can a refactoring specified with this concept be automated?

Due to the unlimited variety of variability mechanisms, it is not possible to evaluate the specification concept for all of them. Nevertheless, the case study performed provides results for the metrics and indicators for the fitness in general.

8.8.1.1. Metric capturing

Unambiguity To decide about the unambiguity of the specification, an interview was performed with four participants (Section 8.5.2). They were provided with an excerpt of the concrete refactoring specification mentioned above and a questionnaire about their comprehension. The questionnaire itself and the complete answers are provided in Appendix B.4.

Completeness The completeness was measured in terms of coverage of types of SoftwareElements to be refactored in the ArgoUML case study. A 100% completeness is achieved if refactoring instructions can be specified for all types of SoftwareElements required to refactor a set of copies into an SPL. This metric depends on the concrete copies under study respectively the intended SPL. Thus, the ArgoUML case study was selected for this evaluation due to the documented feature-specific code. Furthermore, the industrial case study does not represent a clear benchmark for this evaluation, as the vendor has not decided about a final VP design, yet.

Automation To prove the automation, the master student who wrote the specification implemented an according automation. This automation is integrated in the SPLEVO prototype and was evaluated in the ArgoUML case study. The degree of automation is assessed by the compilation errors in the resulting SPL and the manual effort required afterwards to achieve a valid code base.

8.8.1.2. Results

The results of the questionnaire successfully assessed the comprehensibility of the specification concepts. The answers confirmed the validity of the structure but also point out the importance of the quality of the specification itself.

Comprehension All participants successfully answered the questions to prove the comprehension of the refactoring itself. They confirmed the necessity of the examples in general and for the individual instructions. In context of the refactoring instruction for method elements, the participants had to prove their comprehension of a declared function as part of the mechanics. They all returned correct answers but with different details. For example, one reported the function to be obvious while another expected a check of the return type of the method – which is ensured by the overall limitations.

Examples and limitations Some participants mentioned that they used the examples for their overall comprehension (e.g., "Gives a concrete implementation template"). Thus, examples must be chosen carefully to be representative and comprehensible. Similarly, the participants confirmed the necessity and usefulness of the limitation sections. However, the quality and details of the concrete limitations presented in the example were partly confusing (e.g., "Helpful but more detail needed", "... bit confusing, because it's somehow obvious that... ", "I'm not sure whether the list is complete").

Pseudo code Three of four participants noted possible difficulties with pseudo code notations (e.g., "hard to verify/test without translating it to concrete language"). One confirmed the advantage of language independence. In total, two participants declared a neutral feedback about the use of pseudo code, one declared to prefer a programming language, and one mentioned that he could not decide about it without having to implement it. To conclude: Using pseudo code is not invalid. However, using a programming language the target group of a specification is used to might support the comprehensibility of the mechanics. For example, when specifying a refactoring for a company developing applications with the C# programming language, it is reasonable to specify the refactorings in C# as well.

Context information The answers show that providing a limited context in advance influenced the participants' comprehension. This was done to limit the resources required to participate in the interview. However, this did not invalidate the results and only led to some general uncertainties (e.g., "Explanation of what OPTXOR is", terminology such as "implementing element", "...not sure how to identify the two CUs...", "Can this not be fully automated?").

Further remarks One participant explicitly declared the decomposition as helpful for comprehending the refactoring. Another one also noted the classification scheme (i.e., characteristics) and the alternative sections as positive aspects.

Completeness The refactoring specification developed by the student was reviewed and assessed as valid. The Variants of all VPs in the ArgoUML case study are implemented by SoftwareElements with the JaMoPP metamodel types: Statement, CompilationUnit, Import, Field, Condition, Method, Constructor, and Block. All of these types of software elements are covered by the refactoring specification (Appendix A.1). Some of the refactoring instructions defined in the specification include restrictions of their applicability. However, none of these restrictions affected the ArgoUML case study as proven by the evaluation on the possible degree of automation.

Automation In addition to specifying the refactoring, the master student had to develop an automation according to the refactoring specification. This automation was included in the SPLEVO prototype and thus has been applied in the ArgoUML case study. Executing the refactoring resulted in no compilation errors.

A manual evaluation of the automation identified that external dependencies included in resources such as Java Archive (JAR) files are not covered. This did not influence the ArgoUML case study, as all copies include the same dependencies (i.e., the same JAR files). However, such JAR files are not covered by the JaMoPP model and thus also not covered by the model extractions and analyses in the SPLEVO prototype. To cope with this limitation, developers have to manually provide the according resources to the final SPL when the refactoring is performed.

Conclusion As an overall result, the fitness of the refactoring specification concepts is successfully evaluated. Writing a specification according to the concept and in a comprehensible manner was proven as well as the possible coverage and automation. However, the specification concept supports the creation and handling of refactorings, but it is still possible to write wrong or incomprehensible refactoring specifications.

8.8.2. Evaluation Question I.III.2: Variability Mechanism Recommendation

To evaluate the recommendation system with regard to its capability to reduce manual effort and the risk of inconsistent decisions, we use an argumentative approach. The result of the recommendation strongly relies on the assumption that the variability characteristics of the VPs reflect the stakeholders' requirements. Furthermore, the result of the recommendation system depends on the set of variability mechanisms provided by Software Architects as part of an SPL Profile.

Assuming that VP characteristics and available variability mechanics are defined properly, the reduction of the manual effort and the risk of inconsistent implementations can be represented by the following metrics:

- **Variability Decision Effort**: How many decisions have to be made by developers with and without the auto recommendation?
- **Variance of Mechanism Implementations**: How often have mechanisms been selected which are not the optimal choice for a VP?

The former represents a comparison of the worst-case and the best-case scenarios. The worst-case scenario exists in case of all necessary decisions having to be done manually (i.e., no auto recommendation in place). The best-case scenario exists in case of the auto recommendation being able to decide all VPs. The latter represents the possible variance of variability implementation styles between VPs.

Variability decision effort The proposed recommendation system is based on a set of rules matching the variability characteristics of a VP and the variability mechanisms selected in the SPL Profile in the order they are defined in. These rules relate to the number of decisions to be performed by developers.

Depending on the number of VPs n_{VP} and the number of SoftwareElements implementing variants n_{SE} of these VPs, at least $3 * n_{VP} + n_{SE}$ checks are required to decide for variability mechanisms for all VPs. This is a best-case scenario estimation which sets if the first variability mechanism checked for each VP can be applied.

For example, the feature-specific code locations documented by Couto et al. [36] in the ArgoUML case study (Section 8.4.1) conform to 1,967 VPs and 2,282 SoftwareElements implementing their variants. In the best-case, this requires $3 * 1,967 + 2,282 = 8,183$ decisions about criteria being fulfilled or not.

When the auto recommendation is applied, there will be no manual effort except for executing the auto recommendation. The actual time required by a human for a single decision strongly depends on the experience of the developers as well as the usability of the tooling. However, even under the best conditions, the automation will outperform the manual process. Assuming an effort of 1 second to look at a VP and store a decision, more than 2 hours will be saved in case of the ArgoUML case study (i.e., $8,183 * 1\ seconds \approx 136\ minutes \approx 21/4\ hours$).

Variance of mechanism implementations The possible variance of implemented variability mechanisms depends on the number of possible mechanisms, the variety of SoftwareElements implementing the VPs, and the individual programming styles of the implementing developers.

However, to estimate the number of potential variants of implementations we consider information provided in the industrial case study. During the interviews, participant three initially estimated at least 10 different "styles of implementing variability" (i.e., variability mechanisms). He repealed this number and estimated a much higher but unknown number at the end of the interview. Thus, 10 is a reliable minimum number of alternative variability mechanisms. Without knowing the details of these mechanisms, we assume that developers can potentially choose each of them for a VP. However, only one variability mechanism can be the best choice according to the preferences of the software architects. Thus, 9 of 10 alternatives represent non-optimal decisions.

Furthermore, we assume the minimum number of VPs n_{VP} by applying all technical possible merges to each of the studied components. Accordingly, there are $9 * n_{VP}$ potential non-optimal decisions. Table 8.21 summarizes the estimations for the two components under study. As shown, there are 1,710 respectively 4,095 non-optimal possible decisions which can affect the consistency of the SPL implementation. Thus, applying the variability mechanisms recommendation allows for reducing the risk of non-optimal decisions from 1,710 respectively 4,095 to 0.

Component	Variation Points		Potentially Wrong Decisions
	Initial	Merged	$9 * n_{VP}$
Sales	563	190	1,710
Address	1,734	455	4,095

Table 8.21.: Potentially non-optimal variability mechanism decisions

8.9. Evaluation II: Consolidation Process

8.9.1. Evaluation Question II.1: Fitness for Industrial Scenarios

We assessed the fitness of the process for industrial scenarios by three criteria:

1. **Integration**: The activities are seamlessly integrated with each other.
2. **Input**: The required input is available.
3. **Responsibilities**: The responsibilities for the activities can be fulfilled.

The former is proven by the practicability of the SPLEvo prototype. All activities are represented in the prototype. Furthermore, they can exchange the data as described in Section 4.2 without additional adaptations. To prove the second and third criteria, we follow a line of argumentation visualized in Figure 8.7. This line of argumentation allows for assessing the fitness by the appropriateness of the defined roles.

Line of argumentation The SPLEVO consolidation process is defined as a chain of activities. This chain is fit for an industrial application if the activities can be executed and their process internal and process external input is available. An activity can be executed if it is either fully automated and a valid role exists to start it, or it requires manual processing and an according role exists to take care for this. If such defined roles are appropriate for an industrial application, the activities are suitable for an industrial application as well. The process external input is available if the responsibilities are clear for the individual activities. As shown in Figure 8.7, roles are defined by activities they have to execute and the responsibilities for input they have to provide. Accordingly, if the roles fit for an industrial application, the responsibilities are suitable and the activities can be executed. Combined with the availability of the internal input, the overall process can be declared as fit for an industrial application if the roles are appropriate.

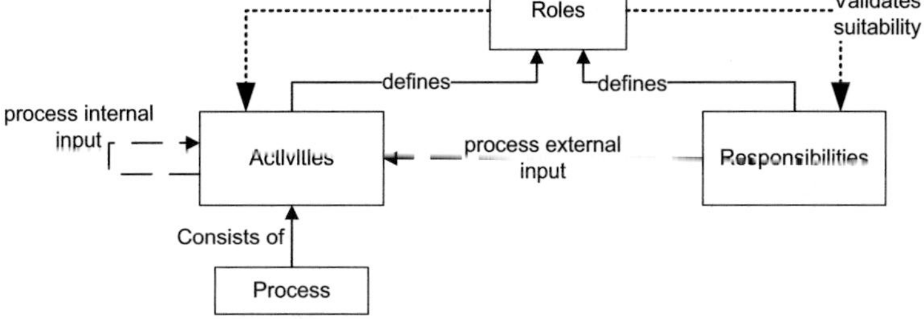

Figure 8.7.: Process fitness for industrial scenarios: Line of argumentation

The roles' appropriateness was assessed by considering the feedback received in the interview workshop as well as in the online survey. The former was designed in an open manner not focused on asking about the roles. The latter was an anonymous survey strictly focused on receiving feedback about the roles. The following subsections discuss the roles in context of the feedback received in the interviews and survey. The original results are provided in Appendix B.2 and Appendix B.3.

8.9.1.1. Software Architect

Interview workshop The participants reported about many different technologies and variability mechanisms currently used in their development. Thus, there is a necessity for a role to keep track of those technologies and mechanisms and decide about new ones to integrate (i.e., architectural decisions). Especially the reported divergence in variability implementations further motivated the introduction of the Software Architect role for the consolidation process.

Survey All survey participants agreed in the availability of a person to fill the role of the Software Architect. Twelve of 18 participants reported concrete positions currently owned by the persons able to fill the role of the Software Architect. Furthermore, they agreed that these persons have the necessary competence and decision-making powers. About half of the participants agreed to feel themselves being able to fill this role.

8.9.1.2. SPL Consolidation Developer

Interview workshop The project manager as well as the developers reported about the preference for developers being able to decide about variability mechanisms on their own. To cope with this requirement and the according skill to understand variability mechanisms, the role of an SPL Consolidation Developer was introduced. Furthermore, a participant reported the requirement for documenting introduced variability. This confirms to the skill of an SPL Consolidation Developer to work with a variation point model.

Survey 13 of 18 participants agreed to know a concrete person to fill the role of an SPL Consolidation Developer. Ten of them named current positions of persons who can potentially fill the role. One participant mentioned the ability of all team members to fill this role. Compared to the Software Architect role, less of the participants agreed to feel themselves able to fill the role. Furthermore, less of them agreed for potential candidates to have the required competences and decision-making powers to fulfill the role, yet. Accordingly, the certainty about the role is lower but can still be assessed as valid.

8.9.1.3. SPL Manager

Interview workshop The interview participants reported about developers checking their introduced variability with the development management and the product management. The SPL Manager role is intended to represent those two perspectives and to provide the required feedback for the SPL Consolidation Developer.

Survey Ten of 18 participants declared to agree to the availability of a concrete person for the SPL Manager role. Eight of these participants also declared current positions of these concrete persons. However, none of the participants totally disagreed to the availability of a concrete person able to fill the SPL Manager role. Furthermore, some of the participants mentioned uncertainty about their decisions in the final feedback. Hence, the disagreement potentially results from the uncertainty about the role itself.

8.9.1.4. Product Manager

Interview workshop The interview participants reported about the product management being aware of the needs of individual projects. Accordingly, the role of a Product Manager was introduced as the stakeholder originally representing the project requirements.

Survey 17 of 18 participants agreed to being able to name concrete persons to fill the role of a Product Manager. Nine participants declared current positions owned by these persons. Only a minority of the participants saw themselves in such a position and a minor uncertainty existed about the availability of the necessary competency and decision-making powers.

8.9.1.5. Software Developer

Interview workshop All interview participants, except for participant 3, described their interest in the code and the resulting code quality. The interest in a long-term code quality is represented by the role of a Software Developer to make it explicit in contrast to requirements in context of an efficient consolidation process.

Survey All survey participants agreed to the availability of a concrete person to fill this role and having the required competency and decision-making powers. Ten participants declared current positions of these persons, confirming this result as well. Concerning the ability to fill this role themselves, the participants split in two groups: About one half agreed, the rest did not. This fits to the participants' balance of development and management origins.

8.9.1.6. SPL Consolidation Consultant

Interview workshop The SPL Consolidation Consultant role was not mentioned in the answers provided in the interview workshop. However, the participants described various ways for addressing a consolidation, such as starting with individual code locations or searching for structures. On the one side, this is about personal preferences and allows for different perspectives for identifying alternative solutions. On the other side, heterogeneous solutions must be prevented to improve SPL maintenance and management. The SPL Consolidation Consultant role was introduced to guide a consolidation process when necessary, especially when a novel approach such as the SPLEVO approach is facilitated.

Survey The answers given by the survey participants represent no clear trend of agreement or disagreement on the availability of a person to fill this role. However, this is acceptable as the role was introduced because of the observable need but not because of a declared necessity. In addition, the need for this role also depends on the process applied. For example, if consolidations are not handled explicitly, there is no obvious need for such a role.

8.9.1.7. Conclusion of Role Evaluation

Correlation with existing roles A correlation between existing roles or positions in traditional software engineering and the agreement to individual SPLEVO roles can be observed. Roles with names confirming to existing roles or positions received a higher agreement (e.g., Software Architect, Product Manager, and Software Developer). Novel roles received less agreement but not total disagreement (e.g., SPL Consolidation Developer and SPL Manager).

Result of applicability The roles defined as part of the SPLEVO process were created by considering information captured during interviews with industrial participants. Furthermore, they were satisfyingly validated in an online survey. The survey itself asked about concrete persons to fill the roles. This type of question is considered to be more restrictive than asking about the validity of the roles, only. It requires not only to understand and support a role but to associate a known person with it. Accordingly, the agreement with the roles themselves is stated to be at least the same or even stronger as reflected by the answers.

Finally, the roles are assessed to be appropriate and, thus, the consolidation process is assessed to be fit for industrial applications.

8.9.2. Evaluation Question II.2: Benefit of Structured Guidance

To evaluate the benefit of the structured guidance of the explicit process, we have reviewed the current situation reported in the interviews and argue for the automation and structure provided by the SPLEVO process. The argumentation is chosen as comparing case studies performing a consolidation with and without the guidance was not possible in the industrial case study.

Reported heterogeneity and overheads The interview participants all reported about the varying implementation of variability in their products. While they reported about common sense techniques to implement variability, they further reported to have no clear definition of when to use a concrete one. Furthermore, several iterations to prove and adapt a new variability with development and product management are reported.

Deduced benefit The proposed consolidation process targets those two reported issues. Specifying an explicit list of variability mechanisms in advance obviously provides a benefit compared to individual implementations for achieving more consistent solutions. Similarly, performing a consolidation in a structured manner and applying the contributions of the SPLEVO approach (e.g., models and analyses) obviously leads to reduced efforts because of the automation and the reduction of feedback cycles for coordinating the variability realization. Furthermore, the clear responsibilities and stakeholders to consider reduce the risk of missing information and support an awareness for consolidations in general. Finally, the required overhead to apply the explicit process can reduce the benefit. However, this overhead depends on the culture of the individual company. Similar to agile processes in general, the SPLEVO approach recommends to apply the process in a lean manner to reduce the overhead as much as possible. Thus, we argue for the benefit of the structured guidance provided by the SPLEVO process.

8.10. Threats to Validity

The following subsections describe possible threats to the validity of the evaluation. However, they were tolerated in order to being able to perform an evaluation to this extent and to provide at least fundamental answers to all identified evaluation questions.

Degrees of freedom in SPL decisions Realizing SPLs allows for many degrees of freedom to cope with individual preferences (Section 2.2). The SPLEVO approach allows for supporting a broad variety of these degrees. While it is not feasible to validate all of them, concrete preferences were assumed during the evaluation (e.g., the specified consolidation refactoring). This comes with a potential risk of differing results when choosing other preferences for the future SPL. However, most of the evaluation questions and metrics were designed for independence of such preferences (e.g., the results returned by the variability or difference analyses).

Types of modifications The case studies performed do not cover all types of modifications. For example, in the ArgoUML case study, no modifications for introducing new member classes exist. Thus, there is a potential risk of types of code modifications being not covered by the case studies performed but influencing the evaluation results. To cope with this risk, the ArgoUML case study was chosen because it covers a variety of different modifications. Finally, the additional industrial case study was performed to reduce the risk even further.

Influence in interviews and surveys The interviews and the survey performed had to cope with several challenges representing potential threats to their validity. First, a higher number of participants would have been desirable, but the required knowledge and experience limited the amount of possible participants. For example, the interviews about the refactoring specification required participants in use with JaMoPP, MDSD, and refactorings. This strongly reduced the number of available participants but allowed for not confusing the participants with new technologies and topics not in the focus of the interviews.

Furthermore, the interviews and the survey were performed only about parts of the overall SPLEVO approach in order to not exceed the time the participants had to invest. Thus, only partial information about the concepts could be presented (e.g., only parts of the refactoring specification). For example, the roles presented in the survey were only summarized and not discussed to their full extent. This represents a potential threat to the validity of the answers. However, the tendencies and qualitative feedback received allow for a reasonable reliability in the results.

Finally, the interviews performed about the refactoring specification concept were influenced by the quality of the concrete refactoring specification provided by the said student. Thus, the interview was designed in a way that reduced the influence of the concrete specification as much as possible.

Validity of argumentation Some evaluation questions could be answered with an argumentative approach only. Case studies and empirical experiments would have been preferred but were not possible due to the unavailability of according setups. However, the argumentative approach allowed for providing at least directing answers for the according evaluation questions.

8.11. Evaluation Summary

The presented evaluation confirmed the validity of the SPLEVO approach and the evaluation results corroborate the overall hypotheses (i.e., Hypothesis I and II).

Hypothesis I.I (Difference Analysis) Hypothesis I.I was corroborated by a 100% recall of the specialized difference analysis, which allows for a fully automated difference analysis phase. Furthermore, considering copy-based customization practices allowed for reducing the manual effort in terms of irrelevant differences by about 18%.

Hypothesis I.II (Variability Design) Hypothesis I.II was corroborated as the Program Dependency Analysis allowed for reducing the manual effort by about 72% on average in the ArgoUML case study and by about 75% on average in the industrial case study. The Shared Term Analysis achieved a benefit of only 10% to 22% in the ArgoUML and even none in the industrial case study. Analyzing relationships based on simultaneous modifications was not possible at all because of the unavailability of according data.

To conclude, analyzing relations between the differences allows for reducing developers' manual effort in general, but the actual benefit depends on the type of relationship under study and the concrete scenario it is used in.

Furthermore, analyzing dependent modifications turned out as the most promising strategy.

Hypothesis I.III (Consolidation Refactoring) Hypothesis I.III was corroborated by the fitness of the proposed concept for specifying the novel type of refactorings for introducing variability mechanisms during copy consolidation. Interviews proved the capability of the concept to specify unambiguous refactorings, and a case study with a concrete refactoring proved its capability for automation. Furthermore, the characteristics considered in the specification concept allow for reducing the effort for selecting variability mechanisms (e.g., approximately 2 1/4 hours in the industrial case study) and reducing the risk of non-optimal decisions (e.g., removing the risk of 1,710 respectively 4,095 non-optimal decisions in the industrial case study).

Hypothesis II (Consolidation Process) Hypothesis II was corroborated by the capability to implement the process and the appropriateness of the roles to execute the activities of the process respectively provide the necessary input. The appropriateness of the roles was proven in interviews and an online survey with four respectively 18 industrial participants. Especially for the three primary roles, nearly all survey participants agreed to being able to name existing persons able to fill these roles. The benefit of the guidance follows from the support of challenges in the current ad hoc consolidation approaches explicitly declared in the interviews.

9. Assumptions and Limitations

This chapter presents the assumptions this thesis proceeds on and discusses the limitations of the approach. The following sections, first, describe the assumptions of this thesis. Afterwards, they discuss the limitations structured according to the possible automation, the approach itself, the prototype, and limitations that are not directly in the scope of this thesis.

9.1. Assumptions as Preconditions

Valid product copies as input The SPLEVO approach assumes product copies that can be compiled and executed. Depending on the infrastructure used by extracting software models, it might be possible to process partial copies or copies producing compiler errors. However, unresolved references can lead to wrong results, such as unmatched type references during the difference analysis.

Consolidation decision It is assumed that the decision whether to consolidate the copies or not has been performed in advance. The approach does not support this decision, especially in terms of strategic management decisions or cost estimation. However, it aims for reducing the manual effort and thus supports a decision to consolidate.

Validity of developer decisions It is assumed that developers make valid decisions when deciding about presented recommendations or editing the Variation Point Model (VPM) manually. For example, developers are able to delete Variation Points (VPs) manually to ignore a specific code variation. This can have a strong impact on the downstream analysis and design recommendations because of VP relationships that will not be detected anymore. The approach does not include any validation of such developer decisions.

Renaming rules and Derived Copies The approach assumes SPL Consolidation Developers to provide rules for any renaming strategies that have been applied during copy-based customization. No automated renaming detection is performed as part of the difference analysis to not risk missing differences and thus invalidating the reliable automation. However, on the one side, tools for detecting naming patterns can be used to support developers in providing such rules. On the other side, if such rules are not provided, the result of the difference analysis is still valid even when existing Derived Copies cannot be detected. Furthermore, the proposed strategies to filter irrelevant differences allow to cope with such misses.

9.2. Limitations of Automation

A fully automated consolidation is not possible in general. At least, it will not result in a satisfying Software Product Line (SPL). From a technical perspective, one can apply the SPLEVO approach in a fully automated manner and accept all recommendations by default. However, individual preferences and the actual need in specific scenarios would be ignored completely. Furthermore, as shown in the evaluation, automatically detecting and aggregating related modifications (i.e., VPs) cannot be done with 100% recall and precision. Thus, the resulting SPL will be non-optimal in the best and invalid in the worst case. As an alternative, the initial VPMs can be used for refactoring, but the resulting SPL will provide too many individual VPs to be handled in practice.

9.3. Limitations of Approach

Individual scenarios There is no "one size fits all" process or analysis configuration to be applied in all scenarios. We identified reasonable configurations during the evaluation, such as the Shared Term Analysis used with detecting shared term clusters. However, even those do not provide benefit for all scenarios, as shown for the Shared Term Analysis in the industrial case study.

Extensive code beautifying Extensive code beautifying, such as renaming and restructuring, can lead to many differences and thus many VPs to handle. As a result, the analysis possibly recommends aggregations including such VPs and reducing the total value for developers. However, the need to review such modifications exists independently from the SPLEVO approach. To cope with this, strategies to filter VPs representing code beautifying have been presented, but a manual investigation is still necessary.

Multi-feature modifications SoftwareElements that have been modified several times for different features can lead to relationships between otherwise unrelated modifications. For example, data items for different features have been added to the initialization of the same list element. From the perspective of the analysis, a valid relationship has been detected. However, a manual investigation is required to handle such cases and thus lowers the benefit of the analysis.

9.4. Limitations of Prototype

Pairwise consolidation In general, companies creating copy-based customizations typically create more than one copy before deciding for a consolidation. Due to the EMF Compare infrastructure used in the SPLEVO prototype, it is currently limited to pairwise comparisons. However, concepts, algorithms, and metamodels of the SPLEVO approach are able to handle more than two copies at the same time.

9.5. Out-of-Scope Limitations

Tests The SPLEVO approach has been developed to consolidate productive code. Test code has been excluded from the scope of the approach as it comes with different characteristics and requirements. For example, it is theoretically possible to consolidate test code by introducing a variability mechanism in the test code itself. However, this would not be sufficient for a test in context of an SPL. Here, a test should not be variable itself but prove the system under test with different configurations.

Consolidation and modernization In practice, consolidation is often performed tightly connected with modernization projects – for example, consolidating product copies and introducing a new version of a framework at the same time. Changing an infrastructure while performing a consolidation can invalidate the assumption of valid product copies because the code might not be free of compilation errors anymore. Furthermore, the effect of continuously changing the implementation during the consolidation process is not clear yet and must be studied in an according scenario.

Part III.

Outlook and Conclusion

10. Related Work

This chapter presents and discusses approaches related to the challenges of consolidating customized product copies as targeted by this thesis and its contributions. The foundations presented in Section 2 are not repeated again.

Figure 10.1 illustrates the main groups of related work aligned to the main phases of the SPLEVO approach. The following sections present the related work according to these groups: Approaches for handling copies in general are presented in Section 10.1. Section 10.2 presents approaches for improving existing Software Product Lines (SPLs) and approaches for analyzing programs are discussed in Section 10.3. The modeling of software variation points is a comprehensive topic related to the SPLEVO approach and is discussed in Section 10.4.

10.1. Handling Copies

Related research on handling customized product copies can be distinguished into three types of approaches: concepts and model consolidation, implementation-aware consolidation, and approaches for extracting feature models from existing product copies or variants.

10.1.1. Consolidation Framework and Process

Concepts for consolidations and model consolidations are on a more abstract level, discussing how to treat design artifacts or describe process for consolidation. They do not provide concrete guidance for consolidating the implementation of the copies.

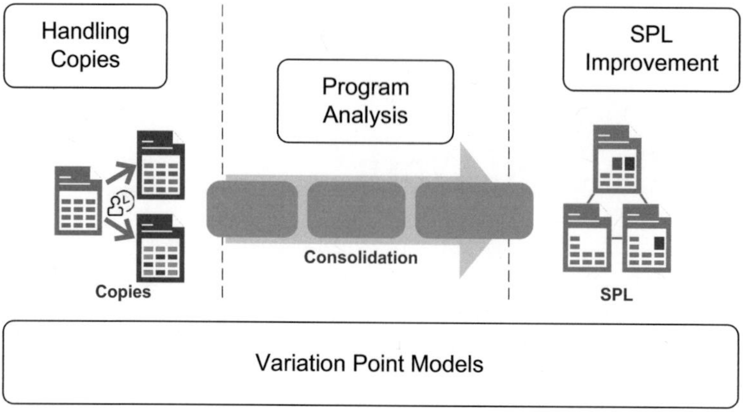

Figure 10.1.: Groups of related work aligned to the SPLEVO approach

Consolidation framework Rubin and Chechik [162, 160] propose a framework to merge customized product variants in general. They describe an algorithm to consolidate the software design models of the product copies based on a formalized "merge-in" operator. Their general algorithm can be adapted to other abstraction levels but a concrete merge-in operator needs to be defined. Their approach does not allow for new feature combinations as it would be possible with the SPLEVO approach with an according variation point design. Furthermore, we identified several challenges, such as the amount of difference and handling technical constraints, which are not reflected by their approach.

Consolidation process Schütz [172] describes a process to consolidate copy-based customized products into an SPL. He describes a general consolidation process comparable to the approach presented in this thesis. He recommends to use an adapted difference analysis and to investigate variability based on reverse engineering tools. However, he remains on the process level and does not name any concrete solutions or implementations for his recommendations as done in this thesis. Schütz [172] claims to use additional non-implementation artifacts such as marketing descriptions or user guides. Considering such documents is a complementary direction to this thesis. While it is not integrated in the SPLEVO approach, the SPL Manager and Product Manager roles are assumed to consider according information manually. Furthermore, approaches such as proposed by Alves et al. [5] could be considered to facilitate such information in context of the variability design.

10.1.2. Implementation-Aware Consolidation

Implementation-aware consolidation approaches consider the implementation of the customized copies and provide guidance for the according challenges.

Reflexion method Koschke et al. [108] propose an approach for consolidating customized product copies by assigning their features to module structures. They propose to use the reflexion method introduced by Murphy et al. [135]. In a second step, they propose to identify copy-specific features based on the different mappings between features and modules. Their approach is limited to scenarios with appropriate module descriptions available. However, it is complimentary to the SPLEVO approach and could be used as an additional relationship analysis if reliable module descriptions are available.

Detecting variation points using dynamic analysis Cornelissen et al. [35] propose to compare the Program Execution Traces (PETs) of the same feature in different variants of a program for detecting variation points in their implementation. These analysis techniques themselves origin from Chen and Rajlich [31], and Wilde and Scully [194]. Their approach is complementary to the SPLEVO and can be used to analyze dependent modification relationships as discussed in Section 6.1.3.1.

Visualization of potential reuse Duszynski [47] propose an approach to analyze existing product copies about their differences and commonalities and provide developers with a visualization of the results to support their reuse decisions. The approach of Duszynski [47] contributes to the field of copy consolidation, as this thesis does. In contrast, Duszynski [47] focus on visualizing information instead of guiding to variability design decisions. However, the two approaches are complementary and evaluating their integration to gain improved usability in terms of visualization and guidance is a reasonable direction of future work.

10.1.3. Feature and Variant Model Extraction

Several approaches have been proposed to extract feature models from customized copies or related products. Some describe this as a first step towards a consolidation (e.g., Ziadi et al. [197], Al-Msie'Deen et al. [134] and Al-Msie'Deen [133]), others use such models for a continuous management of customized product forks (e.g., Rubin et al. [165]).

Feature model extraction from coarse grain differences Ziadi et al. [197] propose a consolidation approach based on reverse engineering a model representation of the product copies, identifying feature candidates based on these models, and manually pruning the candidates as well as adding missing ones. The resulting model is used as a base to build a feature model. The goal of their approach is to support the reverse engineering of feature models from the differences and commonalities of existing product copies. They do not support the consolidation itself. Furthermore, while considering the existing implementations of the product copies to reverse engineer valid model representations, their abstraction is coarse grain (i.e., classes and packages) and does not reflect fine and medium granular differences.

Feature detection from building blocks Al-Msie'Deen et al. [134] and Al-Msie'Deen [133] propose an approach to derive features from object-oriented code based on Information Retrieval (IR) techniques as proposed by Marcus et al. [127] for concept location in general. Their goal is to provide a feature model for supporting a manual consolidation later on. They propose to use Latent Semantic Indexing (LSI) and Formal Concept Analysis (FCA) to identify related software elements based on included terms and derive according features. The approach of Al-Msie'Deen et al. [134] is complementary to the SPLEVO approach and might be integrated as an additional relationship analysis.

However, in their case studies they used sets of product variants each containing all available features except for one. In relation to copy consolidation, this represents a scenario with the same customized features implemented in exactly the same manner in different copies. This setup is beneficial to clustering approaches as several copies provide the same data sets. Accordingly, the benefit of their approach in context of consolidating independently developed copies as targeted by this thesis needs to be evaluated.

Managing forked product variants Rubin et al. [165] target the challenge of handling forked (copied) and customized product copies. Their approach contributes to the field of handling customized copies in general but it is not about consolidating them into an SPL.

Change dependency model Rubin et al. [165] introduce a model called "Product Line Changeset Dependency Model (PL-CDM)" to describe and later query the dependencies between SPL features and their implementation in the product variants. This model relates to the Variation Point Model (VPM) of the SPLEVO approach in terms of identifying varying software elements in the product copies. However, its purpose is to track those differences and not to iteratively build a variability design for consolidation as it is possible with the VPM of the SPLEVO approach.

Facilitating information from Version Control Systems (VCSs) Rubin et al. [165] assume to have a mature VCS in place to receive data to build their model. Rubin et al. [165, page 4] propose to apply program dependency analysis on the change sets captured by this system. They argue for the existence and application of such systems in practice as done for the SPLEVO approach in context of analyzing simultaneous modifications (Section 6.1.3.3). However, as shown in our industrial case study, this assumption does not hold in all cases. Furthermore, commits cannot be assumed as fully reliable indicators in practice. On the one side, one cannot assume that modifications committed at once are about a single feature only (e.g., during offline development). On the other side, Rubin et al. [165] assume all modifications committed to a single branch as related to each other. In the general case, this can be too coarse grain, as a branch might have been created for a specific customer and not for a specific feature only. In contrast to their analysis, the SPLEVO approach is also applicable if no sufficient VCS is in place.

10.2. SPL Improvement

One topic in the area of SPL evolution is the improvement of existing SPLs. Research in this area covers the reverse engineering of feature models, the encapsulation of features within a single code base, and the refactoring of features for improving their variability.

10.2.1. Feature Model Reverse Engineering

Feature models have been proven to support the management of variability especially in highly configurable software systems. However, She et al. [175] and Acher et al. [1] report that feature models are rarely available and creating them manually is error-prone and tedious. Accordingly, approaches to reverse engineer feature models from existing SPLs have been proposed to cope with this challenge. The approaches proposed by She et al. [175] and Acher et al. [1] are representatives in this field.

Building feature model hierarchies She et al. [175] propose an approach for building a feature model structure in terms of hierarchy and dependencies. Their approach requires a list of features and formalized dependencies between them. First, the approach supports the user in manually building a feature hierarchy. To decide for a parent of a feature, the approach recommends reasonable parent features based on the provided dependencies between features and terms shared in their descriptions. When the feature hierarchy is created, the approach automatically detects constraints between the hierarchical features based on the dependencies. The approach of She et al. [175] is complementary to the SPLEVO approach and can be used to support the user in building a hierarchy on top of a flat feature model exported from the created VPM.

Architectural feature models Acher et al. [1] extend the approach of She et al. [175] in the context of architectural models. They aggregate a feature model provided by an architect as well as features and constraints between them derived from the actual components of the system under study. For the latter, they consider each component of a system as a feature, and the feature constraints are derived from the component dependencies. Applying the approach of She et al. [175] to this input, they achieve an architectural feature model including the actual constraints in the system.

Similar to the approach of She et al. [175], the approach of Acher et al. [1] can be used to further extend the SPLEVO approach. The SPLEVO approach has been designed to be adaptable for new technologies, which includes component models (Section 3.4.2). Thus, it would be reasonable to evaluate the benefit of the approach of Acher et al. [1] for analyzing further relationships between variation points. This is comparable to an integration with the reflexion method proposed by Koschke et al. [108].

10.2.2. SPL Refactoring

SPL refactoring approaches are proposed to protect and improve the value of an SPL and its variability over time. A continuous improvement to cope with challenges as evolving variability is described in the problem statement by Juergens and Pizka [89].

Extracting and refactoring product lines with AOP Alves et al. [4] propose a two-step SPL consolidation approach with a focus on refactoring the resulting feature model. First, they propose to manually refactor the existing products to a common core with encapsulated features using Aspect Oriented Programming (AOP) and to manually build an according feature model (i.e., called "SPL bootstrapping"). Afterwards, they refactor the initial feature model to improve its configurability according to the SPL refactoring defined in Alves et al. [3].

SPL Bootstrapping To support the extraction of a shared product core and variable features, Alves et al. [3] recommend deriving feature models from documentation and using the concern location techniques to identify them in the code. In particular, they use the program dependency-based concern location approach proposed by Robillard and Murphy [158]. The names of the features manually derived from the documentations serve as input for the concern location. In contrast, the SPLEVO approach focuses on the extraction of the common core and variable features and, thus, could be used for an extended support for the first step proposed by Alves et al. [3]. Additionally, the SPLEVO approach does not rely on the availability of valid seeds as required by Alves et al. [4, page 77] but uses them if available. As identified in our case studies, this assumption is too limiting.

AOP limitation Alves et al. [4] propose an approach focused on AOP by mapping concerns to aspects. As reported by Gacek and Anastasopoules [64, page 5], AOP does not support run time variability. Furthermore, Kästner et al. [92, 93] report about the limitations of AOP for supporting statements at arbitrary positions in a method body or accessing local variables. The SPLEVO approach is not limited to a specific variability mechanism but allows for specifying intended mechanisms to cope with the need for different variability characteristics.

Solution consistency In the approach presented by Alves et al. [3], the resulting variability design completely depends on the individual capabilities of the consolidating developers, and the realization decision is made upfront due to their approach (i.e., AOP). To cope with the potential risk of inconsistent solutions, the SPLEVO approach explicitly distinguishes between and provides support for variability structure, characteristics, and realization decisions.

Degenerated SPLs Nunes et al. [137] propose an approach for handling degenerated SPLs (e.g., incompatible or redundant product-specific features). Their goal is to support the evolution of an SPL with a focus on product specific adaptations which become incompatible with the core SPL. Nunes et al. [137] propose to analyze the history of the core SPL and the derived products to consider their evolution in the change dimensions of product adaptions and SPL releases. Nunes et al. [137] assume to have an initial feature model available and a VCS providing the required history information. Furthermore, they do not support the initial creation of an SPL by consolidating independently customized product copies.

Trace links and feature impact Eyal-Salman et al. [57] present an approach to identify trace links between features and code artifacts implementing these features. They use a Latent Semantic Indexing (LSI) approach from the field of information retrieval to distinguish between common and differing code parts of the compared variants. Furthermore, they assume to have documented features available to use them as search queries, and their approach is limited to package and class changes. Eyal-Salman et al. [56] extend this approach by predicting features that are influenced by a specific code change. The purpose of their reverse engineering approach is not about consolidating customized copies or designing variability as done in this thesis, but to use trace links for the continuous management of the feature implementations.

10.2.3. Refactoring Specification

The restructuring of existing code to improve its quality properties, such as comprehensibility, is an essential task in software engineering.

Traditional refactoring Fowler et al. [63] provides a fundamental catalog of refactorings (Section 2.4.11). This catalog includes a template for specifying refactorings in a comprehensible manner (Fowler et al. [63, p. 85]). The refactoring specification of the SPLEVO approach is aligned to the template proposed by Fowler et al. [63] because it is widely accepted and well understood (i.e., name, summary, motivation, mechanics, examples). In addition, it adds variability aspects and distinguishes between general information about the variability mechanism introduced and the refactoring of individual software elements. The latter is necessary to process Variation Points (VPs) implemented by different elements at different locations. In contrast, refactorings specified by Fowler et al. [63] target only a specific set of software elements.

Role-based refactoring specification Reimann et al. [156] propose a formal specification of refactorings of models to allow for specifying refactorings in an abstract manner and reuse them for concrete metamodels. In context of this thesis, such a reuse might be useful if the same consolidation refactorings should be specified for similar types of software models. However, the benefit of reusing consolidation refactorings through such an abstraction is not evaluated yet. Furthermore, the approach of Reimann et al. [156] has been initially tested by Daniel [40] for implementing the automation of the conditional refactoring as part of the evaluation of this thesis. This initial test was stopped because of the challenging abstraction and limitations of the current implementation of the approach (e.g., several roles with the same metamodel type were not possible).

10.3. Program Analysis

10.3.1. Feature Location Techniques

Feature Location Techniques in context of SPLs Rubin and Chechik [161] survey existing feature location techniques and their usage for a transition to an SPL. They identify shortcomings of existing techniques, such as their limitation to single code bases. In addition, they describe the potential benefit of adapting and applying these techniques to the field of SPLs. Rubin and Chechik [161] demand to further evaluate those techniques and their benefits for transitions to an SPL approach. The SPLEVO approach presented in this thesis conforms to this direction and provides a concrete strategy for applying such techniques for a consolidation (i.e., a transition to an SPL). Furthermore, the evaluation performed within this thesis provides insight about the benefits of applying some of these techniques.

Feature Location Techniques in general Dit et al. [43] perform an extensive survey on feature location techniques (89 articles from 25 venues) and report open challenges, such as selecting an appropriate technique or the need for further evaluation on specific techniques. Dit et al. [43, page 40] explicitly state the need for further evaluation on the benefit of textual based techniques from the field of Natural Language Program Analysis

(NLPA). The results presented in this thesis contribute to this open challenge and provide insight about the limited benefit of NLPA for locating product-specific features.

10.3.2. Relationship Classification

Program dependency classification Wilde [193] proposes a classification of program dependencies. He distinguishes different types of elements that can depend to each other (e.g., Data Types, Data Items, and Source Files) as well as different strategies to discover them (e.g., textual search, cross referencing, tracing indirect dependencies, and data flow methods).

The types and sources for identifications proposed by Wilde [193] are related to the relationship types the SPLEVO approach proposes for investigation (e.g., simultaneous modifications are not included). However, on the one side, the SPLEVO approach defines program dependencies in a more restrictive way than done by Wilde. They are defined to be implemented with the syntax of a programming language (e.g., represented in a Program Dependency Graph (PDG) or by PET). On the other side, the SPLEVO relationship types cover more types of relationships (i.e., dependencies in the terminology of Wilde [193]). For example, they include not only textual similarities but also relationships resulting from time and issue aspects. The differing classifications are not in contrast to each other but serve different purposes as Wilde classified dependencies in general and the SPLEVO approach does it in context of analyzing VPs.

10.3.3. Clone Detection

Clone detection is one of the major topics related to handling copied code. However, consolidating copies is about identifying the differences between copies and to transform them into variability. Clone detection is about finding similar code to remove their redundancy (i.e., introducing reuse). Hence, the algorithms to handle differences differ and requirements specific to the consolidation context as described in Section 5.1 are not supported at all.

However, clone detection can be used to identify relationships between code fragments as described in Section 6.1.3.2 and for filtering variation points that can be ignored as described in Section 6.1.2. Thus, clone detection is an analysis to be used complementary to the SPLEVO approach.

10.3.4. Difference Analysis

Difference analysis in general and program differences in specific have been targets of research for several years. Also in practice, many solutions have been developed and used. However, the specific needs for consolidating customized code copies are not targeted yet. Hence none of the approaches below targets those needs, but they are related in the context of program difference analysis in general.

State of the practice In practice, identifying differences between code copies is often done with general purpose tools such as GNU Diff introduced by MacKenzie et al. [124]. They are able to analyze any kind of textual artifacts but fail to align their results with programming language structures. Modern development environments such as Eclipse [48] provide comparison tools for specific programming languages respecting the languages' syntax. However, they do not support requirements such as taking renaming into account.

Semantic differences Apiwattanapong et al. [8] define an algorithm respecting programming language structures and Control Flow Graph (CFG)s to filter differences in methods without a change in the methods' observable behavior. With the same goal, Jackson and Ladd [87] study the input and output of methods. In contrast to their approaches, the SPLEVO approach needs to identify all code modifications possibly relevant to introduce variability. For example, code modifications within a method calling a new external dependency might not change the semantic of a method, but the external dependency might need be reflected by variable feature. Furthermore, changes to a systems' status within the method are not reflected in the input and output of a method. However, interpreting the semantic of a difference is complementary to the SPLEVO approach to identify candidates of variation points to filter (Section 6.1.2).

Change types and impacts Fluri and Gall [61] and Fluri et al. [62] have identified different types of code changes and their impact on software evolution. They use heuristics for detecting move operations to improve their analysis results. They report about the benefit of these improvements in the context of their change impact assessment. However, falsely identified move operations potentially lead to missed differences and, thus, contradict a fully automated difference analysis as required in the SPLEVO approach.

Differencing XML software representations Maletic and Collard [125] proposed a generic concept to support difference analysis by querying XML representations of the source code. XML in general and the srcML format used by them in specific provide data structures supporting queries compared to plain textual code representations. However, they propose to apply standard textual difference analysis which requires to interpret the differing structures later on. In contrast, our difference analysis approach allows for an improved difference analysis based on the software elements themselves.

10.3.5. Merging

Merging approaches as motivated by Perry et al. [147] and surveyed by Mens [131] are used to integrate parallel modifications of the same resource with each other (Section 2.4.7.3). From a high level perspective, consolidating customized product copies is a similar task. However, in contrast to traditional merging, consolidation requires to introduce variability mechanisms when integrating the code differences. This is not a straight forward approach and requires to design variability in advance to achieve a useful SPL.

Nevertheless, the field of merging provides techniques that are reasonable to be evaluated to improve the SPLEVO approach. One example is the renaming detection proposed by Malpohl et al. [126] for filtering variation points as described in Section 6.1.2.

10.4. Variation Point Models

Managing variability is one of the major aspects in SPL engineering. Thus several models have been proposed to express variability as introduced in Section 2.3.2. In the SPLEVO approach, software variability and feature modeling from a product and requirements perspective are distinguished as done by Svahnberg et al. [183] (Section 3.2.1). An integration respectively an extensible export to arbitrary feature models is part of the concept.

Existing variation point models As introduced in Section 2.3.2, many mature models exist in the field of software variability. For example, Pohl et al. [149] propose the Orthogonal Variability Model, and the Object Management Group (OMG) is currently working on the Common Variability Language (CVL) [76]. Both conform with the definition of a variation point of Jacobson et al. [88]. Other types of variability modeling techniques such as the UML extension of Gomaa [67] or the "Product Line Changeset Dependency Model" proposed by Rubin et al. [165] have been proposed as well. However, the SPLEVO approach introduces a novel Variation Point Model (VPM) designed to cope with the challenges of a consolidation not covered by the existing models.

VPM: Variation Point Groups The SPLEVO VPM differs from the definition of a variation point proposed by Jacobson et al. [88] and also used in the Orthogonal Variability Model and the CVL. While they use a variation point to identify one or more locations of variability, a variation point in the VPM represents a single location of variability only. In addition, a VariationPointGroup element is proposed to explicitly combine several locations of variability (i.e., variation points). This concept allows for defining the aggregation operators for iteratively improving the variation point design (Section 6.1.1).

VPM: Variation Point Characteristics VPs in the SPLEVO VPM allow for individually assigning variability characteristics and realization mechanisms. For example, a feature might be realized by several VPs. One of them requires to load a component through dependency injection, which would allow for product level extensibility, too. At the same time, another VP of the same feature is about a database connection stored in a configuration file, which requires a completely different variability mechanism.

The CVL proposed by Haugen [76] provides an element named VSpec intended to express characteristics of a variation point. However, the possible characteristics allows specifying a resolution time (i.e., binding time) but without a semantic in the CVL according to Haugen [76]: "resolutionTime : "String [1..1] The latest life-cycle stage at which this VSpec is expected to be resolved, e.g. Design, Link, Build, PostBuild, etc. It has no semantics within CVL.". Furthermore, the extensibility of a VP is expressed by sub types of the VariationPoint metamodel class and the extensibility is expressed by the cardinality of child VSpec elements. In contrast, the SPLEVO VPM allows for defining straight characteristics supporting their automatic evaluation and improved comprehensibility.

VPM: Lightweight for analysis Variation point models are created for different purposes such as configuration or SPL domain analysis. The SPLEVO approach has been created to provide only those infrastructure required in the context of a consolidation and being easy to understand by developers and lightweight to be processed.

11. Future Work

This chapter presents directions for future research that have been discovered in this thesis in general and during the evaluation in specific. The following subsections describe these directions distinguished in four topics. First, Section 11.1 demands for revising and evaluating the SPLEVO approach for continuous Software Product Line (SPL) maintenance. Next, Section 11.3 discusses the adaptation of the SPLEVO approach for specific domains. Afterwards, Section 11.4 demands for studying the usability of relationship analysis tooling. Finally, Section 11.2 argues for extending the refactoring support with reusable abstractions of custom variability.

11.1. Continuous SPL Maintenance

When companies successfully adopted an SPL approach, continuous maintenance and evolution are critical for its long-term success (e.g., Clements and Northrop [33], Böckle et al. [18] and Pohl et al. [149]). In recent years, product-specific adaptations that are not reflected in the SPL have been identified as a challenge in the field of SPL maintenance (i.e., degenerated SPLs according to Nunes et al. [137]). Beside others, they lead to incompatibilities and additional management overheads.

It is a reasonable direction of future work to study the benefits the SPLEVO approach can provide to this challenge. An integration as a round trip SPL engineering would allow for a more efficient reactive SPL approach.

11.2. Custom Variability Mechanisms

In addition to generally applicable variability mechanisms, companies introduce custom infrastructure for configuration management in their products – for example, realizing run time variability configured according to license information stored in a database. The proposed specification concept already allows for specifying an according consolidation refactoring. However, Reimann et al. [156] proposed a generalization of traditional refactorings valuable to reuse according mechanisms for different languages. Based on their findings, it should be studied if a generalization of consolidation refactorings is valuable to simplify the specification of custom variability mechanisms – for example, studying the possibility and value of specifying refactorings for license-aware run time variability in general and mapping this to custom license mechanisms.

11.3. Domain-Specific Adaptations

Software engineering for domains such as embedded systems, mobile applications, or automotive uses specific development techniques and artifacts. This includes Domain Specific Languages (DSLs) and domain-specific variability mechanisms. Investigating in the adaptation of the SPLEVO approach for such conditions possibly allows for exploiting additional information to further improve the analysis and automate the process.

For example, in the field of mobile applications, development infrastructure comes with specific artifacts, such as configuration files, and coding practices, such as libraries, components, or coding styles. This information can provide additional information to find new relationships and identify existing ones more precisely. Furthermore, marketplaces for mobile applications, such as the Apple iTunes or Google Play provide license and payment infrastructure that can be integrated in variability mechanisms. Consolidation refactorings introducing according variability mechanisms could be developed in a reusable manner, which is similar to the refactoring reuse in context of custom variability mechanisms described in the last section.

As a direction of future research, individual domains should be analyzed and case studies to prove the benefit of individual adaptations should be performed.

11.4. Usability for Developers

A critical factor for the end-to-end efficiency of software engineering approaches is the usability and integration in development environments. As observed in our case studies, the accessibility of information and simplicity to provide input can have a big impact on the user acceptance. For example, visualizing the relationships between differences as graph to identify central variation points improved the interpretation of the findings. Similar requirements were reported during the interview workshop.

The observed performance and scalability of the SPLEVO analyses were sufficient for an application throughout the case studies and satisfying for industrial application. However, performance gains, especially enabling real time relationship analyses, would allow for new usability concepts, such as informing developers about related code locations when editing source code. Such concepts could actively force consistent variability implementations.

Many approaches for improved source code processing have been proposed in the field of software analyses. For example, Hunt [84] analyzed differences based on the parse tree of programs only. Investigating in such approaches is reasonable to achieve real time analyses and new usability concepts.

Thus, investigations in new usability concepts and integration with Integrated Development Environments (IDEs) are reasonable directions of future research to further evolve the SPLEVO approach and improve consolidation processes in general.

11.5. Variability and Design Decisions

Introduce variability, in particular implementing a variation point with a concrete variability mechanism is a software design decision. The rational for this design decision is the intention to support the original copy-specific feature in a SPL and to benefit from the SPL advantages.

Research in the field of software evolution has identified benefits from tracing and reusing design decisions to improve design decisions in the future (e.g., Durdik and Reussner [46], Könemann and Zimmermann [106] and Küster and Trifu [116]). Combining this direction of research with the SPLEVO approach might allow for i) tracing the rationale for introduced variation points to guide their future evolution and ii) to further support Software Architects and SPL Consolidation Developers when deciding for variability mechanisms during a consolidation. The former direction has already been sketched in Küster and Klatt [115].

12. Conclusion

This chapter summarizes this thesis, concludes about the hypotheses, and discusses additional insight gained by the evaluation. It starts with a short summary of the topic and its motivation, followed by scientific questions targeted and the hypotheses advanced by this thesis. Afterwards, the chapter summarizes the contributions as well as their evaluation. Finally, additional insight and directions for future work identified by this thesis are presented.

Topic and motivation The presented thesis contributes to the field of Software Product Line (SPL) development based on customized product copies and their challenges for a long-term maintenance and business success. Such customized product copies are a barrier for growth due to redundant maintenance costs and unused potentials of synergy effects and cross selling. To overcome this barrier and benefit from the advantages of a SPL with explicit reuse and variability management, a consolidation of the customized product copies is necessary. Such consolidations are known to be challenging themselves. Corresponding problem statements of too high manual expenses, wasted efforts, and inconsistent implementations have been formulated to guide the presented research.

Scientific questions and hypotheses The scientific questions of which information can support developers to cope with those challenges and how to gather them from the available sources form the basis of this thesis. To target these questions, this thesis has advanced the hypothesis that software analyses can be used to identify related differences and derive recommendations to design the variability of the future SPL. Additionally, it advances the hypothesis that a structured process is not only valuable to prevent coordination overheads but supports a consistent variability implementation. Rubin and Chechik [161] describe in their survey on feature location techniques explicitly the necessity to adopt and evaluate those techniques for supporting the transition to an SPL.

Contributions of the SPLEVO approach To corroborate these hypotheses, this thesis proposes the novel SPLEVO approach. It contributes a fully automated model-based difference analysis that considers copy-based customization-specific practices to improve the results. Additionally, a novel model for iteratively designing variability is introduced and automatically initialized by the difference analysis. Based on this model, the SPLEVO approach provides analyses to recommend design decisions for improving the initial variability design. Furthermore, it proposes a novel refactoring specification concept and a recommendation system to enable a guided refactoring for achieving an SPL with consistently implemented variability. Finally, a consolidation process is specified in terms of activities and stakeholders to reduce overheads and enable efficient decisions.

Evaluation An evaluation based on case studies, interviews, and an online survey has been performed. In the case studies, variants of the industrial-ready open-source modeling tool ArgoUML and copies of a commercial product were investigated. The ArgoUML case study provided pre-documented feature-specific code as a benchmark for the analyses of the SPLEVO approach. In contrast, the copies of the commercial product have evolved over several years under industrial conditions. The interviews and survey have been performed with industrial participants and evaluated different aspects of the approach in context of state of the practice environments

The case studies confirmed the benefit of the analyses in terms of a fully automated difference analysis that is further improved by filtering irrelevant differences by considering copy-based customization-specific practices, such as copies still accessing the code their originate from. Furthermore, analyzing relationships between differences has been proven to be valuable for identifying differences that contribute to the same custom feature and for recommending according design decisions. Nevertheless, the evaluation has identified different degrees of benefit depending on the type of relationship that is analyzed. Here, analyzing program dependencies has turned out as the most promising alternative. Finally, the refactoring specification concept allowed to specify and fully automate a refactoring for introducing variability based on conditional statements.

The interviews and surveys confirmed the applicability and necessity of the proposed process under industrial conditions as existing today. The refactoring specification has been proven to be unambiguous and valuable, but the influence of quality of the concrete specification cannot be neglected. Furthermore, the interviews confirmed the challenges of customized product copies and the state of the practice described by others and motivating this thesis.

In total, the evaluation successfully corroborated the hypotheses of this thesis, gained new insight into the consolidation challenge, and motivated several directions of future research.

Additional insight The new insight on consolidating customized product copies can be summarized as described in this paragraph.

Analyzing relationships between differences is a valuable approach to support a consolidation. Many promising analysis approaches have been proposed in the field of feature location as surveyed by Rubin and Chechik [163, 161]. For example, a variety of analysis of program dependencies, change histories, and textual information are described in their survey. The evaluation performed in this thesis has shown limitations of representatives of these approaches in terms of limited precision, recall, and availability of data to analyze. Furthermore, adaptions were necessary to use them in context of a copy consolidation. Additionally, optimizations such as filter strategies for textual analyses and an extended set of dependencies for program dependency analyses are necessary to improve the findings.

To conclude, The results show that restrictive types of relationships, such as program dependencies, provide more reliable results and are easier to be reviewed as suggestive relationships. Especially textual analysis to identify related code modifications are vague and difficult because of irrelevant terms. Similar results have been shown by evaluating different approaches for change impact analyses (Klatt et al. [105]). This might be an indicator for the value of analyzing program dependencies in general as reported by others before, such as Wilde [193] and Ottenstein and Ottenstein [144].

Directions for future research Several directions for future research have been identified in context of the proposed approach and the consolidation in general. Similar to the consolidation, the continuous maintenance of SPL is an ongoing topic of research activities. Especially to cope with degeneration in terms of product-level adaptations that are incompatible with the SPL is challenging and adapting the SPLEVO approach to this field is a reasonable direction. Furthermore, considering domain-specific conditions should be evaluated for further automation and improved analysis results. Similarly, the generalization of consolidation refactorings similar to the generalization of traditional refactorings as proposed by Reimann et al. [156] is promising to simplify the realization of custom variability mechanisms. Finally, the field of usability engineering is promising for software development in general and has been identified as a reasonable direction to improve consolidation processes.

Part IV.

Appendix

A. Appendix: Refactoring

A.1. Refactoring Specification Example

This section provides an example of a refactoring specification. It was developed, automated, and evaluated in the master thesis of Daniel [40]. The refactoring specified below introduces a variability mechanism facilitating conditional statements. It was developed as part of the SPLEVO approach to evaluate the applicability of the refactoring specification. Furthermore, it was used to prove the automation of such a refactoring in the case studies.

IF WITH STATIC CONFIGURATION CLASS (OPTXOR)

Summary

A refactoring to implement OPTXOR variability based on conditional statements with configuration in a static Java class.

Configuration Mechanism

The configuration is realized using String constants in Java class to be configured before compilation.

Motivation

The resulting code implements variants at one place; hence it improves identifying the executed code.

Supported Characteristics		**Supported Elements**
Binding Time	Compile	**JaMoPP Java Model**
Variability Type	OPTXOR	• CompilationUnit • Import • Class • Interface • Enumeration • Field • Method • Constructor • Block • Statement • Condition
Extensible	No	
Quality Goal by trend		Conciseness

Limitations

Following software elements are not supported because they cannot co-exist:

- Differing class- and interface- signatures (extends, implements)
- Methods with equal names but varying return types
- Fields with equal names but different types
- Local variables with equal names but different types and referencing elements outside the containing variation points.

Alternatives

Example

Two implementations of a statement in a method being combined by introducing variant-specific conditions which evaluate constants provided by a configuration class.

Leading

```
public void doSth(){
  print("Leading");
}
```

Integration

```
public void doSth(){
  print("Integration");
}
```

Refactored SPL

```
public void doSth(){ // Line breaks reduced for the sake of brevity
  if(Config.CONF1.equals("Leading")) { print("Leading"); }
  if(Config.CONF1.equals("Integration")) { print("Integration"); }
}
class Config {
   public static final String CONF1 = "Integration"; // Either "Leading" or " Integration"
}
```

Instruction: CompilationUnit

Summary

An SPL must integrate the compilation units of all variants. Therefore, this refactoring instruction copies the compilation units of the integration copies to the leading copy, if they do not exist, yet.

Preconditions

Location

Element	CompilationUnit
Exclusion	

Implementing Elements

Element	CompilationUnit
Exclusion	

Example

Merges the missing ClassB.java (contained in org.example.somepackage) into the leading Variant.

Leading	Integration
org.example.somepackage: • ClassA.java • ClassC.java	org.example.somepackage: • ClassA.java • ClassB.java • ClassC.java

Refactored SPL

```
org.example.somepackage:
• ClassA.java
• ClassB.java
• ClassC.java
```

Additional Parameters

String: leadingSrcPath: The path to the source folder of the leading copy to add new compilation units.

Mechanics

Iterate over all integration variants and their compilation units. Build the URI representing the path for each compilation unit, create a new model resource at this URI, and place the compilation unit in it.

```
foreach Variant:variant ∈ vp.variants do
   if variant.leading then
      continue;
   endif

   foreach CompilationUnit:cu ∈ variant.implementingElements do
      foreach String:segment ∈ cu.nameSpaces do
         leadingSrcPath ← leadingSrcPath.concatenate(leadingSrcPath, segment);
         leadingSrcPath ← leadingSrcPath.concatenate(leadingSrcPath, getFileSeparator());
      endforeach

      compilationUnitName ← getFileName(cu);
      leadingSrcPath ← leadingSrcPath.concatenate(leadingSrcPath, compilationUnitName);
      Resource:resource ← rs.createResource(URI( leadingSrcPath));
      resource.contents.add(cu);
   endforeach
endforeach
```

Instruction: Import	
Summary	
To allow for a complete single code base, all dependencies must be reflected. This refactoring instruction carries over all imports.	
Preconditions	
Location	
Element	CompilationUnit
Exclusion	
Implementing Elements	
Element	Import
Exclusion	
Example	
Merges the import ExtendedClass from the integration copy into the leading copy.	
Leading	**Integration**
`import com.example.SimpleClass;`	`import com.example.ExtendedClass;`
Refactored SPL	
`import com.example.SimpleClass;` `import com.example.ExtendedClass;`	
Additional Parameters	
Mechanics	
Iterate over the variants and their imports. Add the import to the location of the variation point, if it does not contain an equal import, yet.	

```
CompilationUnit: vpLocation ← vp.location;
foreach Variant:variant ∈ vp.variants do
   if variant.leading then
      continue;
   endif
   foreach Import:import ∈ variant.implementingElements do
      if !vpLocation.contains(import) then
         vpLocation.add(import);
      endif
   endforeach
endforeach
```

Instruction: Class in a Member Container

Summary

The SPL must contain all classes from the leading and integration copies. This refactoring instruction integrates the member classes of integration copies in a specific member container into the leading copy.

Preconditions

Location

Element	MemberContainer
Exclusion	

Implementing Elements

Element	Class
Exclusion	

Example

Merges class A2 into the member container of the leading variant (a class in this case).

Leading	Integration

`public class A {`
`private class A1 {…};`
`}`
	`public class A {`
	`private class A2 {…};`
	`}`

Refactored SPL

```
public class A {
   private class A1 {…};
   private class A2 {…};
}
```

Additional Parameters

Mechanics

Iterate over all integration variants and their classes. Add a class to the variation point location if the location does not contain a class, interface, or enumeration with the same name, yet.

```
MemberContainer: vpLocation ← vp.location;
foreach Variant:variant ∈ vp.variants do
   if variant.leading then
      continue;
   endif
   foreach Class:class ∈ variant.implementingElements do
      if !containsClassInterfaceOrEnumWithName(vpLocation, class.name) then
         vpLocation.add(class);
      endif
   endforeach
endforeach
```

Instruction: Class in a Compilation Unit	
Summary	
The SPL must contain all classes from the leading and integration copies. This refactoring instruction integrates the classes contained in a compilation unit from the integration copies into the leading copy.	
Preconditions	
Location	
Element	CompilationUnit
Exclusion	
Implementing Elements	
Element	Class
Exclusion	
Example	
Merges class B into the compilation unit of the leading variant.	
Leading	**Integration**

`SomeClass.java:`
`private class A {…};`
	`SomeClass.java:`
	`private class A {…};`
	`private class B {…};`

Refactored SPL	

`SomeClass.java:`
`private class A {…};`
`private class B {…};`	

Additional Parameters	
Mechanics	
Iterate over all integration variants and their classes. Add a class to the location of the variation point if it does not contain a class, interface, or enumeration with the same name, yet.	

```
CompilationUnit: vpLocation ← vp.location;
foreach Variant:variant ∈ vp.variants do
  if !variant.leading then
    continue;
  endif
  foreach Class:class ∈ variant.implementingElements do
    if !containsClassInterfaceOrEnumWithName(vpLocation, class.name) then
      vpLocation.add(class);
    endif
  endforeach
endforeach
```

Instruction: Interface in a Member Container	
Summary	
The SPL must contain all interfaces from the leading and integration copies. This refactoring instruction integrates the interfaces of a member container from the integration copies into the leading copy.	
Preconditions	
Location	
Element	MemberContainer
Exclusion	
Implementing Elements	
Element	Interface
Exclusion	
Example	
Copies interface A2 into the member container of the leading variant (a class in this case).	
Leading	**Integration**

`public class A {`
`private interface A1 {…};`
`…`
`}`
	`public class A {`
	`private interface A2 {…};`
	`…`
	`}`

Refactored SPL	

`public class A {`
`private interface A1 {…};`
`private interface A2 {…};`
`…`
`}`	

Additional Parameters	
Mechanics	
Iterate over all integration variants and their interfaces. Add the interface to the location of the variation point if it does not contain a class, interface, or enumeration with the same name, yet.	

```
MemberContainer: vpLocation ← vp.location;
foreach Variant:variant ∈ vp.variants do
   if variant.leading then
      continue;
   endif
   foreach Interface:interface ∈ variant.implementingElements do
      if !containsClassInterfaceOrEnumWithName(vpLocation, interface.name) then
         vpLocation.add(interface);
      endif
   endforeach
endforeach
```

Instruction: Interface in a Compilation Unit	
Summary	
The SPL must contain all interfaces from the leading and integration copies. This refactoring instruction integrates the interfaces contained in a compilation unit from the integration copies into the leading copy.	
Preconditions	
Location	
Element	CompilationUnit
Exclusion	
Implementing Elements	
Element	Interface
Exclusion	
Example	
Merges interface B into the compilation unit of the leading variant.	
Leading	**Integration**

`SomeClass.java:`
`private interface A {…};`
`private interface B {…};`
	`SomeClass.java:`
	`private interface A {…};`
	`private interface B {…};`

Refactored SPL	

`SomeClass.java:`
`private interface A {…};`
`private interface B {…};`	

Additional Parameters	
Mechanics	
Iterate over all integration variants and their interfaces. Add an interface to the location of the variation point if it does not contain a class, interface, or enumeration with the same name, yet.	

```
CompilationUnit: vpLocation ← vp.location;
foreach Variant:variant ∈ vp.variants do
  if variant.leading then
    continue;
  endif
  foreach Interface:interface ∈ variant.implementingElements do
    if !containsClassInterfaceOrEnumWithName(vpLocation, interface.name) then
      vpLocation.add(interface);
    endif
  endforeach
endforeach
```

Instruction: Enumeration in a Member Container	
Summary	
The SPL must integrate the enumerations of all variants, including their constants. This refactoring instruction integrates enumerations contained in a member container from the integration copies into the leading copies. It also merges the constants of enumerations with equal names.	
Preconditions	
Location	
Element	MemberContainer
Exclusion	
Implementing Elements	
Element	Enumeration
Exclusion	
Example	
Missing enumeration AnotherEnum is integrated into the member container of the leading copy. Also shows the integration of enumeration constant B of the integration copy of SomeEnum.	
Leading	**Integration**

`public class A {`
`public enum SomeEnum { A; }`
`}`
	`public class A {`
	`public enum SomeEnum { B; }`
	`public enum AnotherEnum { X; }`
	`}`

Refactored SPL	

`public class A {`
`public enum SomeEnum { A, B; }`
`public enum AnotherEnum { X; }`
`}`	

Additional Parameters	

Mechanics

This algorithm has two key steps: In the first step (first foreach), it collects all available enumeration names from the Variants. It stores their enumeration objects (leading or, if not available, first integration), the constants of that enumeration in all Variants and whether or not it already has a leading implementation.
In the next step (second foreach), it uses the maps to get the enumeration object, adds the missing constants to that object and adds the enumeration to the VP's location if it has no leading implementation.

```
MemberContainer: vpLocation ← vp.location;

Map<String, Enumeration>: enumerationsToName;
Map<String, Set<String>>: constantsToEnumName;
Map<String, Boolean>: leadingToEnumName;

foreach Variant: variant ∈ vp.variants do
   foreach Enumeration:enumeration ∈ variant.implementingElements do
      if enumerationsToName.containsKey(enumeration.name) || variant.leading) then
         enumerationsToName.gets(enumeration.name) ← enumeration;
      endif
      leadingToEnumName.gets(enumeration.name) ← variant.leading;
      foreach EnumConstant: enumConst ∈ enumeration.constants do
         constantsToEnumName.gets(enumeration.name).add(enumConst.name);
      endforeach
   endforeach
endforeach

foreach String: enumName ∈ enumerationsToName.keys do
   enumeration ← enumerationsToName.gets(enumName);
   foreach String: constName ∈ constantsToEnumName.gets(enumName) do
      if !hasConstantWithSameName(enumeration, constName) then
         enumConst.name ← constName;
         enumeration.constants.add(enumConst);
      endif
   endforeach

   if !leadingToEnumName.gets(enumName) then
      vpLocation.add(enumeration);
   endif
endforeach
```

Instruction: Enumeration in a Compilation Unit

Summary

An SPL must integrate the enumerations from any Variant, including their constants. This refactoring instruction integrates enumerations contained in a compilation unit from the integration copies into the leading copies. It also merges the constants of enumerations with equal names.

Preconditions

Location

Element	CompilationUnit
Exclusion	

Implementing Elements

Element	Enumeration
Exclusion	

Example

Missing enumeration AnotherEnum gets integrated into the leading compilation unit. Also shows the integration of enumeration constant B from the integration implementation of SomeEnum into the leading implementation.

Leading

```
SomeClass.java:
public enum SomeEnum {  A; }
```

Integration

```
SomeClass.java:
public enum SomeEnum {  B; }
public enum AnotherEnum { X; }
```

Refactored SPL

```
SomeClass.java:
public enum SomeEnum {  A, B; }
public enum AnotherEnum { X; }
```

Additional Parameters

Mechanics

This algorithm has two key steps: In the first step (first foreach), it collects all available enumeration names from the Variants. It stores their enumeration objects (leading or, if not available, first integration), the constants of that enumeration in all Variants and whether or not it already has a leading implementation.
In the next step (second foreach), it uses the maps to get the enumeration object, adds the missing constants to that object and adds the enumeration to the VP's location if it has no leading implementation.

```
CompilationUnit: vpLocation ← vp.location;

Map<String, Enumeration>: enumerationsToName;
Map<String, Set<String>>: constantsToEnumName;
Map<String, Boolean>: leadingToEnumName;

foreach Variant: variant ∈ vp.variants do
   foreach Enumeration:enumeration ∈ variant.implementingElements do
      if enumerationsToName.containsKey(enumeration.name) || variant.leading) then
         enumerationsToName.gets(enumeration.name) ← enumeration;
      endif
      leadingToEnumName.gets(enumeration.name) ← variant.leading;
      foreach EnumConstant: enumConst ∈ enumeration.constants do
         constantsToEnumName.gets(enumeration.name).add(enumConst.name);
      endforeach
   endforeach
endforeach

foreach String: enumName ∈ enumerationsToName.keys do
   enumeration ← enumerationsToName.gets(enumName);
   foreach String: constName ∈ constantsToEnumName.gets(enumName) do
      if !hasConstantWithSameName(enumeration, constName) then
         enumConst.name ← constName;
         enumeration.constants.add(enumConst);
      endif
   endforeach

   if !leadingToEnumName.gets(enumName) then
      vpLocation.add(enumeration);
   endif
endforeach
```

Instruction: Field	
Summary	
The SPL must contain the fields of all variants. The refactoring instruction integrates fields of all variants into the leading variant. In case of different initial values among the implementations, initialization blocks with conditional assignments get introduced.	
Preconditions	
Location	
Element	MemberContainer
Exclusion	
Implementing Elements	
Element	Field
Exclusion	• Fields with equal names but different types.
Example	
Integrates the missing field b into the leading variant and introduces an initializer block to integrate the initializations from both Variants.	
Leading	**Integration**

`public class SomeClass {`
`private int a = 0;`
`}`
	`public class SomeClass {`
	`private int a = 1;`
	`private int b = 1;`
	`}`

Refactored SPL	

```
public class SomeClass {
   private int a;
   private int b = 1;
   {
      if(Config.CONF1.equals("Leading")){
         a = 0;
      }
      if(Config.CONF1.equals("Integration")){
         a = 1;
      }
   }
}
```

Additional Parameters

Mechanics

The algorithm first adds the import of the configuration class to the containing compilation unit. It then (first foreach) builds maps to store the field objects, their positions within the parent container and their initial values to the field's name. It also stores the field's initial value and the ID of the Variant that it is implemented in.
It then deletes the fields of the leading Variant from the VP's location and generates two blocks (to initialize static and non-static fields). In the following foreach, it adds the fields to the VP's location, removes final modifiers (if applicable) and fills the initializer blocks with Variant-specific conditional assignments if they have more than one initial value. Finally, it adds the initializer blocks to the VP's location if they are not empty.

```
Class: vpLocation ← vp.location;
addConfigurationClassImportIfMissing(vpLocation.containingCompilationUnit);

Map<String,Field>: fieldToFieldName;
Map<String,Integer>: positionToFieldName;
Map<String, Set<Expression>>: initialValuesToFieldName;
Map<Expression, String>: variantIDToInitialValue;

foreach Variant:variant ∈ vp.variants do
   foreach Field:field ∈ variant.implementingElements do
      fieldToFieldName.gets(field.name) ← field;
      positionToFieldName.gets(field.name) ← field.container.indexOf(field);

      if !initialValuesToFieldName.gets(field.name).contains(field.initialValue) then
         initialValuesToFieldName.gets(field.name).add(field.initialValue);
      endif

      variantIDToInitialValue.gets(field.initialValue) ← variant.id;
   endforeach
endforeach

deleteVariableFieldsFromLeading(vp);

Block: nonStaticBlock;
Block: staticBlock;
staticBlock.modifiers.add(new Final());

foreach String: fieldName ∈ fieldToFieldName.keys do
   Field: field ← fieldToFieldName.gets(fieldName );
   int: fieldPos ← positionToFieldName.gets(fieldName );
   List< Expression >: initialValues ← initialValuesToFieldName.gets(fieldName);

   vpLocation.add(fieldPos, field);
   removeFinalModifier(field);

   if initialValues.size > 1 then
      field.initialValue ← null;
      if isStatic(field) then
         createFieldConditionalInitialization(initialValues, staticBlock);
      endif
      else
         createFieldConditionalInitialization(initialValues, nonStaticBlock);
      endelse
   endif
endforeach
```

```
if staticBlock.size > 0 then
  vpLocation.add(staticBlock);
endif
if nonStaticBlock.size > 0 then
  vpLocation.add(nonStaticBlock);
endif
```

```
// ---------------------------------------------------------------------------
// Function: createFieldConditionalInitialization
// Creates a new conition to initialize a field.
Input:  List< Expression >: initialValues; // the initial values of for the field
        Block: block; // the block to add the condition to
Output:
foreach Expression: initialValue ∈ initialValues do
        String: variantId ← variantIDToInitialValue.gets(initialValue);
        String: groupId ← vp.group.id;

        String: conditionString ← "SPLConfig." + groupId + ".equals(" + variantId + ")";
        Condition: condition;
        condition.condition ← expressionFromString(conditionString);

        ExpressionStatement: assignmentStatement ←
                                initialValueToStandaloneAssignment(initialValue);
        condition.ifBlock.add(assignmentStatement);
        block.add(condition);
endforeach
```

Instruction: Method	
Summary	
The SPL classes must contain the methods from all Variants. This refactoring instruction integrates the methods from the integration Variants into the leading Variant.	
Preconditions	
Location	
Element	MemberContainer
Exclusion	
Implementing Elements	
Element	Method
Exclusion	• Methods with equal names but different return types.
Example	
Integrates the method with the double parameter of the integration into the leading variant since it does not contain a method with one double parameter.	
Leading	**Integration**

`public class SomeClass {`
`public void someMethod(){...};`
`public void someMethod(int i){...};`
`}`
	`public class SomeClass {`
	`public void someMethod(){...};`
	`public void someMethod(double d){...};`
	`}`

Refactored SPL	

`public class SomeClass {`
`public void someMethod(){...};`
`public void someMethod(int i){...};`
`public void someMethod(double d){...};`
`}`	

Additional Parameters	

Mechanics
Iterate over all integration variants and their methods. Add the method to the location of the variation point, if the location does not contain a method with the same name and an equal set of parameters, yet.

```
MemberContainer: vpLocation ← vp.location;
foreach Variant:variant ∈ vp.variants do
  if variant.leading then
    continue;
  endif
  foreach Method:method ∈ variant.implementingElements do
    if !hasMethodWithEqualNameAndParameters(vpLocation, method) then
      vpLocation.add(method);
    endif
  endforeach
endforeach
```

```
// ----------------------------------------------------------------------
// Function: hasMethodWithEqualNameAndParameters
// Checks whether a given container has a method with equal name and parameters.
Input:  MemberContainer: memberContainer; Method: method
Output: Boolean: true if such a method was found; Otherwise false.

foreach Method: currentMethod ∈ memberContainer.methods do
  List<Parameter>: paramSet1 ← currentMethod.parameters;
  List<Parameter>: paramSet2 ← method.parameters;

  if !currentMethod.name.equals(method.name) then
    continue;
  endif
  if paramSet1.size != paramSet2.size then
    continue;
  endif

  for i ← 0 to paramSet1.size -1 do
    if !paramSet1.get(i).type.equals(paramSet2.get(i).type) then
      break;
    endif
    if i == (paramSet1.size -1) then
      return true;
    endif
  endfor
endforeach
return false;
```

Instruction: Constructor	
Summary	
The SPL classes must contain the constructors of all Variants. This refactoring instruction merges the constructors of the integration variants into the leading copy.	
Preconditions	
Location	
Element	Class
Exclusion	
Implementing Elements	
Element	Constructor
Exclusion	
Example	
Integrates the constructor with the double parameter from the integration into the leading variant because it does not contain a constructor with one double parameter.	
Leading	**Integration**

`public class SomeClass {`
`public SomeClass(){...};`
`public SomeClass(int i){...};`
`}`
	`public class SomeClass {`
	`public SomeClass(){...};`
	`public SomeClass(double d){...};`
	`}`

Refactored SPL	

`public class SomeClass {`
`public SomeClass(){...};`
`public SomeClass(int i){...};`
`public SomeClass(double d){...};`
`}`	

Additional Parameters	

Mechanics
Iterate over all integration variants. Add the constructors to the location of the variation point, if the location does not contain a constructor with an equal set of parameters, yet.

```
MemberContainer: vpLocation ← vp.location;
foreach Variant:variant ∈ vp.variants do
   if variant.leading then
      continue;
   endif
   foreach Constructor:constructor ∈ variant.implementingElements do
      if !hasConstructorWithEqualParameters(vpLocation, constructor) then
         vpLocation.add(constructor);
      endif
   endforeach
endforeach
```

```
// Function: hasConstructorWithEqualParameters
// Checks whether a given container has a method with equal name and parameters.
Input:  MemberContainer: memberContainer; Constructor: constructor
Output:Boolean: true if such a constructor was found; Otherwise false.

foreach Constructor: currentConstructor ∈ memberContainer.constructors do
   List<Parameter>: paramSet1 ← currentConstructor.parameters;
   List<Parameter>: paramSet2 ← constructor.parameters;

   if paramSet1.size != paramSet2.size then
      continue;
   endif

   for i ← 0 to paramSet1.size -1 do
      if !paramSet1.get(i).type.equals(paramSet2.get(i).type) then
         break;
      endif
      if i == (paramSet1.size -1) then
         return true;
      endif
   endfor
endforeach
return false;
```

Instruction: Block

Summary

The SPL Classes must contain all initializer blocks of all variants. This refactoring instruction merges the blocks of the integration variants into the leading Variant.

Preconditions

Location

Element	MemberContainer
Exclusion	

Implementing Elements

Element	Block
Exclusion	

Example

Integrates a block from the integration into the leading variant because it does not contain the block.

Leading

```
public class SomeClass {}
```

Integration

```
public class SomeClass {
   {
      System.out.println();
   }
}
```

Refactored SPL

```
public class SomeClass {
   {
      System.out.println();
   }
}
```

Additional Parameters

Mechanics

Iterate over all integration variants and their blocks and add them to the location of the variation point.

```
vpLocation ← vp.location;
foreach Variant:variant ∈ vp.variants do
   if variant.leading then
      continue;
   endif
   foreach Block:block ∈ variant.implementingElements do
      vpLocation.add(block);
   endforeach
endforeach
```

Instruction: Statement in a Statement List Container	
Summary	
This refactoring instruction introduces conditional statements that match the SPL configuration to execute Variant-specific statements. Local variable statements declaring a variable that is referenced outside the variation point are placed in front of the conditional statement. The variable is initialized with the default value of their data type and the variant-specific initialization is done inside the conditional statement.	
Preconditions	
Location	
Element	StatementListContainer
Exclusion	
Implementing Elements	
Element	Statement
Exclusion	• Local variable declarations with equal variable names but different variable types and elements outside the containing variation point that have references to the variable.
Example	
The integration method has a different initial value for x and a different argument in the print method. Splits x into declaration and assignment and executes the Variant-specific code in the conditional statements.	

Leading

```
public void method(){
   int x = 1;
   print("Leading:" + x);
   return x;
}
```

Integration

```
public void method(){
   int x = 2;
   print("Integration:" + x);
   return x;
}
```

Refactored SPL

```
public void method(){
   int x;
   if(Config.CONF1.equals("Leading")){
      x = 1;
      print("Leading:" + x);
   }
   if(Config.CONF1.equals("Integration")){
      x = 2;
      print("Integration:" + x);
   }
   return x;
}
```

Additional Parameters

Mechanics

The algorithm first adds the import of the configuration class to the containing compilation unit. It then calculates the position at which the variable elements have to be inserted in the VP's location. It then wraps the statements of each Variant into a condition that evaluates the SPL configuration. If the statement is a local variable statement whose variable is referenced out-side the current VP, it gets split into declaration and assignment, whereas the declaration gets stored and the assignment is done within the If-block. It also removes the final modifier of the variable (if applicable). It then adds the created condition into the VP's location at the previously calculated position.
It then deletes the leading Variant's elements from the VP's location and adds the declaration in front of the first of the generated conditions. Finally, the algorithm checks whether the VP's location is a method and whether it has a non-void return type and all Variants have a trailing return statement. In this case, the algorithm adds a default return statement at the end of the method.

```
StatementListContainer: vpLocation ← vp.location;
addConfigurationClassImportIfMissing(vpLocation.containingCompilationUnit);

addConfigurationClassImportIfMissing(vpLocation.containingCompilationUnit);

Map<String, LocalVariableStatement>: localVariableStatementsToName;

int: variabilityPositionStart ← getVariabilityPosition(vp);
int: variabilityPositionEnd ← variabilityPositionStart;

foreach Variant:variant ∈ vp.variants do
   String: groupId ← vp.group.Id;
   String: variantId ← variant.Id;

   String: conditionString ← "SPLConfig." + groupId + ".equals(" + variantId + ")";
   Condition: condition;
   condition.condition ← expressionFromString(conditionString);

   foreach Statement:statement ∈ variant.implementingElements do
      int: offset ← variant.implementingElements.size -
                              variant.implementingElements.indexOf(statement);
      if statement instanceof LocalVariableStatement
                && isReferencedByPostdecessor(statement, offset) then
         LocalVariable: variable ← statement.variable;
         removeFinalModifier(variable);
         statement ← extractAssignment(variable);
         variable.initialValue ← defaultValueForType(variable.typeReference.target);

         if !localVariableStatementsToName.containsKey(variable.name) || variant.leading then
            localVariableStatementsToName.gets(variable.name) ← statement;
         endif
      endif

      if statement != null then
         condition.ifBlock.add(statement);
      endif
   endforeach
   vpLocation.statements.add(variabilityPositionEnd++, currentCondition);
endforeach

deleteLeadingVariantElementsFromVPLocation(vp);
vpLocation.addAll(variabilityPositionStart, localVariableStatementsToName.values);

if vpLocation instanceof ClassMethod then
   boolean: isVoid ← returnTypeIsVoid(vpLocation);
```

```
   boolean: allVariantsHaveATrailingReturn ← allVariantsHaveATrailingReturn(vp);

   if !isVoid && allVariantsHaveATrailingReturn then
      Return: returnStatement;
      Literal: defaultValue ← defaultValueForType(vpLocation.typeReference.target);
      returnStatement.returnValue ← defaultValue;
      vpLocation.add(returnStatement);
   endif
endif
```

```
// ---------------------------------------------------------------------------
// Function: getVariabilityPosition
// Calculates the position of the variable statements.
Input : VariationPoint: vp
Output: int: The position.

StatementListContainer: vpLocation ← vp.location;

foreach Variant: variant ∈ vp.variants do
   if variant.leading then
      Statement: firstElement ← variant.implementingElements.gets(0);
      return firstElement.eContainer.indexOf(firstElement);
   endif
endforeach

Statement: firstElement ← vp.variants.gets(0).implementingElements.gets(0);
int: posIntegration ← firstElement.eContainer.indexOf(firstElement);

List< Statement >: predecessors ← firstElement.eContainer.subList(0, posIntegration);
predecessors ← intersect(vpLocation, predecessors);

if predecessors.size == 0 then
   return 0;
endif

pos ← searchFirstGroupOccurence(vpLocation, predecessors);
return pos +1;
```

```
// ---------------------------------------------------------------------------
// Function: searchFirstGroupOccurence
// Searches the first occurrence of a given list of statements in a container.
Input:    StatementListContainer: targetContainer, List<Statement>: predecessors
Output: int: If group was found, the index of the last element of the group; otherwise -1.

predecessorPos ← 0;
for i ← 0 to predecessors.size -1 do
   baseElement ← targetContainer.gets(i);
   predecessor ← predecessors.gets(predecessorPos);

   if baseElement.equals(predecessor) then
      predecessorPos++;
   endif
   elseif isVariabilityCondition(baseElement) then
      int: predecessorsSubList ← predecessors.subList(predecessorPos, predecessors.size);
      predecessorPos += countVariableStatements(baseElement.ifBlock, predecessorsSubList);
   endelseif

   if predecessorPos == predecessors.size then
      if predecessor instanceof LocalVariableStatement then
         int: posNextVarCond ← posNextVariabilityCondition(targetContainer, i);
         if posNextVarCond ! = -1 then
            return posNextVarCond;
         endif
      endif
      return i;
   endif
endfor
return -1;
```

```
// ---------------------------------------------------------------------------
// Function: posNextVariabilityCondition
// Finds the position of the next condition that was introduced by this variability
// mechanism and returns its position. Searches elements starting at a given index.
Input:    StatementListContainer: targetContainer; int: startIndex
Output: The position. -1 if nothing found.

for i ← startIndex to targetContainer.size -1 do
   Statement: currentStatement ← targetContainer.statements.gets(i);
   if isVariabilityCondition(currentStatement) then
      return i;
   endif
endfor
return -1;
```

```
// ---------------------------------------------------------------------------
// Function: isReferencedByPostdecessor
// Checks whether a LocalVariableStatement's LocalVariable is referenced
// by a following element in its parent container.
Input : LocalVariableStatement: localVariableStatement; int: offset
Output: boolean: True if a reference was found; false otherwise.

LocalVariabe: variable ← localVariableStatement.variable;
List<Statement>: containerStatements ← localVariableStatement.eContainer.statements;

int: fromIndex ← containerStatements.indexOf() + offset;
int: toIndex ← containerStatements.size;

if fromIndex >= toIndex then
  return false;
endif

List<Statement>: postDecessors ← containerStatements.subList(fromIndex, toIndex);
foreach Statement: postDecessor: postDecessors do
  if hasReferenceTo(postDecessor, variable) then
    return true;
  endif
endforeach

return false;
```

Instruction: Statement in a Condition

Summary

This refactoring instruction integrates variable else-statements in a condition. It introduces conditional statements to execute the Variant code. In case that the variation point has more than one variant, the refactoring wraps those conditional statements into a condition that checks whether at least one of the Variants has been selected.

Preconditions

Location	
Element	Condition
Exclusion	
Implementing Elements	
Element	Statement
Exclusion	

Example

The integration variant has one additional else-if in between. The refactoring introduces a top-level condition to check whether at least one of the Variants has been selected and then executes the Variant-specific code using conditional statements.

Leading

```
public void method(int i) {
   if (i == 0) {
      print("0");
   } else if (i == 2) {
      print("2");
   }
}
```

Integration

```
public void method(int i) {
   if (i == 0) {
      print("0");
   } else if (i == 1) {
      print("1");
   } else if (i == 2) {
      print("2");
   }
}
```

Refactored SPL

```
public void method(int i) {
   if (i == 0) {
      print("0");
   } else if (Config.CONF1.equals("Leading") || Config.CONF1.equals("Integration")) {
      if (Config.CONF1.equals("Leading")) {
         if (i == 2) {
            print("2");
         }
      }
      if (Config.CONF1.equals("Integration")) {
         if (i == 1) {
            print("1");
         } else if (i == 2) {
            print("2");
         }
      }
   } else if (i == 2) {
      print("2");
   }
}
```

Additional Parameters
Mechanics
If the VP has more than one Variant (first if), the refactoring first builds a top-level condition that checks whether at least one of the Variants has been selected. It then adds conditional statements to the condition that integrate the variable statements. In case that the VP has only one Variant (else), the algorithm does not build a top-level condition. It only builds the conditional statements to execute the Variant code. Finally, it adds the condition (either the top-level condition or the Variant-specific one) to the else-branch of the VP's location.

```
Condition: vpLocation ← vp.location;
addConfigurationClassImportIfMissing(vpLocation.containingCompilationUnit);

Statement: elseStatement ← vpLocation.elseStatement;
Condition: variabilityCondition;

String: groupId ← vp.group.Id;

if vp.variants.size > 1 then
   ConditionalOrExpression: orExpression;
   foreach Variant:variant ∈ vp.variants do
      String: conditionString ← "SPLConfig." + groupId + ".equals(" + variant.Id + ")";
      IdentifierReference: identifierRef ← identifierReferenceFromString(conditionString);
      orExpression.children.add(identifierRef );
   endforeach

   variabilityCondition.condition ← orExpression;

   foreach Variant:variant ∈ vp.variants do
      String: variantId ← variant.id;
      String: conditionString ← "SPLConfig." + groupId + ".equals(" + variantId + ")";
      Condition: currentCondition;
      currentCondition.condition ← expressionFromString(conditionString);
      currentCondition.ifBlock.add(variant.implementingElements.gets(0));
      variabilityCondition.ifBlock.add(currentCondition);
   endforeach
endif
else
   String: variantId ← vp.variants.gets(0).id;
   String: conditionString ← "SPLConfig." + groupId + ".equals(" + variantId + ")";
   variabilityCondition.condition ← expressionFromString(conditionString);

   Statement: implementingElement ← vp.variants.gets(0).implementingElements.gets(0);

   if implementingElementinstanceofBlock then
      variabilityCondition.ifBlock ← implementingElement;
   endif
   else
      variabilityCondition.ifBlock.add(implementingElement);
   endelse
endelse

vpLocation.elseStatement ← variabilityCondition;
variabilityCondition.elseStatement ← elseStatement;
```

B. Appendix: Evaluation

B.1. Shared Term Analyzer

B.1.1. Stop Word List: Høst Programmer Vocabulary

The vocabulary for developing Java applications proposed by Høst and Østvold [82] and used as default stop word list in the case studies:

accept action add check clear close create do dump end equals find generate get handle has hash init initialize insert is load make new next parse print process read remove reset run set size start to update validate visit write

B.1.2. Stop Word List: MySQL Prepared

The stop word list of the MySQL database server [142] prepared by splitting apostrophes and removing words with less than three characters.

able about above according accordingly across actually after afterwards again against ain all allow allows almost alone along already also although always among amongst and another any anybody anyhow anyone anything anyway anyways anywhere apart appear appreciate appropriate are aren around aside ask asking associated available away awfully became because become becomes becoming been before beforehand behind being believe below beside besides best better between beyond both brief but mon came can cannot cant cause causes certain certainly changes clearly com come comes concerning consequently consider considering contain containing contains corresponding could couldn course currently definitely described despite did didn different does doesn doing don done down downwards during each edu eight either else elsewhere enough entirely especially etc even ever every everybody everyone everything everywhere exactly example except far few fifth first five followed following follows for former formerly forth four from further furthermore get gets getting given gives goes going gone got gotten greetings had hadn happens hardly has hasn have haven having hello help hence her here hereafter hereby herein hereupon hers herself him himself his hither hopefully how howbeit however ignored immediate inasmuch inc indeed indicate indicated indicates inner insofar instead into inward isn its itself just keep keeps kept know knows known last lately later latter latterly least less lest let like liked likely little look looking looks ltd mainly many may maybe mean meanwhile merely might more moreover most mostly much must myself name namely near nearly necessary need needs neither never nevertheless new next nine nobody non none noone nor normally not nothing novel now nowhere obviously off often okay old once one ones only onto other others otherwise ought our ours ourselves out outside over overall own particular particularly per perhaps placed please plus possible presumably probably provides que quite rather really reasonably regarding regardless regards relatively respectively right said same saw say saying says second secondly see seeing seem seemed seeming seems seen self selves sensible sent serious seriously seven several shall she should shouldn since six some somebody somehow someone something sometime sometimes somewhat somewhere soon sorry specified specify specifying still sub such sup sure take taken tell tends than thank thanks thanx that thats the their theirs them themselves then thence there there thereafter thereby therefore therein theres thereupon these they think third this thorough thoroughly those though three through throughout thru thus together too took toward towards tried tries truly try trying twice two under unfortunately unless unlikely until unto upon use used useful uses using usually value various very via viz want wants was wasn way welcome well went were weren what what whatever when whence whenever where whereafter whereas whereby wherein whereupon wherever whether which while whither who whoever whole whom whose why will willing wish with within without won wonder would wouldn yes yet you your yours yourself yourselves zero

B.2. Interview Workshop

This section summarizes the answers for each question asked during the interview workshop (Section 8.5.1). The summaries have been created from the notes taken during the interviews and proven by the participating employees of the vendor and the independent consultancy. Table B.1 summarizes the positions reported by the individual participants.

Participant	Position
Participant 1	Developer
Participant 2	Developer
Participant 3	Architect / Project Manager
Participant 4	Developer / Architect

Table B.1.: Interview workshop: Participants

Question 1: How do you implement variability today? All participants answered this question in a similar way. In general: either for run time with a custom license mechanism, for compile time by generating code (e.g., for data models), or for load time using configuration files. In specific, many different mechanisms and styles to implement one or the other exist. Participants reported about OSGi Manifest files, properties files, Maven and Spring descriptors, dependency injection, user context and license interpretations and many more. Participant 3 first estimated about ten different ways of implementation, at the end of the interview he repealed this number and estimated an unknown but much higher number.

Question 2: How do you decide for a way to implement variability? All participants answered in a similar way: This is decided by the developer himself. In rare cases, there is an explicit required variability mechanism to use. Most of the time, this is interpreted by the individual developer and later on rechecked with the development management, and in a second step with the product management being aware of the requirements of the individual projects. Participant 3 described from his project management perspective that he would prefer to enable the developers to make the right decisions and to reduce the feedback cycle with the development or product management required by the current process.

Question 3: Imagine you have to consolidate a copied and customized component into a variable software product line. What would you do? All participants responded that they would search for similarities to exclude them for their further processing and focus on the differences. For the second step, the participants reported different strategies they would follow.

Participants 1 and 2 were interested in starting with the code locations one by one, then either directly modifying them with getting warned in case of a problem or being presented with related code locations when focusing on a particular one.

Participant 3 stated that he would be interested in what has changed and why. He described the optimal case of seeing customizations from the user perspective and getting presented with the code contributing to each customization. Remark: He was talking about user interfaces. However, he noted by himself that this demand would be too product-specific and rarely possible, as customizations to be considered are typically very artificial.

Participant 4 described his interest in patterns of similar modifications and to find out which of these implementations would be the best. He motivated his demand by having observed that customizations are often done to similar parts of the software. As some customizations are done better than others, he would try to align the variability he introduces with the best variability pattern identified.

Independent of the strategy they preferred, all participants mentioned some kind of iterative approach, thus releasing them from having to process all modifications at once.

Question 4: How would you like to see the differences and what are you interested in? All participants mentioned the code modifications and higher level structures as well as the relationships, but with different weightings and expectations.

Participant 1 mentioned a good experience with graph-based representations but only for orientation and navigation. Furthermore, graphs must not get too big for being useful. However, for anything else than orientation and navigation he reported to prefer other representations, such as lists, trees, or code.

Participant 2, who would have liked to start right ahead with modifying code, wanted to get actively informed when he performed an invalid modification or missed a related code modification. Thus, he also mentioned the need of a rollback mechanism when realizing a wrong decision.

Question 5: When working with code structures, which level of granularity do you expect to be useful? All participants reported the usefulness of package, class and member granularity for navigation as well as orientation. They all mentioned the statement level as being relevant for the detailed assessment of the modifications, to decide for a specific way of consolidation.

Participant 4 mentioned a drill-down capability to get from coarse grained to more detailed information.

Question 6: What else would you like to have or is important for you in the context of a consolidation? Participant 3 reported about current problems to find the implementation of existing variability when an employee leaves the company, as there is typically no documentation, code comment or tracing of where to find code that relates to a specific variability. Participant 2 described a related requirement to being able to describe why he made a specific variability design decision, for example a decision of grouping two variation points without an obvious dependency.

Participant 4 mentioned an adaptive approach which is able to understand how a developer consolidates a specific customization pattern and recommends other variation points / customizations to consolidate in the same manner.

Participant 2 has liked to have a tool recommending consolidation actions, such as the variability mechanism to implement.

Participant 1 described the requirement to be able to completely ignore specific differences / variation points in the downstream process. He argued for not having to consider the complete system at once, respectively that some modifications are not of interest at all.

B.3. Survey Industrial Applicability

The following sections provide the questionnaire and the original replies. The survey has been performed in German as the target group were German participants. Thus, the survey is shown here in the raw format. Similarly, the answers are presented in German as well. The results are interpreted and given in English in the according subsections of Section 8.

B.3.1. Questionnaire

In the following, the questionnaire pages are displayed. The participants were provided with the same pages except for minor spacing changes to make them fit on the pages here.

0% ausgefüllt

Online Befragung:
Rollen des SPLevo-Konsolidierungsprozeßes

Projektrahmen der Befragung

Das Projekt KoPL und der SPLevo Ansatz haben das Ziel die Konsolidierung kundenspezifischer Software Produktkopien, hin zu einer geordneten Software Produktlinie (SPL) zu unterstützen und damit wirtschaftlicher zu gestalten.

Projektkontext

Kundenspezifische Produktkopien entstehen in der Software-Entwicklung, wenn flexibel und meist mit begrenzten Ressourcen eine bestehende Lösung an kundenspezifische Bedürfnisse angepasst werden soll und daher kopiert und unabhängig vom Original modifiziert wird.

Eine **Software Produktlinie** erlaubt durch den gesteuerten Einsatz von Variabilität (Flexibilität) und Konfigurationsmöglichkeiten verschiedene Produkte aus einer einzigen Produktbasis abzuleiten, ohne diese kopieren zu müssen. Langfristig hilft dies Synergieeffekte zu nutzen und beispielsweise redundante Wartungskosten zu vermeiden.

Um **zu Beginn von der hohen Flexibilität der Kopien** zu profitieren und **langfristig die Vorteile von Produktlinien nutzen** zu können, ist es notwendig die Kopien in eine Produktlinie zu konsolidieren.

Als Teil des SPLevo Ansatzes wurden Rollen (Akteure) identifiziert, die bei einer Konsolidierung generell zu berücksichtigen sind, Aufgaben übernehmen oder Entscheidungen treffen.

Ziel der Befragung

Das Ziel dieser Befragung ist zu ermitteln, wie gut die definierten Rollen in ein heutiges Praxisumfeld übertragen werden können und wie Unternehmen derzeit in Bezug auf Konsolidierungsprojekte aufgestellt sind.

Auswertung und Anonymität der Befragung

Die Beantwortung der Fragen erfolgt anonym.
Die Ergebnisse der Befragung werden im Rahmen einer Promotion am Karlsruher Institut für Technologie (KIT) bzw. FZI Forschungszentrum Informatik, sowie im Rahmen des BMBF geförderten Forschungsprojektes KoPL anonymisiert ausgewertet, veröffentlicht und ausdrücklich nicht mit den Teilnehmern in Verbindung gebracht. Wir würden uns jedoch freuen Sie unabhängig von den Ergebnissen als Teilnehmer an der Studie nennen zu dürfen. Im Falle Ihres Einverständnisses würden wir uns über kurze E-Mail hierzu freuen. Ebenso informieren wir Sie im Nachgang gerne über die Ergebnisse der Befragung, wenn Sie uns dies auch kurz per E-Mail mitteilen.

Ansprechpartner für die Befragung

Benjamin Klatt, FZI Forschungszentrum Informatik
Haid-und-Neu-Str. 10-14, 76131 Karlsruhe
klatt@fzi.de, +49 721 9654-690

Hinweis zum Datenschutz

Die Beantwortung der Fragen und dementsprechend auch die Auswertung erfolgen komplett anonym.
Die Software für den Online-Fragebogen wird von dem unabhängigen Anbieter SoSci Serve GmbH bereitgestellt in einem Rechenzentrum innerhalb Deutschlands betrieben.
Weiter Informationen erhalten Sie unter SoSci Serve GmbH.

Weiter

8% ausgefüllt

Vorkenntnisse und Erfahrungen

Die folgenden Fragen dienen der Einstufung Ihrer eigenen Erfahrungen in der Software Entwicklung allgemein und im Bereich der Software Produktlinien beziehungsweise Software-Konsolidierung im Speziellen. Sie ermöglichen Verbesserungspotentiale, die aus der Befragung hervorgehen, zielgruppengerechter umzusetzen.

1. Welche Tätigkeiten gehören zu ihrem derzeit Aufgabenbereich?

(Mehrfachnennung möglich)

- ☐ Management (Projekt)
- ☐ Management (Produkt)
- ☐ Management (Unternehmen / Bereich / Abteilung)
- ☐ Entwicklung (Produkt)
- ☐ Entwicklung (Lösung) / Beratung
- ☐ Forschung & Lehre (Wissenschaftler)
- ☐ Forschung & Lehre (Student)

2. Bitte geben Sie einige Eckdaten zu Ihrem Arbeitsumfeld an.

Anzahl der Mitarbeiter im Unternehmen: [Bitte auswählen] ▼

3. Wieviel Erfahrung haben Sie in der Softwareentwicklung?

In einem industriellen Kontext ______ Jahre

In Open Source- oder Forschungsprojekten ______ Jahre

Weiter

15% ausgefüllt

Kundenspezifische Produktkopien (?)

1. Wie stark stimmen Sie den folgenden Aussagen über kundenspezifisch angepasste Software-Produktkopien zu?

Bitte bewerten Sie die Aussagen aus Ihrer persönlichen Sicht und wählen Sie den Grad Ihrer Zustimmung. Bitte beantworten Sie die Fragen möglichst zügig und intuitiv.

stimme gar nicht zu — stimme voll zu

	0	1	2	3	4	5
Kundenspezifische Kopien bieten Flexibilität bei der Entwicklung neuer Funktionalitäten.	○	○	○	○	○	○
Kundenspezifische Kopien bedeuten erhöhte Arbeitsaufwände.	○	○	○	○	○	○
Kundenspezifische Kopien sind ein Problem, das wir aktiv verhindern.	○	○	○	○	○	○
Kundenspezifische Kopien bieten eine Möglichkeit Projektdruck entgegenzuwirken.	○	○	○	○	○	○

2. Wie stark stimmen Sie den folgenden Aussagen über kundenspezifisch angepasste Software Produktkopien zu?

Bitte bewerten Sie die Aussagen aus Ihrer persönlichen Sicht und wählen Sie den Grad Ihrer Zustimmung. Bitte beantworten Sie die Fragen möglichst zügig und intuitiv.

stimme gar nicht zu — stimme voll zu

	0	1	2	3	4	5
Kundenspezifische Kopien werden bei uns aktiv vermieden.	○	○	○	○	○	○
Kundenspezifische Kopien werden bei uns aktiv entfernt.	○	○	○	○	○	○
Kundenspezifische Kopien werden bei uns in Kauf genommen wenn es die Projektbedingungen erfordern.	○	○	○	○	○	○
Kundenspezifische Kopien werden bei uns in Projekten gezielt eingesetzt.	○	○	○	○	○	○

Weiter

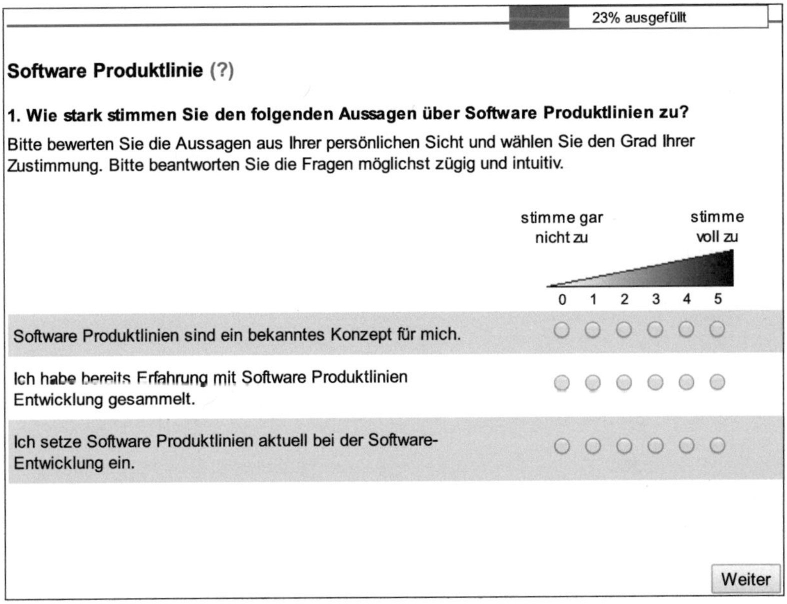

23% ausgefüllt

Software Produktlinie (?)

1. Wie stark stimmen Sie den folgenden Aussagen über Software Produktlinien zu?

Bitte bewerten Sie die Aussagen aus Ihrer persönlichen Sicht und wählen Sie den Grad Ihrer Zustimmung. Bitte beantworten Sie die Fragen möglichst zügig und intuitiv.

	stimme gar nicht zu 0	1	2	3	4	stimme voll zu 5
Software Produktlinien sind ein bekanntes Konzept für mich.	○	○	○	○	○	○
Ich habe bereits Erfahrung mit Software Produktlinien Entwicklung gesammelt.	○	○	○	○	○	○
Ich setze Software Produktlinien aktuell bei der Software-Entwicklung ein.	○	○	○	○	○	○

Weiter

31% ausgefüllt

Konsolidierung kundenspezifischer Kopien (?)

1. Wie stark stimmen Sie den folgenden Aussagen über Ihre Erfahrung mit der Konsolidierung kundenspezifischer Kopien zu Software Produktlinien zu?

Bitte bewerten Sie die Aussagen aus Ihrer persönlichen Sicht und wählen Sie den Grad Ihrer Zustimmung. Bitte beantworten Sie die Fragen möglichst zügig und intuitiv.

	stimme gar nicht zu 0	1	2	3	4	stimme voll zu 5
Ich habe selbst bereits eine Konsolidierung durchgeführt oder war an ihr beteiligt.	○	○	○	○	○	○
Mir wurde über einen längeren Zeitraum (> 2 Monate) von einer Konsolidierung berichtet.	○	○	○	○	○	○
Ich hatte bisher noch keinen Kontakt mit einer solchen Konsolidierung.	○	○	○	○	○	○
Ich hatte einen Einblick in eine Konsolidierung, war aber selbst nicht aktiv.	○	○	○	○	○	○

Weiter

38% ausgefüllt

Rollen im SPLevo Konsolidierungsprozess

Eine Rolle beschreibt die Aufgaben und Verantwortungsbereiche, die von einer Person oder Gruppe von Personen bei einer Konsolidierung übernommen werden. Wenn sich aus ihrer Position spezielle Anforderungen an die zukünftige Produktlinie ergeben, sind diese ebenfalls durch die Rolle beschrieben. Eine Person im Unternehmen / Projekt kann auch mehrere Rollen übernehmen.

Im Folgenden erhalten Sie einen kurzen Gesamtüberblick über die identifizierten Rollen. Anschließend stellen wir Ihnen die einzelnen Rollen kurz vor und stellen Ihnen Fragen zu Ihrer Einschätzung der jeweiligen Rolle.

Rollen Überblick

Die Bezeichnungen der einzelnen Rollen sind an Rollen der allgemeinen Software Entwicklung und deren Aufgabenbereiche angelehnt. Sie werden hier jedoch rein im Kontext der Konsolidierung kundenspezifischer Produktkopien betrachtet. Personen, die eine Rolle übernehmen, können durchaus weitere Aufgaben / Rollen einnehmen.

Rolle	Beschreibung
Software Architekt	Definiert Unternehmens- oder Produktübergreifende Richtlinien (Best Practices) zur Umsetzung von Software Produktlinien.
Konsolidierungsentwickler	Führt die technische Konsolidierung der Produktkopien zur Software Produktlinie durch.
SPL Manager	Ist für die zukünftige Produktlinie aus Produktmanagement Sicht verantwortlich und muss daher auch die Sichtweisen der zukünftigen Anwender und Produktverantwortlichen vertreten.
Produktmanager	Verantwortet ein einzelnes Produkt / eine Lösung, die mit der zukünftigen Software Produktlinie realisiert wird und eventuell vorher schon als Kopie existierte.
Software Entwickler	Wartet und erweitert die Software Produktlinie und realisiert und wartet abgeleitete Produkte und Lösungen.
SPL Konsolidierungsberater	Unterstützt den Konsolidierungsprozess mit angepassten technischen Werkzeugen und Beratung bei der Durchführung.

Weiter

46% ausgefüllt

Rolle: Software Architekt

Im Kontext einer Konsolidierung definitert ein Software Architekt Unternehmens- oder Produktübergreifende Richtlinien (Best Practices) zur Umsetzung von Software Produktlinien.

Aktivitäten

Ein Software Architekt erarbeitet generelle Vorgaben zur Umsetzung von Software Produktlinien. Hierzu gehören empfohlene Mechanismen zur Umsetzung von Variabilität in der Software genauso wie Konfigurationsmechanismen. Außerdem legt er generelle Qualitätsziele für die Konsolidierung fest.

Zuständigkeit (Entscheidungen und Input)

Ein Software Architekt ist für generelle Technologie-Entscheidungen, sowie Strategien zur Umsetzung von Produktlinien zuständig.

Kenntnisse / Skills

Ein Software Architekt benötigt Erfahrung bei der Bewertung von Technologien und zur Entscheidungsfindung. Dafür muss er sowohl die Anforderungen der kurzfristigen Umsetzung als auch der langfristigen Wartung- und Weiterentwicklung berücksichtigen können. Hierzu gehören auch die Fähigkeiten und Strukturen der verfügbaren Entwicklerteams.

---

1. Wie stark stimmen Sie den folgenden Aussagen zur beschriebenen Rolle „Software Architekt“ im Kontext einer Konsolidierung zu?

Bitte bewerten Sie die Aussagen aus Ihrer persönlichen Sicht und wählen Sie den Grad Ihrer Zustimmung. Bitte beantworten Sie die Fragen möglichst zügig und intuitiv.

stimme gar nicht zu — stimme voll zu

	0	1	2	3	4	5
Es gibt eine oder mehrere Personen in meinem aktuellen Arbeitsumfeld, die ich in dieser Rolle sehen würde.	○	○	○	○	○	○
Ich kann mir vorstellen selbst diese Rolle zu übernehmen.	○	○	○	○	○	○
Die Person, die ich in der Rolle sehe besitzt die notwendigen Entscheidungsbefugnisse.	○	○	○	○	○	○
Die Person, die ich in der Rolle sehe besitzt die notwendigen Kompetenzen.	○	○	○	○	○	○

2. Die Personen, die ich in der Rolle des Software Architekten sehe haben folgende Positionen in unserem Unternehmen (Stellenbezeichnung)

Position

Bei mehreren Positionen bitte jeweils eine pro Zeile

Weiter

54% ausgefüllt

Rolle: Konsolidierungsentwickler

Ein Konsolidierungsentwickler führt die technische Konsolidierung der Produktkopien zur Software Produktlinie durch.

Aktivitäten
Ein Konsolidierungsentwickler legt die Rahmenbedingungen einer konkreten Konsolidierung fest, wie zum Beispiel welche Kopien konsolidiert werden sollen. Bei der Konsolidierung selbst erhebt er die Unterschiede zwischen den Kopien und analysiert diese, um die Variabilität der zukünftigen Software Produktlinie aus technischer Sicht zu entwerfen. Er stimmt seinen Entwurf mit dem SPL Manager ab bevor er sich um die technische Umsetzung der SPL kümmert.

Zuständigkeit (Entscheidungen und Input)
Ein Konsolidierungsentwickler entscheidet, was genau mit welchen Parametern konsolidiert werden soll. Er entscheidet über die Gestaltung der Variationspunkte aus technischer Sicht und wählt aus den generell erlaubten Variabilitätsmechanismen die sinnvollsten aus.

Kenntnisse / Skills
Ein Konsolidierungsentwickler benötigt ein grundlegendes Verständnis für Variabilität und Konfigurationsmechanismen. Ihm muss bewusst sein, dass es zwischen einzelnen Code-Veränderungen Zusammenhänge geben kann und diese herauszufinden und zu berücksichtigen sind. Außerdem muss er entscheiden können, welche Kopien zu konsolidieren sind und ermitteln können welches Wissen über diese Kopien noch im Unternehmen existiert. Er muss mit dem Produktlinienverantwortlichen kommunizieren können.

Im Vergleich zu einem "normalen" Entwickler zeichnen den Konsolidierungsentwickler vor allem seine Kenntnisse über Variabilitätsmechanismen, Abhängigkeitsmanagement, sowie die Wartung von Software Produkten aus.

1. Wie stark stimmen Sie den folgenden Aussagen zur beschriebenen Rolle „Konsolidierungsentwickler" im Kontext einer Konsolidierung zu?

Bitte bewerten Sie die Aussagen aus Ihrer persönlichen Sicht und wählen Sie den Grad Ihrer Zustimmung. Bitte beantworten Sie die Fragen möglichst zügig und intuitiv.

	stimme gar nicht zu 0	1	2	3	4	stimme voll zu 5
Es gibt eine oder mehrere Personen in meinem aktuellen Arbeitsumfeld, die ich in dieser Rolle sehen würde.	○	○	○	○	○	○
Ich kann mir vorstellen selbst diese Rolle zu übernehmen.	○	○	○	○	○	○
Die Person, die ich in der Rolle sehe besitzt die notwendigen Entscheidungsbefugnisse.	○	○	○	○	○	○
Die Person, die ich in der Rolle sehe besitzt die notwendigen Kompetenzen.	○	○	○	○	○	○

2. Die Personen, die ich in der Rolle des Konsolidierungsentwicklers sehe haben folgende Positionen in unserem Unternehmen (Stellenbezeichnung)

Position

Bei mehreren Positionen bitte jeweils eine pro Zeile

62% ausgefüllt

SPL Manager

Ein Software Produktlinien Manager (SPL Manager) ist für die zukünftige Produktlinie aus Produktmanagement-Sicht verantwortlich. Er vertritt auch die Sichtweisen der zukünftigen Anwender und Produktverantwortlichen, die nicht direkt am Konsolidierungsprozess beteiligt sind.

Aktivitäten
Ein SPL Manager gibt dem Konsolidierungsentwickler eine Rückmeldung zu seinem Produktlinien Entwurf, in dem er beurteilt, ob die Konfigurationsmöglichkeiten ausreichend aber auch nicht zu umfangreich sind um zukünftig sinnvolle Produkte von der Produktlinie ableiten zu können.

Zuständigkeit (Entscheidungen und Input)
Ein SPL Manager ist dafür zuständig, dass mit der Software Produktlinie später Produkte erstellt werden können, die eine leichte Konfiguration der bisherigen Produktkopien sowie sinnvoller neuer Kombinationen von bisher kundenspezifischen Funktionen ermöglicht. Er vertritt im Prozess damit auch Produkt Manager und Software Entwickler und ihre Anforderungen.

Kenntnisse / Skills
Ein SPL Manager benötigt ein grundlegendes Verständnis von Variabilität und Konfigurationsmöglichkeiten. Darüber hinaus braucht er ein Bewusstsein dafür, dass zu viele feine Konfigurationsmöglichkeiten zwar eine höhere Flexibilität bieten, gleichzeitig aber eine höhere Verwaltungs- und Wartungskomplexität mit sich bringen.

Ganz generell zeichnen den SPL Manager auch seine Kenntnisse des Marktes, sowie der Bedürfnisse und Anforderungen der Kunden aus.

1. Wie stark stimmen Sie den folgenden Aussagen zur beschriebenen Rolle „SPL Manager“ im Kontext einer Konsolidierung zu?

Bitte bewerten Sie die Aussagen aus Ihrer persönlichen Sicht und wählen Sie den Grad Ihrer Zustimmung. Bitte beantworten Sie die Fragen möglichst zügig und intuitiv.

	stimme gar nicht zu 0	1	2	3	4	stimme voll zu 5
Es gibt eine oder mehrere Personen in meinem aktuellen Arbeitsumfeld, die ich in dieser Rolle sehen würde.	○	○	○	○	○	○
Ich kann mir vorstellen selbst diese Rolle zu übernehmen.	○	○	○	○	○	○
Die Person, die ich in der Rolle sehe besitzt die notwendigen Entscheidungsbefugnisse.	○	○	○	○	○	○
Die Person, die ich in der Rolle sehe besitzt die notwendigen Kompetenzen.	○	○	○	○	○	○

2. Die Personen, die ich in der Rolle des SPL Managers sehe haben folgende Positionen in unserem Unternehmen (Stellenbezeichnung)

Position

Bei mehreren Positionen bitte jeweils eine pro Zeile

09% ausgefüllt

Rolle: Produktmanager

Ein Produkt Manager verantwortet ein einzelnes Produkt / eine Lösung, die mit der zukünftigen Software Produktlinie realisiert wird. Gegebenenfalls war diese zuvor auch als Kopie vorhanden.

Während ein SPL Manager übergreifend für alle Produkte verantwortlich ist, so ist ein Produktmanager für eine oder mehrere abgeleitete kundenspezifische Produkte oder Lösungen verantwortlich.

Aktivitäten

Ein Produkt Manager ist nicht direkt an der Konsolidierung beteiligt und daher auch für keine Aktivität im Prozess zuständig.

Zuständigkeit (Entscheidungen und Input)

Ein Produkt Manager kennt die Endanwender-Anforderungen eines Produktes / einer Lösung und stellt diese dem SPL Manager bei Bedarf zur Verfügung.

Kenntnisse / Skills

Ein Produkt Manager kennt ein konkretes Produkt / eine Lösung und kann die Kunden und/oder Endanwender Anforderungen beurteilen. Hat das Produkt vorher als kundenspezifische Kopie existiert, so kann er das aus Produktsicht noch vorhandene Wissen darüber bereitstellen.

1. Wie stark stimmen Sie den folgenden Aussagen zur beschriebenen Rolle „Produktmanager“ im Kontext einer Konsolidierung zu?

Bitte bewerten Sie die Aussagen aus Ihrer persönlichen Sicht und wählen Sie den Grad Ihrer Zustimmung. Bitte beantworten Sie die Fragen möglichst zügig und intuitiv.

	stimme gar nicht zu 0	1	2	3	4	stimme voll zu 5
Es gibt eine oder mehrere Personen in meinem aktuellen Arbeitsumfeld, die ich in dieser Rolle sehen würde.	○	○	○	○	○	○
Ich kann mir vorstellen selbst diese Rolle zu übernehmen.	○	○	○	○	○	○
Die Person, die ich in der Rolle sehe besitzt die notwendigen Entscheidungsbefugnisse.	○	○	○	○	○	○
Die Person, die ich in der Rolle sehe besitzt die notwendigen Kompetenzen.	○	○	○	○	○	○

2. Die Personen, die ich in der Rolle des Produktmanagers sehe haben folgende Positionen in unserem Unternehmen (Stellenbezeichnung)

Position

Bei mehreren Positionen bitte jeweils eine pro Zeile

Weiter

77% ausgefüllt

Software Entwickler

Ein Software Entwickler ist für die Wartung und Weiterentwicklung der Software Produktlinie, sowie der davon abgeleiteten Produkte zuständig. Sind produktspezifische Erweiterungen für die Produktlinie möglich, so werden sie ebenfalls von einem Software Entwickler implementiert und gewartet.

Aktivitäten

Ein Software Entwickler ist nicht direkt an der Konsolidierung beteiligt und daher auch für keine Aktivität im Prozess zuständig.

Zuständigkeit (Entscheidungen und Input)

Ein Software Entwickler kann dem SPL Manager bei Bedarf seine technischen Anforderungen zur Wartung und Weiterentwicklung bei Bedarf zur Verfügung stellen.

Kenntnisse / Skills

Ein Software Entwickler kennt sich mit Fragestellungen der Software Wartung und Weiterentwicklung, sowie der Entwicklung von Erweiterungen für bereitgestellte Schnittstellen aus. Ist ein Software Entwickler auch für die Software Produktlinie selbst zuständig, so kennt er sich mit der Umsetzung von Variabilität und deren Auswirkungen aus.

1. Wie stark stimmen Sie den folgenden Aussagen zur beschriebenen Rolle „Software Entwickler" im Kontext einer Konsolidierung zu?

Bitte bewerten Sie die Aussagen aus Ihrer persönlichen Sicht und wählen Sie den Grad Ihrer Zustimmung. Bitte beantworten Sie die Fragen möglichst zügig und intuitiv.

	stimme gar nicht zu 0	1	2	3	4	stimme voll zu 5
Es gibt eine oder mehrere Personen in meinem aktuellen Arbeitsumfeld, die ich in dieser Rolle sehen würde.	○	○	○	○	○	○
Ich kann mir vorstellen selbst diese Rolle zu übernehmen.	○	○	○	○	○	○
Die Person, die ich in der Rolle sehe besitzt die notwendigen Entscheidungsbefugnisse.	○	○	○	○	○	○
Die Person, die ich in der Rolle sehe besitzt die notwendigen Kompetenzen.	○	○	○	○	○	○

2. Die Personen, die ich in der Rolle des Software Entwicklers sehe haben folgende Positionen in unserem Unternehmen (Stellenbezeichnung)

Position

Bei mehreren Positionen bitte jeweils eine pro Zeile

Weiter

85% ausgefüllt

Konsolidierungsberater

Ein Software Produktlinien Konsolidierungsberater (SPL Konsolidierungsberater) unterstützt die Prozessbeteiligten bei der Konsolidierung durch die Einführung und Anpassung von unterstützenden Werkzeugen.
Bei dem Konsolidierungsberater handelt es sich gegebenenfalls um einen externen Ansprechpartner, der bei Bedarf auch vielen Konsolidierungsprojekten bereitsteht.

Aktivitäten
Ein SPL Konsolidierungsberater ist nicht direkt an der Konsolidierung beteiligt und daher auch für keine Aktivität im Prozess zuständig.

Zuständigkeit (Entscheidungen und Input)
Ein SPL Konsolidierungsberater ist für keine Entscheidungen oder Lieferungen von Input verantwortlich.

Kenntnisse / Skills
Ein SPL Konsolidierungsberater ist Ansprechpartner für Konsolidierungsprozesse; als solcher kennt er sich mit der Durchführung solcher Prozesse, sowie der unterstützenden Werkzeugen, beispielsweise für das Verstehen der Produktkopien oder das Refactoring aus. Er ist in der Lage diese Werkzeuge bei Bedarf auch zu erweitern oder anzupassen.

1. Wie stark stimmen Sie den folgenden Aussagen zur beschriebenen Rolle „SPL Konsolidierungsberater" im Kontext einer Konsolidierung zu?

Bitte bewerten Sie die Aussagen aus Ihrer persönlichen Sicht und wählen Sie den Grad Ihrer Zustimmung. Bitte beantworten Sie die Fragen möglichst zügig und intuitiv.

	0 (stimme gar nicht zu)	1	2	3	4	5 (stimme voll zu)
Es gibt eine oder mehrere Personen in meinem aktuellen Arbeitsumfeld, die ich in dieser Rolle sehen würde.	○	○	○	○	○	○
Ich kann mir vorstellen selbst diese Rolle zu übernehmen.	○	○	○	○	○	○
Die Person, die ich in der Rolle sehe besitzt die notwendigen Entscheidungsbefugnisse.	○	○	○	○	○	○
Die Person, die ich in der Rolle sehe besitzt die notwendigen Kompetenzen.	○	○	○	○	○	○

2. Die Personen, die ich in der Rolle des SPL Konsolidierungsberaters sehe haben folgende Positionen in unserem Unternehmen (Stellenbezeichnung)

Position

Bei mehreren Positionen bitte jeweils eine pro Zeile

Weiter

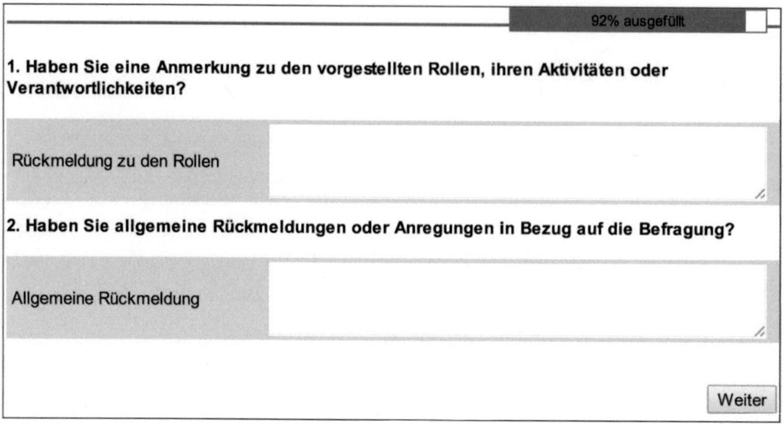
92% ausgefüllt

1. Haben Sie eine Anmerkung zu den vorgestellten Rollen, ihren Aktivitäten oder Verantwortlichkeiten?

Rückmeldung zu den Rollen

2. Haben Sie allgemeine Rückmeldungen oder Anregungen in Bezug auf die Befragung?

Allgemeine Rückmeldung

Weiter

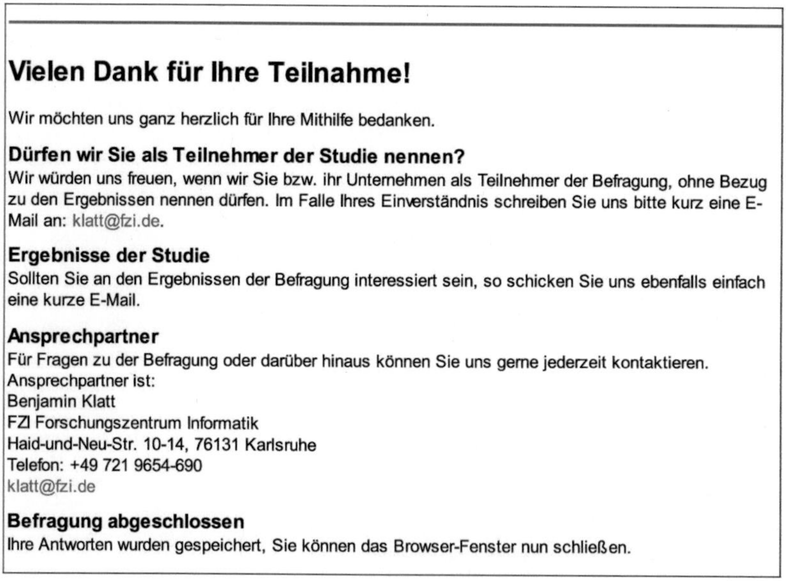
Vielen Dank für Ihre Teilnahme!

Wir möchten uns ganz herzlich für Ihre Mithilfe bedanken.

Dürfen wir Sie als Teilnehmer der Studie nennen?
Wir würden uns freuen, wenn wir Sie bzw. ihr Unternehmen als Teilnehmer der Befragung, ohne Bezug zu den Ergebnissen nennen dürfen. Im Falle Ihres Einverständnis schreiben Sie uns bitte kurz eine E-Mail an: klatt@fzi.de.

Ergebnisse der Studie
Sollten Sie an den Ergebnissen der Befragung interessiert sein, so schicken Sie uns ebenfalls einfach eine kurze E-Mail.

Ansprechpartner
Für Fragen zu der Befragung oder darüber hinaus können Sie uns gerne jederzeit kontaktieren.
Ansprechpartner ist:
Benjamin Klatt
FZI Forschungszentrum Informatik
Haid-und-Neu-Str. 10-14, 76131 Karlsruhe
Telefon: +49 721 9654-690
klatt@fzi.de

Befragung abgeschlossen
Ihre Antworten wurden gespeichert, Sie können das Browser-Fenster nun schließen.

B.3.2. Answers

The following subsections and tables provide the results given by the participants (i.e., "Teilnehmer") of the online survey.

Position	Teilnehmer Nr. 1	2	3	4	5	6	7	8	9	10	11	12	13	14	15	16	17	18	Σ
Management																			
Projekt				1	1	1			1	1	1	1	1	1			1		10
Produkt		1	1			1				1		1					1		6
Unternehm.	1	1	1			1				1	1	1		1	1			1	10
Entwicklung																			
Produkt	1	1		1		1	1			1		1				1	1		9
Beratung	1				1	1	1	1	1	1		1				1	1		10
Forschung																			
Forscher				1													1		2
Student																			0

Table B.2.: Survey participants: Current position (multiple choices allowed)

Teilnehmer Nr.	Erfahrung Software-Entwicklung (in Jahren) Industriell	Open Source / Forschung
1	17	6
2	15	20
3	20	3
4	4	12
5	3	1
6	8	0
7	3	1
8	1	6
9	12	3
10	5	10
11	17	0
12	5	5
13	0	10
14	1	1
15	16	6
16	5	15
17	7	7
18	15	0
∅	8.6	5.9

Table B.3.: Survey participants: Development experience

T-Nr.	Unternehmensgröße (in Mitarbeitern)					
	2-5	6-15	15-40	40-100	100-400	400-1000
1						1
2					1	
3					1	
4					1	
5						1
6					1	
7					1	
8					1	
9					1	
10	1					
11			1			
12		1				
13					1	
14						1
15					1	
16					1	
17					1	
18			1			
Σ	1	1	2	0	11	3

Table B.4.: Survey participants: Company size; T-Nr: Teilnehmer Nr.

	-	Zustimmung				+
	0	1	2	3	4	5
Erfahrung Produktkopien						
Kundenspezifische Kopien bieten Flexibilität bei der Entwicklung neuer Funktionalitäten.	2	3	1	4	5	3
Kundenspezifische Kopien bedeuten erhöhte Arbeitsaufwände.	0	2	1	1	11	3
Kundenspezifische Kopien sind ein Problem, das wir aktiv verhindern.	1	0	2	6	6	3
Kundenspezifische Kopien bieten eine Möglichkeit Projektdruck entgegenzuwirken.	0	2	3	6	6	1
Einsatz Produktkopien						
Kundenspezifische Kopien werden bei uns aktiv vermieden.	0	1	3	4	6	4
Kundenspezifische Kopien werden bei uns aktiv entfernt.	1	7	5	4	1	0
Kundenspezifische Kopien werden bei uns in Kauf genommen, wenn es die Projektbedingungen erfordern.	0	3	0	3	10	2
Kundenspezifische Kopien werden bei uns in Projekten gezielt eingesetzt.	6	4	6	1	1	0

Table B.5.: Survey participants: Experience with the topic
(Likert Scale: 0=No agreement; 5=Full agreement)

	-		Zustimmung			+
	0	1	2	3	4	5
Erfahrung Produktlinien						
Software Produktlinien sind ein bekanntes Konzept für mich.	0	1	1	4	6	6
Ich habe bereits Erfahrung mit Software Produktlinien Entwicklung gesammelt.	1	0	7	3	2	5
Ich setze Software Produktlinien aktuell bei der Software-Entwicklung ein.	6	2	3	4	1	2
Erfahrung Konsolidierung						
Ich habe selbst bereits eine Konsolidierung durchgeführt oder war an ihr beteiligt.	8	1	1	2	2	4
Mir wurde über einen längeren Zeitraum (> 2 Monate) von einer Konsolidierung berichtet.	9	3	1	3	0	2
Ich hatte bisher noch keinen Kontakt mit einer solchen Konsolidierung.	10	2	0	2	1	3
Ich hatte einen Einblick in eine Konsolidierung, war aber selbst nicht aktiv.	9	2	3	0	3	1

Table B.6.: Survey participants: Experience with the topic continued (Likert Scale: 0=No agreement; 5=Full agreement)

Software Architect	- 0	Zustimmung 1	2	3	4	+ 5
Es gibt eine oder mehrere Personen in meinem aktuellen Arbeitsumfeld, die ich in dieser Rolle sehen würde.	1	1	1	2	2	11
Ich kann mir vorstellen selbst diese Rolle zu übernehmen.	6	0	1	4	2	5
Die Person, die ich in der Rolle sehe besitzt die notwendigen Entscheidungsbefugnisse.	0	0	4	3	6	5
Die Person, die ich in der Rolle sehe besitzt die notwendigen Kompetenzen.	0	0	1	4	4	9
Positionen potentieller Personen						

- Chief Architekt, Software Produkt Manager
- PA –> Produktarchitekt ist bei uns schon als Rolle besetzt
- Teamleiter
- Senior Consultant, Project Manager
- CTO, Software Architect
- SE Architekt
- CEO, CTO, Software Architect
- Solution Architect
- Software Architect Platform SDK, Lead Developer Platform SDK
- Software Architekt
- Software Architekt

Table B.7.: Survey Result: Software Architect
(Likert Scale: 0=No agreement; 5=Full agreement)

SPL Consolidation Developer	- Zustimmung + 0	1	2	3	4	5
Es gibt eine oder mehrere Personen in meinem aktuellen Arbeitsumfeld, die ich in dieser Rolle sehen würde.	2	2	1	6	2	5
Ich kann mir vorstellen selbst diese Rolle zu übernehmen.	7	2	1	3	1	4
Die Person, die ich in der Rolle sehe besitzt die notwendigen Entscheidungsbefugnisse.	1	4	3	4	2	4
Die Person, die ich in der Rolle sehe besitzt die notwendigen Kompetenzen.	1	1	2	1	9	4
Positionen potentieller Personen						
• Senior Entwickler, Software Architekt • (Senior-)Entwickler • Senior Consultant, Consultant • CTO, Software Architcct, Software Developer • Softwareentwickler • Software Developer, Software Architect • Developer • Software Architect Platform SDK, Lead/Senior Developer Platform SDK • Software Engineer • das ist bei uns Teamaufgabe, die spezielle Rolle gibt es nicht, wenn mann von dem Mergingtask absieht der mehr oder weniger von einem Personenkreis ausgeführt wird						

Table B.8.: Survey Result: SPL Consolidation Developer
(Likert Scale: 0=No agreement; 5=Full agreement)

SPL Manager	- 0	Zustimmung 1	2	3	4	+ 5
Es gibt eine oder mehrere Personen in meinem aktuellen Arbeitsumfeld, die ich in dieser Rolle sehen würde.	0	6	2	6	0	4
Ich kann mir vorstellen selbst diese Rolle zu übernehmen.	8	4	2	2	0	2
Die Person, die ich in der Rolle sehe besitzt die notwendigen Entscheidungsbefugnisse.	2	4	4	4	1	3
Die Person, die ich in der Rolle sehe besitzt die notwendigen Kompetenzen.	1	4	3	7	1	2
Positionen potentieller Personen						
• Solution Manager • Product-Designer • CTO, Software Architect, Software Developer • Aktuell nicht notwendig • Software, Architect • Consultant • Teamleiter Platform SDK, Product Manager • Product Manager • würde bei uns geteilt durch PO- ProductOwner und PPL - Produktprojektleiter						

Table B.9.: Survey Result: SPL Manager
(Likert Scale: 0=No agreement; 5=Full agreement)

Produktmanager	- 0	Zustimmung 1	2	3	4	+ 5
Es gibt eine oder mehrere Personen in meinem aktuellen Arbeitsumfeld, die ich in dieser Rolle sehen würde.	0	1	0	3	8	6
Ich kann mir vorstellen selbst diese Rolle zu übernehmen.	7	3	2	2	2	2
Die Person, die ich in der Rolle sehe besitzt die notwendigen Entscheidungsbefugnisse.	0	3	3	5	4	3
Die Person, die ich in der Rolle sehe besitzt die notwendigen Kompetenzen.	0	2	2	7	3	4
Positionen potentieller Personen						
• Produkt Owner • PM- Produktmanager • Produktmanager • CTO|Software Architect, Software Developer • Produktmanager • Product Manager, CTO, CEO • Consultant • Product Manager • Product Manager						

Table B.10.: Survey Result: Product Manager
(Likert Scale: 0=No agreement; 5=Full agreement)

Software Entwickler	- 0	Zustimmung 1	2	3	4	+ 5
Es gibt eine oder mehrere Personen in meinem aktuellen Arbeitsumfeld, die ich in dieser Rolle sehen würde.	0	0	0	1	5	12
Ich kann mir vorstellen selbst diese Rolle zu übernehmen.	6	3	1	0	1	7
Die Person, die ich in der Rolle sehe besitzt die notwendigen Entscheidungsbefugnisse.	0	1	2	3	3	9
Die Person, die ich in der Rolle sehe besitzt die notwendigen Kompetenzen.	0	0	0	1	7	10

Positionen potentieller Personen

- Software Entwickler, Senior Software Entwickler, QS Specialist
- Developer / Entwicklungsteam
- Entwickler
- Consultant
- Software Developer
- Softwareentwickler
- Software Developer, Software Architect
- Developer
- Junior/Senior Software Developer
- Software Engineer

Table B.11.: Survey Result: Software Developer
(Likert Scale: 0=No agreement; 5=Full agreement)

SPL Konsolidierungsberater	-	Zustimmung				+
	0	1	2	3	4	5
Es gibt eine oder mehrere Personen in meinem aktuellen Arbeitsumfeld, die ich in dieser Rolle sehen würde.	4	4	3	3	2	2
Ich kann mir vorstellen selbst diese Rolle zu übernehmen.	8	4	2	1	1	2
Die Person, die ich in der Rolle sehe besitzt die notwendigen Entscheidungsbefugnisse.	3	6	4	1	2	2
Die Person, die ich in der Rolle sehe besitzt die notwendigen Kompetenzen.	3	5	3	2	2	3
Positionen potentieller Personen						
• wir haben BA- Businessanalysten und Anforderungsmanager, die könnten sowas machen • Technology Consultant • SE Architekt • Software Architect, CTO • Developer • Software Architect Platform SDK • Software Architekt						

Table B.12.: Survey Result: SPL Consolidation Consultant
(Likert Scale: 0=No agreement; 5=Full agreement)

Feedback Rollen: Rückmeldung zu den Rollen
Entwickler und Tester verschmelzen im Scrum/agilen Umfeld. Würde ich berücksichtigen|Mit fehlen die Rollen Releasemanager und Build&Deployment Manager
Wir arbeiten mit Scrum in Anlehnung an Scaled Agile Viele Rollen sind daraus abgeleitet, und ähnlich
Ja, in unserem Recht kleinen Unternehmen passt die Stellenbezeichnung nicht so gut zu den Rollenbezeichnungen. Auch geht die Qualifikation der Mitarbeiter teilweise über die in der Stellenbezeichnung verbundene Expertise hinaus. Damit ist die vorgenommene Zuordnung mit Vorsicht zu evaluieren.
Grad der notwendigen technischen Tiefe ist bei SPL Manager und Produktmanager sehr offen. Insb. ob die Rolle abschätzen können muss, ob etwas technisch umsetzbar ist, bleibt unklar. Antworten passen nicht immer zur Rollenbeschreibung: Konsolidierungsberater ist für keine Entscheidung verantwortlich -> in Antworten 'hat Entscheidungsbefugnisse'
Feedback Umfrage: Allgemeine Rückmeldung
Immer wieder spannend den Produkt/RoadMap Prozess mit Projekt und Kundeanforderungen unter einen Hut zu bringen. Bin auf die Ergebnisse gespannt
Da bei uns keine SPL eingesetzt werden, konnte ich zu den SPL-spezifischeren Rollen keine vernüntige EInschätzung abgeben.
Je nach Beantwortung der ersten Rollen-Frage 'Es gibt eine oder mehrere Personen in meinem aktuellen Arbeitsumfeld, die ich in dieser Rolle sehen würde.' machen die folgenden Fragen ggf. nicht mehr viel Sinn (z.B. 'ich stimme nicht zu' -> Antworten auf <tab>'Person besitzt...' machen keinen Sinn).

Table B.13.: Survey feedback

B.4. Interview Refactoring Specification

The following subsections provide the questionnaire and the summarized answers of the interviews about the comprehensibility of the consolidation refactoring specification concept (Section 8.5.2). The results are discussed as part of the evaluation in Section 8.8.1. Note: The consolidation refactoring was named "variability refactoring" before. The questionnaire documentation has not been updated to the new name to document the version originally sent out to the participants.

B.4.1. Questionnaire

The following pages present the questionnaire that has been sent out to the interview participants. It was originally sent as a word processor document, and the participants were asked to respond in the word document and send it back. In addition, they received parts of the refactoring specification included in Appendix A.1. In particular, they received the first page containing the general information about the refactoring and the refactoring instructions for Method and Import elements of the JaMoPP metamodel.

Interview: Variability Refactoring Specification Comprehensibility

Introduction

The target of this interview is to evaluate the comprehensibility of a specification concept for a novel type of refactorings.
This type of refactoring is about combining two variants of the same code and introducing a variability mechanism to use the one or the other in the same code base in the future. This includes a configuration mechanism for specifying which alternative to use as well.
Note: This novel type of refactoring slightly differs from traditional refactorings allowing for improving the internal structure of a code without changing its external behavior. Nevertheless, considering the combined variants and the introduced configuration, you are able to configure the original behavior of the code variants. Thus, each of these configurations and the according original code variants provide the same behavior and this novel refactoring conforms to the traditional refactorings.

During the interview, please keep in mind that this interview is focused on the comprehensibility of the specification structure and the provided types of information in general. It is not about assessing the introduced variability and configuration mechanisms itself. Both might be useful in one scenario but inappropriate in another.

Interview Process

The process of this interview is structured in two steps:

1. Answer questionnaire part 1 about your experience
2. Read the refactoring specification
3. Answer questionnaire part 2 about the refactoring specification

The specification you will be provided with covers only a part of the complete refactoring. But the parts you will read are representative for the refactoring specification at all.
The refactoring specification contains two parts:

- **General Information** about the refactoring itself respectively the variability and configuration mechanisms it introduces.
  Intention: Deciding to use this refactoring for a concrete variable code location or not
- **Instructions** how to refactor specific types of software elements.
  Intention: Guide you in performing the refactoring manually or implementing automation for it.

Now, please answer the first part of the questionnaire, then read the provided specification, and continue with the questionnaire afterwards.
Additionally, please do not modify the questionnaire itself and fill out the fields marked with a yellow background. For multiple-choice questions, please select only one answer.

Questionnaire Part 1: Knowledge and Experience
How many years of experience do you have in developing Software?
Industrial: ____ Open Source / Research: ____
Considering software refactorings, how would you rate your personal skills?
☐None ☐Basic ☐Experienced ☐Professional
Considering model driven software development, how would you rate your personal skills?
☐None ☐Basic ☐Experienced ☐Professional
Considering model driven software development, how would you rate your personal knowledge about this model?
☐None ☐Basic ☐Experienced ☐Professional

Questionnaire Part 2: Refactoring Specification

General Information

According to the information you read, when would you apply this refactoring?

Answer:

Describe in two sentences, how the alternative variants can be configured later on.

Answer:

Did you find an example as part of the general information helpful to understand the specified refactoring?

☐necessary ☐ unnecessary ☐ disturbing

Reason:

How do you rate the informal description of the limitations?

☐sufficient ☐ disturbing ☐ expected something else

Reason:

Did you miss anything in the general information part stopping you to decide about applying the refactoring or not?

☐no ☐ yes, I missed:

Refactoring Instructions in general	
	Did you find an example as part of the instructions helpful to understand the specified refactoring?
	☐necessary ☐ unnecessary ☐ disturbing Reason:
	How do you rate using pseudo code and the intention to not limit the way the mechanics are automated or even performing it manually?
	☐positive as it does not limit me ☐neutral ☐I prefer a concrete programming language even if not the one I will use ☐other:
	Did you miss anything in the instructions in general which might stop you in applying them?
	☐no ☐ yes, I missed:

Refactoring Instruction: Import

According to the information you read:
When can you apply this instruction and when not?

Answer:

Is there anything you missed in this specific refactoring instruction?

☐no ☐ yes, I missed:

Refactoring Instruction: Method

According to the information you read:
When can you apply this instruction and when not?

Answer:

The mechanics defines a function. Please give its name and describe in two sentences what its purpose is and where it is called.

Name and description:

Is there anything you missed in this specific refactoring instruction?

☐no ☐ yes, I missed:

	Participants 1	2	3	4	∅
Development Experience (years)					
Industrial	5	2	3	7	4.25
Research / Open Source	15	16	12	5	12
Skills (1=Basic, 4=Professional)					
Refactoring	4	3	4	4	4
MDSD	4	4	4	4	4
JaMoPP	4	4	4	4	4

Table B.14.: Refactoring interview: Participants' experience

B.4.2. Answers

the following tables contain the answers as they were given by the participants. No spelling or grammar correction has been applied to them.

According to the information you read, when would you apply this refactoring?	
1	If I had two different method implementations in copied code and wanted to choose between them before compilation time, I could use this refactoring.
2	When tow (or more) features are alternative (mutually exclusive).
3	When we have a set of implementations of the same component. The used implementation should be selected on compile time. For this selection this refactoring introduces a "controller" acting as a dispatcher.
4	When differences between two variants are located in a single place in the code and when variability can be realized using an IF statement.
Describe in two sentences, how alternative variants can be configured later on.	
1	I would need to change the String constant CONF1 in class Config to switch between variants. Second sentence to address the questions requirement to write two sentences.
2	There is a single class with static members of type String. A concrete selection of a particular feature is described by setting one of a set of possible values for the respective String constant describing the configuration for this feature.
3	Configuration only takes place just before compilation. It can be adjusted by modifying particular fields in a configuration class.
4	Alternative variants can be selected by replacing the values of static string constants in the configuration class. This must be performed at compile time.

Table B.15.: Refactoring interview answers: General infos

Did you find an example as part of the general information helpful to understand the specified refactoring?		
1	necessary	Code reads better than just text (given developers as target audience). Gives a concrete implementation template
2	necessary	Absolutely helpful. Before that, there is much room for own ideas on what the refactoring might do in detail.
3	necessary	Every catalogue contains examples. They are very supportive in understanding the catalogues intention in general and the particular catalogue entry specifically.
4	necessary	A good example is never disturbing and nearly never unnecessary.
How do you rate the informal description of the limitations?		
1	necessary	I find the limitations are quite necessary. But choose them wisely. Some are a bit confusing, because it's somehow obvious that if-statements can not be used for variation on class signatures.
2	/	Intentionally did not mark any option: What I would have wanted was "Helpful but more detail needed". The information that is there is good but it probably only helps when you already have intimate knowledge of variability mechanisms and their limitations.
3	expected sth. else	Did not understand the last limitation. "local variables" a local to what? When being local in a method it doesn't matter if another method contains another local variable with the same name.
4	necessary	The list of given limitations contains representative examples for cases where the refactoring is not acceptable. I'm not sure whether the list is complete, neither can I say that it even should be complete. In any case it is sufficient.

Table B.16.: Refactoring interview answers: General infos continued

Did you miss anything in the general information part stopping you to decide about applying the refactoring or not?		
1	no	No. I also like the classification scheme and the alternatives section. For supported elements I would not refer to JaMoPP but to Java in general
2	yes	Explanation of what OPTXOR is.
3	no	/
4	no	/

Table B.17.: Refactoring interview answers: General infos continued

Did you find an example as part of the instructions helpful to understand the specified refactoring?		
1	necessary	Again, same audience and reason as above
2	necessary	
3	necessary	I like the decomposition oft he overall refactoring. That's why each separate instruction (like adding the imports and merging the methods) is understandable easily and examples are not necessary at all cost. But in general I wouldn't let examples out.
4	necessary	Some instructions can get quite complex. An example never hurts.
How do you rate using pseudo code and the intention to not limit the way the mechanics are automated or even performing it manually?		
1	neutral	Good: not limited to concrete language Bad: hard to verify/test without translating it to concrete language
2	prefer programming language	(Three questions in one. Sort of confusing to give an answer here.)
3	neutral	
4	other	The pseudo code that specifies how to implement the refactoring was of little interest to me as I was not confronted with the task to actually implement the refactoring. I'm not sure whether it will even be required for this task. Translating the pseudo code to a concrete language might be equally hard as implementing the refactoring based from a textual description.

Table B.18.: Refactoring interview answers: Instructions general

Did you miss anything in the instructions in general which might stop you in applying them?		
1	no	
2	no	I am assuming that you would be presented with an identified difference of two copies and then be prompted how to deal with them. In that case, the instructions are fine. Otherwise, it would be helpful on which elements to apply the instructions.
3	yes	Wouldn't stop me but I miss details about the composition of the particular instructions. What ifo ne instruction (like adding the imports) fails? Will the others be executed? Will the whole refactoring fail? What about global pre- and post-conditions in contrast to those of the specific separate instructions?
4	yes	It was not clear how the instructions refer to the refactoring. The refactoring should contain a list of "instruction types" that are required to perform the refactoring.

Table B.19.: Refactoring interview answers: Instructions general continued

According to the information you read: When can you apply this instruction and when not?		
1	I did not find any exclusions in instruction. So I assume I can apply it for all imports oft he involved classes	
2	When there is (at least) one import in the integration copy that is needed by a feature. (I'm only guessing here. Could not find anything specific to when the refactoring can be applied)	
3	This question is misleading: one might answer that it cannot be applied when the integrated variant contains imports already contained in the leading variant. But I expect this check to be performed by the refactoring itself. In general, imports can always be added to a class, can't they? According to the pre-conditions, this instruction can only be executed if the variation points are CompilationUnits.	
4	According to the given information it can be applied always. However, I think this is only true if there are no name conflicts.	
Is there anything you missed in this specific refactoring instruction?		
1	yes	I'm not sure how to identify the two CUs that are to be integrated by this step. Did I miss something here?
2	yes	Explanation on why this procedure (seemingly) needs a manual operation. Can this not be fully automated?
3	no	
4	yes	See above: Detection and handling of name conflicts.

Table B.20.: Refactoring interview answers: Instructions for import elements

According to the information you read: When can you apply this instruction and when not?	
1	Again how do I associate the leading and the integration class? I can apply the refactoring on all methods that are not equal with names and differ in return types. From descriptions it's not clear what happens to method with equal names and parameters. This is somewhat clarified in the mechanics. Also the example description could be clearer in this regard.
2	Apply: When there are multiple methods with the same name and return type but different numer/types of parameters. Cannot apply: When methods have different return types. (please see below)
3	According to the pre-conditions, this instruction can only be executed if the variation points are MemberContainers. Again, I would expect the refactoring tool to reject this instruction in case signatures match, as it can be seen in the mechanics.
4	When variants contain different methods
The mechanics defines a function. Please give its name and describe in two sentences what its purpose is and where it is called.	
1	Name: hasMethodWithEqualNameAndParameters. Checks whether the target container has a method with same name and parameters. Second sentence to address the questions requirement to write two sentences
2	hasMethodWithEqualNameAndParameters() Checks whether a given container has a method with equal name and parameters. (Is this a sanity check?)
3	Name: hasMethodWithEqualNameAndParameters Checks whether a leading MemberContainer contains a method having the same signature as the passed method of a integrated variant. Return types are not checked.
4	Name: hasMethodWithEqualNameAndParameters Purpose: Check whether there is a method with the same signature.

Table B.21.: Refactoring interview answers: Instructions for method elements

Is there anything you missed in this specific refactoring instruction?		
1	no	The structure for the instruction is very well and complete from my perspective. Only the example spec seems not complete/consistent. The name “implementing element” in Pre-Condition is somehow hard to grasp
2	yes	Under exclusion: Explanation that methods with same signature with regard to Koenig lookup are not supported (same number and sequence of types for parameters but, in this case, different implementation).
3	no	
4	yes	The relation to the refactoring is missing. Is this related to the IF WITH STATIC CLASS refactoring?

Table B.22.: Refactoring interview answers: Instructions for method elements continued

Acronyms

AOP Aspect Oriented Programming
API Application Programming Interface
AST Abstract Syntax Tree

CFG Control Flow Graph
CM Change Management
CVL Common Variability Language

DSL Domain Specific Language

EMOF Essential Meta Object Facility
ERP Enterprise Resource Planing

FCA Formal Concept Analysis
FM Feature Model
FODA Feature Oriented Domain Analysis

GQM Goal Question Metric

IDE Integrated Development Environment
IR Information Retrieval

JAR Java Archive

KDM Knowledge Discovery Model
KIT Karlsruhe Institute of Technology

LLOC Logical Lines of Code
LSI Latent Semantic Indexing

MBE Model Based Engineering
MDA Model Driven Architecture
MDD Model Driven Development
MDE Model Driven Engineering
MDSD Model Driven Software Development
MOF Meta Object Facility

NLPA Natural Language Program Analysis

OCL Object Constraint Language
OMG Object Management Group

PDG Program Dependency Graph
PET Program Execution Trace
PLOC Physical Lines of Code
PPA Partial Program Analysis

SCM Software Configuration Management
SLOC Source Lines of Code
SME Small and medium sized enterprises
SPL Software Product Line

UI User Interface
UML Unified Modeling Language
URI Uniform Resource Identifier

V	Variant
VCS	Version Control System
VP	Variation Point
VPG	Variation Point Group
VPM	Variation Point Model

Bibliography

[1] Mathieu Acher, Anthony Cleve, Philippe Collet, Philippe Merle, Laurence Duchien and Philippe Lahire. 'Reverse Engineering Architectural Feature Models'. In: *Proceedings of the 5th European Conference on Software Architecture (ECSA 2011)*. LNCS. Essen (Germany): Springer Berlin / Heidelberg, Sept. 2011, p. 16.

[2] Hiralal Agrawal and Joseph R. Horgan. 'Dynamic Program Slicing'. In: *Proceedings of the 11th ACM SIGPLAN Conference on Programming Language Design and Implementation (PLDI 1990)*. White Plains, New York, USA: ACM, 1990, pp. 246–256. DOI: 10.1145/93542.93576.

[3] Vander Alves, Rohit Gehyi, Tiago Massoni, Uirá Kulesza, Paulo Borba and Carlos Lucena. 'Refactoring Product Lines'. In: *Proceedings of the 5th International Conference on Generative Programming and Component Engineering (GPCE 2006)*. ACM, 2006, pp. 201–210. ISBN: 1595932372.

[4] Vander Alves, Pedro Matos Jr, Leonardo Cole, Paulo Borba and Geber Ramalho. 'Extracting and Evolving Mobile Games Product Lines'. In: *Software Product Lines*. Ed. by Henk Obbink and Klaus Pohl. Vol. 3714. Lecture Notes in Computer Science. Springer Berlin / Heidelberg, 2005, pp. 70–81. ISBN: 978-3-540-28936-4. DOI: 10.1007/11554844_8.

[5] Vander Alves, Christa Schwanninger, Luciano Barbosa, Awais Rashid, Peter Sawyer, Paul Rayson, Christoph Pohl and Andreas Rummler. 'An Exploratory Study of Information Retrieval Techniques in Domain Analysis'. In: *Proceedings of the 12th International Software Product Line Conference (SPLC 2008)*. IEEE Computer Society, Sept. 2008, pp. 67–76. ISBN: 978-0-7695-3303-2. DOI: 10.1109/SPLC.2008.18.

[6] John Anvik and Margaret-anne Storey. 'Task Articulation in Software Maintenance: Integrating Source Code Annotations with an Issue Tracking System'. In: *Proceedings of the 24th International Conference on Software Maintenance (ICSM 2008)*. IEEE Computer Society, 2008, pp. 460–461. ISBN: 9781424426140. DOI: 10.1109/ICSM.2008.4658104.

[7] Sven Apel, Don Batory, Christian Kästner and Gunter Saake. *Feature-Oriented Software Product Lines*. 1. Springer Berlin / Heidelberg, 2013, p. 330. ISBN: 978-3-642-37521-7.

[8] Taweesup Apiwattanapong, Alessandro Orso and Mary Jean Harrold. 'JDiff: A Differencing Technique and Tool for Object-Oriented Programs'. In: *Automated Software Engineering* 14.1 (Dec. 2006), pp. 3–36. ISSN: 0928-8910. DOI: 10.1007/s10515-006-0002-0.

[9] Colin Atkinson, Joachim Bayer, Christian Bunse, Erik Kamsties, Oliver Laitenberger, Roland Laqua, Dirk Muthig, Barbara Paech, Jürgen Wüst and Jörg Zettel. *Component-based Product Line Engineering with UML*. Ed. by Grady Booch, Ivar Jacobson and James Rumbaugh. Vol. 1. 1. Addison-Wesley, 2002, p. 464. ISBN: 0201737914.

[10] Victor R. Basili and David M. Weiss. 'A Methodology for Collecting Valid Software Engineering Data'. In: *IEEE Transactions on Software Engineering* SE-10.6 (Nov. 1984), pp. 728–738. ISSN: 0098-5589. DOI: 10.1109/TSE.1984.5010301.

[11] Don Batory, Jacob Neal Sarvela and Axel Rauschmayer. 'Scaling Step-wise Refinement'. In: *IEEE Transactions on Software Engineering* 30.6 (2004), pp. 355–371.

[12] Ira D. Baxter, Andrew Yahin, Leonardo Moura, Marcelo Sant'Anna and Lorraine Bier. 'Clone Detection Using Abstract Syntax Trees'. In: *Proceedings of the International Conference on Software Maintenance (ICSM 1998)*. IEEE Computer Society, 1998, pp. 368–377.

[13] Stefan Bellon, Rainer Koschke, Giulio Antoniol, Jens Krinke and Ettore Merlo. 'Comparison and Evaluation of Clone Detection Tools'. In: *IEEE Transactions on Software Engineering* 33.9 (Sept. 2007), pp. 577–591. ISSN: 0098-5589. DOI: 10.1109/TSE.2007.70725.

[14] Keith Bennett and Vaclav Rajlich. 'Software Maintenance and Evolution : A Roadmap'. In: *Proceedings of the 22nd International Conference on Software Engineering - FOSE Track (ICSE 2000)*. New York, NY, USA: ACM, 2000, pp. 73–87. ISBN: 1581132530. DOI: 10.1145/336512.336534.

[15] Kathrin Berg, Judith Bishop and Dirk Muthig. 'Tracing Software Product Line Variability – From Problem to Solution Space'. In: *Proceedings of the 2005 Annual Research Conference of the South African Institute of Computer Scientists and Information Technologists on IT Research in Developing Countries*. White River, South Africa: South African Institute for Computer Scientists and Information Technologists, 2005, pp. 111–120.

[16] Thorsten Berger, Ralf Rublack, Divya Nair, Joanne M. Atlee, Martin Becker, Krzysztof Czarnecki and Andrzej Wąsowski. 'A Survey of Variability Modeling in Industrial Practice'. In: *Proceedings of the 7th International Workshop on Variability Modelling of Software-intensive Systems (VaMoS 2013)*. New York, New York, USA: ACM, 2013, p. 1. ISBN: 9781450315418. DOI: 10.1145/2430502.2430513.

[17] Dane Bertram, Amy Voida, Saul Greenberg and Robert Walker. 'Communication, Collaboration, and Bugs: The Social Nature of Issue Tracking in Small, Collocated Teams'. In: *Proceedings of the 13th ACM conference on Computer-Supported Cooperative Work and Social Computing (CSCW 2010)*. ACM, 2010, pp. 291–300. ISBN: 9781605587950. DOI: 10.1145/1718918.1718972.

[18] Günter Böckle, Peter Knauber, Klaus Pohl and Klaus Schmid. *Software-Produktlinien: Methoden, Einführung und Praxis*. dpunkt Verlag, Heidelberg, 2004.

[19] Rainer Böhme and Ralf Reussner. 'Validation of Predictions with Measurements'. In: *Dependability Metrics*. Ed. by Irene Eusgeld, Felix Freiling and Ralf H. Reussner. Vol. 4909. Lecture Notes in Computer Science. Springer Berlin / Heidelberg, 2008, pp. 14–18. ISBN: 978-3-540-68946-1. DOI: 10.1007/978-3-540-68947-8_3.

[20] Jan Bosch. *Design and Use of Software Architectures: Adopting and Evolving a Product-Line Approach*. Vol. 1. 1. Addison-Wesley, 2000. ISBN: 0201674947.

[21] Jan Bosch. 'Maturity and Evolution in Software Product Lines: Approaches, Artefacts and Organization'. In: *Software Product Lines*. Ed. by Gary Chastek. Vol. 2379. Lecture Notes in Computer Science. Springer Berlin / Heidelberg, 2002, pp. 257–271. ISBN: 978-3-540-43985-1. DOI: 10.1007/3-540-45652-X_16.

[22] Jan Bosch, Gert Florijn, Danny Greefhorst, Juha Kuusela, J Obbink and Klaus Pohl. 'Variability Issues in Software Product Lines'. In: *Proceedings of the 4th International Workshop on Software Product-Family Engineering (PFE 2001)*. Ed. by Frank van der Linden. Vol. 2290. Lecture Notes in Computer Science. Springer Berlin / Heidelberg, 2002, pp. 13–21. ISBN: 978-3-540-43659-1.

[23] Pierre Bourque and Robert Dupuis. *Guide to the Software Engineering Body of Knowledge 2004 Version*. Vol. 1. IEEE Computer Society, 2004. ISBN: 0-7695-2330-7. DOI: 10.1109/SESS.1999.767664.

[24] Marco Brambilla, Jordi Cabot and Manuel Wimmer. *Model-Driven Software Engineering in Practice*. Vol. 1. 1. Morgan & Claypool Publishers, 2012, pp. 1–182. ISBN: 9781608458820.

[25] Cedric Brun and Laurent Goubet. *EMF Compare Project*. 2014. URL: http://www.eclipse.org/emf/compare/ (visited on 03/09/2014).

[26] Hugo Bruneliere, Jordi Cabot, Frédéric Jouault and F. Madiot. 'MoDisco: A Generic and Extensible Framework for Model Driven Reverse Engineering'. In: *Proceedings of the 25th IEEE/ACM International Conference on Automated Software Engineering (ASE 2010)*. ACM, 2010, pp. 173–174. ISBN: 9780123749130.

[27] Jim Buffenbarger. 'Syntactic Software Merging'. In: *Software Configuration Management*. Ed. by Jacky Estublier. Vol. 1005. Lecture Notes in Computer Science. Springer Berlin / Heidelberg, 1995, pp. 153–172. ISBN: 978-3-540-60578-2.

[28] Bruno Caprile and Paolo Tonella. 'Nomen Est Omen: Analyzing the Language of Function Identifiers'. In: *Proceedings of the 6th Working Conference on Reverse Engineering (WCRE 1999)*. IEEE Computer Society, 1999, pp. 112–122. ISBN: 0-7695-0303-9. DOI: 10.1109/WCRE.1999.806952.

[29] Kai-Uwe Carstensen, Christian Ebert, Cornelia Endriss, Susanne Jekat, Ralf Klabunde and Hagen Langer. *Computerlinguistik und Sprachtechnologie: Eine Einführung*. Vol. 2. Spektrum Akademischer Verlag, 2010. ISBN: 978-3-8274-2023-7. DOI: 10.1007/978-3-8274-2224-8.

[30] Sudarshan S. Chawathe, Anand Rajaraman, Hector Garcia-Molina and Jennifer Widom. 'Change Detection in Hierarchically Structured Information'. In: *Proceedings of the Proceedings of the 1996 ACM SIGMOD International Conference on Management of Data (SIGMOD 1996)* 25.2 (1996), pp. 493–504. DOI: 10.1145/233269.233366.

[31] Kunrong Chen and Václav Rajlich. 'Case Study of Feature Location using Dependence Graph'. In: *Proceedings of the 8th International Workshop on Program Comprehension (IWPC 2000)*. Limerick , Ireland: IEEE Computer Society, 2000, pp. 241–247. ISBN: 0769506569.

[32] Elliot Chikofsky and James H. Cross. 'Reverse Engineering and Design Recovery: A Taxonomy'. In: *Software* 7.1 (1990), pp. 13–17. DOI: 10.1109/52.43044.

[33] Paul Clements and Linda Northrop. *Software Product Lines : Practices and Patterns*. 6. print. SEI Series in Software Engineering 6. Boston, Mass.: Addison-Wesley, 2007, p. 563. ISBN: 0-201-70332-7.

[34] Inc CollabNet. *ArgoUML Download Count*. 2014. URL: http://argouml.tigris.org/downloadcount.html (visited on 03/09/2014).

[35] Bas Cornelissen, Bas Graaf and Leon Moonen. 'Identification of Variation Points Using Dynamic Analysis'. In: *Proceedings of the 1st International Workshop on Reengineering Towards Product Lines (R2PL 2005)*. 2005, pp. 9–13.

[36] Marcus Vinicius Couto, Marco Tulio Valente and Eduardo Figueiredo. 'Extracting Software Product Lines : A Case Study Using Conditional Compilation'. In: *Proceedings of the 15th European Conference on Software Maintenance and Reengineering (CSMR 2011)*. IEEE Computer Society, 2011, pp. 191–200. DOI: 10.1109/CSMR.2011.25.

[37] Paul Croll, Thomas Pigoski and James W. Moore. *ISO/IEC 14764-2006: Software Engineering - Software Life Cycle Processes - Maintenance*. Tech. rep. IEEE, 2006, pp. 1–46. DOI: 10.1109/IEEESTD.2006.235774.

[38] Krysztof Czarnecki and Ulrich Eisenecker. *Generative Programming: Methods, Tools, and Applications*. Vol. 1. 1. Addison Wesley, 2000, p. 864. ISBN: 978-0201309775.

[39] Barthélémy Dagenais and Laurie Hendren. 'Enabling Static Analysis for Partial Java Programs'. In: *ACM Sigplan Notices* 43.10 (2008), pp. 313–328. DOI: 10.1145/1449955.1449790.

[40] Kojic Daniel. 'Refactoring Specification and Automation for the Consolidation of Customized Product Copies'. Master Thesis. Karlsruhe Institute of Technology, 2014.

[41] Serge Demeyer. 'Object-Oriented Reengineering'. In: *Software Evolution*. Ed. by Tom Mens and Serge Demeyer. Vol. 1. Springer Berlin / Heidelberg, 2008, pp. 91–104. ISBN: 978-3-540-76439-7. DOI: 10.1007/978-3-540-76440-3_5.

[42] WinMerge Developerteam. *WinMerge*. 2014. URL: http://winmerge.org/ (visited on 03/09/2014).

[43] Bogdan Dit, Meghan Revelle, Malcom Gethers and Denys Poshyvanyk. 'Feature Location in Source Code: a Taxonomy and Survey'. In: *Journal of Software: Evolution and Process* 25.1 (Jan. 2013), pp. 53–95. ISSN: 20477473. DOI: 10.1002/smr.567.

[44] Software Technology Group TU Dresden. *EMFText Syntax Zoo*. 2014. URL: http://www.emftext.org/zoo/ (visited on 03/09/2014).

[45] Yael Dubinsky, Julia Rubin, Thorsten Berger, Slawomir Duszynski, Martin Becker and Krzysztof Czarnecki. 'An Exploratory Study of Cloning in Industrial Software Product Lines'. In: *Proceedings of the 17th European Conference on Software Maintenance and Reengineering (CSMR 2013)*. IEEE Computer Society, 2013, pp. 25–34. DOI: 10.1109/CSMR.2013.13.

[46] Zoya Durdik and Ralf Reussner. 'On the appropriate rationale for using design patterns and pattern documentation'. In: *Proceedings of the 9th International ACM Sigsoft Conference on the Quality of Software Architectures (QoSA 2013)*. 1. New York, New York, USA: ACM, 2013, pp. 107–116. ISBN: 9781450321266. DOI: 10.1145/2465478.2465491.

[47] Slawomir Duszynski. 'A Scalable Goal-oriented Approach to Software Variability Recovery'. In: *Proceedings of the 15th International Software Product Line Conference (SPLC 2011)*. New York, New York, USA: ACM, 2011, 42:1–42:8. ISBN: 9781450307895. DOI: 10.1145/2019136.2019185.

[48] Eclipse Foundation. *Eclipse*. 2014. URL: http://www.eclipse.org (visited on 03/09/2014).

[49] Eclipse Foundation. *Eclipse JDT – Java Development Tools*. 2014. URL: www.eclipse.org/jdt/ (visited on 03/09/2014).

[50] Eclipse Foundation. *Eclipse Modeling Framework Project (EMF)*. 2014. URL: http://www.eclipse.org/modeling/emf/ (visited on 03/09/2014).

[51] Eclipse Foundation. *EMF Feature Model*. 2014. URL: http://www.eclipse.org/modeling/emft/featuremodel/ (visited on 03/09/2014).

[52] Eclipse Foundation. *Mylyn – Task and Application Lifecycle Management (ALM) Framework for Eclipse*. URL: http://www.eclipse.org/mylyn/ (visited on 03/09/2014).

[53] Eclipse Foundation. *ZEST*. 2014. URL: http://www.eclipse.org/gef/zest/ (visited on 03/09/2014).

[54] Sven Efftinge and Markus Völter. 'oAW xText: A Framework for Textual DSLs'. In: *Proceedings of the Workshop on Modeling Symposium at Eclipse Summit 2006*. 2006, p. 118.

[55] Eurocontrol. *EUROCONTROL ATM Lexicon*. 2014. URL: https://www.eurocontrol.int/lexicon/lexicon/en/index.php/Main%5C_Page (visited on 03/09/2014).

[56] Hamzeh Eyal-Salman, Abdelhak-djamel Seriai and Christophe Dony. 'Feature-Level Change Impact Analysis Using Formal Concept Analysis'. In: *Proceedings of the 26th International Conference on Software Engineering and Knowledge Engineering (SEKE 2014)*. Vancouver, Canada: Knowledge Systems Institute Graduate School, 2014, pp. 447–452.

[57] Hamzeh Eyal-Salman, Abdelhak-djamel Seriai, Christophe Dony and Ra Al-msie. 'Identifying Traceability Links between Product Variants and Their Features'. In: *Proceedings of the 1st International Workshop on Reverse Variability Engineering (REVE 2013)*. Genova, 2013, pp. 17–23.

[58] C Fellbaum. *Wordnet - An Electronical Lexical Database*. Ed. by Christiane Fellbaum. MIT Press, 1998, p. 423. ISBN: 9780262061971.

[59] Jeanne Ferrante, Karl J. Ottenstein and Joe D. Warren. 'The Program Dependence Graph and its Use in Optimization'. In: *ACM Transactions on Programming Languages and Systems* 9.3 (July 1987), pp. 319–349. ISSN: 01640925. DOI: 10.1145/24039.24041.

[60] David Flanagan. *Java in a Nutshell*. Ed. by Debra Cameron and Mike Laukides. Vol. 5. O'Reilly Media, Inc., 2005. ISBN: 9780596007737.

[61] B. Fluri and H.C. Gall. 'Classifying Change Types for Qualifying Change Couplings'. In: *Proceedings of the 14th IEEE International Conference on Program Comprehension (ICPC 2006)*. IEEE Computer Society, 2006, pp. 35–45. ISBN: 0-7695-2601-2. DOI: 10.1109/ICPC.2006.16.

[62] Beat Fluri, Michael Wuersch, Martin Pinzger and Harald Gall. 'Change Distilling:Tree Differencing for Fine-Grained Source Code Change Extraction'. In: *IEEE Transactions on Software Engineering* 33.11 (Nov. 2007), pp. 725–743. ISSN: 0098-5589. DOI: 10.1109/TSE.2007.70731.

[63] Martin Fowler, Kent Beck, John Brant and William Opdyke. *Refactoring: Improving the Design of Existing Code*. Vol. 1. Addison-Wesley, 1999, p. 464. ISBN: 0201485672. DOI: 10.1007/s10071-009-0219-y.

[64] Critina Gacek and Michalis Anastasopoules. 'Implementing Product Line Variabilities'. In: *Proceedings of the 2001 Symposium on Software Reusability: Putting Software Reuse in Context*. New York: ACM, 2001, pp. 109–117. ISBN: 1581133588. DOI: 10.1145/375212.375269.

[65] Erich Gamma, Richard Helm, Ralph Johnson and John Vlissides. *Design Patterns: Elements of Reusable Object-oriented Software*. Addison-Wesley Professional Computing Series. Addison-Wesley, 1995, p. 395. ISBN: 0201633612. DOI: 10.1093/carcin/bgs084.

[66] pure systems GmbH. *pure::variants*. 2014. URL: http://www.pure-systems.com/ (visited on 03/09/2014).

[67] Hassan Gomaa. *Designing Software Product Lines with UML: From Use Cases to Pattern-Based Software Architectures*. Addison Wesley, 2004, p. 736. ISBN: 0201775956.

[68] Hassan Gomaa and Diana L Webber. 'Modeling Adaptive and Evolvable Software Product Lines using the Variation Point Model'. In: *Proceedings of the 37th Hawaii International Conference on System Sciences (HICSS 2004)*. Vol. 00. C. IEEE Computer Society, 2004, pp. 1–10. ISBN: 0769520561.

[69] Inc Google. *CodePro Analytix*. 2014. URL: https://developers.google.com/java-dev-tools/codepro/doc/ (visited on 03/09/2014).

[70] James Gosling, Bill Joy, Guy Steele and Gilad Bracha. *The Java Language Specification*. 3. Addison Wesley, 2005, p. 688. ISBN: 0-321-24678-0.

[71] Penny A. Grubb and Armstrong A. Takang. *Software Maintenance: Concepts and Practice*. Vol. 1. 1. World Scientific Publishing, 1996, p. 349. ISBN: 978-9812384263.

[72] J. van Gurp, J. Bosch and M. Svahnberg. 'On the Notion of Variability in Software Product Lines'. In: *Proceedings the 2nd Working IEEE/IFIP Conference on Software Architecture (WICSA 2001)*. IEEE Computer Society, 2001, pp. 45–54. ISBN: 0-7695-1360-3. DOI: 10.1109/WICSA.2001.948406.

[73] Graham Hamilton. *Sun Microsystems JavaBeans*. Tech. rep. Sun Microsystems, 1997, pp. 1–114.

[74] Donna Harman. 'How effective is Suffixing?' In: *Journal of the American Society for Information Science* 42.1 (1991), pp. 7–15.

[75] Erik Hatcher, Otis Gospodnetic and Mike McCandless. *Lucene in Action*. Vol. 54. In Action series 2. Manning, 2010, p. 475. ISBN: 978-1933988177.

[76] Øystein Haugen. *Common Variability Language (CVL) OMG Revised Submission*. Tech. rep. Cvl. 2012.

[77] Florian Heidenreich, Jendrik Johannes, Sven Karol, Mirko Seifert and Christian Wende. 'Derivation and Refinement of Textual Syntax for Models'. In: *Model Driven Architecture - Foundations and Applications*. Ed. by Richard F. Paige, Alan Hartman and Arend Rensink. Vol. 5562. Lecture Notes in Computer Science. Springer Berlin / Heidelberg, 2009, pp. 114–129. ISBN: 978-3-642-02673-7.

[78] Florian Heidenreich, Jendrik Johannes, Mirko Seifert and Christian Wende. 'Closing the Gap between Modelling and Java'. In: *Proceedings of the 2nd International Conference on Software Language Engineering (SLE 2009)*. Springer Berlin / Heidelberg, 2009, pp. 374–383. DOI: 10.1007/978-3-642-12107-4_25.

[79] Florian Heidenreich, Jan Kopcsek and Christian Wende. 'FeatureMapper: Mapping Features to Models'. In: *Proceedings of the 30th International Conference on Software Engineering (ICSE 2008)*. ACM, 2008, pp. 943–944. ISBN: 9781605580791.

[80] Susan Horwitz, Jan Prins and Thomas Reps. 'Integrating Noninterfering Versions of Programs'. In: *ACM Transactions on Programming Languages and Systems* 11.3 (July 1989), pp. 345–387. ISSN: 01640925. DOI: 10.1145/65979.65980.

[81] Susan Horwitz, Thomas Reps and David Binkley. 'Interprocedural slicing using dependence graphs'. In: *ACM Transactions on Programming Languages and Systems* 12.1 (Jan. 1990), pp. 26–60. ISSN: 01640925. DOI: 10.1145/77606.77608.

[82] Einar W Høst and Bjarte M Østvold. 'The Java Programmer's Phrase Book'. In: *Software Language Engineering*. Ed. by Dragan Gašević, Ralf Lämmel and Eric Wyk. Vol. 5452. Lecture Notes in Computer Science id. Springer Berlin / Heidelberg, 2009, pp. 322–341. ISBN: 978-3-642-00433-9. DOI: http://dx.doi.org/10.1007/978-3-642-00434-6_20.

[83] Einar W Høst and Bjarte M Østvold. 'The Programmer's Lexicon , Volume I : The Verbs'. In: *Proceedings of the 7th IEEE International Working Conference on Source Code Analysis and Manipulation (SCAM 2007)*. Vol. I. IEEE Computer Society, 2007, pp. 193–202.

[84] J.J. Hunt and W.F. Tichy. 'Extensible Language-Aware Merging'. In: *Proceedings of the 18th International Conference on Software Maintenance (ICSM 2002)*. IEEE Computer Society, 2002, pp. 511–520. ISBN: 0-7695-1819-2. DOI: 10.1109/ICSM.2002.1167812.

[85] ISO, IEC and IEEE. 'Systems and Software Engineering Vocabulary'. In: *ISO/IEC/IEEE 24765:2010(E)* 1.1 (2010), pp. 1–418. DOI: 10.1109/IEEESTD.2010.5733835.

[86] ISO/IEC. *ISO/IEC TR 15846:1998 Information technology - Software life cycle processes - Configuration Management*. Tech. rep. Genève 20, Switzerland: ISO/IEC, 1998.

[87] Daniel Jackson and David A Ladd. 'Semantic Diff: a Tool for Summarizing the Effects of Modifications'. In: *Proceedings of the 10th International Conference on Software Maintenance (ICSM 1994)*. IEEE Computer Society, 1994, pp. 243–252. ISBN: 0-8186-6330-8. DOI: 10.1109/ICSM.1994.336770.

[88] Ivar Jacobson, Martin Griss and Patrick Jonsson. *Software Reuse: Architecture, Process and Organization for Business Success*. 1st editio. Addison-Wesley, 1997.

[89] Elmar Juergens and Markus Pizka. 'Variability Models Must Not be Invariant (Problem Statement)'. In: *Proceedings of the 1st International Workshop on Variability Modelling of Software-intensive Systems (VaMoS 2007)*. Ed. by Klaus Pohl, Patrick Heymans, Kyo-Chul Kang and Andreas Metzger. Limerick, Ireland, 2007, pp. 171–176.

[90] Kyo C. Kang, Sholom G. Cohen, James A. Hess, William E. Novak and A. Spencer Peterson. *Feature-Oriented Domain Analysis (FODA) Feasibility Study*. Tech. rep. November. Pittsburgh, Pennsylvania: Software Engineering Institute - Carnegie Mellon University, 1990, p. 161.

[91] C. Kästner, T. Thüm, G. Saake, J. Feigenspan, T. Leich, F. Wielgorz and S. Apel. 'FeatureIDE : A Tool Framework for Feature-Oriented Software Development'. In: *Proceedings of the 31st International Conference on Software Engineering (ICSE 2009)*. Vancouver, Canada: IEEE Computer Society, 2009, pp. 611–614. ISBN: 9781424434527. DOI: 10.1109/ICSE.2009.5070568.

[92] Christian Kästner, Sven Apel and Don Batory. 'A Case Study Implementing Features Using AspectJ'. In: *Proceedings of the 11th International Software Product Line Conference (SPLC 2007)*. IEEE Computer Society, Sept. 2007, pp. 223–232. ISBN: 0-7695-2888-0. DOI: 10.1109/SPLINE.2007.12.

[93] Christian Kästner, Sven Apel and Martin Kuhlemann. 'Granularity in Software Product Lines'. In: *Proceedings of the 30th International Conference on Software Engineering (ICSE 2008)*. New York: ACM, 2008, pp. 311–320. ISBN: 9781605580791. DOI: 10.1145/1368088.1368131.

[94] David Kawrykow and Martin P. Robillard. 'Non-Essential Changes in Version Histories'. In: *Proceedings of the 33rd International Conference on Software Engineering (ICSE 2011)*. New York, New York, USA: ACM, 2011, pp. 351–360. ISBN: 9781450304450. DOI: 10.1145/1985793.1985842.

[95] Timo Kehrer, Udo Kelter and Gabriele Taentzer. 'Integrating the Specification and Recognition of Changes in Models'. In: *Proceedings of the 14th Workshop Software-Reengineering (WSR 2012)*. Bad Honnef, 2012, pp. 3–4.

[96] Benjamin Klatt. *SPLevo Website*. 2014. URL: http://www.splevo.org (visited on 03/09/2014).

[97] Benjamin Klatt, Zoya Durdik, Heiko Koziolek, Klaus Krogmann, Johannes Stammel and Roland Weiss. 'Identify Impacts of Evolving Third Party Components on Long-Living Software Systems'. In: *Proceedings of the 16th European Conference on Software Maintenance and Reengineering (CSMR 2012)*. Szeged, Hungary: IEEE Computer Society, Mar. 2012, pp. 461–464. ISBN: 978-0-7695-4666-7. DOI: 10.1109/CSMR.2012.59.

[98] Benjamin Klatt and Klaus Krogmann. 'Software Extension Mechanisms'. In: *Proceedings of the 13th International Workshop on Component-Oriented Programming (WCOP 2008)*. Ed. by Ralf Reussner, Clemens Szyperski and Wolfgang Weck. Interner Bereich Universit{ä}t Karlsruhe (TH) 2008-12. 2008, pp. 11–18.

[99] Benjamin Klatt, Klaus Krogmann and Volker Kuttruff. 'Developing Stop Word Lists for Natural Language Program Analysis'. In: *Proceedings of the 16th Workshop Software-Reengineering and Evolution (WSRE 2014)*. Bad Honnef, 2014, pp. 38–39.

[100] Benjamin Klatt, Klaus Krogmann and Christoph Seidl. 'Program Dependency Analysis for Consolidating Customized Product Copies'. In: *Proceesings of the 30th International Conference on Software Maintenance and Evolution (ICSME 2014)*. Victoria, Canada: IEEE Computer Society, 2014, to be published.

[101] Benjamin Klatt, Klaus Krogmann and Christian Wende. 'Consolidating Customized Product Copies to Software Product Lines'. In: *Proceedings of the 16th Workshop Software-Reengineering and Evolution (WSRE 2014)*. Bad Honnef, 2014, pp. 17–18.

[102] Benjamin Klatt and Martin Küster. 'Improving Product Copy Consolidation by Architecture-aware Difference Analysis'. In: *Proceedings of the 9th International ACM Sigsoft Conference on the Quality of Software Architectures (QoSA 2013)*. New York, New York, USA: ACM, 2013, p. 117. ISBN: 9781450321266. DOI: 10.1145/2465478.2465495.

[103] Benjamin Klatt and Martin Küster. 'Respecting Component Architecture to Migrate Product Copies to a Software Product Line'. In: *Proceedings of the 17th International Doctoral Symposium on Components and Architecture (WCOP 2012)*. New York, USA: ACM, 2012, p. 7. ISBN: 9781450313483. DOI: 10.1145/2304676.2304679.

[104] Benjamin Klatt, Martin Küster and Klaus Krogmann. 'A Graph-Based Analysis Concept to Derive a Variation Point Design from Product Copies'. In: *Proceedings of the 1st International Workshop on Reverse Variability Engineering (REVE 2013)*. Genova, 2013.

[105] Benjamin Klatt, K Martin, Klaus Krogmann and Oliver Burkhardt. 'A Change Impact Analysis Case Study: Replacing the Input Data Model of SoMoX'. In: *Proceedings of the 15th Workshop Software-Reengineering (WSR 2013)*. Bad Honnef, Germany, 2013.

[106] Patrick Könemann and Olaf Zimmermann. 'Linking Design Decisions to Design Models in Model-Based Software Development'. In: *Software Architecture*. Ed. by MuhammadAli Babar and Ian Gorton. Vol. 6285. Lecture Notes in Computer Science. Springer Berlin / Heidelberg, 2010, pp. 246–262. ISBN: 978-3-642-15113-2. DOI: 10.1007/978-3-642-15114-9_19.

[107] KoPL Project Consortium. *KoPL*. 2014. URL: http://www.kopl-project.org/ (visited on 03/09/2014).

[108] Rainer Koschke, Pierre Frenzel, Andreas P. J. Breu and Karsten Angstmann. 'Extending the Reflexion Method for Consolidating Software Variants into Product Lines'. In: *Software Quality Journal* 17.4 (Mar. 2009), pp. 331–366. ISSN: 0963-9314. DOI: 10.1007/s11219-009-9077-8.

[109] Heiko Koziolek, Roland Weiss and Jens Doppelhamer. 'Evolving Industrial Software Architectures into a Software Product Line: A Case Study'. In: *Architectures for Adaptive Software Systems*. Ed. by Raffaela Mirandola, Ian Gorton and Christine Hofmeister. Vol. 5581. Lecture Notes in Computer Science. Springer Berlin / Heidelberg, 2009, pp. 177–193.

[110] Josh Kropf. *Java Preprocessor*. 2008. URL: http://www.slashdev.ca/javapp/ (visited on 03/09/2014).

[111] Robert Krovetz. 'Viewing Morphology as an Inference Process'. In: *Proceedings of the 16th Annual International ACM SIGIR Conference on Research & Development on Information Retrieval*. ACM, 1993, pp. 191–202.

[112] Charles W. Krueger. 'The BigLever Software Gears Unified Software Product Line Engineering Framework'. In: *Proceedings of the 12th International Software Product Line Conference (SPLC 2008)* 1.1 (Sept. 2008), pp. 353–353. DOI: 10.1109/SPLC.2008.33.

[113] C.W. Krueger. 'Easing the Transition to Software Mass Customization'. In: *Proceedings of the 4th International Workshop on Software Product-Family Engineering (PFE 2001)*. Ed. by Frank van der Linden. Vol. 1. 512. Springer Berlin / Heidelberg, 2002, pp. 282–293.

[114] Adrian Kuhn, Stéphane Ducasse and Tudor Girba. 'Semantic Clustering: Identifying Topics in Source Code'. In: *Information and Software Technology* 49.3 (2007), pp. 230–243. ISSN: 0950-5849.

[115] Martin Küster and Benjamin Klatt. 'Leveraging Design Decisions in Evolving Systems'. In: *Proceedings of the 14th Workshop Software-Reengineering (WSR 2012)*. Bad-Honnef, Germany, 2012.

[116] Martin Küster and Mircea Trifu. 'A Case Study on Co-evolution of Software Artifacts Using Integrated Views'. In: *Proceedings of the Joint 10th Working IEEE/IFIP Conference on Software Architecture & 6th European Conference on Software Architecture (WICSA/ECSA 2012)*. New York, New York, USA: ACM, 2012, pp. 124–131. ISBN: 9781450315685. DOI: 10.1145/2361999.2362025.

[117] Steffen Lehnert. 'A Taxonomy for Software Change Impact Analysis'. In: *Proceedings of the 12th International Workshop on Principles on Software Evolution (IWPSE-EVOL 2011)*. Szeged, Hungary: ACM, 2011, pp. 41–50. ISBN: 9781450308489. DOI: 10.1145/2024445.2024454.

[118] Liebig, Sven Apel, Lengauer, Kästner and Schulze. 'An Analysis of the Variability in Forty Preprocessor-based Software Product Lines'. In: *Proceedings of the 32nd International Conference on Software Engineering (ICSE 2010)*. ACM, 2010.

[119] Bennett P. Lientz and E. Burton Swanson. *Software Maintenance and Management*. Vol. 1. 1. Boston, MA, USA: Addison-Wesley, 1980. ISBN: 0201042053.

[120] R. Likert. 'A Technique for the Measurement of Attitudes'. In: *Archives of Psychology* 22 140 (1932), p. 55. ISSN: 0006-8993. DOI: 2731047. arXiv: 2731047.

[121] Ernst Lippe and Norbert van Oosterom. 'Operation-based Text-based merge tools'. In: *Proceedings of the 5th ACM SIGSOFT Symposium on Software Development Environments (SDE 1992)*. New York, NY, USA: ACM, 1992, pp. 78–87. ISBN: 0897915550. DOI: 10.1145/142868.143753.

[122] Felix Loesch and Erhard Ploedereder. 'Optimization of Variability in Software Product Lines'. In: *Proceedings of the 11th International Software Product Line Conference (SPLC 2007)* (Sept. 2007), pp. 151–162. DOI: 10.1109/SPLINE.2007.31.

[123] Roberto E. Lopez-Herrejon. *REVE Workshop 2014*. 2014. URL: http://www.isse.jku.at/reve2014/ (visited on 03/09/2014).

[124] D MacKenzie, Paul Eggert and Richard Stallman. *Comparing and Merging Files with GNU diff and patch*. Vol. 2. April. Network Theory Ltd., 2003. ISBN: 0954161750.

[125] J.I. Maletic and M.L. Collard. 'Supporting Source Code Difference Analysis'. In: *Proceedings of the 20th IEEE International Conference on Software Maintenance (ICSM 2004)*. IEEE Computer Society, Sept. 2004, pp. 210–219. ISBN: 0-7695-2213-0. DOI: 10.1109/ICSM.2004.1357805.

[126] Guido Malpohl, James J. Hunt and Walter F. Tichy. 'Renaming Detection'. In: *Automated Software Engineering* 10.2 (2003), pp. 183–202. DOI: 10.1023/A:1022968013020.

[127] A. Marcus, A. Sergeyev, V. Rajlich and J.I. Maletic. 'An Information Retrieval Approach to Concept Location in Source Code'. In: *Proceedings of the 11th Working Conference on Reverse Engineering (WCRE 2004)*. IEEE Computer Society, 2004, pp. 214–223. ISBN: 0-7695-2243-2. DOI: 10.1109/WCRE.2004.10.

[128] Robert C. Martin. *Clean Code*. Vol. 1. 1. Boston, MA, USA: Prentice Hall, 2009, p. 431. ISBN: 987-0-13-235088-4.

[129] Jürgen Meister. 'Produktgetriebene Entwicklung von Software-Produktlinien am Beispiel analytischer Anwendungssoftware'. PhD thesis. Carl von Ossietzky Universität, Oldenburg, Germany, 2006.

[130] Jürgen Meister, Ralf Reussner and Martin Rohde. 'Managing Product Line Variability by Patterns'. In: *Object-Oriented and Internet-Based Technologies*. Ed. by Mathias Weske and Peter Liggesmeyer. Vol. 3263. Lecture Notes in Computer Science. Springer Berlin / Heidelberg, 2004, pp. 153–168.

[131] Tom Mens. 'A state-of-the-art survey on software merging'. In: *IEEE Transactions on Software Engineering* 28.5 (May 2002), pp. 449–462. ISSN: 0098-5589. DOI: 10.1109/TSE.2002.1000449.

[132] Microsoft. *.Net Naming Guidelines*. 2014. URL: http://msdn.microsoft.com/en-us/library/ms229002(v=vs.100).aspx (visited on 03/09/2014).

[133] Ra'Fat Al-Msie'Deen. 'Mining Feature Models from the Object-oriented Source Code of a Collection of Software Product Variants'. In: *Proceedings of the 27th European Conference on Object-Oriented Programming (ECOOP 2013)*. 2013, pp. 1–10.

[134] Ra'Fat Al-Msie'Deen, A-D Seriai, Marianne Huchard, Christelle Urtado and Sylvain Vauttier. 'Mining Features from the Object-Oriented Source Code of Software Variants by Combining Lexical and Structural Similarity'. In: *Proceedings of the 14th International Conference on Information Reuse and Integration (IRI 2013)*. IEEE Computer Society, 2013, pp. 586–593. DOI: 10.1109/IRI.2013.6642522.

[135] G.C. Murphy, D. Notkin and K.J. Sullivan. 'Software Reflexion Models : Bridging the Gap between Design and Implementation'. In: *IEEE Transactions on Software Engineering* 27.4 (2001), pp. 364–380.

[136] Iulian Neamtiu, Jeffrey S. Foster and Michael Hicks. 'Understanding Source Code Evolution using Abstract Syntax Tree Matching'. In: *Proceedings of the 2nd International Workshop on Mining Software Repositories (MSR 2005)* (2005), pp. 1–5. DOI: 10.1145/1083142.1083143.

[137] Camila Nunes, Alessandro Garcia and Carlos Lucena. 'History-sensitive Recovery of Product Line Features'. In: *Proceedings of the 26th International Conference on Software Maintenance (ICSM 2010)*. IEEE Computer Society, Sept. 2010, pp. 1–2. ISBN: 978-1-4244-8630-4. DOI: 10.1109/ICSM.2010.5609561.

[138] Object Management Group (OMG). *ADM Abstract Syntax Tree Metamodel (ASTM)*. Tech. rep. January. Object Management Group (OMG), 2011.

[139] Object Management Group (OMG). *ADM Knowledge Discovery Meta-Model (KDM)*. Tech. rep. August. Object Management Group (OMG), 2011.

[140] Object Management Group (OMG). *Meta Object Facility (MOF) Core*. Tech. rep. April. Object Management Group (OMG), 2014.

[141] Object Management Group (OMG). *Object Constraint Language (OCL)*. Tech. rep. February. Object Management Group (OMG), 2014.

[142] Oracle Corporation. *MySQL Stop Word List*. 2014. URL: `http://dev.mysql.com/doc/refman/5.5/en/fulltext-stopwords.html` (visited on 03/09/2014).

[143] OSGi Alliance. *The OSGi Alliance OSGi Core Release 6*. Tech. rep. June. OSGi Alliance, 2014, p. 450.

[144] Karl J Ottenstein and Linda M Ottenstein. *The Program Dependence Graph in a Software Development Environment*. Vol. 19. 5. ACM, 1984, pp. 177–184. ISBN: 0897911318.

[145] David Lorge Parnas. 'On the Design and Development of Program Families'. In: *IEEE Transactions on Software Engineering* 1.1 (Mar. 1976), pp. 1–9. ISSN: 0098-5589. DOI: `10.1109/TSE.1976.233797`.

[146] Thomas Patzke and Dirk Muthig. *Product Line Implementation Technologies*. Tech. rep. 057. Kaiserslautern: Fraunhofer IESE, 2002, p. 61.

[147] Dewayne E. Perry, Harvey P. Siy and Lawrence G. Votta. 'Parallel changes in large-scale software development: an observational case study'. In: *ACM Transactions on Software Engineering and Methodology* 10.3 (July 2001), pp. 308–337. ISSN: 1049331X. DOI: `10.1145/383876.383878`.

[148] Thomas M. Pigoski and Alain April. 'Software Maintenance'. In: *Guide to the Software Engineering Body of Knowledge*. Ed. by Pierre Bourque and Robert Dupuis. Vol. 2004. IEEE Computer Society, 2004. Chap. Software M, pp. 6–1 — 6–15. ISBN: 0-7695-2330-7.

[149] Klaus Pohl, Günter Böckle and Frank van der Linden. *Software Product Line Engineering: Foundations, Principles, and Techniques*. Springer Berlin / Heidelberg, 2005, p. 468. ISBN: 3540243720.

[150] Lori Pollock, K. Vijay-Shanker, Emily Hill, Giriprasad Sridhara and David Shepherd. 'Natural Language-Based Software Analyses and Tools for Software Maintenance'. In: *Software Engineering, International Summer Schools, ISSSE 2009-2011*. Salerno, Italy, 2012, pp. 102–134.

[151] M. F. Porter. *Snowball: A Language for Stemming Algorithms*. 2001. URL: http://snowball.tartarus.org/texts/introduction.html (visited on 03/09/2014).

[152] M.F. Porter. 'An Algorithm for Suffix Stripping'. In: *Program*. Vol. 14. 3. Emerald Group Publishing Limited, 1980, pp. 130–137. DOI: 10.1108/eb046814.

[153] Princeton University. *WordNet Database*. 2014. URL: http://wordnet.princeton.edu/ (visited on 03/09/2014).

[154] V. Rajlich and P. Gosavi. 'Incremental Change in Object-Oriented Programming'. In: *IEEE Software* 21.4 (July 2004), pp. 62–69. ISSN: 0740-7459. DOI: 10.1109/MS.2004.17.

[155] Daniel Ratiu. 'Domain Knowledge Driven Program Analysis'. In: *Softwaretechnik-Trends* 29.2 (2009).

[156] Jan Reimann, Mirko Seifert and Uwe Aßmann. 'On the Reuse and Recommendation of Model Refactoring Specifications'. In: *Software & Systems Modeling* 12.3 (Apr. 2012), pp. 579–596. ISSN: 1619-1366. DOI: 10.1007/s10270-012-0243-2.

[157] C. Riva and C. Del Rosso. 'Experiences with Software Product Family Evolution'. In: *Proceedings of the 6th International Workshop on Principles of Software Evolution (IWPSE 2003)*. IEEE Computer Society, 2003, pp. 161–169. ISBN: 0-7695-1903-2. DOI: 10.1109/IWPSE.2003.1231223.

[158] M.R. Robillard and G.C. Murphy. 'Concern Graphs: Finding and Describing concerns using Structural Program Dependencies'. In: *Proceedings of the 24th International Conference on Software Engineering (ICSE 2002)*. ACM, 2002, pp. 406–416. ISBN: 1-58113-472-X. DOI: 10.1109/ICSE.2002.1007986.

[159] Chanchal K Roy, James R Cordy and Rainer Koschke. 'Comparison and Evaluation of Code Clone Detection Techniques and Tools: A qualitative Approach'. In: *Science of Computer Programming* 74.7 (2009), pp. 470–495. ISSN: 0167-6423. DOI: DOI:10.1016/j.scico.2009.02.007.

[160] Julia Rubin and Marsha Chechik. 'A Framework for Managing Cloned Product Variants'. In: *Proceedings of the 35th International Conference on Software (ICSE 2013)*. San Francisco: ACM, 2013, pp. 1233–1236. ISBN: 9781467330763.

[161] Julia Rubin and Marsha Chechik. 'A Survey of Feature Location Techniques'. In: *Domain Engineering: Product Lines, Languages, and Conceptual Models*. Ed. by Iris Reinhartz-Berger, Arnon Sturm, Tony Clark, Sholom Cohen and Jorn Bettin. Springer Berlin / Heidelberg, 2013, pp. 29–58. ISBN: 978-3642366536. DOI: 10.1007/978-3-642-36654-3_2.

[162] Julia Rubin and Marsha Chechik. 'Combining Related Products into Product Lines'. In: *Proceedings of the 15th International Conference on Fundamental Approaches to Software Engineering (FASE 2012)*. Springer Berlin / Heidelberg, 2012.

[163] Julia Rubin and Marsha Chechik. 'Locating Distinguishing Features using Diff Sets'. In: *Proceedings of the 27th IEEE/ACM International Conference on Automated Software Engineering (ASE 2012)*. New York, New York, USA: ACM, 2012, p. 242. ISBN: 9781450312042. DOI: 10.1145/2351676.2351712.

[164] Julia Rubin and Marsha Chechik. 'Quality of merge-refactorings for product lines'. In: *Proceedings of the 16th International Conference on Fundamental Approaches to Software Engineering (FASE 2013)*. Springer Berlin / Heidelberg, 2013, pp. 83–98.

[165] Julia Rubin, Andrei Kirshin, Goetz Botterweck and Marsha Chechik. 'Managing Forked Product Variants'. In: *Proceedings of the 16th International Software Product Line Conference (SPLC 2012)*. New York, New York, USA: ACM, 2012, p. 156. ISBN: 9781450310949. DOI: 10.1145/2362536.2362558.

[166] Jorma Sajaniemi and Raquel Navarro Prieto. 'An Investigation into Professional Programmers' Mental Representations of Variables'. In: *Proceedings of the 13th International Workshop on Program Comprehension (IWPC 2005)*. IEEE Computer Society, 2005, pp. 55–64. ISBN: 0-7695-2254-8. DOI: 10.1109/WPC.2005.8.

[167] Ina Schaefer, Lorenzo Bettini, Viviana Bono, Ferruccio Damiani and Nico Tanzarella. 'Delta-Oriented Programming of Software Product Lines'. In: *Software Product Lines: Going Beyond*. Ed. by Jan Bosch and Jaejoon Lee. Vol. 6287. Lecture Notes in Computer Science. Springer Berlin / Heidelberg, 2010, pp. 77–91. DOI: 10.1007/978-3-642-15579-6_6.

[168] Ina Schaefer, Rick Rabiser, Dave Clarke, Lorenzo Bettini, David Benavides, Goetz Botterweck, Animesh Pathak, Salvador Trujillo and Karina Villela. 'Software Diversity: State of the Art and Perspectives'. In: *International Journal on Software Tools for Technology Transfer* 14.5 (July 2012), pp. 477–495. ISSN: 1433-2779. DOI: 10.1007/s10009-012-0253-y.

[169] Klaus Schmid. 'A Comprehensive Product Line Scoping Approach and its Validation'. In: *Proceedings of the 24th International Conference on Software Engineering (ICSE 2002)*. New York, New York, USA: ACM, 2002, pp. 593–603. ISBN: 158113472X. DOI: 10.1145/581413.581415.

[170] Klaus Schmid. 'Scoping Software Product Lines: An Analysis of an Emerging Technology'. In: *Proceedings of the 1st International Software Product Line Conference (SPLC 2000)*. Norwell: Kluwer Academic Publishers, 2000, pp. 513–532. ISBN: 0-79237-940-3.

[171] Arnd Schnieders and Frank Puhlmann. 'Variability Mechanisms in E-Business Process Families'. In: *Proceedings of the 9th International Conference on Business Information Systems (BIS 2006)*. Ed. by W Abramowicz and H Mayr. Bonn, Germany, 2006, pp. 583–601.

[172] Dietmar Schütz. 'Variability Reverse Engineering'. In: *Proceedings of the 14th European Conference on Pattern Languages of Programs (EuroPLoP 2009)*. 2009, pp. 1–6.

[173] Olaf Seng, Frank Simon and Thomas Mohaupt. *Code Quality Management*. dpunkt Verlag, Heidelberg, 2006. ISBN: 978-3898643887.

[174] David C Sharp. 'Containing and Facilitating Change via Object Oriented Tailoring Techniques'. In: *Proceedings of the 1st International Software Product Line Conference (SPLC 2000)*. Ed. by Patrick E. Donohoe. Denver, Colorado: Springer Berlin / Heidelberg, 2000.

[175] Steven She, Rafael Lotufo, Thorsten Berger, Andrzej Wąsowski and Krzysztof Czarnecki. 'Reverse Engineering Feature Models'. In: *Proceedings of the 33rd International Conference on Software Engineering (ICSE 2011)*. New York, New York, USA: ACM, 2011, pp. 461–470. ISBN: 9781450304450. DOI: 10.1145/1985793.1985856.

[176] M Sinnema and S Deelstra. 'Classifying Variability Modeling Techniques'. In: *Information and Software Technology* 49.7 (2007), pp. 717–739. ISSN: 09505849. DOI: 10.1016/j.infsof.2006.08.001.

[177] Pieter van der Spek, Steven Klusener and Pierre van de Laar. 'Towards Recovering Architectural Concepts Using Latent Semantic Indexing'. In: *Proceedings of the 12th European Conference on Software Maintenance and Reengineering (CSMR 2008)*. IEEE Computer Society, Apr. 2008, pp. 253–257. ISBN: 978-1-4244-2157-2. DOI: 10.1109/CSMR.2008.4493321.

[178] Margaret-Anne Storey, L.-T. Cheng, J. Singer, M. Muller, D. Myers and J. Ryall. 'How Programmers can Turn Comments into Waypoints for Code Navigation'. In: *Proceedings of the 23th International Conference on Software Maintenance (ICSM 2007)*. IEEE Computer Society, 2007, pp. 265–274. DOI: 10.1109/ICSM.2007.4362639.

[179] Margaret-Anne Storey, Jody Ryall, R Ian Bull, Del Myers and Janice Singer. 'TODO or To Bug : Exploring How Task Annotations Play a Role in the Work Practices of Software Developers'. In: *Proceedings of the 30th International Conference on Software Engineering (ICSE 2008)*. ACM, 2008, pp. 251–260. ISBN: 9781605580791. DOI: 10.1145/1368088.1368123.

[180] Fabian M. Suchanek. *Javatools Pling Stemmer - Yago Naga Project*. 2014. URL: http://resources.mpi-inf.mpg.de/yago-naga/javatools/doc/javatools/parsers/PlingStemmer.html (visited on 03/09/2014).

[181] Fabian M. Suchanek, Georgiana Ifrim and Gerhard Weikum. 'LEILA: Learning to Extract Information by Linguistic Analysis'. In: *Proceedings of the 2nd Workshop on Ontology Population at ACL/COLING (OLP 2006)*. 2006, pp. 18–25.

[182] Mikael Svahnberg and Jan Bosch. 'Issues Concerning Variability in Software Product Lines'. In: *Software Architectures for Product Families*. Ed. by Frank van der Linden. Vol. 1951. Lecture Notes in Computer Science. Springer Berlin / Heidelberg, 2000, pp. 146–157. ISBN: 978-3-540-41480-3. DOI: 10.1007/978-3-540-44542-5_17.

[183] Mikael Svahnberg, Jilles van Gurp and Jan Bosch. 'A Taxonomy of Variability Realization Techniques'. In: *Software: Practice and Experience* 35.8 (2005), pp. 705–754. DOI: 10.1002/spe.v35:8.

[184] Walter F. Tichy. 'RCS - A System for Version Control'. In: *Software: Practice and Experience* 15.7 (1985), pp. 637–654. DOI: 10.1002/spe.4380150703.

[185] Frank Tip. *A Survey of Program Slicing Techniques*. Tech. rep. Amsterdam, The Netherlands, The Netherlands: CWI (Centre for Mathematics and Computer Science), 1994, pp. 1–65.

[186] F. Van der Linden. 'Software Product Families in Europe: the Esaps & Cafe Projects'. In: *IEEE Software* 19.August (2002), pp. 41–49.

[187] Robbie Vanbrabant. *Google Guice: Agile Lightweight Dependency Injection Framework*. Vol. 1. 1. Apress, 2008, p. 192. ISBN: 978-1590599976.

[188] Markus Völter, Thomas Stahl, Jorn Bettin, Arno Haase and Simon Helsen. *Model Driven Software Development*. 1st ed. Vol. 1. 1. John Wiley & Sons, 2006, p. 446. ISBN: 978-0470025703.

[189] Mark Weiser. 'Program Slicing'. In: *IEEE Transactions on Software Engineering* SE-10.4 (July 1984), pp. 352–357. ISSN: 0098-5589. DOI: 10.1109/TSE.1984.5010248.

[190] Mark Weiser. 'Programmers Use Slices When Debugging'. In: *Communications of the ACM* 25.7 (1982), pp. 446–452. DOI: 10.1145/358557.358577.

[191] David M Weiss and Chi Tau Robert Lai. *Software Product-Line Engineering: A Family-Based Software Development Process*. Vol. 1. 1. Boston, MA, USA: Addison-Wesley, 1999, p. 426. ISBN: 0-201-69438-7.

[192] Bernhard Westfechtel. 'Structure-Oriented Merging of Revisions of Software Documents'. In: *Proceedings of the 3rd International Workshop on Software Configuration Management (SCM 1991)*. New York, New York, USA: ACM, 1991, pp. 68–79. ISBN: 08979144295. DOI: 10.1145/111062.111071.

[193] Norman Wilde. *Understanding Program Dependencies*. Tech. rep. August 1990. Carnegie Mellon University, Software Engineering Institute, 1990, p. 26.

[194] Norman Wilde and Michael C Scully. 'Software Reconnaissance: Mapping Program Features to Code'. In: *Journal Of Software Maintenance Research And Practice* 7.1 (1995), pp. 49–62. ISSN: 1040550X. DOI: 10.1002/smr.4360070105.

[195] Zhenchang Xing and Eleni Stroulia. 'UMLDiff: An Algorithm for Object-oriented Design Differencing'. In: *Proceedings of the 20th IEEE/ACM International Conference on Automated Software Engineering (ASE 2005)*. ACM, 2005, pp. 54–65. ISBN: 1581139934.

[196] Hamed Shariat Yazdi, Pit Pietsch, Timo Kehrer and Udo Kelter. 'Statistical Analysis of Changes for Synthesizing Realistic Test Models'. In: *Proceedings of the Software Engineering (SE 2013)*. Aachen, 2013, pp. 225–238.

[197] Tewfik Ziadi, Luz Frias, Marcos Aurélio Almeida da Silva and Mikal Ziane. 'Feature Identification from the Source Code of Product Variants'. In: *Proceedings of the 16th European Conference on Software Maintenance and Reengineering (CSMR 2012)*. IEEE Computer Society, Mar. 2012, pp. 417–422. ISBN: 978-0-7695-4666-7. DOI: 10.1109/CSMR.2012.52.

The Karlsruhe Series on Software Design and Quality

Edited by Prof. Dr. Ralf Reussner // ISSN 1867-0067

Band 1 **Steffen Becker**
Coupled Model Transformations for QoS Enabled Component-Based Software Design. 2008
ISBN 978-3-86644-271-9

Band 2 **Heiko Koziolek**
Parameter Dependencies for Reusable Performance Specifications of Software Components. 2008
ISBN 978-3-86644-272-6

Band 3 **Jens Happe**
Predicting Software Performance in Symmetric Multi-core and Multiprocessor Environments. 2009
ISBN 978-3-86644-381-5

Band 4 **Klaus Krogmann**
Reconstruction of Software Component Architectures and Behaviour Models using Static and Dynamic Analysis. 2012
ISBN 978-3-86644-804-9

Band 5 **Michael Kuperberg**
Quantifying and Predicting the Influence of Execution Platform on Software Component Performance. 2010
ISBN 978-3-86644-741-7

Band 6 **Thomas Goldschmidt**
View-Based Textual Modelling. 2011
ISBN 978-3-86644-642-7

The Karlsruhe Series on Software Design and Quality

Edited by Prof. Dr. Ralf Reussner // ISSN 1867-0067

Band 7 **Anne Koziolek**
Automated Improvement of Software Architecture Models for Performance and Other Quality Attributes. 2013
ISBN 978-3-86644-973-2

Band 8 **Lucia Happe**
Configurable Software Performance Completions through Higher-Order Model Transformations. 2013
ISBN 978-3-86644-990-9

Band 9 **Franz Brosch**
Integrated Software Architecture-Based Reliability Prediction for IT Systems. 2012
ISBN 978-3-86644-859-9

Band 10 **Christoph Rathfelder**
Modelling Event-Based Interactions in Component-Based Architectures for Quantitative System Evaluation. 2013
ISBN 978-3-86644-969-5

Band 11 **Henning Groenda**
Certifying Software Component Performance Specifications. 2013
ISBN 978-3-7315-0080-3

Band 12 **Dennis Westermann**
Deriving Goal-oriented Performance Models by Systematic Experimentation. 2014
ISBN 978-3-7315-0165-7

The Karlsruhe Series on Software Design and Quality

Edited by Prof. Dr. Ralf Reussner // ISSN 1867-0067

Band 13 **Michael Hauck**
Automated Experiments for Deriving Performance-relevant Properties of Software Execution Environments. 2014
ISBN 978-3-7315-0138-1

Band 14 **Zoya Durdik**
Architectural Design Decision Documentation through Reuse of Design Patterns. 2016
ISBN 978-3-7315-0292-0

Band 15 **Erik Burger**
Flexible Views for View-based Model-driven Development. 2014
ISBN 978-3-7315-0276-0

Band 16 **Benjamin Klatt**
Consolidation of Customized Product Copies into Software Product Lines. 2016
ISBN 978-3-7315-0368-2

Die Bände sind unter www.ksp.kit.edu als PDF frei verfügbar oder als Druckausgabe bestellbar.